BTEC National

Travel & Tourism

BTEC National
Travel & Tourism

**Elise James, Joanne Thirlaway
& Ursula Woodhouse**

Hodder Arnold
A MEMBER OF THE HODDER HEADLINE GROUP

endorsed by
edexcel

This high-quality material is endorsed by Edexcel and has been through a rigorous quality assurance programme to ensure that it is a suitable companion to the specification for both learners and teachers. This does not mean that its contents will be used verbatim when setting examinations nor is it to be read as being the official specification – a copy of which is available at www.edexcel.org.uk

Orders: please contact Bookpoint Ltd, 130 Milton Park, Abingdon, Oxon OX14 4SB. Telephone: (44) 01235 827720. Fax: (44) 01235 400454. Lines are open from 9.00 – 5.00, Monday to Saturday, with a 24-hour message answering service. You can also order through our website www.hoddereducation.co.uk

If you have any comments to make about this, or any of our other titles, please send them to educationenquiries@hodder.co.uk

British Library Cataloguing in Publication Data
A catalogue record for this title is available from the British Library

ISBN: 978 0 340 94573 5

First Edition published 2007.
Impression number   10 9 8 7 6 5 4 3 2 1
Year   2011 2010 2009 2008 2007

Cover photo © Mina Chapman/Corbis

Typeset in 12/14 Minion by Fakenham Photosetting Limited, Fakenham, Norfolk

Printed in Italy for Hodder Arnold, an imprint of Hodder Education and a member of the Hodder Headline Group, an Hachette Livre UK Company, 338 Euston Road, London NW1 3BH.

Contents

Acknowledgements

Joanne Thirlaway
I would like to thank my mother and husband for their support and encouragement.

Elise James
Many thanks to Karen Donohoe for her expertise in cash flow forecasts and budgeting. To Ian, thanks for all the cups of tea and your patience in times of stress. To Harry, my mum and all my family, thank you for your positive and supportive comments.

Ursula Woodhouse
I would like to thank my colleagues and manager for their support and my husband for all his encouragement, help and patience during the writing of this book.

Contributing authors
Ronan Conway has an MA in International Tourism Policy, a BA (Hons) in Leisure Management (Tourism and Recreation), a PGCE in Further Education and is a Member of the Tourism Society (MTS). He worked for eight years in the travel industry and has taught Levels 1–4 in Travel & Tourism for six years. He is currently a lecturer at City & Islington College, London. Ronan wrote Unit 3 The UK as a destination and Unit 11 Sustainable tourism development.

Susan Gelson worked in the aviation industry as air cabin crew and in a variety of ground handling roles. She left the aviation industry to complete a tourism degree and join a further education college as a lecturer in airline and airport operations and cabin crew. Sue is also an external verifier for FE aviation qualifications and works closely with industry as an education consultant to develop aviation qualifications that fit the needs of employers and colleges. Susan wrote Unit 24 Handling air passengers.

Every effort has been made to trace and acknowledge ownership of copyright. The publishers will be glad to make suitable arrangements with any copyright holders whom it has not been possible to contact.

The authors and publishers would like to thank the following:

ABTA Ltd, AITO, Ashdown Forest Tourism Association, BA Museum, Bedes World, British Airways plc, *Daily Telegraph*, easyJet, Exodus, *Financial Times*, First Choice Holidays, *Guardian*, Holiday Which?, *Independent*, LEGO Group, Livewire Magazine GNER, National Trust, Natural England, Northern Ireland Tourist Board, OAG Worldwide Ltd, *Observer*, Page & Moy, Pearson, Press Association, Robin Hood Airport, South Yorkshire Passenger Transport Executive, Tate London, Tate Online, Taylor Nelson Sofres, The Centre for Life, Thomas Cook, Travelsphere, Travel Centre, *Travel Trade Gazette*, *Travel Weekly*, TUI UK Ltd, Tyne and Wear Museums, Universal Studios, VirginHolidays, Visit Brighton, VisitBritain

Artwork:
Figures 3.03, 3.04, 3.05, 3.06, 3.07, 3.08, 3.09, 3.12, 3.13, 7.01, 24.01 and 24.04 by Tony Jones, Art Construction.

Photos:
p4 (left) Charles Bowman/photolibrary.com, (right) © Alan Curtis/Alamy, **p5** © Andrew Fox/Alamy, **p6** (left) © Pawel Libera/Alamy, (right) © Daniel Gustavsson/iStockphoto.com, **p7** © Jack Sullivan/Alamy, **p11** Popperfoto.com, **p12** TopFoto.co.uk, **p14** (left) © Roman Soumar/Corbis, (right) © Danny Lehman/Corbis, **p43** (left) © Alan Novelli/Alamy, (right) © David J. Green/Alamy, **p51** © AM Corporation/Alamy, **p53** Jtb Photo Communications Inc/photolibrary.com, **p54** Anthony Devlin/PA Wire/PA Photos, **p55** (bottom left) © Graeme Purdy/iStockphoto.com, (top right) © Stephen Saks Photography/Alamy, (bottom right) Ingram Publishing, **p56** © Pixfolio/Alamy, **p58** © Steven May/Alamy, **p59** © Paul Hackett/Reuters/Corbis, **p75** © Jon Arnold Images/Alamy, **p82** © Stock Connection Distribution/Alamy, **p85** Wyn Voysey, AA, TopFoto, **p94** © 2007 Voyages Jules Verne, **p124** (top) © Guillaume Dubé/iStockphoto.com, (bottom) © mcx images/Alamy, **p138** James Lemass/Index Stock Imagery/photolibrary.com, **p139** (top) © Alberto Pomares/iStockphoto.com, (bottom) © Jon Hicks/Corbis, **p146** © Dirscherl Reinhard/SuperStock, **p147** (left) © Richard T. Nowitz/Corbis, (right) © Dennis MacDonald/Alamy, **p148** (top) © Goss Images/Alamy, (bottom) © Kevin R. Morris/Corbis, **p149** © Deborah Dennis/Alamy, **p150** © Georgina Bowater/Corbis, **p159** © Joanne Thirlaway, **p164** © David Robertson/Alamy, **p176** (left) Loreto Bay Company, (right) Damian Dovarganes/AP/PA Photos, **p177** (left) © Robert Harding Picture Library Ltd/Alamy, (right) Jim Holmes, AA, TopFoto, **p178** © Jon Arnold Images/Alamy, **p179** © The Photolibrary Wales/Alamy, **p180** © Mike McQueen/Corbis, **p182** © The Photolibrary Wales/Alamy, **p183** © Kevin Jarratt/iStockphoto.com, **p184** © Eric Nathan/Alamy, **p187** © Craig Lovell/Corbis, **p215** (top) © Robbie Jack/Corbis, (bottom) © David Sanger Photography/Alamy, **p220** (left) © Silvio Verrecchia/iStockphoto.com, (right) © Natasha Owen/Fotolia, **p248** © Stephen Saks Photography/Alamy, **p249** (left) © Baz Keeble/Alamy, (right) Chris Nicholson/Robert Harding/Rex Features, **p251** Beatles Story Ltd, **p254** © Dave Jepson/Alamy, **p255** Eureka! The Museum for Children, **p258** © David Crausby/Alamy, **p260** NITB – Northern Ireland Tourist Board, **p275** © Apix /Alamy, **p276** © Christoph Ermel/iStockphoto.com.

Core units

Learning outcomes

By the end of this unit you should:

- know the components of travel and tourism, and how they interrelate
- know the roles and responsibilities of travel and tourism organisations within the different sectors
- understand how recent developments have shaped the present-day travel and tourism industry
- understand the trends and factors affecting the development of travel and tourism.

The components of travel and tourism

Types of tourism

Before you start learning about the travel and tourism industry, it is vital to define the notion of tourism and introduce some basic terms that relate to your studies. According to the UK Tourism Society, tourism is:

> **The temporary, short-term movement of people to destinations outside the places where they normally live and work, and their activities during their stay at these destinations.**

We can distinguish between domestic, incoming (inbound) and outgoing (outbound) tourism; these can be defined as follows:

- *domestic tourism* – travelling within their own country, e.g. a student from Leeds going to the Reading Festival
- *incoming tourism* – tourists from other countries coming to the UK, e.g. a couple from Madrid coming to spend a weekend in London
- *outgoing tourism* – UK residents travelling to other countries, e.g. a family from Bristol going on a skiing holiday to Austria.

Depending on the purpose of travel, we can talk about business trips, leisure trips or VFR (visiting friends and relatives).

The six travel and tourism components

The travel and tourism industry consists of six main components: *accommodation providers, transport providers, visitor attractions, tour operators, travel agents* as well as a wide range of *support services* (trade associations, ancillary services, tourism development bodies and many others).

This unit will look at each component as well as how they work together and how they depend on one another.

Accommodation providers

Among accommodation providers there are hotels (1–7 stars), hostels, motels, camping and caravan sites, bed & breakfasts, holiday parks and campus accommodation. Accommodation providers vary greatly in terms of the products and services they offer, the types of customer they attract, the prices they charge as well as location of their properties and their ownership.

While hotels, especially 4- and 5-star properties, may offer a wide range of services such as room service, concierge, a gym, as well as meeting and conference facilities, a small B&B will only provide a room, sometimes with a bathroom outside the room and one meal a day (i.e. breakfast).

Hotels are more likely to attract business visitors while caravan sites will cater for leisure visitors, such as families. A guesthouse or a farmhouse may be owned by an individual, while hotels, such as the Hilton or the Intercontinental, may be part of large international chains with properties worldwide. A

Fig 1.01 The Savoy hotel, London

Fig 1.02 A campsite

youth hostel offers budget accommodation, while a hotel typically aims at the higher end of the market.

Caravan parks or campsites tend to be located outside city centres where space is not at a premium, while guesthouses and hotels often use city-centre locations and their proximity to the various amenities and transport links as a selling point.

ACTIVITY

Investigate and briefly describe accommodation providers in terms of ownership, products and services, prices and location.

Transport providers

Transport providers can be divided into road, rail, air and water transportation. Each has its own characteristics, advantages and disadvantages.

Air transportation, which mainly developed after the Second World War, can be divided into scheduled, charter and low-cost airlines.

Scheduled airlines, such as British Airways or bmi, operate according to a fixed timetable and normally offer customers a wider selection of destinations (short-haul and long-haul). Services such as meals and allocated seats are included in the price of the ticket.

Low-cost airlines, such as Ryanair, easyJet and Jet2, are also a form of scheduled airline, as they operate to a set timetable, but they do not include as much in the price of their tickets – such as food or allocated seats – as their primary goal is to keep prices down. They also aim to save costs by having a very short turnaround period (spending little time at the airport in between flights), offering a reduced baggage allowance and operating from regional airports.

Charter flights, such as those offered by Thomsonfly and Monarch, tend to be sold mainly as part of a package holiday. Such airlines could either be owned by a tour operator (Thomsonfly is owned by Thomson, for example) or 'chartered' by a tour operator for the purpose of flying its holidaymakers to and from their holiday destinations, following itineraries set by the tour operators.

Road operators, such as coaches, offer a convenient and inexpensive way of travelling in the UK or to the continent. National Express and its continental division, Eurolines, offer a wide selection of routes linking major UK and European cities at affordable prices as long as you do not mind taking longer to get to your destination.

Road travel, however, is dominated by private cars as well as hired vehicles. The largest car-hire companies – Hertz, Avis, Alamo and National – offer a selection of different types of vehicles (e.g. small cars, convertibles) for various durations (one day or one week), often including insurance and charging an all-inclusive price.

Rail operators, such as Eurostar and Virgin Trains, provide a fast and comfortable way of travelling longer distances in the UK and in Europe. Many train companies have now upgraded their trains, providing services for business travellers in their first-class compartments.

Sea operators such as ferries (Brittany Ferries, Sea France) link a number of British ports, such as Dover, Portsmouth and Fishguard, with continental Europe, Ireland and the Channel Islands, and provide sea routes as an alternative to air transport. Ferries have undergone many changes in recent years, particularly following the opening of the Channel Tunnel as they then had to compete with another form of transport. There are also non-sea-going ferries – for example, across the River Tyne.

ACTIVITY

Investigate the products and services, routes and vessels of ferry operators.

Cruises tend to provide a holiday experience rather than being purely a form of transportation. Modern cruise ships now offer a wide range of services on board such as bars and restaurants, sports facilities, shops and entertainment. They provide complete holidays for a variety of customers.

ACTIVITY

Using the internet as well as other media such as newspapers, TV or radio, research recent developments in the transport sector. Be able to present two developments during a class discussion.

Visitor attractions

Visitor attractions can play a large part in a destination's success. They attract visitors and encourage them to stay at a destination longer, thus increasing visitor spending.

There are both natural and man-made attractions. Among natural attractions there are Areas of Outstanding Natural Beauty (AONBs), National Parks, beaches, lakes and beautiful landscapes.

Man-made attractions include purpose-built attractions such as theme parks (e.g. Alton Towers), museums such as the British Museum and heritage attractions such as Maritime Greenwich, galleries (e.g. Tate Britain), stately and historic homes, cathedrals, ornamental gardens, and castles. Such attractions are often owned and/or managed by organisations such as the National Trust or English Heritage.

Fig 1.03 Alton Towers theme park

There are also attractions based on events, which attract tourists to a destination or region. Examples include cultural events such as the Venice Film Festival or sporting events such as the London Marathon or the Olympics.

Attractions such as the National Gallery or the British Museum may offer free admission, while others charge an entrance fee (e.g. Madame Tussauds or Thorpe Park). Paid-for attractions tend to be privately owned while free attractions are usually publicly owned.

Tour operators

Tour operators combine into holidays the various products and services offered by travel and tourism

Fig 1.04 Tate Britain

Fig 1.05 Waterskiing

ACTIVITY

Prepare a list of 20 UK attractions. Identify whether they are natural or built, privately or publicly owned, free or charging an entrance fee.

companies and sell them as packages to customers according to customer preference, need and budget. Tour operators contract accommodation and transport, negotiating lower prices due to the volume of business they can guarantee. Large tour operators also own hotels or airlines in order to have more control over their capacity and offer more competitively priced services to their customers.

There is a wide range of packages offered by tour operators according to their customers' needs and expectations. These could be summer or winter holidays, short-haul destinations (reached within five hours or less by plane from the UK) or long-haul destinations (reached in more than five hours by plane from the UK), suitable for different age groups (i.e. young adults – Club 18–30, over-50s – Saga) or offering different activities such as skiing, diving or hiking.

Tour operators can be divided according to the destinations they offer. These could be: *domestic*, organising services for domestic tourists; *inbound*, organising services for tourists incoming to the UK; and *outbound*, organising services for UK residents travelling abroad.

Tour operators can be further divided into mass market and niche operators. Mass market operators, such as Thomson or Cosmos, offer holidays that appeal to a large number of customers. These could be a two-week package in Spain or a week in the Algarve during the summer months. The niche tour operators devise holidays that cater for customers' specific interests, such as Mediterranean cruises for lovers of ancient history with lectures as part of the cruise programme. The niche operator may also focus on a specific destination such as Essouira in Morocco as opposed to the more established Agadir, or offer a particular activity such as painting or wine-tasting in France.

Travel agents

Travel agents sell different travel and tourism services, such as holidays, accommodation only or train tickets. They also book flights, ferries or car hire, sell additional services such as travel insurance and

Fig 1.06 Sunbathing

Multiple chains, such as Thomas Cook and Going Places, are well known and have branches nationwide, while miniples are usually found in one region of the country such as Yorkshire and Lancashire.

Retail travel agents tend to be located in the high street or in shopping centres, which guarantee them a high volume of passing traffic. They predominantly deal with leisure travellers, offering them the wide range of services discussed above.

Business travel agents deal with business travellers, offering them travel services and making travel arrangements for their trips. Their branches are often located on the premises of the companies they work with and these are called implants. For example, there is a small office of BTI (Business Travel International) UK on the premises of PricewaterhouseCoopers in central London.

Where travel agents handle a large number of calls, they sometimes use out-of-town call centres. Due to lower labour costs, many companies open call centres outside the UK – for example, in India. On the next page there is a case study of an innovative call centre idea implemented by Co-op Travel.

Because of these benefits, home-based virtual contact centres constitute one of the fastest-growing trends in the contact centre market.

> Industry experts estimate that by eliminating office costs and the associated administrative overheads, the home-based contact centre operates at around half the operating costs of a traditional site-based contact centre …
>
> Home-based agents enjoy a net benefit equivalent to a 15 per cent increase in salary – as a result of travel-to-work time being eliminated, greater flexibility and associated work–life balance benefits.

(Source: www.flexibility.co.uk, accessed May 2007)

ACTIVITY

Using the ABTA (The Travel Association, www.abta.com) and AITO (Association of Independent Tour Operators, www.aito.co.uk) websites – as well as other sources – find ten different tour operators. Find out whether they are domestic, inbound or outbound, mass market or niche.

foreign currency, and offer advice about destinations in terms of visas and health requirements.

Depending on the nature of their business, they may operate in the following outlets:

- retail shops
- business shops or 'implants'
- call centres
- online (e-tailers).

Travel agents may operate as independent outlets if they are not a part of a chain. Such shops are normally run by their owners and often have a small number of employees who typically offer a high level of expertise. The majority of travel agents, however, belong to chains, whether multiples or 'miniples'.

Online agents have mostly developed during the last few years with companies such as Expedia, Lastminute.com, ebookers and Opodo. These companies take advantage of modern technologies and customers' preference for booking holidays from the comfort of their own homes via the internet.

Case study

How to run a call centre in the UK

We've all heard about the 'offshoring' of call centres: outsourcing them overseas, especially to the Indian subcontinent – all made possible by new technologies. Even newer technologies, however, raise the possibility of 'homeshoring' – using home-based call centre agents in the UK as a cost-effective alternative.

While these virtual call centres (also called contact centres) cannot compete on labour costs, the reduction in property costs and telephony costs, plus the advantage of having first-language English speakers is now making this a competitive option.

Having 630 ABTA-certified home-based operatives makes the Co-op Travel Group's Future Travel subsidiary the largest virtual contact centre in the UK. And it is convinced of the benefits. According to Peter Healey, technical director of Future Travel:

> **We've reduced staff churn by offering flexible home working to, for example, new mothers returning to work part-time, or older people looking to reduce their hours but not yet ready to retire. In the travel industry, an effective home working centre means that you keep valuable knowledge and experience within the company. Being able to add or reduce lines to fit peak booking times, such as evenings and weekends, means that we can plan capacity.**

Support services

Tourism development and promotion

Tourism development and promotion are mainly carried out by organisations in the public sector, as they tend to be responsible for the support and promotion of the private sector. Organisations such local, regional or national tourist boards are normally involved in such activities.

ACTIVITY

Investigate and describe the roles and responsibilities of VisitBritain.

Trade associations

Trade associations, such as AITO (Association of Independent Tour Operators), ABTA (The Travel Association) and GBTA (Guild of Travel Management Companies) are organisations whose members are privately owned travel and tourism organisations that pay membership fees towards the running costs of the association. Trade associations, in exchange, look after their members' interests and represent their opinions. They also provide a set of rules for their members, often through a code of practice.

Ancillary services

These are services that are offered in addition to the main travel and tourism products as companies strive to deliver the best service to customers. These could include travel insurance, airport parking and money exchange. These enhance the customer's experience and often allow agents to increase their commission.

How the components interrelate

The chain of distribution in Figure 1.07 describes how travel and tourism products and services reach customers. As the travel and tourism industry does not manufacture goods but offers services, at the top of the chain of distribution there are accommodation and transport providers and attractions. The services offered by them are often packaged by tour operators, the wholesalers, and sold through travel agents, the retailers, to customers.

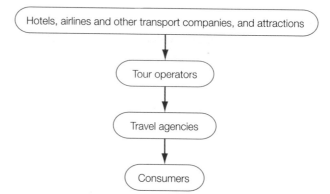

Fig 1.07 Traditional chain of distribution in travel and tourism

However, this is not the only way of distributing travel and tourism products and services; both accommodation and transport providers sell directly to customers, who can book their services by telephone or using their websites.

Customers can also use travel agents, who will book transportation or accommodation directly with airlines or hotels without involving a tour operator. Many tour operators have also taken advantage of the opportunity presented by the internet and started distributing their holidays directly, excluding travel agents completely.

Recent years have seen many other changes to the structure of the travel and tourism industry. A number of organisations in travel and tourism have merged, formed partnerships or taken over other organisations. Intercontinental Hotels took over other holiday chains – for example, Holiday Inn and Crowne Plaza. This is an example of horizontal integration, which means that integration happened at the same level in the chain of distribution.

Organisations also merge with others on different levels in the chain of distribution – for example, a tour operator can take over an airline or a chain of travel agencies. This is called vertical integration. An example of vertical integration is Thomson (a tour operator) which bought Britannia Airways and re-branded it as Thomsonfly.

ACTIVITY

Find current examples of recent mergers, partnership and integration.

Companies join together in order to gain greater market share and offer a wider range of products to their customers, as well as find other ways of distribution so they can make their operations more economical. More economic operation gives them the opportunity to offer customers lower prices and thus compete successfully in the very competitive travel and tourism market.

There are also other forms of working together. For example, airlines form alliances, which is a form of partnership. This does not involve buying one another. Instead they liaise in order to offer a wider network of routes and destinations. Travel agents, often independents, join networks such as Advantage in order to increase their buying power, negotiate better commission levels and thus compete with the multiples.

ACTIVITY

Investigate alliances among airlines such as Star Alliance and One World. How do they work? What are the benefits for customers?

Assessing the outcome

A small number of travel and tourism companies are recruiting for junior positions. The positions are available at a hotel, a tour operator and an online agent, a visitor attraction and a local Tourist Information Centre (TIC). As part of the selection process representatives of those companies wish to assess your understanding of the travel and tourism industry, your research skills and most importantly your current knowledge of all the components as well as how they work together. Prepare a report that covers the above issues.

- Describe (giving examples, including domestic, inbound and outbound tourism) the components of the travel and tourism industry (**P1**).
- Describe the ways that components of travel and tourism interrelate (**P2**).

The roles and responsibilities of organisations within the different sectors

The majority of organisations in the travel and tourism industry belong to the private, for-profit sector. This also means that the majority of organisations are funded privately, either through the sale of goods and services or bank loans required to start or develop the company. In the case of large companies, such as British Airways or the Virgin Group, the funds could also come through the sale of shares. The shares may go up or down in value depending on how the company performs. We call such companies *public companies* as the public can buy their shares, not because they are a part of the public sector.

The main objective of businesses, and therefore the reason why companies trade, is to make a profit and stay in business. This may be achieved in many ways – for example, by ensuring good customer service so customers come back and make recommendations to their friends and family. By doing this, companies ensure sales without spending much on promotion, thus maintaining higher profits. A lot of tour operators ask customers to complete questionnaires at the end of their holidays or feedback cards at the end of their stay at a hotel to establish what met customer expectations and what could be improved.

These objectives can also be achieved by offering competitive prices. Profits may not be high but sales are likely to increase. A number of travel companies closely watch the flight or holiday prices offered by their competitors in order to ensure they can still attract customers.

Another way of ensuring profits is by tightly controlling business expenses – for example, operating from cheaper premises or recruiting staff from abroad. Thomson recently moved its headquarters from Camden, London, to Luton, while a number of hospitality companies now recruit in the new European accession states offering salaries lower than those offered to staff hired in the UK.

Private-sector companies also need to maximise sales. This can be done through promotion and advertising, which can be quite expensive, or through a selection of discounts and carefully set prices as well as through developing customer loyalty. This is also achieved through bringing new products onto the market, ensuring customer interest in your offer.

Companies also aim to increase market share. This is necessary to reduce the impact of competition and increase market control. As discussed earlier, this can also be achieved through horizontal integration.

Organisations are expected to provide service to customers and to other organisations. This is particularly true in the non-for-profit sector where tourist boards offer services to organisations in the for-profit sector by promoting them. They also offer information about their services to clients. An example of this could be a TIC (Tourist Information Centre), which may have a selection of leaflets on B&Bs available in the area. These are given to customers interested in finding information about places to stay for the night.

Organisations in travel and tourism are expected to operate in compliance with various regulations. These could be industry regulations imposed on their members by trade associations such as ABTA. ABTA members need to follow the Code of Conduct that requires, for example, travel agents to respond to a complaint within 28 days.

The CAA (Civil Aviation Authority), the organisation responsible for regulating airports and airlines, ensures that all of them meet safety requirements. It also ensures that all operators offering package holidays that include air travel have the Air Travel Organisers Licence (ATOL). This means that if the company goes bankrupt, customers will recover their deposits and their booking may be re-protected (another tour operator will handle the customer's reservation) using the bond money.

Regulations and legislation do not have to be industry-specific. All companies have to comply with the DDA (Disability Discrimination Act) and Data Protection Act. Their promotional activities, whether in the form of adverts or brochures, have to adhere to Advertising Standards Agency (ASA) guidelines, which expect all promotional materials to be legal, decent, honest and truthful. Failure to do so may result in fines and/or the promotional material having to be withdrawn.

In addition, all organisations (for-profit and not-for-profit sector) have to comply with employment law and issue employees with contracts, offer them paid holiday, maternity leave and other contractual arrangements.

The for-profit sector includes organisations such as airlines, rail operators, coach companies, hotels, holiday centres, theme parks, tour operators, travel agents, car-hire companies and many others. The not-for-profit sector includes the majority of public organisations, regulatory bodies and conservation groups. Their main role is to support and promote the for-profit sector for the benefit of all stakeholders – for example, employees, customers, other organisations and the government. Their funding comes mainly from the government through the Department for Culture, Media and Sport (DCMS) in the form of grants. Their funding may also come from donations, National Lottery grants or membership fees. This means they are not involved in selling and competing for customers although they may subsidise their income by the sale of souvenirs or postcards, renting out their premises, charging for training, etc., or reinvesting the proceeds of commercial operations such as shops.

The main tasks of not-for-profit organisations are:

- introducing common standards
- supporting the travel and tourism industry
- preparing statistics
- promoting destination to potential visitors.

ACTIVITY

Identify the roles and responsibilities of six selected travel and tourism organisations. Identify their sources of funding.

Assessing the outcome

The interview panel from the previous assignment now wants you to demonstrate your knowledge of the roles and responsibilities of travel and tourism organisations from different sectors.

- Describe the roles and responsibilities of travel and tourism organisations from the profit and not-for-profit sectors (**P3**).

Recent developments in travel and tourism

Although people have always travelled, however easy or difficult it was, it is only in the past 50 years that the travel and tourism industry has really developed.

In the past, people had different reasons to travel; for example, a lot of trips were taken for VFR purposes (visiting friends and relatives) or to trade, while leisure travel now dominates the market, offering a wide variety of transport, accommodation and holidays.

Many factors influenced the development of tourism after the Second World War (1939–45). The main ones are related to money, time and technology.

First, the annual 'two-week' holiday (with pay) was established. This meant that for the first time people could take two weeks off a year and still be paid for the time they were on holiday. Naturally, this encouraged many more people to travel.

Fig 1.08 UK tourists on a British beach in the 1940s

Increasing numbers of people were also buying cars, which allowed them to take holidays in the UK or on the continent. Because of this increased mobility, a lot more people were also taking short breaks.

Faster and bigger passenger aircraft were developed, which enabled more and more people to travel to destinations previously out of their reach. In the past, they would have to travel there by sea, which took a long time and was therefore expensive.

As Britain was rebuilt after the war, British consumers had more disposable income, which they spent on travel, and on foreign travel in particular. This, in combination with the development of aircraft, led to the creation of package holidays.

ACTIVITY

Interview some of your older relatives or family friends and find out where they travelled and why.

Legislation

The government saw the potential for tourism to generate income for the British economy. The Development of Tourism Act 1969 confirmed the

Fig 1.09 UK tourists on package holidays in Spain in the 1970s

public sector's involvement in tourism and the role it was going to play – one of encouraging the provision and improvement of tourist amenities as well as encouraging people to visit Britain and people living in Britain to take their holidays there. This was to be done by appointed bodies: the English, Scottish and Welsh Tourist Boards as well as the British Tourist Authority.

Further legislation, such as the Transport Acts 1980 and 1985, contributed to the development of tourism through deregulation and privatisation.

Further pieces of legislation, this time imposed by the European Parliament, further influenced the development of tourism. The Package Travel Regulations of 1992 subjected all tour operators to stricter financial controls and imposed responsibility on them for their customers. These regulations required all operators offering air packages to allocate a sum of money (a bond), calculated on the basis of their turnover, to be placed in the bank in case of financial difficulties. The bond could then be drawn on to refund customers' deposits, pay suppliers or even return passengers otherwise stranded abroad safely home.

More recently, legislation such as the Disability Discrimination Act 2004 has had a great impact on travel and tourism organisations, particularly accommodation and transport providers and attractions, in terms of the necessity to increase accessibility for disabled customers.

Following the introduction of Air Passenger Duty in 1997, the government decided to increase it again from February 2007. We are still waiting to assess the true impact of this increase on all air travel.

> "The hidden costs of flying will rise significantly from February as UK airport departure taxes double. Chancellor Gordon Brown's pre-budget statement announced that economy class passengers will pay £10 on all domestic and European short-haul flights, long haulers will pay £40 and business and first class travellers will have to pay £40 for short-haul and £80 for long-haul flights.
>
> Whether the doubling of airport tax will actually get people to switch to trains – or to not travel at all – is uncertain. Reactions were fairly predictable: environmentalists said it was nowhere near enough, but the angry aviation industry said it was being treated like a cash cow. 'Air passenger duty provides the Treasury with extra funds for general public expenditure without any benefit to the environment whatsoever,' said a British Airways spokesman – ignoring the fact that aviation's contribution to climate change is soaring and is expected to get far worse."

(Source: John Vidal, The Guardian, Saturday, 9 December 2006, copyright Guardian News & Media Ltd 2006)

ACTIVITY

Select three pieces of recent legislation relating to travel and tourism and analyse their impact on the industry.

Product development

In order to ensure a certain level of sales, repeat business and competitiveness, companies in travel and tourism have to develop their product to meet the ever-changing expectations of their customers.

One of the fastest-changing sectors is the airline industry. The most significant change recently has been the boom in low-cost airlines. These offer inexpensive flights to many European cities. The principle behind this is explained in the earlier part of this unit. This increased competition on European routes not only in terms of price but also quality of service, as scheduled airlines responded by attempting to offer better value for money.

Case study

Is low price the only way forward on short-haul routes?

In 1998, British Airways launched a comprehensive range of new services and benefits for 'World Traveller' passengers. New features included seats with adjustable headrests and footrests, and more knee room; and personal video screens for every passenger.

Changes were also introduced on long-haul routes and in cabins, which normally generate the majority of airline revenue on flights – business class and first class.

(Source: www.bamuseum.com, accessed May 2007)

Case study

How to travel in comfort with BA

In August 2000, new Club World 'flying beds' were available on the Hong Kong route. The seats had been well received by customers on the Heathrow–New York JFK route, with significant rises in customer satisfaction ratings for cabin crew, catering, sleep, privacy, comfort and space.

(Source: www.bamuseum.com, accessed May 2007)

Case study

What is World Traveller Plus?

In January 2000 British Airways announced the introduction of a new cabin class, World Traveller Plus. The cabin would offer more space and facilities than World Traveller for a premium on top of the full World Traveller fare.

Apart from the extra leg room, passengers were also offered:

- double hand-baggage allowance (two pieces, 12kg total)
- separate cabin with a maximum of five rows; a personal in-seat entertainment system; laptop power point and individual phone.

World Traveller Plus opened for sale for travel from 29 October, 2000, for services between London Heathrow and New York JFK, Hong Kong and San Francisco.

(Source: www.bamuseum.com, accessed May 2007)

includes transportation, accommodation, all food and drink, activities and entertainment.

As people started taking more holidays, but shorter in duration, more and more operators started offering city breaks.

Destination development

Apart from the well-established short-haul destinations, such as Spain and Greece, gradually long-haul destinations were brought onto the market. Florida, with its theme parks, national parks and warm climate throughout the year became very popular with families. Destinations such as Goa and Thailand offered an opportunity for beach holidays in long-haul locations. Inexpensive accommodation, food and drink at these destinations also contributed to their popularity.

Recently, Eastern European destinations, such as Prague and Croatia, have been added to the variety of popular destinations in Europe, while Cuba seems to be a long-haul hit.

Destinations themselves have started preparing better to receive their visitors: tougher health and safety measures have been introduced, following the EU Package Travel Directive, making operators

The airline industry was not the only one implementing change: a new fast train called Eurostar, linking London with Paris and Brussels, was introduced in 1994, using the undersea tunnel built between Britain and mainland Europe, providing a fast transport route for both foot and car passengers.

Since the introduction of the first two-week holidays to Spain, tour operators have also brought various innovations to the market. Apart from the changes already discussed earlier in this unit, customers can now book an all-inclusive package that

Fig 1.10 Thailand, a popular long-haul destination

responsible for their suppliers. Some destinations also addressed the issue of crime, thus improving their chances of attracting regular business. In many established destinations, such as Spain, there have been improvements in infrastructure, facilities and attractions on offer, making the holidaymaker's stay easier, more enjoyable and providing more opportunities for increased spending.

Fig 1.11 Croatia, a popular new destination

ACTIVITY

ABTA identifies some destinations with potential for growth. Read through this section of ABTA's report on its website using the link below and find out which destinations these are.
What could contribute to their growth in popularity?

(Source: www.abtamembers.org/press/kit/ trends.htm, accessed May 2007)

Technological developments

Various booking systems were created in order to accelerate communication between organisations in travel and tourism and improve the distribution of their services:

- ViewData (used by travel agents and tour operators)

- CRSs (computer reservation systems – used by airlines)
- Global Distribution Systems (e.g. Galileo, Worldspan, Sabre and Amadeus – used by travel agents, tour operators, airlines, car-hire companies and ferry operators).

Other technological advances are linked to the internet. Companies such as airlines, hotels and tour operators offer online booking facilities on secure websites.

In order to allow customers to 'experience' the products and services offered by the travel and tourism industry, 'virtual tours' were devised. These are used by hotels so potential customers can view rooms, common areas and other facilities available on the premises.

Visitor attractions such as the Globe Theatre in London or Chessington World of Adventures also use such tools to allow customers to have a more tangible experience of the services on offer, prior to booking, encouraging them to make a reservation.

Further developments can be observed in the airline industry: e.g. e-ticketing, paperless tickets, self-check-in at airports and online check-in. These help reduce operational costs such as postal bills as tickets no longer need to be posted or replaced if lost in the post. This also reduces the number of check-in staff required as check-in is done remotely or by passengers themselves.

Apart from wide-bodied jets such as the 747 introduced by Boeing in 1969, with its cruising speed of 600 miles per hour and a non-stop range of 7200 miles, larger planes are now being developed. The Airbus A380, with its cruising speed of 500 miles per hour and its 8000 mile range, has already been ordered by a number of airlines, which may either use it to carry more passengers, or to carry passengers in more comfort.

In 1968, some ferry companies introduced hovercrafts, which offer a faster sea connection with France thus competing with airlines, and now, more recently, the Channel Tunnel.

Lifestyle changes

The growth of tourism can also be attributed to lifestyle changes. Higher levels of urbanisation and education encourage us to travel more and further in pursuit of different cultures; having learnt more, we would now like to see it for ourselves. Increased levels of mobility resulting from car ownership as well as the increasing availability of airports, seaports and railway connections help us get around more easily.

Overall we also have more leisure time than our grandparents did. Having various household appliances performing most of our chores and enjoying longer paid holidays gives us more choice as to how we want to spend our leisure time.

Britain is now an ageing society with an increasing number of older people who have more spare time and are willing to spend it travelling. There is now a growing number of companies offering travel and tourism services to mature travellers, e.g. Saga Holidays accepts bookings from customers who are 50 or older, and Page & Moy provides tours to people 45+.

With the increase in the number of single and divorced people, holidays for singles seem to be on the increase, with companies such as Solos Holidays or justyou.co.uk leading the way.

Consumer demand

Overall customer demand for tourism seems to be growing, with increasing numbers of customers being more travelled, having higher expectations, being aware of their rights and not afraid to complain if necessary.

The number of incoming trips has increased too. According to the Office of National Statistics, in 2005 overseas residents made a record 30 million visits to the UK, 2.2 million more than in 2004. While they were here, they spent a record £14.2 billion, an increase of £1.2 billion on 2004.

The number of outgoing trips has also increased. UK residents made a record 66.4 million visits abroad, an increase of 4 per cent on the previous year. UK residents also spent a record amount abroad: £32.2 billion – an increase of 6 per cent on 2004.

This shows that the number of trips taken by UK residents is greater than the number of tourists received in the UK in 2005. Moreover, the amount of money spent by UK residents on their outbound holidays is also greater than the amount of money earned from our incoming visitors. This difference, otherwise called the balance of payments, is negative and adds up to £18 billion. The balance of payments is the relationship between tourism import (outbound trips) and tourism export (incoming trips); it has been negative in Britain for a number of years and seems to be increasing every year.

According to www.tourismtrade.org.uk (accessed May 2007), spending by domestic tourists (i.e. spending by UK tourists within the UK) has now reached the figure of £11.5 billion, with visitors taking a total of 59.3 million trips annually.

Tourism is considered to be one of the largest industries in the UK, approximately 3.5 per cent of the UK economy, and was worth approximately £74.2 billion in 2003.

The number of jobs in travel and tourism also seems to be on the increase, to match customer demand for travel and tourism products and services. According to *Labour Market Trends*, September 2004:

- there are an estimated 1.4 million jobs in tourism in the UK, some 5 per cent of all people in employment in the UK
- approximately 130,400 of these jobs are in self-employment.

Particular growth has been registered in the hospitality and accommodation industries with even greater growth predicted before 2012 when London will be hosting the Olympic Games.

Trends and factors affecting the development of travel and tourism

It is now time to investigate the trends in the travel and tourism industry, attempting to predict where it may go during the next few years. Some of the developments discussed in the earlier part of this unit will provide the basis for this prediction – for example, the number of holidays taken by UK residents seems to be on the increase, with the majority of people taking more than one holiday a year.

Customers now have a wider range of booking methods of which they can take full advantage. According to an ABTA report:

> **The number of respondents who said they were likely to book via the internet in the future had risen by 4 per cent compared with 2002. According to Mintel despite a slowing growth in internet penetration, the way in which the internet is being used and accessed is changing. Mintel reported that travel agents continued to be the most popular booking method for holidays abroad. However, this was changing and the proportion of holidaymakers using this method decreased by 12 percentage points to 49 per cent between 1999 and 2003. Travel agents were gradually losing market share to direct bookings through tour operators (up 3 percentage points) and the increase in independent bookings, particularly those made through the internet.**

(Source: www.abta.com, accessed May 2007)

Apart from the traditional methods such as booking via travel agent, Teletext, or tour operator either by telephone or website, there is now the option of booking via mobile phone, at present restricted to flights only due to the complexity of other services.

The rise in independent travel looks set to continue due to the increasing use of the Internet. According to ABTA, the figures for internet use are:

- 52 per cent of the British population have access to the internet at home
- 44 per cent of adults have used the internet for information about travel and accommodation
- 53 per cent are likely to book a holiday on the internet over the next two years.

This trend also leads to an increased number of so-called 'unpacked' packages – independent arrangements where travellers often combine transport and accommodation for themselves, creating a holiday that meets their particular needs.

Case study

What kind of holiday do we want?

In spite of summer and winter sun holidays', domination of the package holiday market, *a growing number of people are buying activity packages and adventure holidays …*

Beaches for relaxation are the number one request for luxury seekers, whether that's 'barefoot' or 'glitz', but often clients are looking for something more exciting for secondary breaks. Big sporting events have become popular, along with luxury skiing, diving, sailing, golf and spa breaks. Increasingly, 'experiential' holidays that are aspirational, exclusive and unknown are being sought. Round-the-world travel, going to Antarctica or finding gorillas in Uganda are not only expensive, but are literally quite difficult to do and deliberately do not appeal to everyone.

(Source: www.abta.com, accessed May 2007)

There has been steady growth in the use of regional airports. This is mainly due to the continuing expansion of low-cost airlines. It is estimated that the low-cost airline sector in Europe carried around 80 million passengers in 2004, of which over 60 million started or ended their journey at a UK airport.

ACTIVITY

London Luton Airport is one of the UK's fastest-growing airports, with passenger numbers of 7.5 million during the calendar year 2004, an increase of 400 per cent in ten years.
Read about the potential growth of Luton Airport on its website and identify reasons for its popularity and success.
(Source: www.london-luton.co.uk, accessed May 2007)

Factors influencing customer choice

Natural disasters such as hurricanes, tornadoes, earthquakes, droughts and floods as well as volcano eruptions are classified as natural disasters. To a certain extent, they influence customer choice of destinations as nobody wants to holiday in an area struck by a natural disaster, particularly if the essential infrastructure has been destroyed.

Although travel and tourism organisations cannot avoid natural disasters, they can strive to minimise their impacts. Tourists tend to avoid destinations such as the Caribbean during the hurricane season and the industry attempts to encourage travellers by lowering prices during that period.

Every now and then there is a health scare which dissuades travellers from visiting some destinations. Foot-and-mouth disease cost Britain a lot of inbound visitors, estimated at £8.8 billion according to www.lga.gov.uk (accessed May 2007). The outbreak of SARS affected tourism to and from Hong Kong and Canada where the virus spread. The latest example of an epidemic was avian flu, which frightened customers away from destinations such as Turkey.

Case study

Bird flu in Turkey?

Turkey was. . .tipped to be a front-runner in the short/medium-haul market this year, but reports about avian flu in the eastern parts of the country in January 2006 badly affected the early booking period, even though these outbreaks amongst poultry would have no effect on tourists.

(Source: www.abtamembers.org, accessed May 2007)

The most unexpected threat at present seems to be terrorism. Events in New York, Madrid and Bali acted as an obvious deterrent for a number of visitors to those destinations. Terrorist atrocities, and a destination's ability to recover from them may be seen as a real popularity test. Some destinations, in spite of attacks, still attract significant visitor numbers and tourist confidence seems unaffected.

Case study

Are we still scared to go to Egypt?

Bookings to Egypt have again been high, despite the terrorist attack in Sharm el Sheikh in July 2005. Growth has been driven by visits to this top diving destination, even though visits to the ancient sites in either Cairo or the Valley of the Kings are still popular. . . .the exciting scuba diving and year-round sunshine of the Sinai desert present great value for money and excellent hotel accommodation is also securing growth.

(Source: www.abtamembers.org, accessed May 2007)

ACTIVITY

Read through reports in the press of other destinations affected by natural disasters, health warnings or terrorism. Assess the damage caused by them.

More travellers are now choosing their tour operators according to their commitment to environmental issues, therefore some tour operators have learnt to make this their selling point.

Case study

How committed is AITO?

At AITO we take our responsibilities to the environment, to local cultures and to sustainability very seriously. AITO members recognise that the destinations where they provide holidays are the life blood of the industry.

(Source: www.aito.co.uk, accessed May 2007)

With the rise in popularity of low-cost airlines, particularly in Europe, fares have tumbled due to the increased competition and a revised approach to airline operations. Yet cheap travel may soon be a thing of the past due to the proposed 'green' taxes on airlines, which are considered one of the greatest polluters. Other forms of transport, particularly those considered to be 'greener and cleaner', such as rail, may start competing more with air travel.

Development of tourism

Tourism clearly continues to grow, in spite of periods of low demand and the temporary effects of terrorism and natural disasters. With the increase in globalisation, business travel, especially the conference and events market, is on the increase.

There are new generating markets such as Russia, India and China, which the UK is planning to attract.

Cruising continued to grow in 2005 and now makes up about 5 per cent of the travel industry. There has been a 13 per cent increase in cruise passengers choosing to sail from UK ports.

Case study

The future of cruising

It is estimated that 1.5 million British people will take a cruise by 2008. A steady stream of new ships will ensure that a keen cruiser will continue to have plenty of choice. Cruises can be traditional and formal – Cunard has announced that there will be a third *Queen* to join its fleet, *Queen Victoria*, or they can be activity-based and informal – such as *Ocean Village* – and there are many ranges in between. Meanwhile Royal Caribbean Cruise Lines has announced the building of a 5400 passenger megaship.

(Source: www.abtamembers.org, accessed May 2007)

Assessing the outcome

Having reached this stage of your interview, you are now asked to describe the key trends and factors that are likely to have an impact on the development of travel and tourism.

● Describe three key trends and three factors that are affecting or are likely to affect the development of travel and tourism (**P5**).

Improve your grade

If you are reading this part of the unit, you are clearly interested in achieving higher grades. To do so you need to be clear how to get there. This section of the unit endeavours to give you that understanding.

First, we encourage you to do all the activities provided in this unit. They provide a firm basis for your understanding of the travel and tourism industry and for your further research, which will lead you hopefully to a merit or distinction. Without basic knowledge, you cannot achieve higher grades.

You can start off by working on your pass criteria and gradually get to a merit or distinction. For example, criteria **P1**, **P2** and **M1** are linked together. While for **P1** and **P2** you will be describing (*saying how things are*), for **M1** you are expected to explain (*give reasons, answer the why and how questions*). If you are not sure what you are expected to do, check the Glossary at the back of the book to get a better idea.

Having completed all the activities, you will be able to describe different accommodation providers in terms of their products, services, prices and location. This will be sufficient for a pass grade, while heading for a merit you give reasons why accommodation providers work with tourist boards in this country to attract domestic customers. Another example could be why tour operators work with travel agents and how this relationship has recently been changing. This way you will satisfy the requirements of the merit criterion.

When you preparing evidence for **P3**, with some extra work you will also gain **M2** and possibly **D1**. Your task in this textbook requires you to research six selected organisations and identify their roles and funding. If you spend more time on this task and compare the roles and responsibilities of travel and tourism organisations from the profit and not-for-profit sectors, you will satisfy the merit criterion.

Make sure, however, that you select a variety of organisations so there are some similarities as well as differences. If you then wish to take it further, and attempt a distinction, you need to assess (*make value judgements*) how the roles and responsibilities of travel and tourism organisations from the profit and not-for-profit sectors affect their operations. For example, if not-for-profit companies receive money from the government, how does this affect their operation? Do they achieve their objectives, thus satisfying their stakeholders?

When working on **P4** you can also work on **P5**, as some recent developments will influence the immediate future of travel and tourism so you can use them to form predictions and trends. This part of your assignment requires a lot of research as you may not be familiar with various issues and may not understand their significance immediately. Ask your tutor for clarification but also be prepared to do some finding out yourself and do not give up easily. Remember, you are aiming for higher grades! Choose developments that interest you, as you will find it easier to learn about them. You do not need to cover them all: choose the ones you understand and are able to explain (*give reasons, answer why/how questions*). For **D2**, you need to recommend (*make suggestions*) and justify (*give good reason*) how the travel and tourism industry could respond to key trends and factors affecting the future development of travel and

tourism. If you do not have many ideas of your own, speak to people who work for travel and tourism organisations as they deal with similar issues on a fairly regular basis. Don't be put off: try more than one contact, get in touch with the Tourism Society or your local tourist board. Eventually, they will give you some help and inspiration.

Top tips

- You must know the components of travel and tourism before you can begin to explain how they interrelate.
- You must know the sectors, roles and responsibilities of different organisations before you start to compare them or assess their impact.
- You must know about developments before you can explain their impact and recommend how to respond to them.
- You must know what evidence you need to produce (in what form, i.e. report, presentation) and on which topic (e.g. components of the travel and tourism industry).
- You must be clear as to what you are expected to do (e.g. describe, explain, assess) to achieve each criterion.
- You must research and use examples to support your statements.

There are many different types of organisation in the travel and tourism industry. They can be categorised in different ways. There are organisations such as travel agents, tour operators and support services. These are categorised by the products and services they provide. Organisations can also be categorised by the role they play in the chain of distribution, i.e. are they producers, wholesalers, retailers, etc.? Organisations can also be categorised in terms of whether they operate in the public, private or voluntary sector. For this outcome, you need to categorise organisations as either those that are profit-making or those that are non-profit-making.

Features of different types of travel and tourism organisation

Profit

There are many ways to try and determine which organisations are profit-making and which are non-profit-making. One of the key ways to differentiate between them is to look at the objectives of the organisation. Does it state that it aims to make a profit? For example, the Family Holidays Association

(FHA) exists to provide holidays and other recreational activities for those families disadvantaged by poverty. In 2007, it is anticipated that over 1300 families will go on holiday as a result of its activities (www.fhaonline.org.uk). The FHA sets out its objectives as:

- to increase the number of families who have access to holidays
- to research and promote the value of holidays for families experiencing disadvantage
- to increase awareness of the scale and scope of the problem of lack of access to holidays.

British Airways, in its 2005/6 *Annual Report and Accounts*, states, 'a ten per cent operating profit margin remains the financial target'. From these objectives, it can be seen that British Airways can be classed as a profit-making organisation and the FHA as a non-profit-making organisation.

In its simplest terms, a profit is the surplus made by a business when income is greater than costs or revenue exceeds expenditure.

Case study

Profit calculation

Birt Tours organises excursions to the coast during the summer. It costs £500 to hire the coach, which includes the cost of the driver for the day. It paid £150 for a tour guide to accompany the trip. There are 54 seats on the coach. It charges £16 for each customer. For one trip, it sold 44 tickets. In this situation the expenditure was £650 (coach hire and tour guide) and revenue was £704 (44 tickets sold at £16) so the company made a profit of £54.

Income through ticket sales	704
Costs	650
Profit	54

ACTIVITY

Calculate the profit made in the following situations.

1. Marine Museum charges £4.50 for adult entrance and £3 for concessions. It knows it costs £2150 each week in wages and £1945 in overheads (rent, gas, electricity, etc.). In the four weeks of February, ticket sales were as follows:

Week 1   18 adults, 112 concessions
Week 2   66 adults, 239 concessions
Week 3   287 adults, 801 concessions
Week 4   22 adults, 184 concessions

2. The New Heys Hotel has 46 rooms with ensuite facilities. It charges £85 per room per night Monday to Thursday and £69 Friday to Sunday. This includes breakfast. These are the only meals available in the hotel. Each week, staff costs are £3400 and overheads are approximately £5800. In the first week of May, room bookings were as follows:

Sunday   24
Monday   31
Tuesday   46
Wednesday   46
Thursday   39
Friday   29
Saturday   27

It is very rare for an organisation to be able to operate without planning to make a profit or surplus. Even if it were a government-run organisation (public sector), it would be expected that it operate within its budget. Members of organisations such as the National Trust or The Travel Association (ABTA) would not be impressed with management if at the end of the year it asked them for more money because it had operated at a loss. The FHA, as mentioned above, would not meet its objectives if it set out to bring in just enough income to cover its costs. Making a profit, or at least aiming to make a profit, is essential to any business. This ensures they can cover all their costs and if there is any surplus, they can look at improving the products and services they provide.

Distribution of profits

There are many features that can be used to describe organisations. How organisations use their profit is one of those features. Profit-making organisations take some or all of the profits out of the business for the benefit of the owners – for example, by paying dividends to shareholders. For non-profit-making organisations, surplus money is put back into the business. The FHA, for example, will use any 'profit' to pay for more holidays for families in need. It is this distribution of profits that is one key feature that differentiates the type of organisation.

Details of profits and how they are distributed can be found in organisations' annual accounts. Not all organisations have these available for external use but, as you will see later, many organisations do publish their accounts.

Ownership

Another feature of organisations is their ownership. Typically private-sector organisations are classed as profit-making and public and voluntary sector organisations as non-profit-making.

The voluntary sector includes membership organisations, such as ABTA, the National Trust and the International Air Transport Association (IATA), and these are 'owned' by their members. The membership fee they pay entitles them to have a say in the running of the business. There are many membership organisations in the travel and tourism industry and many of these support organisations in a local area, such as the Torbay Hospitality Association (THA) and the Ashdown Forest Tourism Association (AFTA).

ACTIVITY

You work for the local authority in your area and have been asked to set up a membership association for local tourism organisations. Choose a name for your organisation and set your objectives. Investigate the local organisations you would contact to join. Write a letter promoting your organisation, setting out your objectives.

Membership organisations will often be managed by employees but with major decisions taken by elected officials.

The terms 'sole trader', 'partnership' and 'limited company' are often used to categorise organisations. These are terms typically used to categorise private-sector organisations although many membership

Case study

Ashdown Forest
Ashdown Forest
Tourism Association (AFTA)

Ashdown Forest is an area of open heathland on the highest sandy ridge-top of the High Weald Area of Outstanding Natural Beauty (AONB).

This distinctive, nationally valued landscape – of rolling hills draped with small irregular fields, abundant woods and hedges, scattered farmsteads and sunken lanes – can be viewed from many points in the Forest.

The establishment of AFTA has been supported by Sussex Enterprise, Tourism South East and Wealden District Council, all of whom are working to develop a sustainable tourism business network in the area. The association is formally constituted as an unincorporated association and has a management committee.

Case study

The National Trust

The National Trust sets out its approach to appointing and electing its officials in its *Governance Handbook*. The text below shows how the members of the Council are elected.

Elected members of the Council

A postal ballot will be held each year to fill any vacancies on the Council. Applications will be invited through public advertisement in a national newspaper and there will also be an announcement in the National Trust magazine, regional newsletters and on the National Trust website.

The papers for the elections to the Council will be circulated to members of the Trust with the formal paperwork for the Annual General Meeting each year and the results of the ballot will be announced at the Annual General Meeting.

The Council will set up a Nominations Committee to interview the candidates who put their names forward for election to the Council. The Committee will consist of four people. The three members of the Council to serve on the Committee will be elected by the Council by ballot. A fourth member will be independent of the Trust. The Chairman of the Committee can be either a Council member or an external member.

Members of the Committee should not be standing for election to the Council themselves that year and they should not propose or second a member standing for election to the Council.

The Nominations Committee will recommend to the members of the National Trust which of the candidates standing for election it believes would make the most suitable members of the Council. In making its recommendations the Committee will take into account the skills, experience and personal qualities of the candidates and the particular areas in which the Council would benefit from a stronger base of expertise, knowledge or perspective based on a skills audit of existing members of the Council.

The Committee should recognise that the membership of the Council should reflect the breadth and depth of the Trust's work, a wide range of perspectives and the broad spectrum of those with an interest in and a connection to the Trust's work.

It should also bear in mind the need to include enough people with the right background, skills, experience and time to become members of the Board of Trustees.

The Committee will decide whether the recommended list should reflect the number of vacancies or a smaller or larger number. The Committee may decide that guidance to the members of the trust can most usefully be given by matching the number of recommended candidates to the number of vacancies. However the Committee is free to recommend more or fewer candidates than the number of vacancies if it considers that to be appropriate.

The Committee will present a report to the Council on its work before making a recommendation to the membership.

All candidates will submit CVs and personal statements as well as a photograph by the agreed closing date. These will be published in the paperwork for the postal ballot.

Candidates will be interviewed by the Nominations Committee, and if necessary in a two stage process. Interviews will be designed to ascertain whether and to what extent candidates have the qualities and experience required of a Council member.

(Source: www.nationaltrust.org.uk, accessed May 2007)

Case study

ABTA election

ABTA elected a new president in May 2006 as reported by Juliet Dennis in this *Travel Weekly* article (5 May 2006).

Fleming steps up to take ABTA helm

ABTA treasurer Justin Fleming has become the association's new president, replacing Martin Wellings. Fleming, 56, on the board of directors as treasurer since 2005, was the only candidate for the job after Wellings announced he was standing down due to work pressures. Fleming has had two previous stints on the board and has served on ABTA committees since 1987.

In his election address, Fleming said he had the 'time and energy' to tackle issues such as licensing, bonding and membership costs.

Fleming is a non-executive director of Classic Collection Holidays. Until 2000 he was chairman and managing director of Panorama Holiday Group, which he launched in 1987 and sold to MyTravel in 1998.

Meanwhile, ABTA confirmed delays in planning this year's ABTA Travel Convention in Athens due to a change of tourism minister in Greece. 'It's been a slower process than it should have been, but it's back on track,' said a spokesman.

organisations are also limited companies, such as ABTA. Many small hotels or transport operators would be classed as a sole trader or partnership but most travel agents, tour operators and airlines are limited companies. To become a limited company, an organisation must be registered at Companies House (www.companieshouse.gov.uk). Whether it is a private limited company (Ltd) or public limited company (plc) it has to register its name and submit its accounts each year to Companies House. This is a legal requirement and the accounts are then accessible to the general public and not just the owners. Through Companies House, a person can pay a fee and be provided with a copy of the accounts of a limited company. Many organisations present their annual accounts on their website. In addition to financial details, annual accounts can also give you details of organisations' board of directors and, in some cases, senior staff and the roles they undertake, as you can see from the contents page of the MyTravel plc Annual Report of 2006 shown in Figure 2.01.

Contents

01 Overview
Group at a Glance
02 Chairman's Statement
The Operating Review
03 The Financial Review
04 Board of Directors
Directors' Report
Directors' Responsibilities
05 Corporate Governance Report
Remuneration Report
Corporate Responsibility
06 Independent Auditors' Report
Group Income Statement
Group Statement of Recognised Income and Expense
Group Balance Sheet
Group Cash Flow Statement
Notes to the Financial Statements
Five Year Review
07 Independent Auditors' Report
Company Balance Sheet
Notes to the Company Financial Statements
Shareholder Information
Corporate Advisors

Fig 2.01 MyTravel Annual Report & Accounts, 2006

ACTIVITY

Investigate the annual accounts of four travel and tourism plc organisations. List the information that can be found in each.

Public-sector organisations, such as VisitBritain and the Department for Culture, Media and Sport (DCMS) are government-run. The state is their owner

ACTIVITY

Discover the name of the current Secretary of State for the DCMS and any other ministers that have a responsibility for tourism.

and they are managed by employees appointed by the government. The most senior person who manages these organisations is an elected Member of Parliament who is given Secretary of State or Ministerial responsibilities.

Local authorities are also public-sector organisations. Within most local authorities there are departments that have responsibility for tourism, depending upon the importance of tourism to the local economy. In Derby City Council, tourism is the responsibility of the Regeneration and Community department and in Bournemouth Borough Council it is the responsibility of Environment and Economic Services. Employees run the department but the local authority will often have a committee that sets the direction of the department, on behalf of the local people. The committee will consist of elected officials – councillors.

ACTIVITY

Investigate your local authority. Which department has responsibility for tourism? What committee sets policy for tourism? Who are the committee members? What committee does your local councillor sit on?

Assessing the outcome

You work for a local authority and have been asked to set up a database of key travel and tourism organisations. The key features of each organisation will be included on the database.

- Describe the features of a selected profit-making travel and tourism organisation (**P1**).
- Describe the features of a selected non-profit-making travel and tourism organisation (**P2**).

How to complete a cash flow forecast

A cash flow forecast is used to predict when and where businesses might have money problems. It predicts when cash will come in (cash inflows) and when it will go out (cash outflows). A cash flow forecast is normally produced on a spreadsheet using ICT software and is presented in a table. For a cash flow forecast, 'cash' is the amount of money available to fund the day-to-day running of the business. An airline could have aircraft worth millions of pounds but not enough 'cash' to pay staff wages or fund catering for a specific flight. A cash flow forecast does not consider assets such as aircraft, only finance that can quickly be turned into cash.

Table 2.01 shows what a four-month cash flow forecast will look like when complete.

Table 2.01 A basic cash-flow forecast

	Item	Jan	Feb	Mar	Apr
Cash inflows	Sales receipts		5000	35000	35000
	Other receipts	18000			
	Total receipts	**18000**	**5000**	**35000**	**35000**
Cash outflows	Wages and rent	15000	15000	15000	15000
	Other payments	5000	8000	2000	2000
	Total payments	**20000**	**23000**	**17000**	**17000**
Summary	Net cash flow	(2000)	(18000)	18000	18000
	Balance b/f	nil	(2000)	(20000)	(2000)
	Balance c/f	(2000)	(20000)	(2000)	16000

A cash flow forecast has three sections: receipts (cash inflows), payments (cash outflows) and summary (balances).

Cash inflows

For a new business, a cash flow forecast will begin with its start-up capital. For a new hotel, the owner may have set aside £5000 as its working capital so that would be the first item of cash inflow. For an existing organisation planning its cash flow forecast, the starting point will be the amount of money brought forward from its previous forecast.

Once an organisation, such as a hotel, opens for business, it would expect to then start receiving income or receipts – for example, from people booking rooms. A hotel owner would forecast how many rooms they would sell each night over the forecasted period. As a new hotel, it may be difficult to predict this precisely. The owner could look at other limited companies through their annual accounts or may have carried out market research to set up the business. An existing hotel would be able to use previous years' sales figures to help predict future sales. If the new hotel is part of a chain, it will have information related to other hotels in the group that it can use. An organisation will also need to be aware of other factors that could affect sales – for example, long-range weather forecasts, plans for the local area as there may be a new attraction planned or a specific event taking place. These could perhaps bring more people into the area, possibly looking to stay overnight, but it could also mean that potential customers may go elsewhere.

The owner of a new hotel could predict that, as a new hotel, the rooms might not sell well in the first few months but, once established, sales would increase. The same would be true of any new organisation such as an airline or attraction. If the hotel or attraction was in a seaside destination or a seasonal destination – for example, a ski resort such as Aviemore – an organisation may also expect that sales will not be high early and late season when fewer

tourists are likely to visit. This will be reflected in the cash flow forecast.

A cash flow forecast can be detailed in terms of daily or weekly activity. Table 2.02 is an example of how a six-month sales forecast for a new hotel could look. This forecast was based upon the hotel being paid for room occupancy on arrival as with most hotels. Some independent hotels may ask for an initial deposit to reserve the accommodation. Airlines may expect payment in full at the time of booking, travel agents and tour operators receive a deposit when making a booking, with balances paid nearer the time of departure. This can affect cash flow, as shown in Table 2.03

In this example, the hotel still has the same forecasted total sales but the receipts are spread across the period of the forecast with more 'cash' being received into the business earlier. This would allow the hotel to pay off loans earlier or invest in new facilities, if required.

For a hotel, sales may be for the room bookings, but there may also be other sales. If the hotel has a

ACTIVITY

Discuss how the following could affect sales of hotel rooms:
- budget airline introducing services from a local airport
- cruise service from a nearby port with an early-morning departure
- a sponsored 'half marathon' early in July
- a new dinosaur exhibition at the local museum.

ACTIVITY

A regional airline offers domestic services and short-haul international services to Paris, Brussels and Berlin. It is preparing a cash flow forecast. Discuss the factors likely to affect its sales forecast.

Table 2.02 An example of a six-month sales forecast for a new hotel

	Item	Mar	Apr	May	Jun	Jul	Aug
Cash inflows	Hotel room sales receipts	1000	1200	1600	1800	2500	2600

Table 2.03 Six-month sales forecast for a new hotel – deposits taken

	Item	Mar	Apr	May	Jun	Jul	Aug
	Hotel room booking deposit receipts	400	300	300	100	300	100
Cash inflows	Hotel room balance receipts	1000	1000	1600	1400	2000	2500
	Total hotel room sales receipts	**1400**	**1300**	**1900**	**1500**	**2300**	**2600**

restaurant or bar, there will be some sales. Airlines will sell tax-free goods, meals and refreshments. Travel agents will sell foreign currency and other ancillary services such as car hire, theatre tickets, airport hotels and parking. One of the roles of a tour operator's representative is to sell excursions. All of this is in addition to forecasted sales for primary products and services. A cash flow forecast may record these separately.

Value added tax (VAT) is charged by many businesses on the goods and services they provide. The government department HM Revenue & Customs ensures businesses comply with regulations and pay this tax. VAT is charged on the selling price at 17.5 per cent and the business pays that to HM Revenue & Customs. If a hotel planned to charge £50 per night for a room then it would actually have to charge £58.75 (£50 plus 17.5 per cent VAT). This would ensure that once it had paid the VAT, the planned £50 is held by the organisation. A business has to register for VAT and it is usually recorded and paid every three months (quarter). VAT does not apply to all services – for example, passenger transport and insurance. It is therefore important to check if the goods and services to be provided have to charge VAT.

There may be other taxes that have to be considered, such as insurance premium tax paid on insurance sales, that may affect the cash flow forecast of travel agents and tour operators.

A cash flow forecast would include VAT separately, as can be seen in Table 2.04.

Cash outflows

There are many items of expenditure that a business has to pay to cover the costs of running the business. These include overheads such as electricity, gas, rent, council tax, etc. Expenditure will also include staff costs. These may vary over the period of the cash flow forecast. If low sales are anticipated early in the season, fewer staff will be needed. Many airlines and tour operators will employ temporary staff because of the seasonal nature of their business. Some attractions may employ casual staff, used only to cover for a specific event. In addition to staff, there may be other costs – for example, airlines need to buy in food and drink they want to sell. These can often be purchased before there is any income to cover the costs, which is why start-up capital is needed. These costs will also need to be predicted and added to the cash flow. Some of these costs may be fixed, such as council tax, but others may vary according to the number of sales that are made or they may increase with inflation.

Loan repayments are another cash outflow. If an organisation has taken out a loan to get started, a bank or other organisation will want to be repaid. Another outflow might be made through capital purchases. This is when you buy something for your business that will have some value – for example, a computer for an attraction, new beds for hotel rooms, a new ship. There may be a one-off payment or there may be credit terms where the cost is spread and paid for monthly or by some other term (Table 2.05).

Table 2.04 Six-month sales forecast for new hotel, VAT included

	Item	Mar	Apr	May	Jun	Jul	Aug
Cash inflows	Hotel room sales receipts	1000	1200	1600	1800	2500	2600
	VAT	175	210	280	315	438	455
	Total receipts	**1175**	**1410**	**1880**	**2115**	**2938**	**3055**

Table 2.05 Six-month cash inflows and cash outflows for a hotel

	Item	Mar	Apr	May	Jun	Jul	Aug
Cash inflows	Hotel room sales receipts	1000	1200	1600	1800	2500	2600
	VAT	175	210	280	315	438	455
	Total receipts	**1175**	**1410**	**1880**	**2115**	**2938**	**3055**
Cash outflows	Overheads	1000	1000	1000	1000	1000	1000
	Staff costs	300	500	500	500	700	700
	Raw materials	150	250	250	250	300	300
	VAT payments			665			1208
	Total payments	**1450**	**1750**	**2415**	**1750**	**2000**	**3208**

Table 2.06 Six-month cash flow forecast for hotel

	Item	Mar	Apr	May	Jun	Jul	Aug
Cash inflows	Hotel room sales receipts	1000	1200	1600	1800	2500	2600
	VAT	175	210	280	315	438	455
	Total receipts	**1175**	**1410**	**1880**	**2115**	**2938**	**3055**
Cash outflows	Overheads	1000	1000	1000	1000	1000	1000
	Staff costs	300	500	500	500	700	700
	Raw materials	150	250	250	250	300	300
	VAT payments			665			1208
	Total payments	**1450**	**1750**	**2415**	**1750**	**2000**	**3208**
Balances	Net cash flow	(275)	(340)	(535)	365	938	(153)
	Balance b/f		(275)	(615)	(1150)	(785)	153
	Balance c/f	(275)	(615)	(1150)	(785)	153	0

Balances

For both cash inflows and cash outflows there are totals shown, as in Table 2.05. The point of a cash flow forecast is to calculate the net cash flow. This is the difference between the cash inflows and cash outflows each month – the money in and the money out. The net outflow calculated for each month is then 'carried forward' to the following month. This is then 'brought forward' for that month's calculation. This is shown in Table 2.06.

Once the cash flow forecast is complete, the business can then start planning for the future. In Table 2.06, the forecast shows that the hotel will not start making any surplus until June but that will be needed to cover the losses made in the previous months. There is an overall surplus in July but this is needed to pay VAT in August. After six months, the hotel breaks even. It can now look at its cash flow forecast to make decisions about the future. This will be discussed in more detail in the final section of this unit.

Assessing the outcome

Reena has decided to set up her own business as a homeworker for a telesales travel agent. Her plan is to work from home Monday to Friday 9–5. She has a computer but will need to pay for an extra telephone line and rental costs and these are £105 to install a new line and rental is £41 per month. £350 must be paid to the telesales travel agent for the initial contract and £50 per month for administrative support. She is advised that if relying only on the agency for contacts, sales will generate approximately £14,000 worth of holidays per month and she will be paid 10 per cent commission on sales. VAT must be paid on commission. Any sales generated through her own contacts will be paid at 15 per cent commission. She wants to buy a laptop so that she can make appointments to visit customers in their own home and has found one for £695 but she wants to wait three months to be able to find the clients. She knows she will need to promote her services so after two months she plans to pay £300 for leaflets and business cards. She has £500 available for start-up costs.

- Complete a cash flow forecast for a minimum of a six-month period (**P3**).

How to plan a travel and tourism project within financial constraints

For a business to survive, it must operate within its means. It must not overstretch itself financially, spending money it does not have. One reason why a cash flow forecast is used is to try to predict or anticipate if there are times when the business may go into debt so that it can put in place measures to limit this.

In large organisations, each department may have a budget to operate within. The budget sets out the financial constraints of its operations. Departments must not spend more than their budgets. If a department wants to increase its expenditure, it would somehow have to raise new income to cover the additional costs. One way to do this is by charging other departments for the use of its facilities. For example, a catering department may charge £1.50 for each coffee or £100 for room hire for a meeting held by another department in the same organisation.

In addition to ongoing running costs, departments may be given specific projects and these would also need to be completed within financial constraints. A marketing department might be given a new product to promote with a budget, a tour operator's product

development team might be given a budget to investigate new destinations, a museum curator might be given a budget to introduce a new exhibit. A project may also be to introduce a new appraisal system for staff or to develop a customer service policy. Regardless of the project, there will be financial constraints.

When provided with a budget, it is useful to set out a plan, similar to a cash flow forecast, identifying all possible items of expenditure. This is likely to require some research to obtain details of potential costs. When doing so, additions such as VAT must be taken into account. Depending upon the timescale involved in the project, it is also advisable to make some provision for inflation. Prices may increase and if this is not considered, the budget may be exceeded. A budget plan is also advised to include an amount to cover contingencies. A promotional campaign may need an extra series of adverts if it looks as if sales are not progressing as planned, and if this additional cost is not included in the plan, the funding won't be there. If a tour has planned to include a picnic in an excursion and the weather turns out to be rainy, alternative plans will need to be made and this may incur additional costs. Any plan that may require expenditure in another currency will also need to take into account possible exchange rate changes.

ACTIVITY

Below are brief details of two travel and tourism projects. Add more details to the projects and identify the planned expenditure items and also contingencies:
- a residential student tourism conference
- a full-day jeep safari excursion including lunch and drinks.

Objectives

When a project is set, it may or may not come with specific targets or objectives to be achieved. An objective is set to make clear to all involved what they are attempting to achieve. Setting an objective also helps to evaluate the project on completion, i.e. has the project achieved what it set out to achieve?

It may be that a team are given a project with a broad aim but without specific objectives. The project team would start by setting out specific objectives to be achieved to meet the overall aim. One or more individuals involved in the project would discuss and decide what these should be. Objectives needs to be SMART (Figure 2.02).

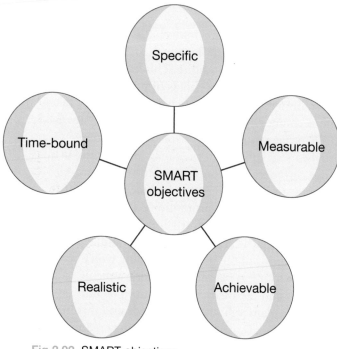

Fig 2.02 SMART objectives

If a general objective is set, such as 'raise awareness', it is difficult to plan how this can be achieved. How do you measure if awareness is raised? Is there a particular group of people whose awareness must be raised? Is there anything in particular to raise awareness of? How can awareness be raised if the current level of awareness isn't known? By being specific it assists in ensuring the objective is measurable. By giving a precise amount by which profit is to be increased or a number of tickets to be sold, the project can more easily be evaluated at the end. Did the profit increase to the amount stated in the objective? Were the intended number of tickets sold?

All objectives have to be achievable. There is no point setting an objective that you know is beyond what could be achieved, given the budget and timescales you are working to. Objectives also have to be realistic and have a set timescale and deadline for achievement. To say that an objective is to hold a student conference but with no deadline for when it will be held makes the objective meaningless.

Timings

If objectives are SMART, then they include timings and that is an important part of any project. A project could mostly achieve its objectives but if these are achieved three months behind target, this may incur additional costs or be a complete failure. If a leaflet is being planned to launch a new ride, say, but isn't printed and distributed until the day of the launch, the money it has cost is wasted as no potential customers will see the leaflet until after the launch. There have been many high-profile cases of projects that have failed to be completed by the deadline, such as the Millennium Bridge, Wembley Stadium and the Airbus A380.

Failure to meet a deadline could mean that objectives are not met. There should be a deadline for each objective to be achieved and for each stage involved in meeting an objective. The more detail that can be included the better. A research project that simply states 'three weeks to research and one week to write the report' is too vague. The plan in Figure 2.03 is more realistic and useful.

Case study

EADS promises Airbus reform after another superjumbo delay

The crisis at EADS intensified yesterday when its board and key airlines said deliveries of the Airbus A380 superjumbo would be delayed for up to another year, further damaging the plane-maker's credibility. The world's biggest plane is now two years behind schedule.

EADS shares tumbled more than 11% this morning when trading opened in Paris but had recovered to €20.96 by lunchtime, a fall of 7.5%.

The A380 delays, caused by inadequate tools used on the 500km of electronic wiring in each superjumbo, will cut free cash flow by €6.3bn, putting added pressure on Airbus's ability to fund the new €8bn A350 long-haul jet designed to match the runaway success of Boeing's 787 Dreamline.

Emirates, the biggest customer with an order for 43 A380s, said it had been advised by Airbus of a further 10-month delay and Lufthansa, the second biggest with an order for 12, and Air France, with 10 on order, said their planes would be a further 12 months late.

Tim Clark, the Emirates chief executive, said it would not get its first planes until August 2008. 'It's a very serious issue and the company is now reviewing all its options.' But sources insisted the Dubai-based airline had not yet decided to cancel its order or seek compensation.

It is thought within the industry that Emirates, the fastest-growing airline, could decide to sustain its growth plans by leasing other planes to fill the gap left by the late deliveries of the A380.

(Source: David Gow, The *Guardian*, 4 October 2006, copyright Guardian News & Media Ltd 2006)

Timings should always be set, taking into account possible failures to meet deadlines, and then contingencies should be put in place (Figure 2.04).

The key is to anticipate everything that can possibly go wrong and work back from the deadline date, allowing sufficient time at each stage.

ACTIVITY

Discuss the implications to Airbus of failing to meet its planned deadline.

Week 1

- Three hours' initial research, identifying possible sources of information, listing priorities
- Four hours' research on topic 1, using internet
- Two hours' planning questionnaire, identifying sample
- Questionnaires in post by Friday afternoon

Week 2

- Three separate two-hour sessions in the library researching journals and local newspapers
- Three hours' further research on internet
- Identify contacts for interview – allow three separate one-hour sessions to arrange meetings

Week 3

- Review questionnaire results four hours: one hour setting up database and three hours inputting results
- Interview meetings, each one hour

Week 4

- Review all findings and select relevant information: two hours
- Prepare outline report: two hours
- One day for reflection
- Two hours' word processing
- Another two hours' word processing

Fig 2.03 A research project timetable

Outcome: Leaflets to be distributed 15 March.

Printers to produce leaflets one week in advance.

Possible problems: Printers have a fire in the building and are unable to meet the deadline.

Contingency plan: Have list of alternative printers available. Be prepared to have to pay extra for last-minute request.

Fig 2.04 Contingency plans

ACTIVITY

A product development team of a major tour operator is planning to visit a Caribbean island to research the possibility of its inclusion in a new brochure. They will take photographs of hotels and attractions. Details must be available by 1 October. They are advised at the end of July. Three members of the team will travel. Two members of the team will stay in the UK.

Put together a timed plan to complete the research. Anticipate all potential problems that could occur and suggest contingencies that should be put in place to deal with them.

Assessing the outcome

A group of ten students from France are planning to arrive on an exchange visit to your local area. They will arrive on a Monday afternoon and leave on the following Sunday morning. They are all aged 14 or 15 and will stay with local families. Room and breakfast will be provided by the families, and dinner on the day of arrival and on two evenings during the stay. Three days will be spent in school and lunch will be provided. The students have been asked to each provide £100 towards the costs of leisure activities and other meals. They will arrive in five weeks and have asked for an itinerary to be sent to them ten days before they arrive.

- Plan a travel and tourism project within financial constraints (**P4**).

How a travel and tourism organisation gains competitive advantage

There is a difference between knowing something and understanding it. To know that Ibiza is popular with young adults is one thing but to understand why means there needs to be knowledge of the destination and knowledge of the psychology of young people and their needs and wants. Understanding would relate the two together. Understanding means you know why, you are able to give a reason. This section will therefore require you to go beyond simply finding information about an organisation: you will need to consider why organisations operate in the way they do.

This section assumes that travel and tourism organisations will seek to gain competitive advantage. The *Cambridge Advanced Learners Dictionary* (2005) states that an advantage is 'a condition giving a greater chance of success'. This means that a competitive advantage is having a better chance of success than competitors. This learning outcome is about how they use this to achieve their aims.

An earlier section of this unit considered how organisations set SMART objectives. Aims are more general than an objective but they are still something an organisation is trying to achieve. An aim might be to raise awareness or be seen as environmentally friendly but these are too vague to be an objective as they are not specific and measurable.

There are many ways organisations seek to gain competitive advantage. One of the most common is to make prices lower than those of competitors. Travel agents often use this approach as can be seen from the First Choice website (Figure 2.05).

Seeing this might attract customers away from a competitor who is charging more for the same or similar product. This gives competitive advantage but does it give competitive advantage to achieve its aims? It depends on the organisation's aims. If the organisation's aim was to increase profit, this would not help. Reducing prices would potentially reduce profits as costs might not be reduced. If the aim was to increase market share, selling products and services at lower prices than competitors could achieve the aim because if you are taking customers away from a competitor, then you are increasing your sales to the

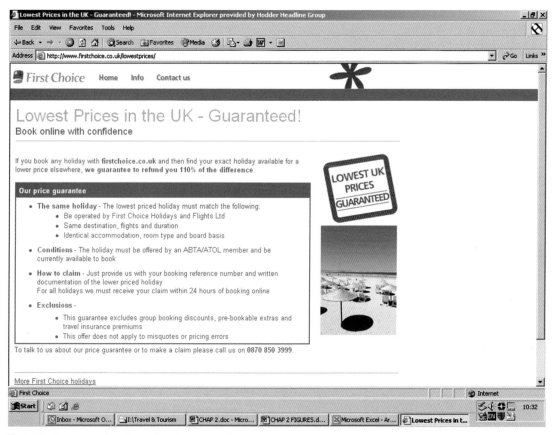

Fig 2.05 First Choice promotes lowest price guarantee

detriment of a competitor: your sales increase as their sales decrease. The market stays the same but your share of it increases. If you are attracting new customers to the market, you are encouraging people to buy who previously couldn't afford it, the market is increasing and you are also increasing your share.

There are other ways that organisations seek to gain competitive advantage but as this outcome is particularly about organisations using these to achieve their aims, this will be the starting point of any considerations made.

For profit-making organisations, there is one main aim: to make a profit. As discussed earlier, many organisations will aim to make a profit. Any activities undertaken to meet that aim would need to be those that can increase profit. Generally, profits increase with price rises but a rise in prices could lead to customers going to a competitor, and reduce sales. This could lead to a lower profit rather than an increase in profit. To increase prices, customers would have to feel they are receiving added value, getting something extra for their money.

ACTIVITY

Investigate transport organisations competing for the same route and find out how they compete on the quality of their products and services.

The Mandarin Oriental Hotel Group is a chain known for its luxury. The Oriental Singapore was voted among the 'top hotels in Asia 2006' in the Condé Nast Traveller Readers Choice Awards. The hotel 'provides for every necessity without question' according to its website. Overleaf are details of the Harbour Suites in the hotel, available from £350 per night:

Tastefully decorated, the distinctively appointed and spacious Harbour Suite is furnished with a unique mix of rich wood and Asia-influenced antiques. Floor to ceiling windows offer breathtaking views of the harbour.

- Wireless high speed internet access
- LCD television in living room
- Sophisticated surround sound systems, offering CD and DVD options
- In-room safe with laptop rechargeable access
- Spacious work desk
- Dual-line telephones with IDD and voicemail
- Separate living room
- Daily selection of local and international newspapers
- Bathtub and a separate glass enclosed shower
- Plush terry bathrobes and slippers
- Tea and coffee making facilities
- Hair dryer and Mini bar
- Personalised in-room registration

Fig 2.06   Harbour Suite

Case study

Gulfair chefs

Flights of fancy with your own personal Sky Chef

When you fly First Class with us, you're in for a really mouth-watering experience. In addition to the warm and friendly service from our cabin crew, you'll receive individual attention from our inflight Sky Chef.

Having trained at some of the world's top hotels, our team of over 100 Sky Chefs introduce a fine dining experience. All the refinements of a five-star restaurant, but with unparalleled views at 35,000ft.

Once you've had a chance to browse our newly enhanced menu, the Sky Chef will come and discuss the options and how you would like your choice served. Dishes range from a delectable range of appetisers, a choice of European and Middle Eastern dishes combined in a contemporary style and the ever-popular Arabic mezze selection.

When you've made that difficult selection, the Sky Chef will then prepare it for you personally, as well as recommending an accompanying beverage from our Sky Cellar. There're all the usual soft drinks, plus excellent wines, spirit and, of course, vintage champagne.

After your entrée, you can indulge in a fresh cheese platter or, if you've room, one of our Sky Chefs' delicious desserts. A tea or coffee to finish, and it's the perfect meal.

This exclusive personalised service is available on A330 wide-bodied flights throughout the Gulf Air network and on A340 wide-bodied flights on selected routes throughout the network.

(Source: www.gulfairco.com, accessed May 2007)

The Dorchester Hotel in London is one of the most luxurious in the capital. Rooms there can cost more than £2000 per night.

ACTIVITY

Investigate the products and services provided at the Dorchester and compare them to those of the Oriental Singapore. Discuss which is most likely to gain competitive advantage to achieve its aim of increasing profits.

ACTIVITY

A hotel group wants to offer higher-quality products and services while maintaining the same level of profit. You work in the product development department at head office and have been asked to attend a planning meeting to review the current provision in the hotels. You have been asked to make suggestions as to how the group could develop its products and services to encourage more sales but with limited additional costs. You will need to describe your suggestions in detail and explain how each of them could meet these aims. For your explanation you must say why your proposal would meet the aims.

In addition to providing better value for money and higher-quality products and services, an organisation may also use different promotional techniques to increase profits. Any form of promotion will incur costs and so to use this approach to gain competitive advantage, an organisation would need to increase sales sufficiently to cover those additional costs. Advertising is generally the most costly promotional technique to use. Alton Towers advertises on national television. The cost of producing an advert and then paying for advertising time, for example at the seasonal opening of the park, could exceed £100,000. At £25 entry fee, an extra 4000 people paying full price would need to come to the park to cover the advertising costs; 4001 people could lead to increased profit, but only if there are no additional costs. If all 4000 arrive on one day the theme park may need extra staff issuing tickets, more staff working in catering outlets, more cleaners, etc. More than 4000 extra customers would then be needed to cover all additional costs. If the extra visitors were spread over a month it would have less impact on staffing. Alton Towers could also consider that, with more people coming to the park, each person is likely to spend money – for example, on refreshments and merchandise – and this could increase revenue and, possibly, profit.

Other ways of promoting would include direct mail, public relations and personal selling. You will learn more about these in Unit 5. These techniques are popular with non-profit-making organisations as they can incur less cost than advertising. Many non-profit-making organisations are membership organisations such as the National Trust and they have details of members. As they have a membership list, they know who to contact through direct mail. They could do this through email with limited costs or by sending a leaflet. Members will have an interest

Case study

World Heritage Sites

World Heritage Sites are places of international importance for the conservation of mankind's cultural and natural heritage. In 2005, there were 812 World Heritage Sites, including 26 in the UK and overseas territories. Examples include the Great Wall of China, the Pyramids, the Great Barrier Reef, Venice and the Tower of London. World Heritage Sites are places that need to be preserved for future generations, as part of a common universal heritage. The World Heritage Convention was established in 1972 by UNESCO (United Nations Educational, Scientific and Cultural Organisation). The World Heritage List set up by the Convention includes natural sites, and a wide variety of cultural sites such as landscapes, towns, historic monuments and modern buildings.

in the organisation achieving its aims as this is why they became members. They will believe in protecting historic properties. They are likely to respond to requests for additional donations or to attend special events and purchase merchandise.

This shows that although all organisations may use promotion to gain competitive advantage to achieve their aims, the techniques used may differ due to the different aims, finance available and the type of customer.

ACTIVITY

Gaining World Heritage Site status would give an attraction competitive advantage, particularly if aiming to raise awareness and enrich community identity. Wearmouth Jarrow will be the UK's nomination in 2009. Explain how achieving World Heritage Site status will give it competitive advantage in achieving the above aims.

ACTIVITY

An airline is planning to introduce a new route from Birmingham to New York with flights operating weekly. Assess how advertising its new service on television during the FA Cup Final would give it competitive advantage to achieve its aim of increasing profits.

For many non-profit-making organisations, one aim could be to achieve sustainable development or to ensure operations are environmentally friendly. The Green Tourism Business Scheme gives details of 'green' tourism awards. Gaining recognition from receiving an award could also give an organisation competitive advantage.

ACTIVITY

Have a look at the 'Tourism Awards' section of the Green Tourism website (www.greentourism.org.uk) and investigate the awards available for green tourism. Find one travel and tourism organisation that has received an award for green tourism. Explain how achieving this award has given it competitive advantage to achieve its aims.

Assessing the outcome

You work for the Natural History Museum, a non-profit-making organisation. Its aims are:

- to increase community involvement
- to increase access to resources
- to increase revenues.

You have been asked to look at how the museum could gain competitive advantage to achieve its aims. You have been asked to research two other attractions: one profit-making and one non-profit-making.

- Explain how a chosen non-profit-making organisation seeks to gain competitive advantage to meet its aims (**P5**).
- Explain how a chosen profit-making organisation seeks to gain competitive advantage to meet its aims (**P6**).

Improve your grade

There are four learning outcomes for this unit, each of which covers a different topic. Each topic is assessed at merit level and two of them also extend into distinction level.

Features of organisations

For two of the merit tasks (**M1** and **M4**), you have to be able to make comparisons. Basically, making comparisons means finding similarities and differences and then explaining why they exist. Some people find it useful to make comparisons by setting information out in a table.

For **M1**, you have to compare the features of a profit-making and non-profit-making organisation. If you were designing a table to make the comparison, you would start by identifying what you want to compare. For **P1** and **P2** of this unit, you will have already described the features of these types of organisation. You will have described ownership, liability, distribution of profits, control, sources of finance and the documentation needed. These, then, are the features you will compare and could be put into the left-hand column of a table. You could then put in what you have found for your profit-making organisation and what you have found for your non-profit-making organisation. It might initially look something like Table 2.07.

If you simply completed the table in Table 2.07, you would not be making a comparison, you would be describing the features of each organisation. You may have taken this approach to meet your pass criteria. For a table you need at least one more column added – one where you make a comparison. You could add a number of columns, taking into account that you must explain the similarities and differences you find (as in Table 2.08).

Table 2.07 Comparisons of organisations

	National Trust	easyJet
Ownership		
Liability		
Distribution of profit		
Control		
Sources of finance		
Documentation needed		

Table 2.08 Similarities and differences between organisations

	National Trust	easyJet	Similarities and differences identified	Similarities and differences explained
Ownership				
Liability				
Distribution of profits				
Control				
Sources of finance				
Documentation needed				

It is likely that you will have identified, and therefore need to explain, more differences than similarities. One similarity might be that both a non-profit-making organisation such as the British Museum and a profit-making organisation such as Thorpe Park use sales of merchandise as a source of finance. Why is that? The British Museum relies on government grants to operate and makes no charges for entrance. Its grant is insufficient to operate in the way it would like – for example, undertaking research and collecting new exhibits. It would need to make additional sales in order to finance achieving its overall aims. One of Thorpe Park's key objectives is to increase profit levels in order to satisfy investors who want to take a share of the profits. It will operate in a way that maximises sales in order to increase profits. Although they both have one source of finance that is the same, the reason for having that source of finance is different. There are other sources of finance each company uses. The comparison made would therefore be more detailed but each aspect would be explained, as shown in the example above.

ACTIVITY

Investigate the sources of finance for Thorpe Park and the British Museum. Explain the similarities and differences.

Cash flow forecast

Earlier in this unit, you learned how to complete a cash flow forecast. A cash flow forecast can be used to identify potential problems. It would be wonderful if a cash flow forecast showed that an organisation would always be making money. Unfortunately, for many organisations, that is not the case. In some cases, a cash flow forecast might indicate problems are likely to arise such as insufficient funds to make the VAT payments due quarterly or not enough to pay wages because of low sales in early or late season. Some organisations may produce a cash flow forecast to see if or when they can afford to buy new equipment such as upgrading computers for a travel agency or refurbishing rooms in a hotel.

In the basic cash flow forecast shown in Table 2.01 on page 25, the business will be in profit by the end of April but the first three months are predicted to be 'in the red'. This is because there were no sales receipts in the first month (January) and they were very low in February compared to March and April. This is one potential problem identified that has occurred and this is because it is a new company trying to get established. There are also potential problems with expenditure. No sales are anticipated in January but wages are being paid out. This is wasting money that doesn't need to be spent. If sales only start in February, then some costs could be saved in January by not employing staff until February. This would put the net cash flow carried forward at the end of January in profit. It would still mean that at the end of February there would be a deficit but it would be a lot less than in the original cash flow forecast, and in March, the organisation would be in profit again. This has highlighted only one problem with two possible reasons for the problem but it has also suggested a solution to that one problem – to start staff one month later. This proposal is also justified as there was an explanation to show how that change would make a difference. This could be supported by a revised cash flow forecast showing the implications of the change, as shown in Table 2.09.

At merit level, you will need to work with a cash flow that covers a six-month period and that has at least three problems. For distinction, there should be a detailed suggestion for how each problem could be dealt with. These should be justified. An updated cash flow to show the implications of your suggestions could be used to prove or substantiate your justification.

ACTIVITY

Interpret the cash flow forecast in Table 2.10 by explaining any problems and suggesting how they could be dealt with, justifying your recommendations.

Travel and tourism project

M3 requires an explanation to be provided of the project that has been planned. An explanation means you have to give reasons. For each part of the plan there will need to be a reason for how it meets the

Table 2.09 Cash flow forecast for a hotel

	Item	Jan	Feb	Mar	Apr
Cash inflows	Sales receipts		5000	35000	35000
	Other receipts	18000			
	Total receipts	**18000**	**5000**	**35000**	**35000**
Cash outflows	Wages and rent	10000	15000	15000	15000
	Other payments	5000	8000	2000	2000
	Total payments	**15000**	**23000**	**17000**	**17000**
Summary	Net cash flow	3000	(18000)	18000	18000
	Balance b/f	nil	3000	(15000)	3000
	Balance c/f	3000	(15000)	3000	21000

Table 2.10 Six months' cash flow forecast for hotel

	Item	Mar	Apr	May	Jun	Jul	Aug
Cash inflows	Hotel room sales receipts	1000	1200	1600	1800	2500	2600
	VAT	175	210	280	315	438	455
	Total receipts	**1175**	**1410**	**1880**	**2115**	**2938**	**3055**
Cash outflows	Overheads	1000	1000	1000	1000	1000	1000
	Staff costs	300	500	500	500	700	700
	Raw materials	150	250	250	250	300	300
	VAT payments			665			1208
	Total payments	**1450**	**1750**	**2415**	**1750**	**2000**	**3208**
Balances	Net cash flow	(275)	(340)	(535)	365	938	(153)
	Balance b/f		(275)	(615)	(1150)	(785)	153
	Balance c/f	(275)	(615)	(1150)	(785)	153	0

objectives and how this can be achieved within financial constraints. The starting point could be explaining how the objectives could be achieved within financial constraints. Were your objectives SMART? If so, then you have already considered if they were realistic and achievable. You might want to include a cash flow forecast to help explain how the timing of your project would meet financial constraints. The cash flow forecast isn't an explanation but it might help you to think through the finances and you can use the cash flow forecast to refer to in your explanation.

Competitive advantage

This topic is assessed at **M4** and **D2**. For **M4** you will need to compare how two organisations seek to gain competitive advantage. You have already described two organisations at pass level so you have the information you need to be able to make the comparison. Earlier in this section, you were advised what is required for a comparison. The comparison needed for this criterion is more complex. You may have chosen organisations with different aims and completely different approaches. There are no clear criteria that lend themselves to being set out in a table, as there were with features of organisations, but it is worth doing some planning in advance. Were any objectives similar? If so, your starting point could be to compare approaches taken to achieve similar objectives. The second stage might be to compare approaches that were similar but perhaps used to achieve different aims. For example, both organisations might have used advertising but one aimed to increase sales and the other to raise awareness of a community project. A key difference might be that one advertised on TV and another in a local newspaper. This might be because the profit-making organisation – for example, an airline – is trying to attract customers from all over the country and its product is exciting and can be seen through moving images like people stretching out in their 'beds' or playing games on computers or watching films on seat-back screens where sound and vision are important. A local museum may want to show only local people what is planned and a photograph may be sufficient. Finances available for promotion may

also be different and this can lead to differences in the approaches taken.

For distinction, you have to make suggestions. You might want to do some 'blue sky thinking'. This means opening up your mind, imagining new possibilities, thinking 'outside the box'. On a blank sheet of paper, in the centre, write one of your chosen organisation's aims. On one side, note what is already being done and then on the other add your ideas. At this stage, don't worry about ideas being feasible, i.e. will it work? Just put all your ideas down. Some might be ridiculous. To achieve its aim of offering a luxury service, you might suggest an airline turns all seats into first class. This would not be feasible as the cost of making the change would increase prices and to create the level of space necessary for everyone would probably mean half the seats are lost – and half the income. The idea might not be feasible (although Silverjet has introduced this as part of its range for flights to New York) but it is a starting point. From there, you can start to think about other luxury items that could be included with limited costs such as toiletry bags on board long-haul flights. This might include disposable toothbrush and small tube of toothpaste, towelettes, ear plugs and eye masks all in a small bag. If purchased in bulk, this could probably be purchased by an airline for approximately £3 per bag but it might make customers feel they have had a better-quality service.

Try to ensure your final ideas are in keeping with the general nature of the organisation. It is difficult to justify a suggestion that a top-rated airline should offer a 'no frills' approach to its service or a five-star hotel should start charging for internet access or remove its Michelin-rated restaurant when these are well established. Always explain how your suggestion will enable the organisation to gain competitive advantage to meet its aims.

Top tips

- You should compare by finding similarities and differences and then explaining why they exist.
- You should use SMART objectives.

Learning outcomes

By the end of this unit you should:

- be able to use sources of reference to provide information on UK destinations
- know the location of the main UK gateways, tourist destinations and geographical features
- understand the appeal of UK destinations
- understand the needs of UK domestic and inbound tourism markets and the ways in which the UK meets those needs
- understand recent key trends and factors (both external and internal) affecting the UK inbound and domestic tourism markets.

The UK as a 'tourism product'

Tourism is very important to the UK economy, providing jobs and investment throughout the country. Increasingly, overseas tourists are choosing the UK for their holidays while more and more British people are choosing to take short weekend and city breaks within the UK. This unit will be internally assessed and will provide you with an overview of the UK tourism product, its customers and the factors that affect tourism to and within the UK.

You will need to complete a portfolio that demonstrates your understanding of the various places of interest and the importance of tourism to the UK. In doing this, you will develop your ability to use a range of reference materials such as brochures, atlases and guide books in order to accurately locate key destinations, gateways, transport links and the geographical features that are important for attracting tourists to a variety of destinations in the UK. You will show how the differing needs of domestic tourists and the various types of inbound tourists are met by the UK 'tourism product'. Finally, you will need to describe how recent trends in UK domestic and inbound tourism are affected and influenced by worldwide events.

Using reference sources to provide information

When working in the travel industry, you will need to refer to a wide range of sources on a daily basis in order to help the customer plan their holiday. In this section you will learn about the typical sources of information you could use. When preparing your portfolio, you should use all of these and, in addition, you should keep a logbook of newspaper articles that you read and travel programmes that you watch that relate to your assignment. Also, it is important to remember that in your portfolio your work should include a bibliography giving details of what reference materials were used, how and where they were used throughout the unit.

Atlases

Atlases and maps are essential when working in a travel agency, tour operator, tourist information centre or any other travel and tourism organisation. It will not be possible to know the exact location of every place in the UK, however so long as you have a good atlas or a map you should be able to locate the place you are looking for. All good atlases will have an index at the back of the book giving an alphabetical listing of all the major places in the UK including a page number and a grid reference indicating where on the page to locate the destination. These grids consist of longitudinal lines, going from north to south and latitudinal lines crossing from west to east. These lines will be either numbered or lettered, thereby allowing you to find the square in which your destination is located simply by using the grid reference in the index.

Internet

Since the late 1990s, the internet has become an essential tool in the travel and tourism industry. Vast amounts of data and information are stored on the World Wide Web and are easily accessible within seconds. Although some journals and reports require subscriptions and membership, most information is free and up to date. All the UK tourist boards have their own websites – for example, the VisitBritain (formerly the British Tourist Authority) website can be found on www.visitbritain.com.

Brochures

When researching information on tourist destinations in the UK, it is important to obtain brochures, which are small booklets containing descriptions, pictures, lists of events and the key features of an area. All national and regional tourist boards produce brochures and you can also get very good information from tour operator brochures, as these will often be more targeted at specific markets and will generally focus on the main selling points that give the destination appeal rather than including all the features the area has to offer.

Statistical data

When researching information on the UK tourism market, you will need to obtain facts and figures on tourist activity, such as:

- volume and spending of tourists
- purpose of tourism in the UK
- holiday tourism in the UK
- average expenditure
- tourism spend by category
- duration of all tourism trips
- month of all tourism trips
- seasonality of all tourism trips
- distribution of domestic tourism by government office region,
- origin of tourists by government office region
- accommodation used by tourists
- serviced accommodation used
- occupancy levels

- booking characteristics
- transport used within the UK
- age profile
- social profile.

By analysing these figures over a period of different years, you will be able to establish a pattern or trend, which may indicate that tourism figures are increasing or decreasing. This will be covered in greater detail in the final learning outcome on key trends and factors affecting the UK inbound and tourism markets.

Timetables

Most tourists requiring public transport will need information on times – for example, for trains, coaches, flights and ferries. Although the larger book versions of timetables are gradually being replaced by online information, (e.g. www.transportweb.com) or telephone-operated information services (e.g. National Rail Enquiries: 08457 484950), most travel organisations will still retain an office copy of directories such as the *Thomas Cook European Rail Timetables* in case of equipment failure.

Destination guides

Books such as *The Rough Guide to England* or *Lonely Planet Britain* provide visitors with comprehensive information on the main attractions in each of the regions throughout the country, a short summary of the local history of the area, recommended itineraries that visitors should take and the contact details for transport and accommodation providers in the area. The descriptions usually give a more authentic account of a destination than the tourist board promotional material. Lonely Planet guides in particular have a reputation for being brutal in their critiques and usually manage to upset a number of tourist boards and locals in their publications (see the case study on the opposite page).

ACTIVITY

Look in the Lonely Planet or similar guide book and read what it says about where you live. Do you agree or disagree with what it says?

Case study

UK Lonely Planet winners and losers

Here are some of the Lonely Planet winners and losers:

Fig 3.01 Liverpool: a winner

Fig 3.02 Worcester: a loser

For its shopping, eating, drinking and dancing attractions, Leeds is labelled as the 'Knightsbridge of the North'. And, according to the guide, Liverpool has thrown off its reputation as a city 'full of smart-arse scallies who would as soon nick your car as tell you a joke'. North of the border, Glasgow is described as having soul, thanks to its 'unique blend of friendliness and warmth, urban chaos, black humour and energy' while its sister city Edinburgh, is praised for its 'unique blend of culture, sophistication and architecture, fused together in a remarkable location'.

In contrast, the guide book describes Worcester, as 'smothered by modern architectural blunders and possessed of a rather soulless centre'. Lincoln's 'unattractive and depressing suburbs don't do the city's tourist authorities any favours'. However the biggest condemnations are reserved for Douglas, the capital of the Isle of Man. It is described as being a 'run-down relic of Victorian tourism with fading B&Bs'.

(Source: *Lonely Planet Britain*, 2003)

Other sources

Some reports, statistics and website articles you may use for your research can become out of date due to new tourism products and initiatives introduced to boost tourism to a destination. Therefore, it is very important to read travel trade press such as *Travel Weekly* or *Travel Trade Gazette*, or the Sunday newspaper travel supplements such as those in *The Sunday Times*, the *Independent on Sunday* and the *Mail on Sunday*. By doing this you will be able to keep up to date with what is happening in UK tourism today, what the factors are affecting tourism and what the reasons are behind trends in UK inbound and domestic tourism.

ACTIVITY

Each week put together a portfolio of interesting articles you have found concerning UK inbound and domestic tourism. Use the full range of sources and discuss your results with your teacher and classmates. These will become very useful later in your assignment, particularly when you attempt the **P5/M3/D2** criteria.

The location of the main UK gateways, tourist destinations and geographical features

For anyone planning to work in the travel and tourism industry, a basic knowledge of the geography of the UK is essential. In many cases you will not have the time or the opportunity to refer to your reference materials so you will need to have a broad awareness of where places are without the aid of a map or an atlas. In this section you will study the following UK gateways, tourist destinations and geographical features:

- airports (including three-letter codes)
- seaports
- coastal resorts
- historical or cultural cities and towns
- islands
- lakes/loughs/lochs
- National Parks
- rivers
- mountain ranges or upland areas
- woodland areas and forests.

Gateways

In order to develop a successful inbound tourism industry any country needs to be easily accessible. The points at which these overseas tourists enter the country through airports, seaports and train terminals are called gateways. The UK has a good supply of gateways and in this section you will learn where the main ones are.

UK airports/three-letter codes

For convenience and ease of communication all airports in the world have three-letter codes that are used to identify them. You will need to know where the main airports in the UK are (Figure 3.03) and what their three-letter codes are.

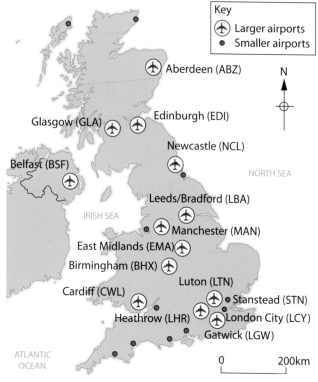

Fig 3.03 UK airports

ACTIVITY

Using an atlas, plot the following airports and their codes on a blank map: Heathrow (LHR), Gatwick (LGW), London City (LCY), Stansted (STN), Manchester (MAN), Birmingham (BHX), East Midlands (EMA), Cardiff (CWL), Edinburgh (EDI), Glasgow (GLA), Luton (LTN), Belfast (BFS).

Fig 3.04 UK ferry ports

Seaports

As the UK is an island surrounded by water, many incoming tourists from the continent choose to travel here by ferry for touring holidays, bringing their car or motorcycle with them. You will need to know what the main ports are that these incoming tourists might use as gateways into the UK (Figure 3.04).

ACTIVITY

Using an atlas, plot the following seaports on a blank map: Dover, Folkestone, Larne, Stranraer, Holyhead, Pembroke, Fishguard, Harwich, Portsmouth, Plymouth.

The Channel Tunnel

Since the opening of the Channel Tunnel in 1994, visitors have been able to choose to board the Eurostar train in Paris or Brussels and be in London in approximately two and a half hours. In 2007, St Pancras station will have replaced Waterloo station as the London terminus for the Eurostar. This will provide better access with connecting trains to the rest of the country. Tourists preferring to drive to the UK can alternatively board the Eurotunnel train with their car at Calais and be in Folkestone within 35 minutes.

Tourist destinations

The UK has a rich supply of natural and built attractions, and you will need to know the location of the main highlights of the British tourism product.

Capital cities

The United Kingdom is made up of the countries of England, Scotland, Wales and Northern Ireland (Figure 3.05). Like most capital cities, Belfast, Cardiff, Edinburgh and London are buzzing, exciting cities with museums, theatres, shops, galleries and an exciting nightlife to keep all ages satisfied.

Coastal resorts

Up until 50 years ago, British seaside resorts were very popular with domestic holidaymakers (Figure 3.06). However, since the introduction of cheap package holidays to the Mediterranean they have fallen into

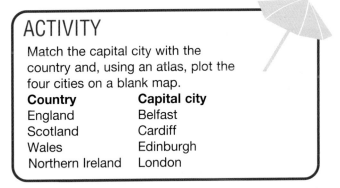

ACTIVITY

Match the capital city with the country and, using an atlas, plot the four cities on a blank map.

Country	Capital city
England	Belfast
Scotland	Cardiff
Wales	Edinburgh
Northern Ireland	London

decline. Despite this, British coastal resorts have responded to the challenge in recent years. Now over 140 beaches in the UK have Blue Flag status for water quality, facilities and safety.

ACTIVITY

Using an atlas, plot the following seaside resorts on a blank map: Brighton, Southend, Newquay, Great Yarmouth, Scarborough, Bournemouth, Torquay, Blackpool, Whitby, Llandudno.

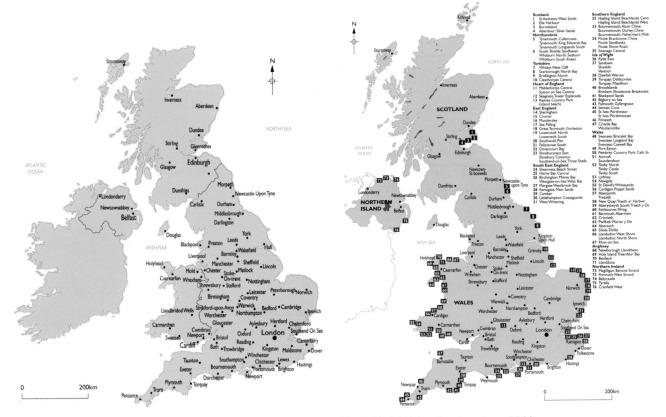

Fig 3.05 Major UK towns and cities   **Fig 3.06** UK blue flag beaches, 2003

Cultural or historical towns and cities

The UK tourism product consists largely of Britain's rich culture and history. Many towns and cities that offer castles, historic buildings, art galleries and museums, or have associations with famous people or events have become popular tourist destinations.

> ### ACTIVITY
> Using an atlas, plot the following cultural or historical towns and cities on a blank map: Bath, Oxford, Cambridge, Stratford-upon-Avon, York, Canterbury, Winchester, Chester, Warwick, Lincoln.

Geographical features

Rivers

Britain's rivers provide opportunities for fishing, boating and scenic routes for countryside walks along riverbanks. Many riverside towns and cities have developed a sentimental and romantic attachment to their rivers, which are often immortalised in songs and poems.

> ### ACTIVITY
> Using an atlas, plot the following rivers on a blank map: Thames, Trent, Clyde, Tay, Severn, Lagan, Avon, Ouse, Tyne, Mersey.

Mountain ranges and upland areas

Mountain climbing and hill walking are popular activities for those tourists more interested in outdoor, adventure-type holidays. This would mainly appeal to domestic tourists and is very important in many rural areas where there are very few alternative sources of employment for the locals (Figure 3.07).

National Parks

The first National Park was established in the Peak District in 1951; by the time the South Downs becomes the newest member in 2007, there will be 15 National Parks in Britain. National Parks cover 10 per cent of the land in England and Wales and just over 7

> ### ACTIVITY
> Using an atlas, plot the following mountain ranges and upland areas on a blank map: Pennines, Cairngorms, Brecon Beacons, Snowdonia, North-West Highlands, Grampian Mountains, Southern Uplands, Cumbrian Mountains, Chiltern Hills, Cotswold Hills, Cheviot Hills, Mendip Hills.

> ### ACTIVITY
> Using an atlas, plot the following National Parks on a blank map: Exmoor, Dartmoor, North York Moors, Yorkshire Dales, Peak District, New Forest, Pembrokeshire Coast, Lake District, Northumberland, Brecon Beacons, Snowdonia.

per cent of the land in Scotland (Figure 3.08). They are characterised by dramatic landscapes of mountains, valleys, moors and coasts. Their functions are to preserve and conserve our natural heritage as well as to encourage the public to enjoy the countryside more. For further information on National Parks, see www.nationalparks.gov.uk.

Islands

Surrounding Britain are a number of interesting islands with rugged landscapes where visitors can escape to. Smaller islands may have only a limited ferry service, particularly in the winter months.

Lakes and other bodies of water

As an island, Britain has some excellent bays for sailing, especially along the south coast. Inland there

> ### ACTIVITY
> Using an atlas, plot the following islands on a blank map: Inner Hebrides (Skye, Islay, Jura, Mull), Outer Hebrides (Lewis, Harris, North Uist, South Uist, Barra, Benbecula), Arran, Isle of Wight, Isle of Man, Isles of Scilly, Channel Islands (Jersey, Guernsey, Alderney), Orkney Islands, Shetland Islands.

Fig 3.07 UK geographical features

Fig 3.08 UK National Parks

ACTIVITY

Using an atlas, plot the following lakes and other bodies of water on a blank map: Loch Ness, Lake Windermere, Lough Neagh, Lake Ullswater, Loch Lomond, Poole Bay, Bristol Channel, Carmarthen Bay, Barnstaple/Bideford Bay, Lyme Bay.

ACTIVITY

Using an atlas, plot the following woodland areas and forests on a blank map: Epping Forest, Forest of Dean, Sherwood Forest, New Forest, Delamere Forest, Thetford Forest, Moray Forests, Forests of the Solway Coast, Queen Elizabeth Forest Park.

are also a number of lakes, which provide very scenic and relaxing holiday attractions for tourists.

Woodland areas and forests

For nature lovers, the woods of Britain provide opportunities for walking, mountain biking, horse riding and picnics (Figure 3.09). There are opportunities to learn about the fauna and flora that inhabit these woodland areas as many visitor centres will provide guided walks and events.

Assessing the outcome

VisitBritain is preparing a tourist guide book to the UK and you have been asked to prepare a set of maps that show the main gateways, tourist destinations and geographical features of the UK. As a tourism expert you would be expected to locate these gateways, destinations and features without the aid of research resources.

- Locate gateways, tourist destinations and geographical features of the UK without the aid of reference material (**P2**).

The appeal of UK destinations

The location of a destination and its natural features (e.g. lakes, mountains, waterfalls), accessibility (e.g. transport routes) and attractions (e.g. historic buildings, theme parks) are all factors that can play a vital role in encouraging tourism to a destination. In this section you will learn what these factors are and how important they are to the appeal of a destination. In your portfolio you will need to select two destinations.

Please note, in your portfolio the destinations you choose as evidence for **P3/M1** cannot be the same as those used as evidence for **P4/M2/D1**.

Natural appeal

An area that can offer unique scenery and an attractive landscape has the potential to become a tourist destination. In addition to the National Parks mentioned earlier, there are 40 Areas of Outstanding Natural Beauty (AONBs) in England and Wales with

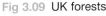

Fig 3.09 UK forests

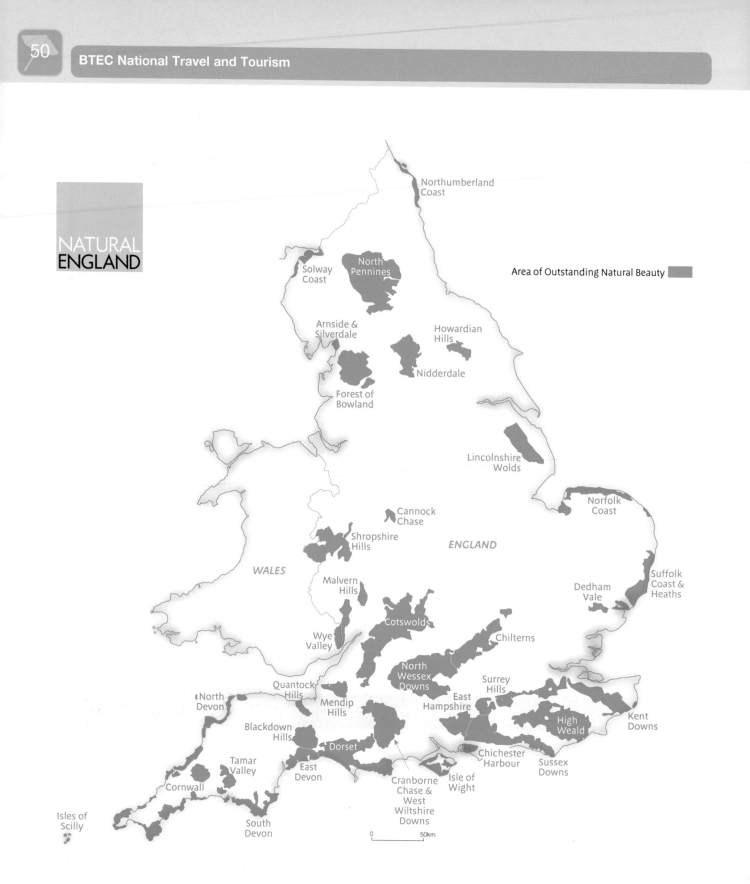

Fig 3.10 Areas of Outstanding Natural Beauty in England

nine in Northern Ireland – for example, the Shropshire Hills and the Antrim Coast and Glens (Figure 3.10). There is also an equivalent 40 National Scenic Areas in Scotland, such as Ben Nevis and Glencoe. As the name implies, these are areas of such outstanding natural beauty that they are selected as conservation areas to preserve their character for future generations. These areas can include features such as, forests, hills, mountains, valleys, gorges, moors, lakes, rivers and waterfalls. Examples of these areas that have promoted their natural beauty to appeal to tourists can be found in the earlier section on geographical features. For further information on Areas of Outstanding Natural Beauty, visit www.aonb.org.uk and for more on National Scenic Areas in Scotland, visit www.snh.org.uk.

Built attractions

Britain's tourist product is based to a large extent on our rich culture and heritage. Many tourists come from all over the world every year to visit towns and cities that appeal to those keen to learn more about our past (see the section above on cultural or historical towns and cities). An example is the historic walled city of Chester, which offers the Roman amphitheatre, Beeston Castle, Chester Cathedral, the Grosvenor Museum, the Gateway Theatre, the stately home of Tatton Park, as well as the famous Tudor houses along The Rows. However, destinations such as Chester need to be able to offer something for younger children in order to attract the family market

Fig 3.11 The Rows, Chester

too. Chester does this through offering modern facilities and attractions such as Chester Zoo, Ragamuffins Play Centre, the Odeon Cinema and Alton Towers theme park nearby.

Location

Another feature that gives a destination appeal is its location and in particular its proximity to tourism-generating areas and gateways. For destinations focusing on the domestic tourism market, a major advantage would be how close they are to the major cities and areas of high population density. The top ten most populated cities in the UK are listed in Table 3.01.

Tourist destination areas that are within a couple of hours' driving time from these cities will obviously

Table 3.01 Top ten most populated cities in the UK		
1	London	7,172,091
2	Birmingham	977,087
3	Leeds	715,402
4	Glasgow	577,869
5	Sheffield	513,234
6	Bradford	467,665
7	Edinburgh	448,624
8	Liverpool	439,477
9	Manchester	392,819
10	Bristol	380,615
(Source: Census, 2001)		

Fig 3.12 UK motorways

Fig 3.13 UK railway network

have greater appeal for the day-tripper market because of the convenience they offer. For those destinations that are close to one of the air or sea gateways (see the earlier section on gateways), this will likewise open up the potential to attract overseas tourists coming into the UK.

Transport links

Having a good supply of natural and built attractions, however, is not enough. If the destination does not have good transport links, then it will lose its appeal to many tourists as it will not be convenient to get to. Transport links include major road networks such as motorways (Figure 3.12) and rail links to other major towns and cities in the UK (Figure 3.13). For those destinations targeting incoming tourists, good transport links to air and sea ports (see the earlier section on gateways), are also very important, especially to airports that support budget airlines offering low-cost fares to the destination. Transport links, however, does not just cover those that permit access to the destination, but can also mean *within* the destination. Towns and cities with a good public

transport system such as, for example, the London Underground, will have a big advantage over those cities that do not. Many tourist towns, such as Stratford-upon-Avon, are now developing park-and-ride schemes for visitors to ease the traffic congestion in town centres caused by day-trippers.

Assessing the outcome

VisitBritain is hosting a delegation of Chinese travel agents on a familiarisation trip to the UK. You have been asked to prepare a presentation on three different types of destination (capital cities, coastal resorts and cultural/historical towns and cities) and describe the factors and features that give them appeal. You will need to demonstrate your ability to use a range of sources of reference to research the information and use these throughout your presentation.

- Describe the appeal of two UK destinations (**P3**).
- Use appropriate reference materials to provide information on UK destinations (**P1**).

Case study

Travelling to Brighton

Fig 3.14 Brighton seafront

This example shows the excellent transport links available to tourists visiting the coastal resort of Brighton.

By coach: Express coaches from London to Brighton take about two hours and regular National Express services depart from London Heathrow and Gatwick airports.

By train: Brighton is just under an hour from London Victoria and there are direct services from Scotland, the north-west, the Midlands, the West Country and South Wales.

The PLUSBUS ticket is also available to visitors who wish to combine train and bus travel. Simply ask for a *PLUSBUS ticket for Brighton* when buying your train ticket and you can make as many journeys as you like on all local Brighton buses on the day your ticket is valid. Prices start at £2 for an adult ticket. Brighton offers an award-winning bus service, making the PLUSBUS ticket a great way to get around town, as well as save money.

By air/car: Brighton is just 30 minutes by road or rail from London Gatwick International Airport and 90 minutes by road from London Heathrow. In addition, Sky South operates regular scheduled flights to destinations in the Channel Islands and France throughout the year from Brighton City Airport.

By Eurostar: Travel by Eurostar from France and Belgium to London Waterloo and then on to Brighton via London Bridge station. Journey time is approximately four hours.

By sea: Brighton is just 20 minutes by road or 25 minutes by rail from the port of Newhaven where a ferry service operates to Dieppe. The Channel Tunnel and major ports of Dover, Folkestone, Portsmouth and Southampton are between one and two hours away by motorway.

(Source: Visit Brighton)

The needs of UK domestic and inbound tourism markets

Tourism is very important to the British economy, whether this is domestic tourism, involving British residents holidaying in the UK, or inbound tourism where visitors come here on holiday from overseas. As with any business, success is dependent on meeting customers' needs and keeping them satisfied. Although most tourists will have similar needs, it is important for you to be aware that the needs of domestic tourists can often be different to those of incoming tourists, and within the inbound market itself there are significant differences between different nationalities in terms of their specific needs.

In this section (**P4**) you will be required to describe the needs of two different types of domestic tourist markets (e.g. business, families) and, for inbound tourists, you will need to consider the needs of two different overseas markets (e.g. Chinese, American) for both business and leisure travellers. Although many of these needs will be similar (e.g. a desire to visit heritage attractions), you could also show an awareness of cultural differences between the visitors. Please note, in your portfolio the destinations you choose as evidence for **P4/M2/D1** cannot be the same as those used as evidence for **P3/M1**.

Domestic tourism market needs

When considering the needs of the domestic market, it is useful to refer to the different types of customer.

Business

Business tourism can be very important to a destination and the needs of the business tourist are quite different to those of the leisure tourist. Businessmen and businesswomen will travel to a destination for work reasons – for example, to attend conferences and events, exhibitions and meetings. A destination that seeks to attract this market will need to have venues large enough to accommodate large numbers of conference delegates with state-of-the-art audio-visual equipment, e.g. videoconferencing facilities. As delegates will be travelling from different parts of the country, the destination will need to have good transport links, such as motorways and rail links to the major cities, e.g. Birmingham. Business travellers will normally be expected to work late in the evenings so hotels will need to provide late check-in as well as early, and preferably express, check-out services. They will usually work in their bedrooms so they will require room service and internet access so they can work uninterrupted.

Groups

In the tourism industry a group is generally regarded as ten or more people. Groups can be either leisure tourists, e.g. a school trip visiting the Manchester Museum or a coach party on a touring holiday of the Scottish Highlands, or they can be business tourists attending a special event, e.g. delegates attending the World Travel Market exhibition in London. Despite these differences, they will have a number of similarities: primarily that they will want to do things together. This can mean providing them with coaches to transport them around, booking them a private seating area in a restaurant, making group bookings for them on a train or at a visitor attraction, providing them with a tour guide or tour leader or checking them in and allocating them bedrooms close together in a hotel, etc.

Families

Family holidays and the visiting friends and relatives (VFR) markets are important contributors to the domestic tourism industry. As family groups can include three different generations their needs can be quite difficult to meet, particularly when the age range is quite large. Elderly and disabled visitors with mobility difficulties may seek quieter, less crowded destinations where there are not too many steps or hills, and the activities that they enjoy will generally be more relaxing, such as visiting museums or art galleries. However, children and teenagers will want more energetic activities such as going to theme parks, zoos, beaches and play centres. Parents will look for leisure parks or holiday camps with leisure facilities and swimming pools on-site, which can offer organised activities for the children as well as evening

Fig 3.15 A Butlins holiday camp

entertainment for the adults and childminding services. Hotels targeting this market will need to provide larger bedrooms or interconnecting rooms as families will want to stay as close together as possible.

Individuals

For many consumers, the 'cash-rich, time-poor' society we live in has meant that they do not have time to take extended holidays; this has resulted in the growth of the city break market. Tourist towns and cities that understand the needs of individuals and couples are able to capitalise on this trend. Essential to this market are good rail and coach transport links to the destination and a reasonable public transport system within the destination itself. This is important as increasingly single people are becoming more confident about travelling alone; this is what has become termed the lone traveller market. These tourists may not have a car or may not want to drive to the destination, preferring to relax on the train during the journey. Hotels are responding to this trend and it is becoming increasingly common for accommodation providers not to charge a single-person supplement for rooms used for sole occupancy. These travellers are generally more adventurous and motivated by a desire to experience something new. Destinations that target this market usually package together a set of natural or built attractions into a consistent special interest theme and use this theme as their unique selling point (USP), to differentiate themselves from competitor destinations – for example, The Beatles Story in Liverpool.

Inbound tourism market needs

Incoming tourists will have many general needs that are the same as those of domestic tourists, whether business travellers coming into the UK to attend meetings or conferences or leisure travellers here on holiday. However, they do have some significant differences, which you will learn about in this section.

Transport

The most obvious difference between domestic and incoming tourists is that overseas tourists need to travel here first. In order to do this they will need to have access to gateways convenient to the destinations they intend travelling to. If they are driving, they will need to have ferry ports where they can 'drive-on, drive-off' with their cars or alternatively they can take the Eurotunnel to Folkestone (see the earlier section on gateways). If they are planning on flying, they will need convenient access to international and regional airports. All international airports in the UK also offer car hire services (such as Hertz, Dollar, etc.) where incoming tourists can pick up a car on arrival and drop it off on departure. These are called fly-drive holidays and are very popular with independent travellers who like to have the freedom to make their own arrangements.

Uniquely British

Britain's tourism product is mainly its heritage and culture, and incoming tourists are drawn to our historic buildings and castles, cathedrals and other visitor attractions such as the Tower of London, Buckingham Palace and St Paul's Cathedral. The stereotypical images of Britishness, such as red phone boxes, red buses, beefeaters and 'bobbies' promoted by national and regional tourist boards to reinforce the brand image provide the UK with its USP. Local and national customs and traditions, such as the Changing of the Guard, the Trooping of the Colour and morris

Fig 3.17 Edinburgh Castle

dancing, along with special events such as the Edinburgh Tattoo, Hogmanay, the Chelsea Flower Show, the Oxford and Cambridge boat race and the Wimbledon tennis championship appeal to incoming tourists' special interest needs to experience the unique British culture.

Accommodation

Incoming tourists visiting Britain need reassurance about the quality of the hotels and bed and breakfasts they will be staying in. In order to provide this, VisitBritain, the Automobile Association (AA) and the Royal Automobile Club (RAC) have combined to produce a harmonised star rating scheme for hotels as well as a diamonds scheme for guest accommodation such as bed and breakfasts, guesthouses, farmhouses and inns. The new grades are expected to appear for the first time in 2008 accommodation guide books. Whereas in the past, schemes used a one- to five-star rating system based primarily on facilities, the new scheme also incorporates the quality of the accommodation in its assessment. In Scotland and

Fig 3.16 Buckingham Palace

Fig 3.18 Fish and chips

Fig 3.19 A four-star rating

Wales, the schemes are slightly different in that the focus is more on the quality rather than the quantity of the facilities. This reflects the difficulty in classifying converted stately homes and castles which, although luxurious, can lack some of the modern facilities such as lifts. For accommodation providers aiming to attract overseas tourists, it is also important to have multi-lingual staff as well as brochures and signs in the languages of the major tourist-generating markets, such as French, German, Italian and Spanish.

Case study

VisitBritain market profile: Japan

'Makeinu' are basically a Japanese version of 'Bridget Jones' – single and childless working women older than 30. However, according to Japan Tourism Marketing (JTM), within this label there is a new group of women that is being watched by the travel industry: the 'ohitorisama' (single-not-young lady) who travel alone by choice, and for them Britain ranked second only to New York as the most preferred destination to visit alone. 'Ohitorisama' tend to be in their thirties and forties, many of them are highly successful single career women, who see travelling alone as a way of rejuvenating themselves. They prefer to be on their own, at their own pace and not bothering with the plans of others. These women enjoy dining and having a drink on their own, and visiting galleries and theatres alone. They are prepared to stay at a hotel alone so as to be pampered and enjoy the beauty treatments offered. They have been targeted by Japanese travel firms such as ANA, JTB and Jalpak for language study tours and cooking classes in London.

ACTIVITY

- Based on the VisitBritain market profile of Japan, what are the needs of the typical 'ohitorisama' market segment?
- What British destination do you think would best suit this type of tourist? Give reasons for your answer
- What are your needs when on holiday in this country and when abroad?
- What are the needs of different types of tourists, such as business people, the elderly, families and groups?

Assessing the outcome

You have been appointed as the new business development manager for a large tour operator. Your first task is to prepare a report on potential new business markets describing what their needs are. You need to select two inbound and two domestic markets for your company to target. You will need to deomonstrate your ability to use a range of reference sources to research the information and use these throughout your report.

- Describe the needs of the UK domestic and inbound tourism markets (**P4**).
- Use appropriate references materials to provide information on UK destinations (**P1**).

Key trends and factors affecting the UK inbound and domestic tourism markets

In order to understand the size and scale of UK inbound and domestic tourism, every year the figures for numbers of tourists arriving and the revenue they generate are recorded and studied carefully by both the government and the travel and tourism industry. These figures are then compared to the statistical data for previous years in order to determine trends in the markets in order to plan for the future. Therefore, it is important to be able to interpret statistics accurately, establish their meaning and implications, and explore the reasons behind the trends in order to be able to form conclusions on the basis of this evidence. The reasons for these trends can be caused by a wide range of internal and external factors that can affect tourism, either to encourage or to discourage inbound and domestic tourists. In this section you will need to research and identify recent trends and the reasons for these trends in UK domestic and inbound tourism.

Analysing key trends

When analysing key trends in UK inbound and domestic tourism, it is normal to study statistical information over the previous ten-year period in order to make an effective year-on-year comparison. The type of statistical data usually used would be figures relating to the number of inbound and domestic visitors the UK receives each year, the amount of income generated by inbound and domestic tourism, their average length of stay, their countries and regions of origin, and the purpose of their visits. Websites that are particularly useful sources of up-to-date and relevant statistical information include:

- Star UK – www.staruk.org.uk
- VisitBritain – www.tourismtrade.org.uk/Market IntelligenceResearch
- Office for National Statistics – www.statistics.gov.uk.

Examples of UK tourism statistical data
General overview

Tourism contributes approximately £85 billion to the UK economy each year and sustains over 2 million jobs both directly and indirectly (source: Labour Market Trends, April 2005). The number of visits made to the UK by overseas residents in 2005 was the highest ever recorded: 30.0 million, with visitors spending a record £14.2 billion. These figures reflected a doubling of visitor numbers between 1985 and 2005 and an increase in visitor spending by overseas residents of 8 per cent in constant price terms in the same period. They also show a healthy recovery for the UK tourism industry from the 18 per cent decline between 2000 and 2001, and the small recoveries in the two subsequent years (source: Office for National Statistics). Tables 3.02–3.04 and Figure 3.20 show examples of tourism statistical data.

Table 3.02 Volume and spending of domestic tourists, 2004

	Trips/visits	Nights	Spending
	Millions	Millions	Millions
UK residents	126.6	408.9	24,357

(Source: Star UK)

Table 3.03 All tourism visits 2001–03

	Visits (millions)	Spending (£ millions)
2001	22.84	11,306
2002	24.18	11,737
2003	24.72	11,855

(Source: Star UK)

Table 3.04 The top five overseas markets for the UK in 2005			
Country	**Visits (000s)**	**Country**	**Spend (£m)**
USA	3438	USA	2384
France	3324	Germany	998
Germany	3294	Irish Republic	895
Irish Republic	2806	France	796
Spain	1786	Spain	697
(Source: VisitBritain)			

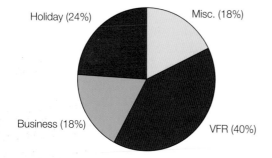

Fig 3.20 Irish Republic: breakdown of visits by purpose of visit in 2005
(Source: VisitBritain)

Factors affecting UK inbound and domestic tourism markets

In order to understand the reasons for these trends, it is important to consider the factors that affect incoming and domestic tourism to the UK. Some of these factors are internal, to do with the UK itself, and some are external to do with the global economy, competitor destinations and the generating countries themselves. In this section you will study some of these internal and external factors.

Factors internal to the UK

Factors that are internal to the UK that have had a discouraging affect on incoming and domestic tourism could include health scares such as the bird flu in Norfolk in April 2006 and Suffolk in February 2007 or, more seriously, the foot and mouth outbreak of 2001 which had a very negative impact on domestic tourism. Tourist concerns over health and safety became even more pertinent following the 7 July 2005 bombings on London transport. Less dramatic, though none the less damaging for the

incoming tourist market, has been the strength of the pound sterling in relation to the US dollar and the Euro, since its introduction in 2002, thus making the UK an expensive destination to visit.

On the other hand, internal factors that have encouraged tourism have been successful marketing campaigns such as the 2006 Enjoy England 'Discover the Secrets of England's Best Kept Short Breaks' campaign, as well as an intensification in 2005 by VisitBritain to encourage North Americans to travel to Britain throughout the year, not just during the summer peak period. The rapid growth of budget airlines has also contributed both to making Britain more accessible to the emerging Eastern European markets and to encouraging the dispersal of domestic tourists to regional airports such as, Ryanair's Stansted–Newquay route.

Fig 3.21 A Ryanair aeroplane

Finally, the quality of the UK tourism product has improved in recent years as a result of a number of initiatives such as, the increased emphasis on quality in the new harmonised star rating scheme for accommodation providers; improved levels of customer service as a result of programmes such as Welcome Host, which is offered through the Regional Tourism Organisations, and the improvements to Britain's beaches, which by 2007 had resulted in 93 beaches in England and Northern Ireland obtaining the international Blue Flag status for cleanliness and environmental management techniques.

Factors external to the UK

There are, however, factors that are beyond the control of the UK tourist industry, which have nevertheless had an affect on levels of incoming tourism. As mentioned earlier, unfavourable exchange rates between sterling and both the Euro and the US dollar have made the UK an expensive destination for key North American and European markets in recent years. This has been brought about by rising inflation, higher unemployment and a slowing down of the economies in these countries, factors that are all external to the UK.

As was mentioned earlier, the growth of budget airlines, on the one hand, provides an opportunity to attract emerging markets in Eastern Europe, however this equally provides a threat to the UK in that these countries are also emerging as competitor destinations as UK tourists avail themselves of cheap flights abroad rather than take domestic holidays in Britain. To compensate for this, in January 2005 the UK received Approved Destination Status (ADS) from the Chinese government, thereby easing travel restrictions for Chinese citizens to the UK. This has also enabled VisitBritain to establish offices in Hong Kong, Beijing and Shanghai to 'market Britain as a distinctive destination within Europe'.

The value of the Chinese tourist market can be witnessed from World Tourism Organization (WTO) figures which indicate 'that the number of tourists leaving China has risen by a million every year since 1998' (source: www.visitbritain.com, accessed May 2007). In 2003 this represented just over 20 million visitors and Britain's share of that market was 0.6%. However the WTO forecasts that by the year 2020 this figure will have risen to 100 million and if Britain can improve its market share to just 1%, then this 'would generate approximately £1 billion for the British economy and create around 25,000 new jobs' (source: www.etoa.org, accessed May 2007).

Fig 3.22 Chinese tourists in the UK

Fig 3.23 Travel trade press: *Travel Trade Gazette* and *Travel Weekly*

Case study

A record year for UK inbound tourism

In the aftermath of the July 2005 bombings in London, few in the travel and tourism industry thought that the UK might come out of it unscathed. Yet this is almost exactly what did happen – at least in terms of inbound tourism.

Admittedly, domestic tourism suffered badly from the bombings – especially in the UK capital. In fact, the domestic market was already performing below trend growth in the months leading up to 7 July, and has been declining steadily in terms of arrivals and spending in London since its peak of 2000. Visit London says the year-end trend would have been negative without 7/7, but the bombs clearly compounded the problems, with anecdotal evidence suggesting that domestic visits fell by as much as 30 per cent in July and August 2005. Preliminary estimates now point to a 6.3 per cent drop in arrivals and a 4 per cent fall in spend for the full 12 months of 2005.

In contrast to the domestic tourism market, UK inbound tourism chalked up a record year. Provisional figures from the Office for National Statistics point to an 8 per cent increase in arrivals for the country overall, to almost 30 million, and a 9 per cent rise in visitor spending, to £14.3 billion (€20.7 billion). Arrivals in London are estimated at 14.3 million, up 7 per cent, with spending rising 6.4 per cent.

The only disappointing source region for the UK in 2005 was North America, which fell by 3 per cent to 4.2 million arrivals. Western Europe, meanwhile – which accounts for nearly two-thirds of total inbound arrivals – increased by 8 per cent to 19.3 million.

However, the best growth by far – of 18 per cent to 6.4 million – came from the 'rest of world' region, which includes all long-haul source countries, excluding North America, plus Eastern Europe. South-East Asia, India, Russia and Eastern Europe were all strong performers in 2005 and, as a result, VisitBritain has decided to step up its marketing and promotional investment in 11 new and developing markets in these regions.

In the case of Eastern Europe, much of the growth can of course be attributed to the continuously increasing 'no-frills' airline capacity into the UK, especially from the new member countries of the European Union. And Russia's growth has come from all sectors – business travel and visits to friends and/or relations (VFR), as well as study trips and holidays. In 2004, Russia had already recorded a 20 per cent increase in arrivals in the UK and a 17 per cent rise in overnight volume, and preliminary estimates point to another year of double-digit growth in 2005.

China was none the less disappointing – largely because expectations following the granting of Approved Destination Status (ADS) were unreasonably high within the UK travel industry. But there were also far more teething problems with ADS than anticipated – for the UK as for other European countries. India, on the other hand, appears to have surpassed all expectations, recording a 53 per cent rise in visitor spending in the UK last year.

(Source: *Travel Daily News*, Wednesday, 15 March, 2006)

Assessing the outcome

You work for the Department of Culture, Media and Sport (DCMS) and you have been asked to prepare a report for the travel media describing tourism trends within the UK incoming and domestic tourism markets. Provide statistical representations such as tables, graphs and pie charts reflecting these trends and describe the internal and external factors influencing these trends. You will need to deomonstrate your ability to use a range of reference sources to research the information and use these throughout your report.

- Describe external and internal factors influencing recent key trends in the UK inbound and domestic market (**P5**).
- Use appropriate references materials to provide information on UK destinations (**P1**).

ACTIVITY

In groups, read about the above trends in the travel trade press and discuss what you think are the reasons for the factors affecting the growth/decline of the different tourist markets.

Improve your grade

Referring to your assessment grid, you will note that the criteria are grouped together according to the topics described opposite. Higher grades are awarded for greater levels of depth, evaluation, analysis and reasoning.

P3/M1 – Destination appeal

The merit criteria (M1) is an expansion of the answer provided for the pass criteria (P3) and the same destinations should be used, however the difference between the two is one of specificity and depth. At merit level, the answer is more detailed, with reference to the appeal of two UK destinations for both domestic and inbound tourists, and the inclusion of more specific facts and figures using a wider range of reference sources such as atlases, timetables, the internet and brochures. For example, whereas at pass level you might make the general point that the destination was accessible to large centres of population, at merit level, you would need to include specific details regarding which airports/motorways/roads/rails link to which cities, with population figures for those generating areas. Likewise, at pass level, you could describe the various features of a destination, whereas at merit level you would be expected to explain the unique selling points and the importance of these features to the overall appeal of that destination to both domestic and inbound tourists.

P4/M2/D1 – Tourist needs

Although at pass level (P4) you would only be expected to give a general description of the needs of four different types of customers, at merit level (M2) you would need to give specific details and the unique selling points of four UK destinations and explain how these would meet the needs of the four different types of domestic and inbound markets you described. You would need to research carefully any new products such as visitor attractions or initiatives such as urban regeneration projects, which have been introduced into the destination area that could contribute towards meeting those markets' needs. Examples could include the promotion of Asian shops and markets in Southall, West London, that would appeal to the Indian market or the Banglatown curry festival in Brick Lane, East London, that would appeal to the Bengali market.

For you to upgrade this to distinction level (D1), you would need to broaden your answer to not just explaining why the four destinations would appeal to the four target markets but give your own evaluation of whether you think the UK as a whole is attractive to these markets. You would still use the same examples as you provided for the P4 and M2 criteria as evidence to support your conclusions but you would also be expected to justify how new transport routes, regional airports and your own suggestions and recommendations could lead to an increase in appeal among the specified tourist markets for the UK tourism product. Note that the destinations you select as evidence for M2/D1 cannot be the same as those used for P3/M1.

P5/M3/D2 – Statistical analysis

The difference between pass (P5) and merit (M3) is that, whereas at pass level you are only expected to describe the reasons for trends and the factors affecting these trends, at merit level the emphasis is more on the analysis of these factors. You will need to include a minimum of three external factors and three internal factors and you will need to provide detailed and reasoned conclusions on the effect these have on recent key trends in the UK inbound and domestic tourism markets. In addition, you will be expected to have demonstrated more research. Whereas at pass level you only needed a minimum of three sources of data, at merit level you will need a wider variety of sources such as media reports, industry publications and relevant websites.

Distinction level (D2) differs from merit level slightly in that the emphasis shifts from analysing the current impacts of these internal and external factors to an evaluation of the likely impact of these external and internal factors on the future of UK inbound and domestic tourism. For example, at merit level you might highlight as an external factor the emergence of new markets – for example, the Chinese and Russian markets. At distinction level, you could argue that in the future the Chinese market is predicted to grow quite rapidly as a result of the easing by the Chinese government of travel restrictions abroad, whereas the Russian market may grow more slowly as Russian citizens may still have difficulty in acquiring visas for foreign travel.

Top tips

- You should show a deeper level of learning, doing full research.
- You should make use of a wide variety of sources.
- You should keep a portfolio of your information sources.

Learning outcomes

By the end of this unit you should:

- know the principles and benefits of good customer service in travel and tourism
- understand how travel and tourism organisations adapt customer service to meet differing customer motivations
- be able to demonstrate customer service skills in travel and tourism
- be able to demonstrate selling skills appropriate to the travel and tourism industry.

Customer service in travel and tourism

One characteristic of the tourism product is its intangibility – it cannot be touched or experienced. A great deal of the tourism product is service-related. A train ticket guarantees to get a customer from a departure point to a destination but if the train arrives late or there is no seat available, a customer is not pleased with the service. The next time they make a journey, they will buy a ticket from another train operating company or even a coach company or airline. This is one of the consequences of an organisation providing poor customer service – the customer goes elsewhere. The customer may pass on their bad report to others such as colleagues, friends and family and so more customers may be lost.

Many organisations offer similar products and services and it is often the quality of service that distinguishes one organisation from another. Knowing the principles of excellent customer service can ensure these are delivered to customers of a selected organisation so that the organisation remains competitive.

Principles of customer service

It isn't easy to determine what makes excellent customer service. Talking to different customers about their experiences can often provide a description of a situation but this cannot always summarise the key points that led to excellent or poor customer service.

Case study

" When I got through the airport, excited about finally arriving in India after a ten-hour flight and two-hour delay, I saw a sea of clipboards and frantically sought one with the name of my tour operator. Eventually I found, right at the back, a faded sticker on a sheet of paper. When I found the person holding the paper, I thought I had arrived at a clubbers' paradise – just at closing time. I wondered if the flight had arrived on time whether they would have still been at the club or in bed. They didn't have my name on a list but told me to get on the coach and they would sort it out later. I had booked it three months before! How could they not have my name? The transfer coach was disgusting. It didn't look as if the rubbish had been cleared in weeks and the rep did nothing but moan about the heat all the way to the hotel. "

One of the key principles of good customer service is that customers get a positive first impression.

In addition to first impressions, there are other principles of customer service. One of these is company image. This includes branding and use of colour and also the company's efficiency.

An organisation's premises is also part of its image and can suggest a certain standard of customer service. For many travel and tourism organisations, such as airlines or train operators, the premises in which they

ACTIVITY

In the case study on the previous page, the customer is unhappy with the service received. Discuss the consequences of this poor customer service to the tour operator and to the overseas representative in the resort. Describe how the tour operator in the example could use the principle of positive first impressions to provide quality customer service. Discuss how this revised description would benefit the employee and the customer.

ACTIVITY

One way that the efficiency of transport companies is measured is by their punctuality. The Civil Aviation Authority produces airline punctuality statistics. Flightontime.info produces an analysis of these statistics. Investigate the efficiency of Virgin Airlines in terms of its punctuality. Discuss the benefits of a transport operator working efficiently and punctually to both the customer and the staff on board.

are based are not accessed by the customer and are not relevant. For accommodation providers or attractions, however, their premises are also their product.

Cleanliness of premises is a key principle of excellent customer service. An attraction covered in litter or a hotel room with dirty towels in the bathroom are both examples of an organisation's premises suggesting poor customer service is provided. Consider working in such an environment. Someone working in a TIC sitting next to a desk constantly messy and full of coffee cups is likely to be embarrassed when dealing with a customer, even if their own desk is clean and tidy.

ACTIVITY

Discuss how an organisation's premises can assist in providing excellent customer service and how this benefits an organisation.

Customers have many needs and meeting these needs is a key principle of excellent customer service. Some of these may be specific to the organisation and the type of product and service offered. Some may be specific to the type of customer. Consider two customers wanting to make a booking through a travel agent for a flight from London to Bangkok. One customer is a business person, the other is booking for herself and her young child, aged 15 months. There are two organisations involved in meeting their needs: the travel agent and the airline. What are their needs from the travel agent? The business person is likely to need a speedy service and clear and accurate information in response to questions about service provided. Is that any different to the other customer? Both may want to make their booking by telephone rather than face-to-face; certainly the business person will not be happy to come away from the office and the customer with a young child may feel uncomfortable, anticipating the child crying, and may be unable to come in alone. The questions they have about the service may be different but they would still expect clear and accurate answers.

ACTIVITY

Describe the needs of each customer from the airline. How might an airline meet those needs? Describe how the employee of an airline benefits from meeting those needs.

Methods to monitor and evaluate

Organisations will set standards for the quality of customer service they expect to provide. They will use different methods to monitor the level of service actually provided and evaluate the service against the standards they expect. The methods they may use include mystery shoppers and questionnaires.

A mystery shopper is someone posing as a real customer. They may be employed by the organisation and trained to assess or evaluate the quality of customer service they experience or an organisation may pay for the services of a specialist organisation. Mystery shopping can be done face to face, by telephone or email to reflect the way a customer accesses the organisation. The mystery shopper will be given the quality criteria to be used for the evaluation. Some organisations will weight the different criteria based on what they consider to be the priority. A call centre, for example, may give more weighting to speed of service and accuracy of service than cleanliness and hygiene. An attraction might put more emphasis on the latter.

ACTIVITY

ACTIVITY

Identify the key criteria that could be used for an airline or a hotel. Discuss the weighting you would give to each criterion identified.

Setting benchmark standards is an important part of monitoring and evaluating customer service. Organisations have different ways of setting the benchmark. Some may set minimum standards that must be achieved and if these are in place, the criterion has been met. Alternatively, an organisation may decide to grade the quality from 1 to 5. In these cases, clear benchmark standards would be set for each of the marks awarded.

ACTIVITY

Travel Weekly is a travel newspaper. Each week there is a feature where it conducts a test by a mystery shopper of different travel agents in a town or city. It uses a 'scoring system', as shown in Figure 4.01.

Set the benchmark standards to be used for each of the quality criteria in the scoring system.

Mystery shopper scoring system

25%	External/internal appearance
25%	Sales technique
10%	Availability check
20%	Product knowledge
10%	Details explained
10%	Request matched

Fig 4.01 *Travel Weekly*'s mystery shopper scoring system

One disadvantage of using a mystery shopper is that it only evaluates the service provided over a short space of time and this may not reflect the quality of the service provided if measured over a longer period of time. It also only evaluates the quality of customer service as delivered to one type of customer. It will not represent, for example, how customer service is delivered to a group or to, say, young couples, unless a range of mystery shopper exercises are undertaken.

An alternative approach may be to use a questionnaire or survey. This would involve either interviewing customers or asking them to complete a questionnaire relating to the service they received. This gives a wider range of viewpoints to be considered and also gives the customer's perspective. The customer, though, is not trained to know the benchmark standards. One customer's view of the level of service expected to award 'excellent' may be very different from another's. A customer used to travelling on a charter service could be very impressed with the service in economy class of Singapore Airlines, voted world's best airline for 11 consecutive years (*Travel and Leisure* magazine). A customer used to travelling first class with Singapore Airlines who has to travel economy class could be disappointed with the service. Each could therefore give a very different mark in a questionnaire.

A questionnaire or telephone interview would be structured in the same way as a mystery shopper test, identifying quality criteria and setting benchmark standards.

ACTIVITY

Produce a questionnaire that could be used as part of a survey to evaluate customer service in a travel and tourism organisation.

Assessing the outcome

A theme park is currently reviewing its customer service to make improvements, if needed. You have been asked to research how other travel and tourism organisations provide customer service. Implementing changes will have costs. The organisation needs to know the benefits of customer service in each organisation you investigate to ensure the costs of making changes are worthwhile.

- Describe how the principles of customer service and methods used to monitor them are applied in two different travel and tourism organisations (**P1**).
- Describe the benefits of good-quality customer service and the consequences of poor service to two different travel and tourism organisations (**P2**).

How customer service can meet differing customer needs

Excellent customer service is provided when all the customer's needs have been met. For example, a tour operator will consider all possible customer needs to produce a package holiday. It will have ensured all needs are met by providing:

- flights from a range of UK airports

- transfers at the destination from the airport to their accommodation, possibly by taxi or limousine and not just by coach

- accommodation ranging from serviced to self-catering, with different levels of quality from one to five stars

- the services of a representative to help if there are any problems

- a range of activities a customer can participate in, ranging from excursions to an activity programme or children's clubs.

An employee of a travel agent may consider they have given good customer service when they have recommended a holiday that meets customer needs:

> I delivered excellent customer service to the customer. He came in wanting a two-week holiday to Spain for him and his family this summer. I asked how much he wanted to spend and if he had any preferred destination. He told me the family had been to Benidorm before and really enjoyed it but his children were growing and he needed better accommodation. I recommended a holiday to Benidorm but this time in a four-star hotel with a kids' club.
>
> *(Tom, travel consultant)*

A customer, however, may have a different view of this experience:

> I was happy with the Benidorm holiday. We did enjoy the last holiday there. I was a bit concerned that, with the children growing, it wasn't really what we wanted. I wanted something lively with plenty going on but maybe more family-orientated rather than suitable for young adults. I was worried that my children, who are now 15 and 16, would want to go out and enjoy the nightlife and I really wanted more of a family holiday. I was happy with the four-star hotel as I did want better accommodation but I was thinking of self-catering to give us a bit more freedom so we could go out and enjoy Spain a bit more, like visiting villages and eating in local tapas bars.
>
> *(Guy, customer)*

Now it seems that perhaps the customer service wasn't as good as the employee thought. In this example, the customer has stated some of his needs but others were unstated and some of them were implied. With good customer service, all needs will be met, so it is important to find out not just stated needs but also those unstated and implied.

- *Stated needs* are those that are declared, specified, articulated in words. For example, 'I really need a rest' or 'I need a seat with more leg room.'

- *Unstated needs* are those that are not said. They may be known but not specified perhaps because of embarrassment or uncertainty. It may also be that they are not stated because it is assumed that someone is aware of them. For example, a customer with a physical disability may not mention the need for disabled access to a plane or rooms with disabled facilities because they assume that because they are sitting in a wheelchair, the travel agent will know this.

- *Implied needs* are hinted at or suggested. For example, a customer arriving in a taxi at a hotel struggling to carry three heavy bags might expect that a porter would see they have a need for help with carrying the luggage and shouldn't need to go and ask for help.

A need can be defined as something that is necessary or a requirement. This is different to a want, which is really a wish or desire. If we are thirsty, our need is for liquid or rehydration but our want might be for a cup of tea or a glass of lager. A business person may need to be in contact with their office, but their want is to be able to use their mobile phone during a flight. With excellent customer service, both needs and wants are fulfilled, i.e. the need is met by providing what is wanted. Excellent customer service can also be as a result of showing how the need can be met using alternative methods to those wanted.

ACTIVITY

Working in pairs, you are going to participate in two role plays: one in a tourist information centre and one on a cruise ship. In one role play, you will be the customer, and in the other you are the employee. Each of you anticipates your customer role and prepares for the role-play situation by writing down a list of needs. For each situation, one of you takes on the role of the customer, responding to questions asked by the one taking on the role of the employee. You should state some needs, imply some needs and leave some needs unstated. Through questioning, the employee should determine all of your needs. At the end, compare the needs identified with those originally written down.

ACTIVITY

Here are some needs a person may have. Describe different ways these needs could be met:
- to get to New York
- to rest overnight when driving from Kent to Scotland
- to write a report when on a flight to Thailand
- to have a relaxing holiday
- to see what the destination is really like.

Motivation

A customer's needs, and especially their wants, are often affected by their motivation to travel. Physical motivation is generally linked to 'health tourism'. Following the Industrial Revolution, physical motivation related to the need to get away from the towns to get fresh air in the country. In Victorian times, seaside resorts became popular as people felt the sea waters could meet their health needs. Nowadays, Caribbean islands are said to meet the needs of those with busy, stressful jobs needing relaxation. Destinations such as India and Latvia are meeting tourists' health needs by providing operations at low cost. Smile Stylers, based in Kerala, India, is just one example of an organisation promoting this new form of health tourism by combining dental care with a pleasurable holiday.

Health tourism is a growing trend and, increasingly, tour operators are developing packages to meet the needs of health tourists, but these are not widely available. Travel agents need to be more aware of this new trend and have product knowledge of what is available. If a customer is planning to travel to India for an operation, they will need a visa. The Indian High Commission in London requires applications in person but there is also a postal and fax service. A travel agent could arrange the visa to assist the customer. They could also arrange for a local agent in the destination to make contact on arrival or once in the hospital to assist if there are any problems. They could also arrange meet-and-greet parking at the airport so that the customer doesn't have to get on a busy bus to find their car on return.

ACTIVITY

Describe other services a travel agent could provide to a customer motivated to travel for health reasons, and explain how each meets their needs.

C.J. Holloway (2006), in *The Business of Tourism* (Pearson) related travel motivation to the following five basic needs:

- physical
- cultural
- interpersonal
- status and prestige
- commercial.

Status and prestige are increasingly important in today's society, and travel and tourism organisations must consider how they can meet these motivational needs.

Williams and Zelinski (1970) in 'On some patterns in international tourist flows', *Economic Geography*, 46(4), 549–67, proposed another way of categorising travel motivations. They claimed that customers are motivated by 'push' and 'pull' factors.

Push factors come from the generating area: the location from which a tourist departs. The stage of economic development, e.g. affluence, mobility, holiday entitlement, is critical in motivating people to travel, i.e. 'pushing' them into becoming tourists. Those in advanced economies have the time and money to be able to be tourists and their way of life suggests a need to 'get away from it all'.

Pull factors are about the receiving area: the destination to which the tourist travels. Accessibility,

Case study

Quality service

Sophie Grace watches satellite TV and is besotted with celebrity and the lives of the rich and famous. She wants luxury in everything. When she visits a travel agent, it is not just the holiday she wants to be luxurious, she wants the agents to offer a quality service. A travel agent could respond to this by providing an appointment service where clients are guaranteed one-to-one advice and information from the manager. A room could be made available for this to take place and refreshments provided on arrival. In the room there could be internet access and a DVD player so that the customer is able to view holiday DVDs. Destination guides such as Fodor's travel guides and magazines such as *Vogue* could be made available to the customer. The customer could then be offered contact via a dedicated phone line that gives them direct access to the manager at all times.

ACTIVITY

Explain how a train company could provide a level of service to meet the needs of Sophie Grace.

attractions, amenities, relative costs and marketing and promotion are all significant elements in 'pulling' a tourist to a specific destination.

ACTIVITY

The Chinese economy is growing and that has created a push for more business people to travel. Liu Xiang is one of a growing number of Chinese citizens who travels for business. How have travel and tourism organisations adapted to offer customer service to business travellers coming to the UK from China?

Assessing the outcome

A travel magazine is planning to produce an article on customer service.

- Describe how differing buyer behaviour and customer types, motivations and needs can influence the service provided by two travel and tourism organisations (**P3**).

Customer service skills in travel and tourism

It is one thing to know and understand the theory of customer service, it is another to be able to apply that knowledge and understanding. When a customer is in front of an employee, or on the telephone, can the employee listen to what they are saying to work out their implied needs or spot whether they need more information? There is a range of skills that need to be developed to be able to apply customer service effectively.

Personal presentation

There are many different types of situation when customer service skills need to be developed but, whatever the situation, when dealing directly with customers, personal presentation is an important part of providing customer service. For this reason, many travel and tourism organisations provide uniforms for their staff to ensure they are presented appropriately. In some organisations, this may be a business suit – for example, in a travel agency – but this is not always the case. Customers would not be impressed if they found a safari tour guide, or a presenter of a dolphin show at an attraction dressed in a business suit. They would expect something more practical.

If an organisation were providing a uniform, it would also expect the uniform to be well presented. There is no point in airlines providing cabin crew with a smart uniform if, when worn, it looks like it was kept in a carrier bag and crew members' hair is a mess and their shoes are muddy. So, in addition to providing uniforms, organisations may also specify presentation requirements. In some organisations, you cannot wear any jewellery or it is limited, e.g. no tongue piercings.

Case study

Dress code

Here is a part of the dress code for the South Yorkshire Passenger Transport Executive.

Dress code

1. Policy
1.1 All employees are required to be clean and display a neat and tidy appearance. When there is any possibility that they will have direct contact with customers/clients, they must look smart and well groomed. This policy applies to all Passenger Transport Executive employees.

2. Recruitment Procedure
2.1 On recruitment, and again on subsequent changes of job, the Human Resources department will outline the standards of dress that will apply.

3. Front-Line Staff with Customer Contact
3.1 In front-line positions, employees are required to wear Transport Executive uniforms. The uniform must be worn throughout working hours, and be maintained in a neat and tidy condition. Hair must be kept clean and tidy. Offensive styles and colours are not acceptable.

ACTIVITY

Complete the dress code in the case study, including information under headings on uniform maintenance, non-front-line staff, management, jewellery and body art, personal hygiene and failure to comply.

Personal presentation is an essential element of demonstrating customer service skills. Not all situations with customers are face to face. Some situations are dealt with by email and also by telephone, and personal presentation is also important in these situations.

ACTIVITY

A call centre is planning to introduce a dress code. Produce an email to all staff explaining why a dress code should be introduced.

Personal presentation is also about the environment in which employees operate. A customer meeting a representative to discuss a problem and finding that on the desk is make-up and a drink and that the documentation to be completed is at the bottom of a carrier bag would be justified in thinking that quality customer service will not be delivered.

When preparing to provide customer service, it is important to consider the resources needed and ensure they are available or can be located. The working environment should always be checked for cleanliness and tidiness.

First impressions

Having a uniform and a high standard of personal presentation is one way an employee can give a positive first impression, but this can also be down to the initial welcome. When answering the telephone, does a simple 'Hello' or 'Good morning, Parador Hotel, Dori speaking, how may I help you?' suggest the higher-quality customer service. Greetings such 'How may I help you?' are positive and suggest that help will be forthcoming. Giving a name helps to establish rapport with the customer. A customer wouldn't normally be greeted in the same way in a face-to-face situation or through an email.

ACTIVITY

Prepare an introduction to a customer for a face-to-face situation. Prepare an introduction to a customer when writing an email.

Creating a welcome is an important part of an initial greeting. It can be communicated through personal presentation, the words used and also through body language. If in a tourist information centre (TIC), staff are sitting together in a group chatting when a customer comes in, and one turns round but doesn't get up from their seat, will the customer feel welcomed? A good welcome might be for the employee to get up from their chair and approach the customer, welcome them, introduce themselves and then ask them to take a seat.

For a customer to feel positive about the service they receive, rapport has to be developed. Rapport can be defined as mutual understanding or trust and agreement between two or more people, or a close connection and sympathetic understanding. In some situations, rapport is not instant, it could take time to develop over several meetings. Overseas representatives have the luxury of time as their customers will generally be on holiday for one or two weeks. If, however, a customer has a problem early in their holiday, then rapport needs to be established quickly to ensure the customer has confidence that the problem will be resolved and for them to be open enough to give the detailed information required.

As a starting point, to establish rapport, the employee could introduce themselves to the customer, ask the customer their name and respond with their own name in same way. For example, if the customer says 'Mrs James', then the employee should also give their surname and not just first name. The customer sets the tone and level of respect and the employee should respond accordingly. Letting the customer set the tone and pace of the meeting allows them to feel they have control. A customer should be allowed to talk about things and divert away from the main point, and not made to think there are better things for an employee to be doing. The employee should gently direct them back to the purpose of the meeting. To gain a mutual understanding, questioning can be used to find common points of reference. It can also determine an appropriate style of communication. Questioning shouldn't be an interrogation, it is ideally a conversation. Once rapport is established, questioning becomes more meaningful as answers are more honest and more information provided.

Listening to the customer is important at all times, but more so when communicating by telephone as there is no body language that can be used to confirm understanding of the emotional state or real intentions of the customer. Listening means not only taking note of the information presented but also what else is being communicated through pauses and silences, tone and language used.

Complaints

It is essential to establish rapport when dealing with a complaint. A customer needs to feel there is empathy

ACTIVITY

In Figure 4.02 are a number of statements a customer may make to an overseas representative or cabin crew. Working with a partner, you should attempt to communicate one of the messages in the left-hand column conveying an emotion from the right-hand column. First, complete this face to face with your partner, where body language can be used. Second, complete the activity back to back (simulating a telephone call) where you are relying on oral communication only. Note any differences in the quality of communication.

Statements	Emotions
I want the chicken	Bored
Follow me	Happy
You will really like that	Anger
I have hurt my ankle	Panicked
How much is that?	Sad

Fig 4.02 Communication test

ACTIVITY

Not all communication is made face to face. It is important to recognise a customer emotion, whatever form of communication is used. Consider this description of a situation encountered by a customer:

> **I arrived at the resort to find the weather was boiling hot. My room was on the 15th floor and the lift wasn't working. My children were on the fourth floor. Breakfast was available between 0700 and 0900. It was waiter service.**

Write a letter outlining the situation. Select one of the emotions shown in Figure 4.02 and show that emotion in the letter you write.

for their situation. Establishing a rapport can help to calm down a situation. Acknowledging a complaint by asking for more than the basic information shows an interest in the issue, although questioning shouldn't seem like an interrogation. Consider a customer meeting a resort representative to tell them the hotel room they have just checked into is dirty and then being asked lots of detailed questions about how dirty and where the dirt is. They may feel like they are not being believed. To calm down the situation, the rep could ask to go to the room where they could find out for themselves so that they could then deal with it on the customer's behalf. It shows empathy but also gives the customer time to calm down and the rep time to establish a rapport with the customer on the way to the room. When dealing with a complaint, an employee should not apologise for the organisation as it suggests fault when that may not be the case. Apologising for the inconvenience or their loss, however, shows empathy and helps to establish rapport. A complaint should always be acknowledged, whether face to face or in writing. It is always useful if a complaint dealt with face to face is followed up with a written acknowledgement. The customer should be advised that the matter will be investigated, even if it appears their complaint isn't valid. The time at which the complaint is made is not the time to tell the customer they were at fault. The customer should always be advised of the next stage in the process and when that stage will be completed, so they have a time frame to work to, and so does the employee. A professional image should always be maintained when dealing with the complaint.

If complaints are made in writing, the same approach should be followed. A letter of response needs to have the same professional image as if dealt with face to face.

Selling skills appropriate to the travel and tourism industry

Most travel and tourism organisations are commercial operations. They operate to sell their goods and services and make a profit. This applies whether it is a tour operator putting together a package holiday, a travel agent selling foreign currency or a National Trust property selling membership. Organisations employ marketing staff to promote their products and services and develop them to meet the needs of their customers but they also rely on front-line sales staff to sell on their behalf.

There are many different situations that provide opportunities for selling products and services.

Assessing the outcome

You work as an overseas representative. At the end of your welcome meeting, a family comes to find out more information about car hire as they are planning to visit one of the attractions. The family includes two young children and a baby.

You work as a train manager for a train operator. You have just heard that there is a fault with overhead lines further along the rail track. You don't know when it will be fixed. You make the announcement to the passengers. As you walk through the first carriage you are stopped by a number of customers with queries about onward connections, length of delay, access to refreshments, etc.

You work as a travel consultant for an independent travel agent. A business person telephones complaining about a flight booking you have made. The ticket didn't allow access to the first-class lounge, the luggage allowance was 5kg less than advised and a charge of £240 has been made and also the expensive bottle of whisky that was being taken as a gift was confiscated going through security.

A family of two adults and two young children were unhappy that on arrival at a hotel they were allocated two rooms: one on the tenth floor and the other on the seventh floor. They had requested adjoining rooms on a low floor as one of the children is claustrophobic and cannot travel in lifts. They have written a complaint about this.

- Use customer service skills to provide services to customers in two different travel and tourism situations (**P4**).
- Deal with two complaints (one of which must be in writing) (**P5**).

Organisations will expect front-line staff to look for opportunities to increase sales. Here are some examples.

- A hotel receptionist will welcome and check in guests who have made accommodation reservations. On check-in, they will offer the opportunity to book a table in the restaurant to increase sales.
- Budget or 'no frills' airlines will expect their cabin crew to ensure safety of customers but also to sell products and services such as snacks and refreshments as well as tax-free goods.

- A tour guide will take customers on a specified tour describing specific sites and on arrival at an attraction will attempt to sell entrance tickets.
- A travel agent dealing with a booking enquiry to Florida may try to sell car hire and tickets to attractions such as DisneyWorld.

Some of these sales opportunities take place prior to departure and others after departure.

ACTIVITY

Describe two examples of sales opportunities that a cruise company could present to a customer prior to departure and two examples of sales opportunities after departure.

When selling products and services, it is helpful to know the stages of the sales process (Figure 4.03). By knowing these stages, skills can then be developed to apply this knowledge when dealing with sales situations.

Building rapport and establishing customer needs and expectations have already received some coverage earlier in this unit. It should be remembered that the process of building rapport is ongoing. At any point, rapport could be lost, perhaps through being too pushy with the sales technique, so it is essential that throughout the sales process the customer service skills that have been developed are applied, together with the selling skills.

A key stage in the sales process is to present features and benefits. Features are the facts or details of what is provided – for example, there are 400 rooms in the hotel, all rooms have internet access, seats on the plane have a seat pitch of 31 inches. This is useful information and provided the information is factually correct, it assists the sales process and can ensure quality customer service. As part of buyer behaviour, many customers have information needs. Outlining or describing features is meeting information needs. The features presented may also clearly match the customer's stated needs. For example, a customer may state they need a four-star hotel with a pool. Describing features shows that these needs are met.

Presenting benefits takes the sales process beyond simply presenting facts and information. It is used to show how a feature provides an advantage, gain or

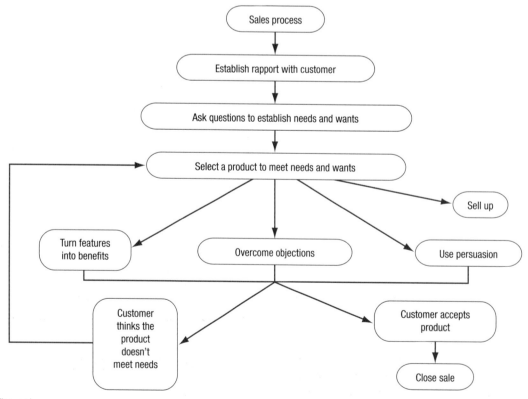

Fig 4.03 The sales process

improvement. It is used to show how it meets or even surpasses needs. When presenting benefits it is important to listen to the customer's stated and unstated needs.

Case study

Needs and wants

A couple tell a travel consultant they are planning their honeymoon and specify a destination but not the accommodation. The features of a four-star hotel are presented with a description of the pool, restaurants, room facilities, etc. The benefits might be that the hotel doesn't have a 'kids' club' so they will not be surrounded by lots of children when on honeymoon, suggesting it is a more peaceful hotel. This may then appeal to their unstated needs for a relaxing and romantic holiday.

A family tell an overseas representative in Florida that they want tickets to the theme parks both in Orlando and on the Gulf Coast. The rep could then present the features of car hire but in presenting the benefits would tell them how difficult it is to find public transport, how long it might take to travel by bus to the Gulf Coast, how a car is convenient and allows them to travel when they want, how they can stop off on long journeys to accommodate the children and how it provides flexibility to visit other attractions such as the Space Center.

Presenting benefits should stir the emotions of the customer but the information must still be factually correct and not contravene legislation such as the Trade Descriptions Act. The tourism product is often intangible so it is important to try to give a sense of what will be experienced. The use of support material such as photographs or video clips can help to present both features and benefits. The more senses a customer uses, the more likely it is to appeal to their emotions. Consider these two descriptions:

> Oh, yes, I've been to the Caribbean. We went last year, it was great. A lovely hotel and great beaches. We bought lots of souvenirs from the local market.

> Oh, last year we went on this amazing week's holiday to St Kitts, in the Caribbean. The hotel was fantastic with the most beautiful aroma of fresh flowers as we left our room each morning. The sky was a stunning blue and as we lay on the soft sandy beach, we could hear the Caribbean Sea lapping against the shore. As we swam in the warm sea, you could spot brightly coloured fish in the water. All along the road into town were market stalls where local people were selling local goods. You could almost taste the coconut and bananas being roasted as you walked along.

Which description would give the most appeal? The second description is attempting to appeal to different senses: sight, hearing, taste, smell and touch.

ACTIVITY

Discuss which part of the second description is linked to each sense. Describe a holiday or other tourism experience you have had, ensuring your description would appeal to all senses.

One of the key stages of the sales process, then, is to turn features into benefits.

ACTIVITY

You are an overseas representative in Kerala, India. You have presented the features of the following excursions at your welcome meeting:
- elephant washing – full day, return coach, wash an elephant, long, sandy beach
- backwater cruise – half day, in the backwaters, view local villages, meet local people
- party night – evening, includes drinks and pub games
- Bekal Hole Aqua Park – full-day, by coach, three hours each way.

A family with two teenage children approaches you after the welcome meeting. Role play with a colleague how you would present the benefits of the excursion above you feel is most appropriate. You could repeat this activity with different types of customer.

Overcoming objections

It is essential when involved in the sales process that detailed product knowledge is developed. This ensures that features presented are factually correct and that the appeal of the product or service is understood so that benefits are presented.

The sales process so far, then, involves developing product knowledge and establishing a rapport with the customer. Features and benefits will have been presented to show how the customer needs that have been discovered and highlighted could be met. The next stage, therefore, should be the sale, yet, sometimes a customer objects to a proposal. Here are some reasons why customers raise objections to making a sale:

- on principle
- product incorrect
- unclear
- change of plan
- cost.

ACTIVITY

For each type of objection shown above, describe a specific example a customer might provide. For each example, present a counter-argument to the customer.

It is important to be aware of possible objections and look for signs of these as early as possible in the sales process. This might be through checking body language, listening to the tone of the conversation that may be changing or explicit statements made by the customer. Spotting possible objections before they are stated provides the opportunity to consider how they might be overcome. Objections should be anticipated so that when presenting features and benefits potential objections could be discussed early in the process rather than waiting until the end.

Closing the sale

As soon as the customer has indicated that they have decided to buy, the sale should be closed. In many cases, however, a customer doesn't clearly indicate their decision and the sales person needs to look for signals. When a customer asks questions such as 'Will you take a cheque?' or 'How much deposit do I need to pay?' then they have either decided or are close to deciding to buy. If a group of customers are involved, they may look at each other, raising eyebrows, smiling

or nodding. These are all buying signals. If at this point, the sales person continues trying to sell, this could take them out of 'decision made' mode. It could start to put doubts in their mind.

Assessing the outcome

You work as a travel consultant with an independent travel agency based in the Midlands, known as a specialist in selling cruise holidays. An elderly couple come into your agency looking to book a cruise holiday to celebrate their 50th wedding anniversary. They can stay for up to three weeks. Role play how you would determine their needs, and sell a product to meet these needs.

- Demonstrate selling skills in a travel and tourism situation (**P6**).

Improve your grade
Customer service and selling skills

It is your practical application of customer service and selling skills that will be critical to achieving higher grades in this unit. When dealing with customers, it is essential to be able to work independently. This means you have to deal with customers in all situations yourself without support and guidance from others. You also need to be confident when dealing with customers. This is difficult when you know you have to work without help. It is easier to be confident if you know there is someone around to help.

The key to confidence is preparation. Poor preparation leads to poor performance. If you research to ensure you have excellent product knowledge, you are more likely to be confident that you can respond to any query the customer may have.

You should also prepare to give a positive first impression. If you look the part, you are more likely to feel the part. The customer will have confidence in you and that can give you confidence in yourself. Consider your dress for the situation. Adopting a role where you sit in a coat or sports wear when taking on the role of hotel receptionist or cabin crew will not help your confidence.

You should also remember that first impressions and personal presentation includes your working

ACTIVITY

For each role play situation you will be involved in, prepare a dress code.

ACTIVITY

A group of people arrive at Thorpe Park. They include two female adults and four children. The children are aged 4, 7, 10 and 15. The 15 year old has a physical disability and uses a wheelchair.

Consider the information and advice the customer is likely to need from this situation and research the information to be able to respond to any customer information needs.

environment. Have you got all the resources to deal with the situation? Do you have all documentation available that you may need to complete and do you know how this should be completed? Have you considered other resources that could help deal with a situation? If your role is cabin crew, do you have a copy of a flight manifest; as an overseas representative, do you have a rooming list? Have you considered how you will find answers to questions from a customer if you don't know the answers? Remember you have to be independent, you can't ask people for help.

ACTIVITY

You work as a tour guide in your local town or city. You have been asked to give a group of overseas students a tour of the main parts of the town centre. List the resources that may be helpful when dealing with this group of customers.

To achieve higher grades you will have to deal with different types of customer. If you are dealing with a group, then are you need to ensure you are communicating with each of them and not just one person. Look at everyone in the group and keep eye contact. When closing a sale, check that all in the group are showing signs that their needs are fully met.

If the group includes children, let them feel involved, show them pictures, ask them questions. Consider your welcome. If the client is elderly, is it appropriate to start with 'Hiya, mate, sit yourself down.' Don't assume because they are elderly that they are infirm and want a quiet holiday. Allow the customer to tell you if they have a problem that needs to be considered but perhaps warn them about situations. Consider strategies for dealing with customers with sensory impairments. For those with visual impairments consider how you would portray an image without showing pictures.

ACTIVITY

You are working as an overseas representative when a customer with a visual impairment asks for information about the backwater cruise excursion. You usually use the photograph below to present features and benefits.

Fig 4.04 Kerala backwater destination

Consider how you would deal with the customer in this situation.

As you practise for your assessment, you are likely to be involved in a number of role-play situations. You may have also have been involved in real situations, perhaps through work experience or part-time work.

It is useful to review your performance each time. A form, such as the one shown, could help you to judge your performance and plan for areas that may need improving. Is there a particular type of customer you have difficulty with or a certain aspect of situations that you struggle with, such as establishing rapport?

Evaluating customer service

In addition to applying your customer service and selling skills, there is another part of the unit to be addressed to access higher grades. One of the merit criteria builds on how the principles of customer service are applied in different organisations and how

Performance review form

Communication	
Language	
Pitch and tone of voice	
Pauses/silences	
Body language	
Listening	
Personal presentation	
Dress	
Hygiene	
Personality	
Confidence	
Attitude	
Friendly manner	
Rapport	
Documentation	
Accuracy	
Appropriate	
Confidentiality	
Meeting customer needs	
Information/assistance	
Response to type of customer	
Helpful	
Needs identified	
Questioning	
Meet and greet	
First impressions	

to meet the needs of different types of customers. Customer needs are considered in the second outcome and the principles of customer service in the first outcome. Comparisons, finding similarities and differences and explaining why they exist, are needed for this merit criterion. You are therefore comparing how the two organisations meet customer needs. A starting point could be to consider the needs of different types of customers. These may be different because of different types of organisations, but some may be similar – for example, needing accurate information on wheelchair access. Starting with similar needs of customers may provide you with sufficient detail to be able to meet the criterion provided that how these are met by the two organisations is explained. Similar needs may not mean that they are dealt with in similar ways. There may be differences in approaches. If you don't find enough similarities and differences, you might want to look for the similarities in what they do and how that might meet different customer needs.

For the distinction criteria (**D1**), you will have to evaluate the customer service of two organisations.

This means making judgements about how good or bad the service is. You should use the quality criteria and benchmark standards of the organisations covered in the first outcome to complete this, explaining and giving reasons for each judgement you make. In order to make recommendations, review your evaluation. Start with where you have identified a weakness and suggest in detail how you would develop this part of their customer service. Show how your suggestions would lead to improvements so that you are justifying them. You might be able to find evidence of how a different organisation made the changes you proposed and how this benefited them.

Top tips

- If you look the part, you are more likely to feel the part.
- First impressions and personal presentation can make a difference.
- Develop your ability to read between the lines to recognise unstated needs and wants.

Specialist units

Learning outcomes

By the end of this unit you should:

- understand the factors affecting marketing in travel and tourism
- know the marketing mix (the 4 Ps) of a travel and tourism organisation
- know how to conduct a marketing research activity for a travel and tourism organisation
- know how to arrange a promotional campaign for a travel and tourism organisation.

Factors affecting marketing in travel and tourism

Environmental policies

Various factors affect the way organisations run and market their products and services. The way businesses are run is increasingly becoming of interest to consumers, who may choose the company on the basis of its environmental policies and its attitude to local providers and communities instead of solely being influenced by the lowest price. A recent example of a company demonstrating involvement in environmental issues in response to customers' concerns is the Virgin travel firms with their pledge to combat global warming, see the newspaper extract below.

Branson to invest $3bn in climate fight

Sir Richard Branson on Thursday pledged to invest $3bn in profits from his transport businesses over the next decade to fight global warming.

In a gesture that underlines mounting corporate interest in being associated with measures to address climate change, the flamboyant British entrepreneur said he was 'starting the ball rolling' on environmental reform because 'global warming could literally wipe out the world'.

He said he became convinced of the need for action after Al Gore, the former US vice- president, visited him at his home.

However, his commitment will differ from the high-profile philanthropic donations of Bill Gates and Warren Buffett, both of whom are donating money made from their business empires to a variety of aid projects.

Sir Richard said he would divert all profits from his five airline and train companies over the next 10 years to a series of commercial ventures designed to produce renewable energy and limit environmental damage.

The money would be invested via a Virgin-style venture capital model, using the structure of his subsidiary Virgin Fuels to fund projects and then reinvest profits, a spokeswoman said.

Among the projects Sir Richard will invest in are an environmentally friendly airline fuel and research on using enzymes to make ethanol and butanol.

An aide said he would meet his $3bn pledge even if these profits were not sufficient.

(Source: www.ft.com, 21 September 2006)

Another company that has converted customers' environmental concerns into solutions is one of the so-called 'big three', First Choice:

> **[First Choice] has announced it will go ahead with its carbon offsetting scheme.**
>
> **The First Choice scheme, in which passengers have to opt out if they do not want to take part, encourages holidaymakers to pay £1 per adult and 50p per child when they book.**

(www.travelweekly.co.uk, accessed May 2007)

A range of legislation has been introduced to protect customers, e.g. Trade Description Act 1968, Consumer Protection Act 1987, Data Protection Act 1984. Legislation specific to the travel and tourism industry includes the Package Travel Regulations 1992. Such legislation introduces some basic measures of customer protection and makes it compulsory for companies to comply with it.

ACTIVITY

Research the above acts and legislation and describe their main points.

Another way of enforcing customer protection is through trade associations that devise their own codes of practice, e.g. the ABTA Code of Conduct.

Political factors

A number of political factors affect companies' marketing strategies. These could be the variety of legislation, whether national or European (such as the Package Travel Regulations mentioned earlier), and could also be a political situation in specific countries such as terrorist threats or acts of terrorism. Such events can be both unexpected and sudden and result in tour operators switching from one destination in favour of others, even if it is only a temporary move. The Foreign and Commonwealth Office (FCO) website offers regular travel advice about regions and countries and their potential dangers to UK residents. The advice given in the box on the opposite page is current as of April 2007.

The threat of terrorism has resulted in a number of actions which were supposed to increase security and

Case study

The ABTA Code of Conduct

The ABTA Code of Conduct is binding on all Members. Its primary aims are to ensure that the public receives the best possible service from Members, and to maintain and enhance the reputation, good name and standing of the Association and its Members.

The Code of Conduct includes the following forms:

- Liability Insurance Notification
- Retail Monitoring
- Standards on Brochures and Booking Conditions, including Brochure Monitoring
- Standards on Surcharges includes Notification of Intention to Surcharge and Surcharge Calculations
- Standards on Websites and Online Trading including Website Monitoring.

The guidance document that accompanies the Code of Conduct is intended to build up over time as a full guide to best practice in the travel industry. Refer to www.abta.com/articlesandcode.shtml.

make travelling safer. Such measures are not always popular or easy to implement. As we saw during summer 2006, these normally inconvenience travellers, cause delays and make travelling slower and less pleasant, and yet such measures are essential to maintain customer confidence in travelling.

Fig 5.01 Safety actions can lead to delays and cancellations

Countries the FCO advises <u>against all</u> travel to:

East Timor (Democratic Republic of)
Ivory Coast
Somalia

Countries the FCO advises against <u>all travel</u> to <u>parts of</u>:

Afghanistan	Iran
Albania	Iraq
Azerbaijan	Israel and the Occupied Palestinian Territories (OPTs)
Burundi	Lebanon
Cameroon	Mali
Chad	Nigeria
Colombia	Pakistan
Congo (Democratic Republic)	Philippines
	Russian Federation
Eritrea	Sri Lanka
Ethiopia	Sudan
Georgia	Uganda
India	
Indonesia	

Countries the FCO advises against <u>all but essential</u> travel to:

Central African Republic
Haiti
Lebanon
Liberia

Countries the FCO advises against <u>all but essential</u> travel to <u>parts of</u>:

Afghanistan	Libya
Angola	Mauritania
Armenia	Niger
Bangladesh	Nigeria
Burundi	Russian Federation
Chad	Rwanda
Congo	Sudan
Congo (Democratic Republic)	Thailand
	Uzbekistan
Guinea	Yemen
India	Zambia
Iraq	
Israel and the Occupied Palestinian Territories (OPTs)	

(Source: www.fco.gov.uk, accessed May 2007)

Transport chaos across the UK

Britain's airports are experiencing different levels of disruption because of the security threat, with Heathrow particularly badly hit. Prepare for delays at all airports and follow our guidelines on what you can pack. All easyJet flights have been cancelled for the rest of the day.

If you want to get on a plane, you will be hand searched, your footwear and anything you are carrying will be x-ray screened. Pushchairs and walking aids will also be x-ray screened, and only airport-provided wheelchairs may pass through the screening point. Passengers must carry items in see-through bags.

Luton
Delays on most flights. Passengers coming to the airport tomorrow should not carry hand luggage and should be prepared for delays.

Stansted
Lengthy delays and cancellations. Check-in and hand search processes are severely affected, and this will continue throughout the day.

Gatwick
Some cancellations and disruption, with an average delay of 1 hour 40 minutes. Check-in and hand search processes across both North and South Terminals are affected, and this will continue throughout the day.

London Heathrow
Severe disruption. All short-haul inbound flights have been cancelled. In-bound long-haul flights continue to operate but with severe delays. Check-in and hand search processes across all four terminals are severely affected, and this will continue throughout the day.

Manchester
Once past security, everyone can shop normally and take their purchases on board except for passengers travelling to the USA. On US flights no liquids can be taken on board – this applies to perfumes, alcohol, drinks and anything with liquid content.

Glasgow and Edinburgh
The airports are both experiencing some cancellations and disruption, with an average delay of 90 minutes for international flights and 40 minutes for domestic flights. There are no flights to Heathrow Airport.

(Source: The *Telegraph*, 11 August 2006)

August terror threat to cost BA £100m

British Airways is expected to reveal this week that the cost of the disruption arising from the terrorist threat to air travel in August is close to £100m, more than double the figure it has announced so far.

A fall in the number of premium transatlantic passengers, particularly those transferring to other flights at Heathrow, is the cause of the increase, according to analysts. Business travellers have been put off travelling through Heathrow because of restrictions on hand baggage, a ban on carrying liquids on flights and increased security checks. The drop is forecast to cut BA's half-yearly profits by 10 per cent from last year's £261m.

Last month the airline announced that the financial impact of the threat, in which terrorists are alleged to have planned to blow up airliners in mid-air, was £40m during August. BA had to cancel 1,280 flights because of disruption to London airports, and added that there had been an effect on forward bookings.

One leading analyst said: 'August is not the end of it. I think there will be at least a £50m impact in September. Premium transfer traffic is significantly weaker for British Airways. Lufthansa and Air France will have seen an increase as a result. A 5–10 per cent reduction in transatlantic Club World [business class] traffic has a significant impact on BA's bottom line.'

BA, along with other airlines, including Ryanair, have been highly critical of the government and airport operator BAA over the introduction of heightened security measures. Passengers have faced lengthy delays due to increased screening and checks. Hand luggage was initially banned, although small bags were later allowed, and restrictions on carrying toiletries on flights were imposed.

At the end of last month, EU transport security officials agreed to an easing of the restrictions on liquids, to take effect from the beginning of this month.

BA has become used to announcing one-off costs due to operational difficulties in the summer months. At last year's half-yearly results it announced that unofficial strike action by about 1,000 ground staff, in support of workers dismissed by catering company Gate Gourmet, had cost it between £35m and £45m because of flight cancellations during the peak August holiday period.

It added that a similar amount had been lost in 2004, thanks to disruption, while in 2003, £40m was lost over more unofficial industrial action.

(Source: Oliver Morgan, The *Observer*, Sunday, 29 October 2006, copyright Guardian News & Media Ltd 2006)

Apart from the disruption and inconvenience caused to passengers, the threat of terrorism may be responsible for considerable losses of revenue.

Economic factors

There are various economic factors that affect the marketing objectives of many travel and tourism organisations. Changes in taxation may be one as additional taxes have to be added to the ticket price. This may discourage people from travelling, particularly price-driven travellers.

The Balearic Islands introduced an environmental tax of €1.00 per person per day. The money was supposed to be used for re-creating tourism in the Balearics and transforming what was once a mass tourism destination into a more sustainable one. This resulted in many customers and tour operators switching sales and choosing other destinations, refusing to pay the tax and support the idea. The tax was eventually withdrawn.

ACTIVITY

The increase in fuel prices is something that can seriously affect the economic well-being of airlines, cruise companies and coach operators. Investigate the number of recent fuel increases. What do you think is their impact on customer numbers, prices and running of organisations?

Another economic factor could be the rate of exchange. Many UK companies set the prices of their foreign package holidays months in advance, relying on currencies to remain at the same level. If, however, the rate of exchange changes to become less favourable, they will get fewer euros or US dollars for their pounds, and they stand to lose a lot of money as legally they are unable to increase the prices of holidays that have already been paid for. On the other hand, a more favourable exchange rate may account for unexpected profits.

Case study

How to combat global warming?

The government is believed to be considering a range of measures to cut greenhouse gas emissions following the publication of the Stern Review, which warns of the devastating economic impact of global warming.

Environment Secretary David Miliband has written to Chancellor Gordon Brown suggesting a levy on cheap flights to help reduce carbon dioxide emissions.

However, Cheapflight.co.uk's Soskin accused Labour of only trying to make up political ground lost to the Tories on the environmental debate. 'The Stern report is about global warming, which is a serious issue. But on the specific issue of aviation, the fact is it only contributes 3% of greenhouse gas emissions. If you got rid of aviation, you would still have the other 97% to deal with.'

He said putting a levy on air travel in the UK alone would have no impact on carbon emissions. 'There is no point unless everybody else is doing it. It is not something that the UK government has the power to do by itself.'

Soskin said that, although emissions from aircraft were rising, this was because passenger numbers had escalated. In fact, the aviation industry has worked hard to make aircraft cleaner and cut emissions per passenger, he said.

He backed the development of bio-fuels for aviation and an industry-wide voluntary scheme to encourage passengers to offset carbon emissions by investing in alternative energy or tree-planting.

If the government goes ahead with increasing aviation duty on environmental grounds, the industry should produce a 'robust' response, Soskin said.

(Source: Ian Taylor, *Travel Weekly*, 21 December 2006)

Social changes

In other units, e.g. Unit 1, you learned about various social changes that affect the travel and tourism industry. There is an increasing number of older people with greater amounts of free time and disposable income, and this shapes the travel and tourism products and services on offer. The money spent by older people is commonly referred to as the 'grey pound'.

There is a growing number of people who choose to live or travel on their own, hoping to meet like-minded people during their holidays and not being penalised by a huge single supplement.

There are now more people travelling more often, not just on family holidays but also with friends, due to the greater availability of transport and the lower price of holidays. This is the reason short breaks and weekend breaks have become so popular and why there are many companies offering them for a wide range of customers, from budget breaks or independent holidays through to luxurious packages.

Technological factors

Technology has a great impact on the travel and tourism industry. There have been many transport developments such as faster trains, e.g. Eurostar, and bigger and faster planes, e.g. Concorde (although this has now been withdrawn from commercial

Fig 5.02 Eurostar trains allow fast access across the Channel

operation). Wider choices permit customers to select the transport method best suited to them.

Great changes have also been seen with regard to computer systems. Developments such as computer reservations systems and online booking systems have forced companies, whether hotels, tour operators or travel agents, to rethink their distribution methods and ways of getting products and services to their customers.

The sheer amount of information available on the internet, and the speed at which news and information now travel, forces companies to be up to date with destination changes, updates, etc., and installing devices such as kiosks, webcams and the like has helped travel and tourism companies combat the intangibility of their products.

Competition between companies as a result of the technological changes actually happens on more than one level and is no longer restricted simply to price or innovative products but also how easily information is available.

Assessing the outcome

As part of your training for the post of assistant manager, you need to prove to your manager that you are aware of a selection of factors you need to consider when running an independent travel agency.

- Explain the factors affecting marketing, using examples from different travel and tourism organisations (**P1**).

The 4 Ps of a travel and tourism organisation

The marketing mix is otherwise referred to as the '4 Ps', these being *product*, *place*, *price* and *promotion*. Such factors need to be 'mixed' or come together to ensure that an organisation achieves its marketing aims, such as maintaining the level of sales, increasing profits, etc.

As the majority of travel and tourism organisations are commercial, it is vital that they achieve their aims and objectives as otherwise they may go out of business. When one of the 'Ps' is mismatched, then the whole mix is affected. For example, if luxurious holidays are sold at unexpectedly low prices, this will not be perceived as a good deal. Potential customers may wonder what has been compromised to achieve such a low price. If a visitor attraction is difficult to find, it may not attract many visitors although it may have a lot to offer them. If a hotel charges the same prices throughout the week, it may be too 'cheap' for business travellers and too expensive for leisure ones, thus missing out on the opportunity to attract either type. If products and services are advertised in the wrong medium – for example, club class fares in a teenage magazine – naturally the expected level of sales will not be reached. This is why it is important

for companies to carefully combine their product, place, price and promotion.

Product

When we talk about product, what do we actually mean? The product of an organisation is any goods and services it has on offer, for which customers normally pay directly or indirectly. For example, accommodation with private bathrooms, a city break to Paris, a scary ride at a theme park or advice about the climate at a destination offered by the travel agents are all 'products' of travel and tourism organisations.

All products have their characteristics, otherwise called features, making it easy for customers to recognise them and therefore attract people to buy them.

Different characteristics may be important to different types of customers. For example, a young couple may be looking for a romantic destination for their weekend which is why they choose a short break in Paris with dinner for two, while an elderly couple may not feel comfortable searching for information about destinations on the internet and therefore prefer to book through travel agents, benefiting from their advice.

Some characteristics may not be sufficient for customers to book or purchase the product. For that to happen, it needs to have so-called USP (unique selling point), which means some distinctive characteristic that differentiates it from the product of its competitors. For example, Sandals offers holidays to couples, and children are not welcome in its resorts. This is its USP as some couples may not want to spend time on holidays with families and opt instead for 'an adults-only' holiday.

> ### Couples Only All-Inclusive Resorts
>
> **Sandals is a collection of 12 of the most romantic resorts on the Caribbean's best beaches, created exclusively for couples in love, in Jamaica, St. Lucia, Antigua and The Bahamas. Enjoy an astounding array of land and watersports, including unlimited golf and scuba diving.**

(Source: www.sandals.com, accessed February 2007)

The creation of distinctive characteristics can also be achieved by the creation of a brand, and reinforced by its name, logo, packaging, particular colours, etc.

One of the problems with the travel and tourism product is that it is mainly intangible. This means that it cannot be touched or experienced prior to purchase; we cannot test the legroom or how comfortable the seats are on the aeroplane for a flight we have just booked; nor can we test the customer service skills of the guide who will be with us on our holiday. This places a huge responsibility on how travel and tourism products are promoted and sold. The promotion must emphasise the features and benefits of the product and encourage customers to purchase it.

The travel and tourism 'product' is also perishable. This means that if is not purchased and used by a certain date, we can no longer sell it. If 10 per cent of the rooms are not booked for tonight, we will not be able to make money out of them tonight, if there are 15 empty seats on a plane flying to Seville tomorrow and if they are not sold by then, we have lost money. This is why companies offer last-minute discounts as they prefer to sell the remaining rooms or seats for a fraction of the price instead of making no money at all.

Whether we like it or not, all products follow a life cycle, which means that the level of sales and profits they generate differs (Figure 5.03).

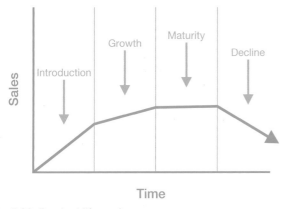

Fig 5.03 Product life cycle

(Source: www.learnmarketing.net, accessed May 2007)

Price

Deciding what price to charge is a difficult task, setting prices correctly requires careful consideration. The initial decision may prove to be wrong so prices may need to be adjusted.

The price is what customers are prepared to pay for products and services, while the cost is what you pay your suppliers. The difference between the costs businesses incur and the prices they charge customers is the mark-up or profit. Prices are not just set by customer demand but also modified by competition as businesses are unable to charge more for the same type of service than their competitors. If they do, they may risk losing customers or not attracting them in the first place. For example, if you compare the fares offered by two airlines flying to the same destination or the price offered by two hotels in a similar location, these tend to be very similar as those organisations need to ensure competitiveness.

There are various pricing policies travel and tourism companies may use. Among them are market penetration, market skimming pricing or the most common, such as competitive pricing, variable pricing or discounting. Let us have a brief look at some pricing policies; you may wish to investigate others in your own study time.

One of the policies we shall be looking at is discounting a full price. This is done to encourage particular types of customers to come and buy the products; e.g. museums offer student discounts and hotels offer reductions to their regular customers.

Travel and tourism organisations also have special offers, which tend to be valid for a specific period of time only and introduced to encourage an otherwise slow market. British Airways often organises a sale after a busy period, such as Christmas.

Many organisations also use seasonal or variable pricing to stimulate sales in quiet seasons and maximise profits in high season.

We are all familiar with the peak and off-peak prices of which we sometimes take advantage. However, sometimes we cannot change the time when we can travel, hence the high prices at times of highest demand, e.g. summer or bank holidays.

Place

It is important to recognise that place does not refer to a destination but can be referred to as the location and availability of products and services as well as the methods by which those products and services are distributed to customers.

Selecting the right location is very important for any organisation. Certain locations project a certain image, e.g. a posh area or a central area, and these can contribute considerably to the success of the organisation through increased sales.

The availability of public transport as well as the availability of parking are also important and may determine how many customers organisations are likely to attract and to what type of customers they are likely to appeal. If you operate in a rural or remote area you may also have difficulties recruiting staff or finding suppliers.

Some locations are also selected for the type of climate they offer. If the choice is not available, businesses (such as outdoor activity centres in Britain, being dependent on an unreliable climate that they are unable to change) need to have a contingency plan so their visitor numbers are not affected.

Finally, the local population may appear friendly and welcoming towards tourists or may act in an unfriendly and even hostile manner, thus making tourists' stay unpleasant and discouraging them from returning to the destination.

ACTIVITY

Investigate attitude changes during recent years towards British tourists in some Spanish, Greek or Cypriot resorts. What caused this change? How is it demonstrated?

The location may also be affected by planning regulations or future plans for the area. If organisations have difficulties in obtaining planning permissions, and a hotel may wish to expand by adding another swimming pool, they may be unable to complete their marketing objective.

Place also includes the way products and services are distributed to customers. This was discussed in detail in Unit 1.

Promotion

Promotion is what we mainly associate with marketing. Promotion is how we make customers aware of the existence of a business and how that

ACTIVITY

Find organisations that distribute using a variety of channels. Does this contribute to the success of their marketing mix?

business communicates information about the availability of its products and services. There are various promotional methods (techniques), which means how we go about promoting the organisation.

Advertising

Advertising is probably that part of promotion that everybody is very familiar with. Companies advertise their products using different media, such as TV, radio, the internet, newspapers and magazines.

ACTIVITY

Identify the advantages and disadvantages of advertising using different media. Focus on the effectiveness of reaching your target markets not solely on costs.

Public relations

Public relations is a form of promotion that aims to maintain or improve the public image of an organisation. This can be done through interviews in the press, or using press releases where the organisation communicates its most recent improvements or developments. This may also be achieved through the use of community relations, through supporting various community initiatives or through the use of corporate communication by means of logos, certain colours or merchandising.

A part of public relations is referred to as media inclusion. This is often used by travel and tourism organisations, as it is an inexpensive way to gain exposure to a large number of potential clients. For example, New Zealand received a large number of tourists after being used as the location for the *Lord of the Rings* film trilogy.

Sales promotions

Sales promotions are used to intensify sales or encourage certain types of customers; these may be in the form of price reductions, free gifts, special offers, competitions, incentives, loyalty schemes and many others.

Direct marketing

Direct marketing is a form of promotion that reaches out directly to customers. This may be by email, post or telephone. It is normally aimed at previous customers whose details are available on the company's database.

Promotional materials

Promotional materials are the actual items organisations produce as a part of their promotional campaign. These include leaflets, adverts, press releases and many others.

Conducting market research

Market research is a vital part of any marketing strategy. It provides information about customers and markets, the effectiveness of promotional campaigns and many other aspects of how any travel and

Assessing the outcome

As you know, the marketing mix is hard to get right but it is vital to do so if we want to meet out marketing objectives. As a new marketing executive of Liverpool John Lennon Airport, describe its marketing mix. The airport would like to be more successful and this is why it has invited you to make some recommendations.

*   Describe the marketing mix of a selected travel and tourism organisation (**P2**).

tourism organisation may operate. Market research is the necessary preparation to establish how much customers are prepared to pay, what products they are likely to buy, what they perceive to be good value for money and to assess the competition. Before embarking on any market research tasks, companies or specialist research agencies must set marketing objectives. These usually involve identifying:

Fig 5.04 Direct marketing literature

- customer needs
- new and existing markets
- trends and fashions
- changes in markets
- opportunities for market and product development
- competitors
- effectiveness of promotional activities.

Once it has been established what is to be researched, companies can choose their methods. There are two basic types of research: primary and secondary.

Primary research, otherwise known as field research, obtains information directly from customers by means of surveys, questionnaires, observations and focus groups, and produces new evidence. Surveys can be done by post, telephone, on the internet or in person on a face-to-face basis. They reach a large number of customers, especially postal surveys, but the response rate may be low. Personal surveys have to limit the number of questions asked, as otherwise customers will not be willing to participate.

Observations are a form of research during which customers' reactions to products are observed and recorded by skilled market research experts. Focus groups involve a group of people encouraged to discuss their opinions about specific products or services. This can provide detailed feedback but it is time-consuming and expensive.

Secondary research, also called desk research, obtains information from existing sources. It can be relatively cheap and easy to carry out but it may not be organisation-specific, up to date or as relevant as primary research. Secondary research may use internal or external sources. Among internal records there may be sales records, usage figures, customer databases and customer feedback in the form of compliments or letters of complaint. External sources include: government publications, press reports, trade journals such as *Travel Weekly* or *Travel Trade Gazette*, professional associations such as ABTA or the Tourism Society, or commercial market research organisations such as Mintel or Gallup, which compile and sell reports about various sectors.

Producing suitable documentation is key to any successful market research. Whether you produce questionnaires, observation checklists, focus group reports or feedback cards, it is vital to ask the right questions, which allow you to collect appropriate data that can be then analysed and evaluated by organisations. You may need to consider the length of your questionnaire – namely, how many questions people will be prepared to answer. You also need to consider the layout, as questions should be in a logical

Case study

Market research at Thistle Hotels

Thistle Hotels encourages customer feedback. In its opinion, this is the best way for it to know what customers think about its products and services.

Upon departure each customer is requested to complete the feedback card shown opposite.

The cards are later analysed by head office so it can monitor customer satisfaction and improve performance acting upon the feedback from customers. There are only few carefully selected questions, which take less than five minutes to complete even when customers are checking out early in the morning, rushing to their meetings or to the airport, catching their plane at the end of their trip.

Thistle Hotels welcomes both positive as well as negative feedback as it believes that a lack of complaints results in a loss of business, as customers will go away without complaining and will never come back, finding an alternative accommodation provider.

Another form of research carried out by Thistle Hotels is the so-called 'mystery guest', a person sent by head office to stay at the hotel to test all products and services on offer. He/she would use as many services as possible to evaluate them all. Needless to say, the staff, including the general manager, do not know who the mystery guest is, so they try equally hard to please all customers. Once the mystery guest has stayed at a hotel, it will receive a report from head office criticising its shortcomings and/or praising its strengths.

According to the manager: 'Monitoring the quality of services, being proactive, winning over the competition and encouraging customer feedback is the only way forward, if we want to maintain existing customers and gain new ones.'

6

Please take a few seconds to rate your experience with us. Just *X* the appropriate box.

Q1. Thinking about everything you look for in a hotel, how would you rate this Thistle Hotel?

Very poor		Poor		OK		Good		Excellent	
☐ 1	☐ 2	☐ 3	☐ 4	☐ 5	☐ 6	☐ 7	☐ 8	☐ 9	☐ 10

Q2. If you had not chosen this Thistle Hotel on this occasion, which one of these alternatives would you most like to have chosen? *Note: It doesn't matter if you haven't stayed there before*

☐ Hilton ☐ Marriott ☐ Crowne Plaza ☐ Moat House

☐ Millennium & Copthorne ☐ De Vere ☐ Holiday Inn ☐ Other hotel Please specify:

Q3. How important to you is the decision as to which hotel chain you stay in?

☐ Not at all important ☐ Slightly important ☐ Moderately important ☐ Very important ☐ Extremely important

Q4. Thinking about everything you look for in a hotel, how would you rate the hotel you chose in Q2?
Note: It is your impression we would like, it doesn't matter if you haven't stayed there before

Very poor		Poor		OK		Good		Excellent	
☐ 1	☐ 2	☐ 3	☐ 4	☐ 5	☐ 6	☐ 7	☐ 8	☐ 9	☐ 10

Q5. Please rate this Thistle hotel on the following:

	This Thistle Hotel ☹ 1	2	☺ 3	4	☺ 5
Service at check out (prompt, friendly & efficient)	☐	☐	☐	☐	☐
In-room heating/ventilation	☐	☐	☐	☐	☐
Efficacy & promptness of service in the bar	☐	☐	☐	☐	☐
Quality of restaurant service	☐	☐	☐	☐	☐
Overall cleanliness of bedroom/bathroom	☐	☐	☐	☐	☐
Would you recommend Thistle Hotels to a friend/business colleague	☐	☐	☐	☐	☐

Q6. If you were to stay in this area again, which one of these statements would be most appropriate?

☐ There would be many reasons to stay at this Thistle Hotel again
☐ I'm unsure: there would be reasons to stay at this Thistle Hotel again, but also reasons to stay elsewhere
☐ I would prefer to stay at another hotel

Q9. How many of your last five hotel stays were at a Thistle Hotel?

☐ One ☐ Two ☐ Three ☐ Four ☐ Five

Q10. How many nights do you spend in a hotel in an average month?

☐ Less than 1 ☐ 1 ☐ 2 ☐ 3 ☐ 4 ☐ 5 ☐ 6 ☐ 7 ☐ 8 ☐ 9 ☐ 10 ☐ 11+

Q11. Please state the main purpose of your visit:

☐ Business ☐ Leisure

order. You also need to be clear as to how you want the answers to be recorded: in the form of multiple choice, closed or open questions or perhaps using 'semantic differential', which asks respondents to select a phrase or word most closely describing their opinion. You need to decide whether you wish to collect quantitative data (numbers) or qualitative (opinions).

You may wish to carry out a pilot questionnaire before starting your research exercise. You need to pay attention to when you expect people to complete your feedback card or questionnaire and how many people will be prepared to participate and for how long. Having collected your data you need to analyse and therefore decide on the number of people you wish to use for your research. Having interpreted the data, you also need to evaluate the findings, which means draw conclusions for your company as well as make recommendations.

Target market

The target market is a particular market segment, a specific group of customers who share similar characteristics that a marketing campaign will focus on. Customers can be segmented according to their demographics, i.e. age, sex, ethnic grouping, family circumstances. This form of segmentation relies on the study of the make-up of the population and illustrates how society is changing.

Another form of segmentation is dividing the population according to socio-economic considerations (Table 5.01).

When preparing a marketing plan, ensure you are clear about the following.

- What does the organisation want to find out?
- Who is its target market?
- What methods does it choose to use?
- How suitable are these methods?
- What documentation will be required?
- How many questions, what kind of questions, how will you be recording answers, etc.?

Table 5.01 Socio-economic groupings	
Class A	Senior managers and professionals, such as managing directors of large firms, doctors and lawyers
Class B	Intermediate or middle-level managers and professionals, such as managers of leisure centres, teachers and accountants
Class C1	Supervisory or junior management, administrative or clerical positions, including office managers, receptionists, computer operators and qualified fitness advisers
Class C2	Skilled manual workers, such as electricians and carpenters
Class D	Semi-skilled and unskilled manual workers, such as cleaners and construction workers
Class E	Others with low incomes, including casual workers and those dependent on state benefits and pensions

- How do you plan to analyse the findings?
- What will your recommendations be?

ACTIVITY

Alton Towers wishes to introduce a new ride to cater for 5–12 year olds. The marketing department has been asked to conduct research into possible rides that will be of interest to this age group.
- Suggest a suitable research technique to use, and give reasons for your answer (you may choose more than one technique).
- What are the strengths and weaknesses of your chosen technique?

Assessing the outcome

Tradewinds wishes to find out the types of short breaks and holidays as well as new destinations its customers may wish it to introduce in its next year's brochure. Plan its research activity, monitor and evaluate to benefit truly from the information you have collected.

- Prepare a plan and documentation for a market research activity in a travel and tourism organisation (**P3**).
- Conduct a market research activity for a market research activity (**P4**).

Organising a promotional campaign

Promotion plays a hugely important role in any travel and tourism organisation's marketing activities. It requires a lot of planning and often requires huge expenditure. It is therefore essential that any promotional campaign is well thought through and carefully executed. Companies often devise a unique 'promotions mix'; this is a mixture of promotional techniques and materials believed by a company to be effective when communicating information about products and services to its customers.

Promotional techniques include:

- advertising
- displays
- public relations
- sales promotions
- direct marketing
- sponsorship
- personal selling
- holiday brochures.

Companies tend to use different methods as different methods are likely to attract a variety of customers. For example, direct email can be sent to customers whose email addresses are available on the company database, while television advertising will reach many potential customers nationwide.

As discussed earlier in this unit, promotional materials such as brochures, leaflets, advertisements and posters are produced by companies to support their chosen promotional techniques. They may produce more than one type of promotional material to support individual techniques – for example, an advertisement in a national newspaper as well as an advertisement on TV.

Promotional materials have to be designed carefully and should demonstrate an organisation's commitment to quality and customer service. They need to be checked for spelling and grammatical errors and present correct information at all times. Prices should be updated if required and if some facilities are not available this should be clearly stated. More importantly, promotional materials also need to be designed following the so-called AIDA principle, where A stands for attention, I for interest, D for desire and A for action. This means that any promotional material ought to attract *attention* by displaying bright colours, bold writing or pictures of celebrities. Promotional materials should be able to raise *interest* either by the use of humorous statements, the inclusion of special offers or in numerous other ways. They also ought to create *desire* in customers to buy the product or use the service. This can be done by means of fantastic descriptions whetting the appetite and persuading customers to buy. The last A is *action*, which means that promotional materials need to give contact details such as telephone number, email address or directions and ways of getting to the destination. For more information, a website address may also be given.

Each type of promotional material varies in design. For example, brochures include more information than leaflets and therefore one needs to be more selective when designing leaflets. Posters and outside displays normally have large pictures, as people often see them from cars or buses, and limited text as it may be difficult to read them. Merchandising items need to display an organisation's logo clearly. Newspaper adverts tend to be black and white while magazine ones are in colour. Radio adverts may not be ideal for advertising holiday packages as listeners will not be able to see the destination, but TV advertising may fail to focus on a particular group of customers as TV adverts target a wide audience. When writing direct marketing emails or letters, those that work best are addressed to customers using their name instead of Mr or The Occupier. The same principle applies when advertising on the internet. Press releases should be written in the third person and try to encourage visitors.

Before any promotional campaign, companies set various promotional objectives. These could be:

- to create brand awareness of specific products and services
- to make customers aware of products' characteristics
- to persuade customers to buy the product or use the service
- to encourage customers to develop brand loyalty
- to encourage customers to continue to buy the product and to recommend it to others
- to raise awareness of the organisation or improve the organisation's public image.

When organising a promotional campaign, one has to consider carefully where to place advertisements. For example, a local attraction may be wasting money advertising on television or in a national newspaper while a budget holiday would fail to attract the right audience if advertised in glossy magazines such as *Vogue*.

Another way of targeting various market segments is to create different promotional materials for different types of customers. Voyages Jules Verne offers a selection of brochures, e.g. Scientific Interests, No Single Supplement, Le Weekend Extraordinaire, etc. (Figure 5.05). This is the only way organisations can focus on the needs and expectations of a specific target market.

Fig 5.05 Voyages Jules Vernes travel brochures

Timing

Timing is another important factor to be taken into consideration when organising promotional campaigns. The more carefully selected the timing, the greater the likelihood that a larger part of the target audience is able to see the promotion and buy the product. For example, trips to theme parks are often advertised during children's TV programmes or programmes suitable for families, while sports clothes manufacturers tend to place their adverts during important sporting events such as football games. Companies also have to consider when customers start thinking about buying the product. Teachers often plan residential trips scheduled to take place after Christmas at the beginning of the academic year. Tour operators therefore send information about their tours at the end of the previous academic year to ensure they are ready for the teachers' return from summer holiday. They may also follow up with phone calls or another brochure later on in September if the academic institution is likely to travel but has not yet placed its order.

Budget

Another factor affecting promotional campaigns is budget. Promotion, being very expensive, may take a large chunk of the travel and tourism organisation's profits. In principle, promotion and all the investments made should be returned in higher customer numbers and larger profits. This only happens if promotion has been successful. It is important to identify all promotional costs clearly. Apart from advertising costs, promotion can also include:

- printing and production costs
- staff costs
- postage
- stationery
- engaging external agencies in organising PR
- products and incentives handed out as part of the promotion.

Regardless of the cost in the current competitive environment, promotion is a must; easyJet did not mind being presented in some unfavourable situations during the *Airline* TV series, as bad publicity is better than none, according to its owner, Stelios Haji-Ioannou.

Monitoring

How do we know whether our well-planned promotional campaign is running well and whether all the time and money invested will return some economic benefits? Firstly, we need to proofread any information to be printed. Printers will not take responsibility for mistakes that have not been found and corrected prior to printing. The errors, unfortunately, may be of a serious nature, such as prices being too low – resulting in the company losing money – or too high resulting in the company losing customers who may look for more competitive options. Secondly, incorrect information may make the company liable for possible legal action. Monitoring will also involve checking when adverts are scheduled to appear, as they will be worthless the night after the event and there is no point showing them when your target market is not at home.

As part of monitoring, companies also have to ensure that posters or other displays are in good condition. A torn poster may not offer enough information. Moreover it may convey the message that the company does not follow through, which may not fill future customers with confidence. The leaflets on display either in TICs (Tourist Information Centres) or in hotels also need to be topped up regularly – there is nothing worse than empty space in the place where brochures are supposed to be – demonstrating that the company is unable to cope with the level of interest. Will it be able to cope with its customers?

Evaluating

It is important to evaluate promotional techniques in order to establish which promotions mix works best for the company. This can be done in a number of ways. Any time a customer places a booking, they can be asked how they heard about the attraction, facility or promotion. Market research can be carried out as to which promotional method or which medium was particularly successful for promoting your products and services. You could ask customers various questions in order to establish their demographic or socio-economic profile. One of the most common methods of evaluating is placing vouchers on leaflets, which can be handed in when making a booking or entering the attraction. Companies can then count the number of vouchers exchanged for bookings to see how well this particular promotional method has worked. Such vouchers normally have individual serial numbers, which allow companies to identify the origin of the vouchers, e.g. which TIC or hotel handed them out. Another form of evaluation is checking the number of tickets sold, the number of hits on a website or admissions during the period you advertise. It is also advisable to check sales and income figures in comparison to the same period last year or the pre-promotion period to identify any increases as a result of the campaign.

Plan

When planning a promotional campaign, you need to ask yourself the following questions.

- What is it you want to communicate to your customers?
- Who are the customers you wish to communicate your message to?

Case study

London Zoo

London Zoo is a charity whose income is self-generated. It relies on revenue raised through visitors and other revenue-generating exercises such as banqueting, conferences and animal adoption. The zoo has a marketing strategy that aims to develop the loyalty of its customers, differentiate London Zoo from all other attractions in London and communicate to the wider public that London Zoo provides a fantastic experience worth spending time and money on.

ACTIVITY

Identify the most effective promotional mix for London Zoo. Analyse the advantages and disadvantages of your chosen promotional mix.

- What promotional technique would be most effective for your target market?
- What promotional materials would most support the promotional technique you have selected?
- What promotional techniques and materials can you afford?
- What would be the best time to run your promotion?
- How can you monitor your promotional campaign?
- How can you evaluate your promotional campaign?

Always provide an explanation for your choices.

Improve your grade

If you are reading this part of the unit you are clearly interested in achieving higher grades. To do so, you need to be clear how to get there. This section of the unit endeavours to give you that understanding.

First, we encourage you to do all the activities provided in this unit. They offer a firm basis for your understanding of marketing in the travel and tourism industry and for your further research, which will lead you hopefully to a merit or a distinction. Without basic knowledge you cannot achieve higher grades. You can start off by working on your pass criteria and gradually get to a merit or a distinction.

Assessing the outcome

As always, British Airways will be launching its after-Christmas sale. As a marketing trainee you have been asked to prepare some suggestions and present them to your boss and team. This task is your first serious assignment and whether you will be offered a permanent position after your training has been completed depends on your performance.

- Plan a promotional campaign for a selected travel and tourism organisation to achieve stated marketing objectives (**P5**).
- Design a press release to be published in *Travel Trade Gazette* in connection with a previously designed promotional campaign.
- Prepare an item of promotional material as part of a planned promotional campaign for a target market (**P6**).

The assessment criteria can be grouped together – for example, you can work on **P1**, **M1** and **D1**. For **P1** you need to explain (*give reasons, answer the why and how questions*) the factors affecting marketing of travel and tourism organisations. Only once you have written a general explanation can you analyse (*say what they are and then draw conclusions*) the constraints, focusing on a specific organisation, a travel agency, airline or visitor attraction. Do not write the whole explanation again but select what affects your organisation – for example, if you choose a travel agency you will analyse the significance of ABTA and its Code of Conduct. If your conclusions are well drawn and valid, you will be awarded a merit, otherwise you will have a high pass. It is worth a try.

Having analysed the constraints for a merit, you will now need to recommend (*make suggestions*) how the selected travel and tourism organisation could adapt to the factors affecting marketing. This is your distinction task. If you are not sure what conclusions to draw or what recommendations to make, you may need to do some research. This is very much recommended at this level of study. The research undertaken can be reading books, journals or newspapers to establish how companies have been affected in the past and what they have done to cope with the constraints. You could also talk to people employed in travel and tourism, and if any of them come to give a talk, then be sure to ask questions. Apply your findings to your organisation when writing an analysis or making recommendations.

The next part of your assignments can also be worked on jointly as **P2** links with **M2**. For **P2** you need to describe (*say how it is*) the marketing mix of an organisation. Select an organisation that interests you so you enjoy finding out about it. You may also choose an organisation in your locality so you will be able to visit it in case you have any additional questions. When describing its marketing mix, keep asking yourself questions about why they do it this way. Does it bring them business? Do they have a successful brand? Are they successful at promoting their organisation? Why do they charge certain prices? Why are they based where they are? Is there anything they could do better and why? Before you realise it, you will not only have described the 4 Ps but also explained how the 4 Ps work together.

You can work on **P3** and **P4** together. In the earlier part of this unit there is guidance on how to prepare a plan. You should have one market research objective but you may use more than one method. Make sure that what you research is what the organisation may want to know otherwise you will struggle to provide the explanation needed for **M3**. To achieve **M3**, you will have to explain (*give reasons, answer the why and how questions*) how you planned your research and why. When explaining, give reasons why the organisation may want to know what you are researching. Give reasons for choosing the market research methods. How effective can they be? What are their benefits or drawbacks? Give reasons why you produced a certain type of documentation, whether it collects a lot of information or is quick and effective. Give reasons for your design in relation to the objective of your market research or type of customers you will be interviewing (if you simply find it more attractive this is not a valid reason). For **D2**,

you should make recommendations (*make suggestions*) as to how the organisation can use the results of the research. Having explained what they have learnt, now you have to suggest what they can do with the knowledge, i.e. how they can improve the way they operate and become more successful.

Criteria **P5**, **P6** and **M4** can be worked on together as they all refer to promotional campaigns. In the earlier part of this unit there is guidance on how to prepare a plan. You should not have more than two promotional objectives and you should use more than one method and material, creating thus a promotion mix. To achieve **M4**, you will have to explain (*give reasons, answer the why and how questions*) how you planned your campaign and why. When explaining, be clear why you want to communicate your message to this type of customer. Explain why you have chosen certain promotional techniques and promotional materials. How effective could they be? For your merit task, you need to particularly scrutinise the factors affecting the campaign, such as budget and time, and explain their effect. Provide reasons why you suggested monitoring or evaluating the campaign in a certain way.

Top tips

- You must present the factors before you start analysing, and especially before you start making recommendations.
- You must prepare your plan and documentation and conduct the activity before you start explaining how the plan and documentation will meet the market research objectives, or make recommendations how the organisation can use the research findings, otherwise you will have nothing to explain.
- You must describe the 4 Ps before you start explaining how they work together.
- You must know what evidence you need to produce (in what form, i.e. report, presentation) and about which topic (components of the travel and tourism industry).
- You must be clear as to what you are expected to do (e.g. describe, explain, assess) to achieve each criterion.
- You must research and use examples to support your statements.

Preparing for employment in the travel and tourism industry

Career opportunities in the travel and tourism industry

The terms career, employment and job opportunities are often used without full consideration of their meaning. To be able to know about career opportunities, it is important to understand the difference between these terms to ensure they are used appropriately. *Collins Dictionary* (2006) defines each of these as follows:

- a *career* is a path through life, a profession or occupation chosen as one's life work
- a *job* is an individual piece of work, a task or an occupation
- *employment* is a person's work or occupation.

By comparing these definitions, it can be seen that there is a clear difference between these terms. Job and employment opportunities are about specific opportunities. A career opportunity is one that provides more than just employment, more than just a job. It provides the opportunity for development and progression, for advancement and promotion. It is about employment throughout life.

It can be difficult to plan for a career as this can depend upon when and if opportunities become available as well as the training and development needed to prepare for the next career move. Also, a career plan can only be based on what is known about potential employment opportunities when a career is started. Ten years ago, opportunities to work as cabin crew were limited to a few scheduled airlines but with the growth of low-cost airlines, air travel has expanded and there are now new opportunities available. Some 20 years ago, few people would have prepared a career plan to work in computing as computers were not widely used in industry. Career plans will evolve as new opportunities become available and as interests, skills and qualities develop.

For most people, a career starts 'at the bottom' with people aiming to 'get higher' or 'move up the career ladder'. But what does this mean? Within each organisation there are different levels of responsibility. These are mainly classed as operational, supervisory, management and senior management. These levels of responsibility are shown overleaf in Figure 6.01 in relation to a multiple travel agency.

A career starting at the bottom, therefore, means starting with employment at operational level such as a foreign exchange cashier and can progress to senior management level such as regional manager. As can be seen in Figure 6.01, this career progression may be achieved within the same organisation. This is also shown in the first case study on the next page.

In addition to the job duties and responsibilities changing throughout a career, the skills and qualities needed also change. To enable an employee to progress within an organisation, an employer may provide appropriate training and development opportunities to allow for these skills and qualities to be developed.

As with the example of Krissy in the case study, to progress in a career, at each stage different qualifications, experience, skills and attributes will be needed. This applies even more if that career takes you into different sectors of an industry or into different industries.

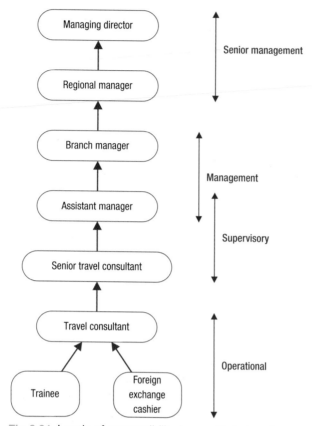

Fig 6.01 Levels of responsibility in a multiple travel agency

Case study

Krissy started her career joining a travel agency aged 16. After two years of 'on the job' training, she became a travel consultant with two years' ABTA experience and an NVQ Level 2 in Travel Services. She then progressed to be senior travel consultant, assistant manager and then manager within the same agency. Over the 11 years that she worked for the organisation, she found her hours of work changed. She was always expected to work Saturdays but as her branch was in a major shopping centre, she also had to work Sundays and late evenings. She eventually became regional manager, as the agency had a number of branches.

ACTIVITY

Research the duties and responsibilities of each job as Krissy progressed through her career.

Compare the duties and responsibilities of each job, highlighting similarities and differences. Explain why differences occur.

ACTIVITY

Explain how the skills and qualities Krissy needed would have changed as she progressed throughout her career.

Case study

Soren's career

Soren started in travel and tourism when he was at school, working during summer holidays at a theme park as a ride assistant. It was only minimum wage but he always thought it would be more enjoyable than working in hospitality, where most of his friends worked. When at university, he got a summer job for two seasons working as an overseas representative on a campsite. He only got one day off a week, but it was a great place in the south of France and he had a good time. He wasn't highly paid but he found he didn't need to spend too much, as his accommodation was provided. At the end of each season, he was able to get a discounted holiday with the company he worked for, so he went skiing. When he left university, he got a job working for a local authority as a tourism development assistant but it was on a fixed-term basis as it was bidding for Cultural Capital of Europe status. Just as he was starting to get used to regular money, the job finished because the bid was unsuccessful. He was again looking for work in the travel and tourism industry. He found a job as a marketing assistant in a train company and was there for some time until he became marketing manager, responsible only to the marketing director. Free train travel throughout the UK meant he was able to travel widely at weekends. He then moved to one of the major tour operators working as a marketing manager and then marketing director before taking up the role of managing director for a large chain of travel agencies. (See Figure 6.02.)

When changing jobs to progress in a career, there are a number of factors to consider. These include seasonality, temporary and fixed-term contracts, working hours, levels of pay and job perks.

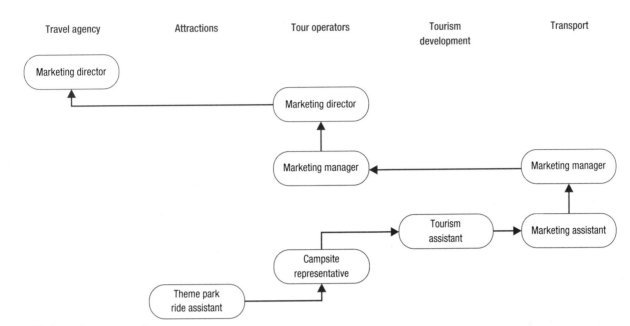

Fig 6.02 Soren's career path

ACTIVITY

Describe the factors that Soren would have had to consider with each job change he made.

Jobs

You can find details of jobs in many different places – for example, in a job centre, local newspaper, shop window, recruitment agency and in trade journals such as *Travel Weekly* and *Travel Trade Gazette* (see Figure 6.03).

Each vacancy gives information about the job, its duties and responsibilities. This information can be presented in different ways.

An advert for a travel sales adviser set out duties and responsibilities as 'to ensure that every customer has the perfect holiday, you'll sell products from our entire range in order to achieve individual sales and profits targets and offer exceptional customer service. In this role you will have daily involvement in selling services and products from the entire product range while continually offering advice and providing exceptional customer service.'

A recruitment advert for the position of museum curator listed some of the duties and responsibilities as follows.

- Supervises the accessioning, cataloguing, indexing and storing of archaeological specimens.

- Oversees the development and coordination of guided museum tours for adults and schools and educational programmes, lectures and workshops.

- Secures financial support for museum events and daily operations.

- Develops and implements publicity and marketing strategies for the museum.

- Oversees the development and implementation of an automated inventory system for the museum's collections.

- Provides technical information to other professionals about the Pueblo Grande ruins.

- Supervises the design and preparation of museum exhibits and displays.

- Supervises the museum volunteer programme.

- Prepares budgets, written reports and forms related to museum operations.

- Performs bookkeeping functions for museum operations.

- Provides technical information and lectures to classes and visitors concerning early Phoenix, Arizona, Indian History and Archaeological procedures.

- Demonstrates continuous effort to improve operations, decrease turnaround times, streamline work processes, and work cooperatively and jointly to provide quality seamless customer service.

CaribCruises
Number one for Caribbean Cruises

Ticketing Consultant

Based in North London, the UK's No 1 cruise operator is looking for an experienced Amadeus Ticketer to join our small but expanding team. The successful candidate will have proven nett and published ticketing experience, excellent communication skills, a high attention to detail and an ability to work towards strict deadlines and targets.

Please email your CV with a covering letter to ticketing@caribcruises.net.

KERALA TOURS | **Regional Sales Executive**
Wales and Ireland

The UK's leading specialist tour operator for quality holidays to India and the Far East is looking to recruit an experienced Sales Executive to develop our customer base in Wales and Ireland.

Professionalism, dynamism and a desire to succeed are some of the qualities we are looking for. A strong working knowledge of the tourism product of India and the Far East is desirable but not essential as training can be provided for the candidate with the right qualities.

Benefits include company car, mobile phone, laptop and very competitive salary with bonuses.

If you are looking for a career with an established, quality tour operator, send your CV to Kerala Tours 1, Grays Street, Basildon, Essex SS14 3PG.

Classic Travel urgently require a **Senior Travel Consultant** for a busy independent office in Carlisle. Must be experienced in arranging quality holidays for discerning clientele. Knowledge of Galileo would be an advantage but not essential. Excellent salary. Please reply to T Elyounoussi, Classic Travel, High Street, Carlisle CA1 1AN.

---

hci

Holiday Club International (hci) is a dynamic holiday club representing leading accommodation providers worldwide. We currently have a vacancy for:

Accounts Manager South America
Working within the team you will take full responsibility for the sales and marketing of our resorts in South America. The ideal candidate will have a strong knowledge of the tourism product and providers and be confident in negotiating at all levels, implementing promotion and incentive campaigns and liaising with senior management.
You will need to have at least five years' industry experience, be numerate and experienced in sales, marketing and operations.
The job requires regular domestic and international travel. A competitive salary and benefits will be offered.
If interested send a letter of application with details of your current remuneration to hci, Which Lane, London WC1B 5DN.

Fig 6.03 Jobs in travel and tourism

To find out about the entry requirements for a specific job, contact usually has to be made with the organisation to obtain a person specification. This gives information about the type of person the organisation is looking for. Few vacancies give details of training and development and progression opportunities. This is something that has to be investigated by looking into the operations of the organisation. How many offices or branches are there? This can suggest the possible opportunities for progression. Does it have a Human Resources or Personnel Department and is training a part of its responsibilities? This could mean the organisation takes the training of its staff seriously and is prepared to invest in their development.

Entry requirements

Most people would like to start a career as early as possible. Studying for any qualification could be considered the first point in a career as it is starting the training process. The skills, knowledge and qualities needed are being developed and the qualifications needed to enter a career could be

achieved. For some, further qualifications might be needed, like a degree or qualifications related to technical skills like Galileo or Welcome Host.

ACTIVITY
Investigate the specific qualifications that are available for entry into the different sectors of the travel and tourism industry. Produce a table showing these qualifications and the types of job they provide entry to.

In some cases, age is an entry requirement. Jobs that involve overnight accommodation legally require an employee to be 18 years or over. This is because a person under 18 years is legally a minor and the employer would be required to take on parental responsibilities. Many key jobs in travel and tourism have minimum age requirements but this may also be because employers consider that maturity is a key quality to be able to fulfil the duties and responsibilities of the job. Life skills, the ability to use initiative and keep calm in a crisis, are qualities that develop with age and employers may consider these to be critical to the job. An arbitrary age may be set when employers consider that appropriate qualities will have developed with age.

ACTIVITY

Cabin crew and overseas representatives are examples of jobs that have a minimum entry requirement. Explain why the duties and responsibilities of each of these jobs and the skills and qualities needed would require a minimum age on entry.

ACTIVITY

Listed below are job titles taken from *Travel Weekly* over a four-week period. Discuss the experience needed for three of these jobs.
- Corporate travel consultant – travel agency
- Airfares consultant – call centre
- Key account executive – airline
- Golf sales consultant – specialist tour operator
- Cruise coordinator – travel agency
- Foreign exchange sales manager – travel agency.

Assessing the outcome

You work for a tour operator that has just vertically integrated with an airline. It is already vertically integrated with a travel agency and also has several hotels in Mediterranean destinations. You work in human resources and have been asked to put together an e-newsletter to all staff indicating the career opportunities that exist within airlines, tour operators, hotels and travel agents.

- Describe career opportunities for four sectors of the travel and tourism industry and produce a description of two chosen jobs (**P1**).

Many entry requirements are more generic and apply to any job at a particular level. For example, both travel consultants and resort representatives are operational-level positions and both require good oral communication skills as much of their work involves dealing with customers face to face. These requirements may change as an employee progresses to the next level when they may be required to have written communication skills to be able to produce detailed reports. A travel agency manager and overseas resort controller would need skills in leading a team, problem solving and number skills. Those intending to progress in a career would need to think about how to develop those skills. Many organisations have succession planning and provide opportunities to develop skills though training or job enlargement (extra responsibility) or job rotation.

As stated earlier, a career is about moving from job to job. When developing a career, a person would look at a job title to determine if they were suitable and if it would provide career development opportunities. It is expected that a job title would give an indication of the scope and level of the job. An indication of the level of job can suggest the skills, experience and attributes needed. A job title can assist in deciding whether it would be interesting or suitable, however, with some job titles, such as passenger services assistant for a ground handling agent or logistics manager for a tour operator, the duties and responsibilities are less clear without further information.

Recruitment and selection procedures

The term 'recruitment and selection' is used when discussing the process that organisations follow to bring new staff into their company. You usually see the terms recruitment and selection together but they actually refer to two different parts of the process. Recruitment is the process for finding and attracting suitable applicants and selection is the process of screening applicants to ensure that the most appropriate applicant is hired.

There are many stages involved in recruitment and selection and it is important to know what is involved at each one. At this level of study, this knowledge should relate to an organisation's rather than potential employee's perspective. In some organisations, specialist staff, such as human resources personnel, may undertake all aspects of the process. In other organisations, however, a range of staff may be involved in one or more stages in the process. For those staff, even if only involved in the recruitment rather than selection stage, it is essential that they see how the activities they undertake fit into the whole process. A member of staff may be asked to assist in conducting an interview and, if they don't understand the person specification and why it is there, it could be difficult to make an objective judgement about selecting the right applicant. As well as needing to understand the process from an organisation's perspective, potential employees may also find it useful to know about the process so that they can prepare effectively for the job of their choice. Knowing how to use a job description and person specification to prepare for being interviewed can ensure they correctly anticipate questions that may be asked and have appropriate answers prepared.

Job analysis

There is often an assumption that the start of the recruitment and selection process is quite straightforward: someone leaves and their job is advertised. It is not that straightforward, however. If a member of staff leaves, they might not automatically be replaced. The organisation may take the opportunity to review the position. Should the job be changed? Should they be looking for something different from the staff involved? The process of recruitment should start with a job analysis, leading to the development of a job description and person specification.

ACTIVITY

Review the information in the case study on the right. Identify the internal factors to be considered and then the external factors to be considered.

Job analysis should be an ongoing activity. The analysis in the case study is arising because of Tom moving to be an assistant manager. An effective organisation doesn't wait for someone to leave before it undertakes a job analysis. In this branch, it could have been looking to recruit a cruise specialist and/or reduce staff before Tom's promotion. If an assistant

Case study

Job analysis

Tom has been at a travel agency for four years, working as a travel consultant. In all the time he has worked there it has been the same team: three full-time travel consultants, an assistant manager and a manager. Tom has now been promoted to assistant manager of another branch and will be starting his job in a month. In the four years that Tom has worked for the agency, sales have reduced slightly each year and are now 10 per cent down on when he started. Research suggests that this is because customers are now booking holidays on the internet. In the last year, the agency has had 20 per cent more enquiries and 15 per cent more sales on cruise holidays.

By starting the recruitment and selection process with a job analysis, the travel agency can now consider whether it really needs five full-time staff in the office. If sales are down 10 per cent, then that is equivalent to half a full-time member of the existing team. If Tom is simply replaced, and someone is given a full-time, permanent position, their wages will have to be paid even if sales continue to go down. What if sales continue to go down? In another four years they could be down another 10 per cent. Does the agency need to replace Tom at all? Could the position work if it was part-time? When Tom leaves, the branch then has two full-time staff, an assistant manager and a manager. Is an assistant manager still needed? Could a senior travel consultant carry out that role? As cruise holidays are now more popular, should there be someone who is a specialist in selling cruise holidays? All these questions arise from an analysis of the situation. Internal and external factors are taken into account to determine the questions to be asked. The answers to those questions will be used to determine if a job vacancy actually exists and, if it does, what type of job it will be.

manager isn't needed at this branch, he or she could have been moved to another branch where the vacancy existed.

Job analysis is the first stage in the recruitment process for an organisation. Table 6.01 shows how the other stages of recruitment and selection fit into the whole process. It highlights the stages where the potential employee or applicant, as well as the organisation, are involved. From this it can be seen

ACTIVITY

A ground handling agent at a regional airport works with leading scheduled and charter airlines. Each year they recruit 20 new ground handling staff to work as passenger services assistants. All staff are seasonal appointments with about 20 per cent offered permanent positions at the end of the season. New appointments start in March with training for two weeks and they are then available for work. Staff work shifts covering 0400 to 1100, seven days per week. In light of recent terrorist threats, security at airports has been tightened. The airport where the ground handling agent operates has agreed to introduce 24-hour operations from May of next year and has submitted a tender to a new airline operating international long-haul services. Discuss how the external factors given in this information could be used in a job analysis of passenger services assistants.

that the recruitment stage is effectively the domain of the organisation. The applicant is only really involved as the selection part of the process commences.

Table 6.01 Stages in the recruitment process

	Organisation	Applicant
Recruitment	Job analysis	
	Job description	
	Person specification	
	Communicate the vacancy	Researching opportunities
Selection	Shortlisting	Producing a CV, speculative enquiries, responding to advertisements
	Interview	Preparing for interviews, attending interviews
	Job offer	Responding to job offers
	Induction	Start job

Communicating the vacancy

This stage in the recruitment process is the first stage where there is interaction between the applicant and organisation. The applicant will be made fully aware of the job description and person specification once they have specified an interest in the position but they will need to have an idea about what the job involves and the type of person the organisation is looking for before they specify an interest. When communicating the vacancy, therefore, the organisation will have to use sufficient information from the job description and person specification to be able to attract suitable applicants. Communicating the vacancy is still part of the recruitment and not the selection process.

There are many different ways of communicating a vacancy. Traditionally this was through newspaper advertising but more recently the internet has been used.

Customer Support Consultant

Our client, a technology specialist within the travel industry, is looking for a support consultant to work in its support team in its Durham-based offices. The job role is to provide technical/customer service support for its SABS product (Search Availability Booking System). You will also liaise with the development team with regard to any system enhancements required. Our client is looking for an individual with a strong background in the travel industry, preferably within, or knowledge of, tour operations as you will be liaising on a regular basis with UK tour operators, making sure that all data is correct and up to date. You should also have knowledge of the ViewData system and have an understanding of the software needs for travel clients. You will also be dealing with customer queries and should therefore have good communication skills, an interest in technical issues relating to automated software packages and the ability to logically resolve any technical issues that occur. A generous salary and benefits are offered for the successful candidate.

(Source: adapted from www.aaappointments.com, accessed May 2007)

Fig 6.04 An informative job advert

Not all vacancies are communicated with this much information (see, e.g., Figure 6.04 overleaf).

Fairways Golf Tours
Sales Executive
Working in central London office for one of UK's leading golf tour operators. Salary + lucrative commission £25–35k Sales/travel experience beneficial. Full training given with good benefits. Must be passionate about golf. CVs to golf@fairwaystours.co.uk for attention of Rob Granger.

Fig 6.05 A brief job advert

Shortlisting

Having communicated information about a vacancy, the process now is about selection. An organisation can receive applications for a vacant position in different ways, for example from a CV, speculative letter or completed application form. Whichever form they decide to use, they will review the applications once received to decide which ones should be shortlisted to attend for interview. The organisation will match the information provided in the application to the requirements of the person specification. An applicant would need to be aware of this part of the process when preparing their application.

ACTIVITY

Compare the two approaches to communicating the vacancy. Which is more informative? Which is likely to encourage the right person to apply?

ACTIVITY

Often, in an application form, there is a section where the applicant is asked to give 'any other relevant information'. Prepare a statement that should be given in this section of an application form for the position shown opposite in Figure 6.06.

ACTIVITY

Discuss other ways an organisation can communicate information about a job. Find an example for each way discussed and compare the differences in each approach.

Not all aspects of an applicant's experience, skills and qualities can be assessed in an application form or CV. Some parts of the applicant's match against the person specification may be left until the interview stage. Organisations will identify the experience, skills and qualities that can be assessed at the application stage and the shortlisting process will focus on those.

ACTIVITY

Look at the information in the extracts from a job description and person specification in Figure 6.06 opposite. Use the information given to design two recruitment advertisements. Design one to appear in a travel journal such as *Travel Weekly* and another to appear on a recruitment agency website.

ACTIVITY

Review the person specification in Figure 6.06 and determine which requirements can be assessed through an application and which will be assessed at interview.

Job description
Directorate: Cultural Services
Post title: Tourist Information Assistant (full time, 37 hours)
Post No: CS23GG
Responsible to: Tourist Information Centre Manager
Responsible for: Tourism Services – Tourist Information Centre Rhyl

Purpose of job: to provide tourist/visitor information services for the Swansea bay area.
Main duties:
1. To provide tourist information services at Rhyl Tourist Information Centre:
- answering tourist enquiries
- operating accommodation booking services
- cash handling
- selling merchandise
- maintaining stocks of promotional materials
on a rota basis, over a 7 day week period including statutory holidays.
2. To provide tourist information services for Rhyl in other locations, as and when required:
- at events
- holiday exhibitions.
This will involve a change of location as and when required.
3. To assist other members of Tourism Services, as and when required, in order to achieve the general tourism service objectives.
4. To undertake all duties in compliance with local authority guidelines:
- ensure that safe systems of work are complied with in accordance with the health and safety strategy and the provisions of the Health and Safety at Work Act
- ensure that all activities are operated in accordance with the Equal Opportunities policy and equal opportunities legislation
- participate in performance reviews on a quarterly basis.
5. The post holder may be required to undertake other duties that can reasonably be assigned within capability and grade, including working where necessary in other units within the department.

Closing date: 15/06/2007

Person specification
Post title: Tourist Information Assistant
Directorate: Cultural Services
Performance requirements

	Essential	Desirable
Educational Qualifications	General education to GCSE standard	C.o.t.i.c.c.
Technical Competence	*A good working knowledge of the local tourism product proven experience of working in a customer-focused environment is essential *Experience of cash handling	*The ability to speak a European language *Knowledge of the regional (i.e. Mid Wales) tourism product
Experience	*Experience of working in an existing T.I.C.	*Experience of staffing exhibitions *Knowledge of local government structure, processes and procedures *Experience of working in a busy and often demanding environment *Some experience of working within a marketing and/or tourism environment
Skills & abilities	*Proven high standard of interpersonal skills *High standard of literacy *Excellent communication skills – both verbal and written *The ability to contribute to and work as part of a team *The ability to work on your own initiative	*Thorough knowledge of modern communication systems, e.g. MS Office, Inter/intranet, databases, etc. *Copy-writing and proof-reading skills *Ability to be able to respond positively to changes in the working environment
Special requirements		*Clean, full driving licence *Welsh speaking

Fig 6.06 Job description and person specification

A candidate assessment form will be completed by those shortlisting applications for interview, to show which applicants have the essential and/or desirable characteristics (Figure 6.07).

The candidate assessment form is then a record that can be used if there are any legal challenges to the process – for example, an unsuccessful applicant claiming discrimination.

ACTIVITY

Work with two or more of your peers that have completed the earlier task of producing a personal statement. Complete the candidate assessment form overleaf, Figure 6.07, to determine who would be invited to interview. Assume all applicants have the essential and none has the desirable qualifications.

Assessing the outcome

You work for a theme park. All departments have previously been responsible for their own recruitment and selection process and have used their own staff and systems. The general manager has asked you to produce a system that could be applied across the whole park.

- Describe the stages of the recruitment and selection process (**P3**).

Applying for employment in the travel and tourism sector

As can be seen from the section on the recruitment and selection process, there are many different approaches that organisations take to recruit and select staff. From the point of view of potential applicants, the selection part of the process is used to persuade a potential employer that they are the most suitable applicant. Before applying for a job, a

Candidate Assessment

Job Title ------------------------------------ Candidateís Name ------------------------------------ Internal/External (delete as applicable) ------------------------------------ Assessor's Name	A+ – Exceeds all essential & desirable criteria A – Exceeds most of essential & desirable criteria B+ – Exceeds some of essential & desirable criteria B – Meets all essential & desirable criteria C+ – Meets all essential criteria & some of desirable criteria C – Meets all essential criteria but none of desirable criteria D – Fails to meet essential criteria

Rating	Evidence from Assessment
	1. Skills and abilities
	2. Experience
	3. Knowledge
	4. Qualifications & Training
	5. Attitude/Disposition
	6. Other Requirements
	<u>Overall Assessment</u>

Recommendation for appointment   YES/NO (delete as applicable)

Assessor's signature --- Date --------------------

Fig 6.07 A sample candidate assessment form

potential applicant will consider if it is worth applying. First, they will decide if they are interested in the job, and its terms and conditions. Then they would think about whether they could do the job and would they be successful if they applied. They may send for a job description and person specification to help them decide if they are going to make an application. They may then go through an informal personal audit to see if they are able to do the job.

Personal skills audit

A person can conduct a personal skills audit each time they think about applying for a job but it is useful to do this in advance to save time. Going through this helps with the application process as you consider all your strengths and weaknesses. There are a number of things to consider with a skills audit – for example, attributes, skills, experience, qualifications and achievements.

Skills

There are a number of skills that employers are looking for. Some of these are generic in that they would apply across a number of different jobs such as communication, use of IT, number, teamwork, problem solving and self-development. Others are more specific and may be called technical skills – for example, ability to use a piece of software or design or use a piece of equipment. The level and range of technical and generic skills needed will vary with different jobs. In considering career plans, it is important to obtain as much information as possible about the range of possible skills needed and conduct a personal skills audit against all possible technical and generic skills that may be needed.

When conducting a skills audit for generic skills it is useful to have benchmark standards to judge against. The standards for the generic skills mentioned earlier can be found on the Department for Education and Science (DfES) website (www.dfes.gov.uk) and that of most awarding bodies (such as Edexcel). These are often updated to reflect current practice. For a skills audit, a person will judge their ability against the standard stated. It is easy to be subjective (look at things from their own viewpoint only) but this may then mean that if they were tested in an interview or when they started their job they

couldn't complete a task. It is important to have an objective view (from other people's perspective). When looking at the standards, consider the evidence available. Can the audit be substantiated? This means, can it be proved that the standard has been met? Where is the evidence?

ACTIVITY

Figure 6.08 overleaf shows the Standards for Communication at Level 3. Discuss the type of evidence that could be used to demonstrate the standards have been met.

When conducting a personal skills audit, it is useful to develop a pro forma or template that could be completed. There is no standard pro forma to use as different people have different career goals and so would need to focus on different skills and attributes etc. For example, if a personal skills audit relates to a plan to gain a job as an overseas representative, then IT skills are not significant but if planning to work in tourism development or tourism marketing, they will be. It is difficult to audit against a standard if the standard required isn't known. A person cannot say if they are a good communicator if they don't know what level of communication is needed. In order to complete a skills audit, the first stage would be to collect evidence about the level of skill and qualities etc. achieved and then draw a conclusion about where they fit based on the available evidence. Effectively, they are evaluating or measuring against criteria.

Figure 6.09 overleaf shows part of a personal skills audit for Luke and Joyce who are studying for BTEC National Travel and Tourism.

Each student has referred to his/her involvement in a group activity for a school project. Here are some comments from other students in the same group about Joyce:

- 'Bossed us all around'
- 'Kept telling us what to do'
- 'Always had to do it her way, never anyone else's'
- 'Couldn't attend meetings at that time, told her that I couldn't as had to do other things, would only have meetings then'

Speaking and listening	Take part in a group discussion.	• Make clear and relevant contributions in a way that suits your purpose and situation. • Respond sensitively to others, and develop points and ideas. • Encourage others to contribute.
	Make a formal presentation of at least eight minutes using an image or other support material.	• Speak clearly and adapt your style of presentation to suit your purpose, subject, audience and situation. • Structure what you say to progress logically through each stage of your presentation. • Use an image or other material to support or enhance what you are saying.
Reading for information	Read and synthesise information from at least two documents about the same subject.	• Select and read relevant documents. • Identify accurately, and compare, the main points, ideas and line of reasoning. • Present your own interpretation of the subject in a way that is coherent and brings together information from different documents to suit your purpose.
Writing	Write two different types of documents each one giving different information about complex subjects. One document must be at least 1,000 words long.	• Select and use a format and style of writing that is appropriate to your purpose and the complexity of the subject matter. • Organise material coherently to suit the length, complexity and purpose of the document. • Spell, punctuate and use grammar accurately. • Make your meaning clear.
Use of images	Use at least one image either to obtain information or to convey information in one of the written documents.	

Fig 6.08 Key Skills Level 3 Communication

Joyce			
Skill	Level required	Current level	Evidence
Teamwork	Level 3	Level 2/3 Already achieved level 2.	Worked as a group on project. Led the team. Organised all activities. Led the meetings. Attended all meetings. Was there on the day. Set everything up etc.

Luke			
Skill	Level required	Current level	Evidence
Teamwork	Level 3	Level 2 at listening but probably more level 1 at others. Not very assertive to move things forward – more of a willing participant.	Attended all meetings at school project, part of a team at Saturday job, also plays football on a Sunday and trains with a team on Tuesdays. Also plays in a 5-a-side league.

Fig 6.09 Personal skills audits

- 'Wouldn't let me do anything, always had to do all the good things herself'
- 'Constantly complained about other team members not pulling their weight'

Here are some comments from other students in the same group about Luke:

- 'Listened when we moaned about Joyce and suggested how to cope with her'

- 'Gave me good feedback on an assignment I was working on'
- 'Suggested ways in which we could deal with a problem'
- 'Attended all team meetings but didn't really say anything in any of the meetings'

Luke also received comments from a member of his football team:

- 'At half-time helped us work out new tactics and we scored within ten minutes of restart'
- 'Never lets us down with 5-a-side, always there'

> **ACTIVITY**
>
> Discuss which personal skills audit was the most honest and objective. How would you judge their teamwork skills?

The application process

There are many different methods that an organisation can use as part of the application process. Some may simply use a CV to determine suitability. This may limit the potential applicant as most CVs focus on experience and qualifications only and not skills and qualities. It may be useful to adapt a CV for each application and give details of experience gained rather than just a job title as this may not clearly indicate the duties and responsibilities held. Some organisations may ask for a letter of application. This can speed up the application process as the organisation doesn't have to wait for the application form, job description and person specification to be sent out to potential applicants. It is also cheaper for the organisation as it doesn't have to print and post out application forms but it is difficult for the organisation to standardise as letters will vary and need to be closely scrutinised. This can be time-consuming. When constructing a letter of application, it is crucial, therefore, that the applicant writes the letter to have immediate impact and be clearly self-promoting in key areas. Effectively it is an application form without relevant boxes and headings. It can be useful to take a standard application form and construct a letter of application to cover the same information. Application forms are mainly used by larger organisations as they know exactly where to look when checking the information against a person specification. Most application forms have a section for 'additional information'. This usually takes the form of a box and is where information not included elsewhere should be stated. The completed application form is used to shortlist applications. If the 'additional information' section is constructed with subheadings taken from the person specification, the organisation can then easily check if essential and desirable requirements have been met. It can also assist the applicant as they can review their abilities as they

construct this part of the application. Experience and qualifications are usually asked for separately on an application forms so this section is about skills and attributes.

Interviews

If invited to an interview, the applicant has demonstrated they have met or could meet the essential requirements and some desirable requirements of the person specification, or more than most other applicants. If shortlisted for interview, the organisation considers the applicant may have the potential to meet the requirements of the job. At interview, the applicant must show they have the skills and qualities needed for the job over and above the information on the application. A good interview will ensure each person shortlisted is asked the same questions and all questions should relate to the specification and not the application form of each applicant.

> **ACTIVITY**
>
> Look again at the requirements of the person specification in Figure 6.06. Prepare the questions to be asked of this candidate at interview.

An applicant can prepare for interview by completing the same task, by reviewing the person specification they have been given and anticipating the questions to be asked. Unfortunately, not all organisations produce a person specification; this will require the candidate to anticipate the skills, qualities and experience needed to do the job and use this to prepare for interview.

> **ACTIVITY**
>
> Working in groups, prepare a person specification for the job and the questions to be asked at interview for the position of overseas representative.

In an interview, many organisations will present an applicant with a problem-solving scenario and judge them against what the organisation considers to be an appropriate response, particularly if they are applying for a supervisory or management position. It is difficult to prepare for this in the same way as you can prepare responses to likely questions.

ACTIVITY

Here are two problem-solving scenarios that could be asked at interview. Prepare a response to each.

You are a senior travel consultant. In the last month, one of your staff has been late to work seven times. Twice, the member of staff has been found in the back office on the phone. The telephone bill has arrived showing a number of overseas telephone calls have been made. Other staff are complaining their colleague is not pulling their weight. This member of staff, though, has made the highest sales this month.

You are working as a train manager on the Exeter to London service. There are problems with overhead lines and the train is stuck outside Reading. You know from going through the train and checking tickets that many passengers have onward connections at Reading and London, and some have ferries and trains to get from Southampton. There has already been a 20-minute delay and you don't know how much longer it is going to be before the train can start again.

ACTIVITY

A tour operator has written a person specification that states 'outstanding sales skills'. It also requires 'high level of customer service skills'. It has set an interview question, 'Can you give me an example of a sales situation where you have demonstrated outstanding sales skills?', to enable applicants to demonstrate they have the first essential requirement. One applicant gave this response:

> **When I was at the airport this man checked in and he had excess luggage so I told him he would have to pay £5 for each extra kilo. He was really annoyed about it as he said he didn't have excess luggage but I told him if he didn't pay he wouldn't be getting on the plane so in the end he gave me the money.**

Discuss how the interviewers would judge the applicant against the two essential requirements of the person specification.

Assessing the outcome

You are currently preparing your career plan. You need to identify your planned career goals and follow this with a personal skills audit. Consider one of the jobs in your plan and how you would demonstrate your suitability at the application and interview stage.

- Produce a personal skills audit in preparation for employment (**P2**).
- Demonstrate suitability for employment during different stages of the job selection process (**P4**).

Factors that contribute to an effective workplace

Ensuring that the workplace is effective is not only the responsibility of management. Those working in any supervisory role – for example, as senior resort representative, team leader, senior travel consultant, purser – also have responsibility for ensuring the effectiveness of the workplace: both the staff and the environment in which they operate. If staff are ineffective and they are complaining it is too cold, it is not their fault the workplace is not effective. If a supervisor has organised a rota that gives too many staff a day off work, they are responsible for the workplace being ineffective. The same applies if too many staff are in work and they cannot all have access to the equipment. If a member of staff is demotivated because they are bored with their job or because they were passed over for promotion, it is the supervisor or manager's responsibility to keep them working effectively.

Working environment

There are many theories about how the working environment can contribute to effective working. Senior staff in an organisation have to make those theories a reality within the organisation. Abraham Maslow is a motivation theorist whose ideas could be applied to employees in the travel and tourism industry. Maslow claimed all people have needs that must be satisfied but that there is a hierarchy of those

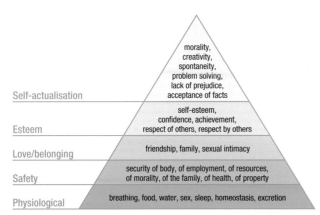

Self-actualisation — morality, creativity, spontaneity, problem solving, lack of prejudice, acceptance of facts

Esteem — self-esteem, confidence, achievement, respect of others, respect by others

Love/belonging — friendship, family, sexual intimacy

Safety — security of body, of employment, of resources, of morality, of the family, of health, of property

Physiological — breathing, food, water, sex, sleep, homeostasis, excretion

Fig 6.10 Maslow's hierarchy of needs

needs (Figure 6.10). Those needs that are lower in the hierarchy have to be satisfied before those higher up the hierarchy.

What this means is that there is no point getting staff to think about being good team members if they don't have their basic needs met, such as those for safety and food and water. A member of staff under threat of redundancy will be less effective because their safety needs are not being met. Making staff wait until 14.30 before they are able to have a refreshment or lunch break after having started work at 09.00 may mean that their basic physiological needs are not met and so they are likely to be ineffective before that time.

ACTIVITY

Discuss with colleagues other situations in the travel and tourism industry where Maslow's theory could be applied. Suggest how organisations in the travel and tourism industry apply Maslow's theory in such situations.

Working relationships

Many aspects of how working relationships affect effectiveness are also related to the working environment, as shown earlier. Teamwork is a key part of working relationships. Not all jobs appear to be about teamwork. Some flights only have one member of cabin crew but they are actually working as a team with the pilot and also with despatch staff or the ground handling agent at the departure and arrival airports.

It is the role of the manager or supervisor to nuture their team so as to ensure harmony. If an employee is not happy with another team member, this can stop them being effective. An employee may stop coming into work and may delay completing tasks and passing on messages because they don't enjoy talking to another person. The person responsible for the team needs to be alert to potential conflicts and take appropriate action before they arise, as well as deal with any conflicts encountered.

Case study

Prioritising needs

It is essential that cabin crew work as a team to fulfil the functions on board an aircraft, such as ensuring the safety of passengers, serving food and drink and selling tax-free items. Although each crew member may have their own area, i.e. a set of seats that have to be served, good teamwork would mean that if one member completed their service before the other, then the latter would be assisted in completing their duties.

Consider then a crew member that has been on board for six hours of an eight-hour flight. Throughout the flight they have been dealing with problems such as passengers needing a blanket and headphones not working. They have served drinks, pre-dinner drinks and water, and when lights were off for people to sleep, there were then problems with a passenger with a baby, and then there was heavy turbulence and the cabin crew and passengers had to remain seated. Next, there were several passengers ill as a result of the turbulence. After the six hours of non-stop working, it is time to serve breakfast. Cabin crew have had no time for food or drink.

What is their priority? If they finish their section before the others, should they be good team members and help others, or take a drink and something to eat? Maslow suggests they should take a drink. If there is more turbulence, do they help a colleague or strap themselves in? Maslow suggests their own safety needs will be a priority.

Case study

Teamwork

Overseas representatives (reps) may have sole responsibility for a hotel but there may be a children's rep in the hotel and they are part of a team for the tour operator providing support for all customers staying there. Overseas reps provide support for the children's rep by providing information on their services at a welcome meeting and the children's rep can offer support to deal with minor problems that customers are experiencing – for example, if a rep has to accompany a customer to the police station because they have lost their passport. The rep may be the only member of staff for their organisation in the resort but they are still part of a team for the destination as there will be other staff in that destination that will support their role and who they can support. For example, resort office staff could deal with customers who are hospitalised following an accident to allow the rep to fulfil airport duties; the resort office will rely on them submitting their liquidation reports and receipts by the deadline to enable them to complete their duties effectively. The UK office staff are also part of the destination team, offering support by providing information about arrivals but they will also expect the rep to support them if they are investigating a complaint made by a customer, to ensure they meet legal requirements in terms of deadlines met.

ACTIVITY

Staff duties

A holiday hypermarket is split into different sections, each focusing on different products – for example, there is a cruising, a long-haul, domestic and a city breaks section. There is also a general section that sells package holidays and ancillary services such as car hire and attractions tickets. Each member of staff sees himself or herself as the specialist but if there are too many customers for one section, then the staff in the general section will have to deal with them. Sales targets are given to each member of staff and they receive bonuses if these are exceeded. All staff have the same target, which is related to sales turnover (the total amount of sales they make). Staff on the cruise and long-haul sections always meet their targets but staff in other sections often fail to meet their target. This is causing some conflict and it has been noticed that staff on the general section are not referring customers with long-haul and cruise enquiries to the specialist section. At a recent staff meeting, staff on the domestic section said they were unhappy that they never get the opportunity to go on any promotional events or familiarisation visits related to overseas destinations. One of the cruise specialists had just come back from a cruise of the South China Sea. The general staff complained that when they are busy, specialists in other departments are not taking telephone calls on their behalf or offering any support. They claim that although the holidays they sell are not as expensive as cruise or long-haul, they make more additional sales such as car hire and airport hotel stays and this should be taken into account when setting targets. The staff responsible for foreign exchange kept quiet throughout the meeting; they don't have targets and their only role is to sell currency. Each department has a team leader and there is an assistant manager and manager in the branch.

Describe how this situation could be dealt with by management.

Incentives

For many people, the main reason for work is money. Their career aspirations are about getting jobs that pay more. Some theorists argue that money (wages) is the key motivator for all staff. Offering commission on excursion sales for representatives or sales of tax-free goods for cabin crew is how some organisations in the travel and tourism industry apply this theory. Money is one incentive. Another reason that people work in the travel and tourism industry is the opportunity to travel. Free or discounted travel is one of the key perks, or incentives. For example, as a member of the Travel Agents Travel Club (TATC), a membership organisation for travel agents, you will be offered exclusive holidays and discounted airfares.

Travel incentives, such as familiarisation visits, are becoming more limited as organisations become more commercially orientated. These incentives incur costs to the organisation. Staff who want to take advantage of incentives offered by airlines, hotel chains or tour operators may have to pay their own costs and take the time as holiday. Some organisations will pay all costs, give spending money and allow such trips to take place in company time.

ACTIVITY

Read a copy of the *Travel Trade Gazette* or *Travel Weekly* and identify all incentives to staff featured either in articles or advertisements.

ACTIVITY

A theme park is planning to introduce incentives to all its staff, whether or not they work directly with customers or sales. Discuss ways of offering incentives. Rank each of your incentives in terms of the most costly to the organisation. Select the three suggestions with the lowest costs to the organisation and produce an article for the staff newsletter describing what staff will receive and what they need to do to receive it.

Assessing the outcome

You work in the Human Resources Department of a major airline.

- Describe the factors that contribute to an effective workplace in travel and tourism organisations (**P5**).

Improve your grade

One of the benefits of attempting to achieve higher grades in this unit is that you will be better prepared when applying for employment in travel and tourism. Consider each stage in the recruitment process described for **P3**. For each stage where an applicant is involved in the process, consider what would be good practice. For example, when preparing an application for a job, what should be done to ensure the application is successful in being shortlisted? You might find it helpful to complete this part of the **M2** criterion before you attempt **P4**. Preparing guidelines for success before you attempt to demonstrate your suitability for employment in different stages in the recruitment and selection process, could assist you to do this effectively. There is another part to **M2**: to use the guidelines to evaluate your performance in **P4**. This part can only be completed after **P4** is complete. At this stage, you are evaluating your performance in the process rather than your suitability for the job; that is a distinction criterion requirement. For **M2**, you are evaluating against the guidelines you have produced. It is not a requirement that you have followed your guidelines but you must make an objective judgement. It may be that you failed to consider the requirements of the job description when preparing for interview. If you stated this was one of the guidelines for success, then you should evaluate that in not doing this you were not prepared for a problem-solving scenario relating to leading a team; you weren't aware of this part of the job. This is a valid statement to make in an evaluation. Objectivity and honesty gain you credit; attempting to suggest your approach was perfect when mistakes were made will not. In order to be objective, it may be helpful to find evidence and refer to specific examples of how you followed or failed to follow guidelines.

At distinction level (**D1**), the evaluation you make should be in relation to your suitability for the chosen job. Effectively, this will require you to complete a personal skills audit against the requirements of the person specification. For each essential and desirable requirement, you should make an objective judgement, ensuring you have evidence to substantiate your claims. Your teacher may have completed an assessment checklist and provided feedback that you could use. On completion of the skills audit, you may find that there are some of the essential or desirable requirements that you don't have. For each of these, produce a separate document – a training and development plan. Describe, for each of these, the action you could take to develop the weaknesses identified. The plan should identify specific actions and timescales. These should be described and not simply stated. For example, it is not sufficient to simply state a qualification – a description of what the qualification includes is also required, together with details of locations where the qualification can be taken. To simply state, 'I need to have customer service training' will be insufficient as there is no description. Are there specific training sessions that can be attended? If so, how long do they last, what do they include, where do they take place, when are they held? The action plan should be detailed.

Top tips

- Consider what would be good practice – the correct way of doing things – in the recruitment and selection process.
- Always identify specific actions and their timescales in career development plans.

Learning outcomes

By the end of this unit you should:

- know the key factors of the European travel market
- understand the factors determining the appeal of leisure destinations in the European travel market
- know how to segment the European travel market by leisure experience
- understand the factors affecting the development of the European travel market.

Key factors of the European travel market

There are many ways in which the countries that are classed as European can be defined. The first is by considering which ones make up the continent of Europe. A continent is a continuous land mass. As the *Science and Technology Encyclopaedia* states:

> **Although long called a continent, in many physical ways Europe is but a great western peninsula of the Eurasian landmass. Its eastern limits are arbitrary and are conventionally drawn along the water divide of the Ural Mountains, the Ural River, the Caspian Sea, and the Caucasus watershed to the Black Sea. On all other sides Europe is surrounded by salt water. Of the oceanic islands of Franz Josef Land, Spitsbergen (Svalbard), Iceland, and the Azores, only Iceland is regarded as an integral part of Europe; thus the north-western boundary is drawn along the Danish Strait.**

Figure 7.01 overleaf shows the countries that are considered to be European.

The European Union is a union of a number of European countries founded to enhance political,

ACTIVITY

Look at the map in Figure 7.01 and name the countries that can be found on the European continent.

economic and social cooperation. It was originally formed of six countries (Belgium, France, Italy, Luxembourg, the Netherlands and West Germany) in 1952 as the European Coal and Steel Community (ECSC) and has evolved over time to extend its membership to other countries and take on different forms, including the European Economic Community (EEC), the European Community (EC) and, more recently, the European Union (EU).

Currently all members are countries of the continent of Europe although there are countries from other continents interested in joining, including Morocco and Turkey. The possibility of Turkey becoming a member, even though most of the country is in Asia, has been considered by the European Union. As the European Union itself reported in MEMO/06/411 in November 2006: 'Turkey has improved its ability to take on the obligations of membership. In most areas some progress was made. However, fulfilment of short-term priorities under the Accession Partnership is lagging behind in many areas.'

ACTIVITY

Research the membership of the European Union. Locate these countries on a map indicating the order in which they joined. Also on the map, show those countries currently being considered for membership.

Two other ways of classifying European countries are by considering the Eurozone and Schengen

Fig 7.01 Europe

Agreement. The Eurozone is the name used to specify those countries that have adopted the Euro as their currency. As EUROPA, the portal for the European Union, states: 'History was made on 1 January 1999 when eleven European Union countries (later to become twelve) irrevocably established the conversion rates between their respective national currencies and the Euro and created a monetary union with a single currency, giving birth to the Euro.'

The name 'Schengen' originates from a small town in Luxembourg. In June 1985, seven European Union countries signed a treaty there to end internal border checkpoints and controls. More countries have joined the treaty over the past years. At present, there are 15 Schengen countries, all in Europe.

ACTIVITY

Find the names of the Schengen countries and locate them on a map.

Destinations and gateways

When considering the European travel market, in addition to identifying the countries that constitute Europe, regardless of the definition used, it is also important to consider the destinations that tourists travel to and the gateways that provide access to those destinations.

Airports are one of the key types of gateway used by UK tourists visiting European destinations, particularly seaside resorts and cities. Each airport in the world is designated a unique three-letter code to ensure that it can be clearly differentiated from other airports in cities with similar or the same names. For example, Paris is the capital of France but in the USA there are towns called Paris in the states of Missouri, Texas and Kentucky. There is also a Paris in Ontario, Canada. Paris, France, has three airports so to clarify which airport is being referred to, each is given a code: Charles de Gaulle is CDG, Orly is ORY and Le Bourget is LBG. The OAG *World Airways Guide* can be used to find the three-letter codes of airports or to find what airport a three-letter code relates to. You can also find three-letter codes on most airline, airport and e-travel agents' websites, such as Ryanair.

Popular seaside destinations are usually those situated along the Mediterranean and Aegean coasts. These are featured in the summer sun and winter sun brochures of major tour operators. A glance at a contents page will usually show the resorts that are featured.

Details of popular tourist towns and cities can be found in short break and city break brochures. Also, there are organisations that provide statistics on the popularity of European tourist towns and cities, an example of which is shown in Table 7.01.

Gateways to countryside areas are less likely to be airports as tourists visiting these areas generally want to explore. They are more likely to take their own transport and so require access to Europe from the UK by ferry across the English Channel or the North Sea. There are ferry ports along the south coast of England that provide access to northern France and Spain. For those living in the north of England and in Scotland, services from Newcastle and Hull will lead

> **ACTIVITY**
>
> Collect the summer sun brochures of ten different tour operators and compile a list of seaside resorts. Note those that appear in all brochures and those that appear in some only.

> **ACTIVITY**
>
> Mr and Mrs Woodley live in Leicester and are planning a holiday to the Black Forest in Germany. They want to travel by car so that when they reach the forest they can travel around easily. Assess the suitability of different ferry routes that may be available to them.

Table 7.01 Hotel benchmark global ranking index

Ranking	City	RevPAR US$ 2006	% change to 2005
1	Venice	211	10.5
2	Paris	199	14.7
3	Dubai	196	14.4
4	Rome	185	13.2
5	Doha	179	20.0
6	London	179	19.1
7	Moscow	176	15.0
8	Geneva	166	8.6
9	Hong Kong SAR	164	20.5
10	Tokyo	161	-1.3

to gateways in Holland and Belgium or Scandinavian countries such as Sweden and Denmark. Details of popular countryside areas can be found in self-drive brochures such as *French Life* (Figure 7.02).

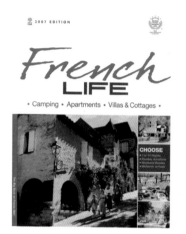

Fig 7.02 *French Life* brochure

Popular countryside areas are also those designated as areas of protected landscape.

Winter sports destinations are accessed via a range of gateways. Ski holidays are popular with school trips; school groups will tend to travel to the destination by coach and will use the ferry routes already mentioned. In addition, many tourists prefer to travel by air to the resorts.

ACTIVITY

What are key airports used for European winter sports destinations?

The 'snow train' is another way of accessing winter sports destinations. Eurostar is now well established for its services to Paris, Lille and Brussels, but it has also introduced its snow train service which goes direct from London Waterloo to a choice of three destinations in the French Alps.

ACTIVITY

A family plan to travel to La Plagne in the French Alps for a skiing holiday during February half term. There is one adult and three children, aged 4, 7 and 11. Assess the suitability of travelling by train or plane to reach their destination.

With cruising increasing in popularity, new cruise ships are being developed to cope with the additional capacity. Ships are becoming bigger. Norwegian Cruise Lines (NCL) is due to launch its 'supership' *Independence of the Seas* for its maiden voyage in mid-May 2008, alternating 14-night 'Mediterranean Treasures' and 'Italian Mediterranean' itineraries. Ports of call for the Mediterranean Treasures itinerary include Gibraltar; Barcelona, Spain; Nice, France; Florence/Pisa, Italy; Sardinia, Italy; Lisbon, Portugal; and Malaga and Vigo, Spain. Guests on the Italian Mediterranean cruises will experience the destinations of Gibraltar; Cannes/Monte Carlo, France; Florence/Pisa, Rome and Sardinia in Italy; Seville and Vigo, Spain; and Lisbon, Portugal.

For some cruise itineraries, the starting point may be in the UK. The Thomson Cruise 'Baltic Capitals' sets sail from Newcastle (Figure 7.03).

Case study

EUROPARC

EUROPARC was founded in 1973 under the official title 'Federation of Nature and National Parks of Europe', and has since grown to become the recognised, professional organisation for European protected areas. An independent, non-governmental organisation, its membership brings together the organisations responsible for the management of over 400 protected areas. They provide details of protected areas; for example, the following parks are EUROPARC members in Poland:

1. Bialowieza National Park
2. Jura Landscape Park
3. Polish Zarzad Glowny Tourism Company
4. Slowinski National Park
5. Tatra National Park
6. The Board of Polish National Parks
7. Wigry National Park.

You can find out more on www.europarc.org.

Case study

50 per cent growth in European cruise passengers predicted

The popularity of cruising is forecast to grow by nearly 50 per cent to 4.5 million Europeans in 2010. The prediction came from European Cruise Council chairman Pier Luigi Foschi, speaking at the Seatrade Europe conference in Naples. The European cruise market has seen consistent growth year on year with 2005 showing a 13 per cent rise to more than 3.2 million passengers. Trends show that holidaymakers are seeking easy-to-reach areas that are off the beaten track including destinations such as the Black Sea and the Atlantic Islands. By the end of the year, 56 ships will have cruised the Mediterranean and this is anticipated to increase to 63 ships by the end of 2007. Foschi said: 'The UK is still leading the way with over one million cruisers in 2005.'

(Source: *Travel Mole*, 24 October 2006)

ACTIVITY

Locate the destinations of the *Independence of the Seas* on a map of Europe. Compare the destinations of this ship with those of a Thomson Mediterranean cruise and those offered by easycruise.

For most itineraries, however, 'cruise and fly' is offered. This requires tourists to fly to the departure port for the cruise. The gateways used are similar to those used for summer sun destinations.

ACTIVITY

Investigate the gateways used for the itineraries of the *Independence of the Seas*, easycruise and Thomson Mediterranean cruises.

Fig 7.03 Thomson's 'Baltic Capitals' cruise route

Factors determining the appeal of leisure travel destinations in Europe

To determine the appeal of a destination, it is important to consider those factors that make it attractive, that make tourists want to visit that particular destination. Climate is often considered to be a factor that makes Mediterranean destinations appealing. Warm winters and hot, dry summers are attractive to those fed up with the 'cold, grey days' that can be experienced in the UK. There are destinations popular with UK tourists, however, where climate is not part of the appeal. If a tourist in Paris is asked why they chose to visit the city, climate is unlikely to be a reason given in many responses. The factors that determine the appeal will therefore vary according to the destination selected. To understand the factors that give appeal, it is important to discriminate between those factors that simply exist and those that contribute to appeal. Factors affecting appeal include accessibility, geographical features and attractions (both cultural and economic). This section of the unit will consider three of these factors.

Accessibility

There are a number of aspects to consider in connection with the accessibility of a destination. It is possible to access any destination but if it involves many changes and several days or hours to get there, the destination will not be appealing to most tourists unless there are other key factors that exist. For some destinations, the fact there are a range of transport options available can make it appealing. Paris is accessible by plane from most regional airports in the UK. Most UK airports have more than one departure each week and in some cases there are several departures each day such as from Bristol International Airport (Table 7.02).

A tourist can also have a choice of different airlines (Table 7.03).

Access to Paris is also available by train via Eurostar. This departs from London Waterloo station. This may be appealing to those living in London but, for other tourists, to access Paris by rail will require a train to London and a transfer across London to Waterloo station. The planned development of a new Eurostar terminal at St Pancras should add to the appeal of using rail to get to Paris. The new services from St Pancras will be launched in November 2007 and, according to the Eurostar website, the journey

Table 7.02 Scheduled flights from Bristol to Paris, Charles de Gaulle										
Departure	**Arrival**	**M**	**T**	**W**	**T**	**F**	**S**	**S**	**Flight number/Airline**	
06:30	09:00	X	X	X	X	X	X	—	AF2073 Air France	
07:30	09:50	X	X	X	X	—	—	—	U26219 easyJet	
07:40	10:00	—	—	—	—	X	—	—	U26219 easyJet	
10:40	13:10	X	X	X	X	X	X	—	AF1373 Air France	
13:10	15:30	—	—	—	—	—	X	—	U26221 easyJet	
14:00	16:20	X	X	X	X	X	—	—	U26223 easyJet	
14:45	17:05	—	—	—	—	—	—	X	U26223 easyJet	
17:25	19:55	X	X	X	X	X	—	X	AF1673 Air France	

(Source: www.bristolairport.co.uk, accessed May 2007)

Table 7.03 Airlines offering flights to Paris, Charles de Gaulle, from Manchester

Airline	Code	Type	Terminal
Air France	AF	Scheduled	2
Flybe	BE	Scheduled	3
Jet2.com	LS	Scheduled	1

Table 7.04 New journey times for the Eurostar from St Pancras

	Current fastest	Nov. 2007 fastest
London–Paris	2 hours 35 mins	2 hours 15 mins
London–Brussels	2 hours 15 mins	1 hour 51 mins
London–Lille	1 hour 40 mins	1 hour 20 mins

will be on average 22 to 25 minutes quicker (Table 7.04).

As Paris is an inland destination, it is not directly accessible by sea, although to travel to Paris by road, tourists from the UK will need to use ferries, hovercraft or the Eurotunnel to cross the English Channel to France. Once in France, there are a number of direct motorways via which to access Paris by road.

ACTIVITY
Investigate the motorway routes to Paris from French ports.

The fact that Paris is accessible by so many methods of transport is one of the factors that give it appeal. Most tourists can find a type of transport that meets their needs in order to access Paris.

Some other destinations, such as those in Turkey, are limited in terms of the types of transport available. Marmaris is one of Turkey's most popular summer destinations for UK tourists but accessibility is not one of the key factors that gives it appeal. Although it is possible to access the destination by road, rail, air and sea, realistically tourists will travel to the resort by air.

ACTIVITY
Investigate access to Marmaris by road, rail and sea.

Dalaman airport is the closest to Marmaris: flights from UK regional airports will take between four and four and a half hours. Flights mainly depart once or twice each week and they are generally available only from the larger regional airports such as London Gatwick, Birmingham and Manchester. Once at Dalaman airport, there is then almost a two-hour transfer to Marmaris. Taking into account possible travel times to the UK departure airport, check-in times and time to transfer from Dalaman to transfer transport, a tourist could be travelling for more than eight hours, yet Marmaris is still appealing to many tourists. Accessibility is clearly not a key factor in this appeal.

Geographical features
These include aspects of landscape that are natural, such as mountains, lakes, cliffs and coastlines. It is when considering this factor that the appeal of Marmaris can be seen: 'With a stunning setting in a natural bay surrounded by wooded mountains, Marmaris is one of the largest and best-developed of Turkey's resorts.' In this description from a Thomson brochure, the geographical features of Marmaris are not only described but also presented in a way that shows how these features give Marmaris appeal to tourists. The coastline is a significant factor in giving appeal to many Mediterranean destinations but it is the mountains of the Alps that give appeal to many destinations in France, Austria, Switzerland and Italy (Figures 7.04 and 7.05).

ACTIVITY

Investigate the accessibility of Les Deux Alpes in France. Find out how to get there by road, rail, sea and air. Assess whether accessibility is a key factor in the destination's appeal.

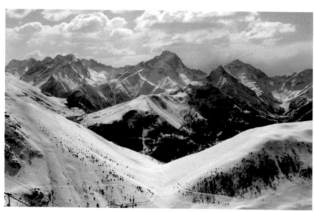

Fig 7.04 The Alps in winter

Fig 7.05 The Alps in summer

The images in Figures 7.04 and 7.05 show that mountains can give a destination appeal to both summer and winter tourists. Mountains give appeal in the winter when covered in snow as they provide opportunities to participate in a range of winter sports activities, the most popular being skiing and snowboarding. Tourists are not just attracted by the views of the mountains, the structure of each mountain can differ and provide a different experience. Advanced skiers will want mountains that provide more challenging skiing conditions and beginners will find more gentle slopes appealing.

ACTIVITY

Research winter sports destinations in Europe. Identify three destinations that can provide challenging ski conditions for advanced skiers and three destinations for beginners. Describe the key features that differentiate the selected destinations.

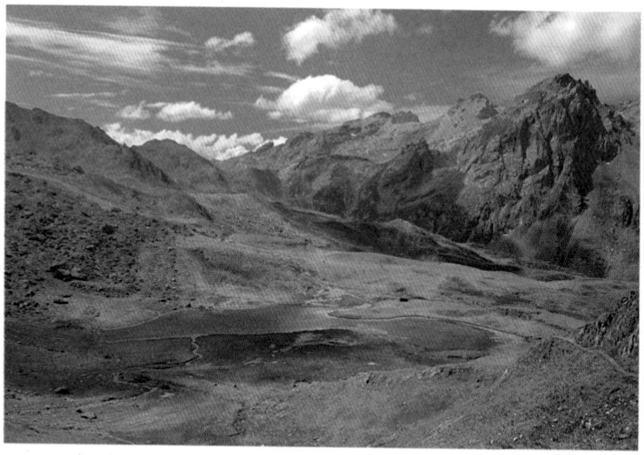

One feature of a ski destination that gives it appeal is if it provides skiing directly from a hotel rather than needing to travel by cable car or other form of transport to access the slopes. Some destinations are popular because they are positioned on glaciers that can give year-round skiing. The Grande Motte glacier is one of the key geographical features that gives Tignes in France its appeal.

ACTIVITY

Discuss how geographical features of mountains, as shown in Figure 7.05 give appeal to destinations in the summer.

Climate, including temperature and rainfall (precipitation), is a key element of geographical features as it is the geography that influences the climate. The appeal of climate in the winter can vary. For some destinations, precipitation can make a destination unappealing. The Balearic Islands would not be as appealing if most winter days were rainy, but without precipitation in mountain resorts there would be no snow and the destination loses its appeal. Many tourists will investigate the snow reports when booking late sales for skiing holidays and will look at climate trends when making advance bookings. A poor year for snow in a destination can adversely affect its future appeal.

Case study

The Alps

Here in Europe the main feature of the Alps seems to be that the big snowfalls come later. You used to be safe in early January but now that is no longer so. On the other hand, a late holiday around Easter seems to be a rather less risky proposition. There also seems to be a larger variance between the east and west Alps, though the data is unclear.

Thousands of skiers and snowboarders are changing their holiday plans and visiting the resorts of Bansko, Borovets and Pamporovo in Bulgaria due to poor snowfall in the traditional Alpine resorts (www.bulgarianproperties.com).

(Hamish McRae, *Independent*, 8 March 2005)

When considering the impact of climate on appeal, consideration should also be given to the effect of global warming. There is concern that Mediterranean summers will be too hot and dry to be able to sustain tourists, and mountain areas will suffer from lower snowfalls.

ACTIVITY

Investigate the European resorts most likely to be affected by global warming.

Cultural

There are many aspects of culture that give a destination appeal. These can include religious links, sports events, national and regional activities, as well as food and drink. For most countries, a traditional dish can be identified: moussaka in Greece, chocolate in Belgium, pasta in Italy and sangria in Spain are just some examples.

When visiting a destination, a tourist may seek out these traditional food and drinks but they are generally not attracted to the destination solely because of the food and drink. One country, though, known for its food and wine is France. For many tourists, this is one of the factors that makes destinations within that country appealing.

ACTIVITY

Identify the traditional food and drink of ten European countries.

Religion is another key aspect of cultural appeal. Many tourists visit Rome and particularly Vatican City because of its association with the Catholic Church. There are many Christian pilgrimage sites in Europe, including Santiago de Compostela and Lourdes. The southern Spanish region of Andalucia still has remnants of its Islamic past.

Case study

Lourdes: Experience the Jubilee Year of 2008

Why celebrate the 150th anniversary of the Apparitions?
In 1858, in a cave situated below the town of Lourdes in the south of France, the Blessed Virgin Mary appeared, in person, on eighteen occasions to Bernadette Soubirous, a very poor 14-year-old girl from Lourdes. The first apparition took place on 11th February and the last took place on 16th July. In 2008, Lourdes will celebrate the 150th anniversary of the Apparitions.

What happened in Lourdes after the Apparitions?
'Go, tell the priests to have a chapel built here and bring people here in procession'. 'I am the Immaculate Conception'... These words, spoken by the Blessed Virgin Mary to Bernadette, are the root of the international attraction of Lourdes. Each year, 6 million people, from every continent, come to Lourdes. Their primary purpose is to visit the Grotto of the Apparitions, the place where the Blessed Virgin Mary and Bernadette spoke with each other, in order to confide their lives to the Mother of God. Lourdes is a place of hope.

(Source: www.Lourdes2008.com, accessed May 2007)

ACTIVITY

Select a religion and investigate destinations in Europe that would be appealing because of their religious links.

Traditional events also give a destination appeal. Many events have been taking place for centuries and these give a destination greater appeal because of its heritage.

Segmenting the European travel market by leisure experience

In Europe, there are different types of destination with different features that give them appeal. Part of the appeal that these destinations have is the experiences they give a tourist when visiting. Destinations may be selected specifically because they provide for these experiences. These experiences could be cultural, adventure, activity, cruise and events. Activity, adventure and events will be considered in this section.

Activity experiences

There are many different types of activities that can be undertaken in European destinations. Golfing holidays are increasingly popular but are still considered specialist holidays. A golfing holiday is one where the main reason for the holiday and therefore the major part of the tourists experience, is related to golf. This is different to a holiday with golf where the tourist is mainly looking for another experience but an excursion or additional activity may be playing or watching golf. The Association of Independent Tour Operators (AITO) lists tour operators that specialise in golfing holidays. Golfing holidays will typically include flights or transport to the destination and transfers to the accommodation. Accommodation will usually be included on or near to one or more golf courses. In addition, green fees will be included, together with tee-off bookings. A round of 18 holes of golf can last four to five hours so the activity takes up most of the tourist's day. At the most popular golf courses, it is difficult to fit in tee times and often people have to start late at night as the courses are so popular. Having an organisation to make arrangements ensures that more time can be spent playing golf. The Portuguese Algarve is one of the most popular destinations for golf. To be popular, a destination must have high-quality golf courses, such as those used on the PGA European Golf Tour.

The destination must also have a warm, dry climate. Temperatures that are too hot are not good for golfers who can be outside for several hours at a time. Golf holidays are popular with groups and many organise their own tournaments.

ACTIVITY

Find golf courses used on the PGA European Golf Tour and find tour operators that will organise golfing holidays to these destinations.

The major tour operators do not specialise in golfing holidays but do feature holidays with golf in their brochures. First Choice offers these types of holiday as well as other activity holidays. The extract below is from the golf section of its website, www.firstchoice.co.uk/groups/golf (accessed May 2007).

> **Tee-off on holiday; the wonderful year-round climates, great locations and preferential golf course rates of our golfing destinations make them a perfect choice for friends, families and colleagues wanting a fun groups holiday.**
>
> **Why book your group a golf holiday with First Choice?**
>
> - **Locations near great golf courses**
> - **Pre-bookable tee-off times**
> - **Golf equipment hire and lessons often available**
> - **Discounted golf club carriage**

ACTIVITY

Investigate the other activity holidays available with First Choice.

La Manga is a purpose-built resort in Spain developed for activity holidays. Golf, tennis, cricket and football are all available at the resort.

ACTIVITY

Investigate the activities that can be experienced on a tennis holiday at La Manga.

Diving is another popular type of activity holiday. For tourists experiencing a diving holiday, a Professional Association of Diving Instructors (PADI) licence is needed. This involves classroom-based and water-based tuition and can take as long as five days to achieve. Some destinations will provide PADI training on arrival but this can limit the amount of time then available for diving in resort.

ACTIVITY

Investigate what is involved in PADI training. Find out the nearest PADI course to where you live.

Case study

Malta

The Maltese Archipelago of Malta, Gozo and Comino is a popular European diving destination. Aquatours is a specialist operator in diving holidays to Malta. It claims the destination offers:

> **Excellent potential for both beginners and experienced divers. With their natural harbours, sheltered bays and creeks, cliffs, caves, reefs and wrecks, the islands invite you to explore – the possibilities are endless. With a huge variety of dive sites just a stone's throw away from each other, you will be able to explore a variety of underwater worlds. Underwater visibility of 30 metres is not uncommon in the spring months. Sea temperatures average around 24°C in the summer and around 15°C in the coldest period of January to March, so divers can enjoy the delights of Malta and Gozo the year round.**

ACTIVITY

Mark and Keiko have two children who have now left home to go to university. They are planning their first holiday without their children. For the first time, they don't have to look for child-friendly destinations with entertainment and activities for the children. They are both keen walkers and are looking for a destination that can meet their needs. They walk regularly at weekends. Suggest a destination that is suitable for walking activities.

Adventure experiences

An adventure is an undertaking that involves danger, risk and/or excitement. To some tourists, even flying to the destination would be considered an adventure but generally adventure experiences are more specialised than being transported to the destination.

Caving

There are many caves that can be visited in Europe and these are generally appealing because of their links with prehistoric times. The Lascaux Caves on the western edge of the Massif Central in France are among the most famous for their prehistoric paintings discovered in 1940. The caves are now closed because of the deterioration caused by so many visitors but a reproduction has been developed.

Many caves can be accessed with guided tours but this doesn't provide sufficient adventure for many tourists. Caving, also called spelunking (from the technical term, 'speleology'),

> is about exploring the untouched underground world, and discovering natural beauty in rock formations caused by millions of years of the earth's natural wear and tear. Because the eco-system of caves is so fragile, extreme care has to be taken to ensure the preservation of these uniquely beautiful areas. When experts discover caves, they use special safety equipment, however, most of the caves available to the public are safe and can be enjoyed at any skill level.

(Source: Hostel Bookers)

Cave diving

According to Scuba Travel:

> The Dordogne region has been at the forefront of European cave diving developments and exploration for decades. The depths of Emergence du Russel, for example, were plumbed in the 1970s to more than 70m. Toe-curling epic dives have been executed using innovations such as half a dozen 'jumbo-rigged' 20-litre cylinders, twin re-breather gear and doubled-up underwater scooters. People have successfully penetrated thousands of metres into these systems, reaching amazing depths of 80m during dives that have lasted several hours. Some of these adventures are testament to the teamwork of dedicated diving groups while others are the achievements of rugged individuals.

Case study

Green Mountain holidays

According to the Green Mountain holiday brochure:

> The caving programme is especially made for people who want to explore and discover the richness of Romania's caves. Romania has an enormous variety of caves (over 12,000!) and by exploring the caves of the Apuseni Mountains, we will only touch the top of the iceberg. Depending on the success of the programme, further explorations will be made the following years. Caving in Romania is not visiting nicely prepared tourist caves but visiting them as the first explorers have seen them. That means that you'll have to climb, use ropes, to crawl and to creep to see the splendid beauty of them.

ACTIVITY

Investigate other European destinations where tourists can experience cave diving.

Skiing

For those seeking adventure, skiing no longer meets their needs. Extreme skiing is what provides the risk and danger. Speed skiing in Les Arcs in France is one form of extreme skiing and heliskiing is now available in Europe.

Case study

Zermatt, Switzerland: Alpin Center Zermatt

Ever buzzed the Matterhorn? UIAGM-certified guides will take you on some of the most scenic flights on earth, followed by great skiing and an excellent cheese course to finish. One flight, one run on the Monte Rosa CHF 330/220 Euros. Three flights/three runs from CHF 510/340 Euros.

ACTIVITY

Investigate other types of extreme skiing that are available in Europe. Locate destinations where these adventure holidays take place.

ACTIVITY

Investigate the options available for a group of motorcyclists to take their classic motorbikes from South Wales to Gedinne in Belgium. Provide details in terms of approximate journey times and costs.

Event experiences

Attending or participating in sports events are popular experiences. There are many sports that have events in Europe. There are European Championships in sports such as athletics, football, rugby (union and league), squash and even kayaking and sea angling. Tourists will travel to be part of these events either to participate or to spectate. There are specialist operators that will organise holidays to these events. For example, to watch England play football abroad, a tourist must be a member of England Fans, which will make all arrangements for a trip.

There are also major sporting events held in Europe that are part of world championships, such as skiing, the football World Cup and Formula 1 racing.

ACTIVITY

Investigate the location of the European rounds of the Formula 1 Championships. Locate these on a map. Investigate tour operators that organise holidays to these events.

Motorcycling is also a popular sport and the World Superbike Championships has several rounds each year held in Europe. Carl Fogarty of the UK won the World Championship a record four times. In 1999, 120,000 fans turned up to watch him race at Brands Hatch, England, and 30,000 travelled to Assen in Holland. Motorcycle racing is not only a popular spectator sport, it is also a participation sport. The International Historic Racing Association (IHRA) organises a number of races each year that attract amateurs from all over Europe. The Classic Belgium TT is held each September in Gedinne.

There are other types of event that have historical significance to a country or destination.

Case study

The Palio in Sienna

'Piazza del Campo' is still used today for the famous Palio horse race. It takes place every year on 2 July and 16 August. The Palio is run to celebrate the miraculous apparition of the Virgin Mary in whose honour the very first Palio was run on 16 August 1656. The Palio was run for the first time in 1701 in honour of the 'Madonna dell Assunta' the patroness and Advocate of Siena through all the tragic events since she protected the Siennese militia at the famous battle of Monteaperti on 4 September 1260, against the Florentines.

The Palio is a historical secular tradition strictly connected with the origin of the Contradas of Siena (districts into which the town is divided) each having their own government, coat of arms, sometimes titles of nobility, emblems and colours, festivities and patron saints. Originally, there were about 59 'Contrade'; now only 17 remain, ten of which take part in the historical pageant and in the race at each Palio (seven by right and three drawn by lots).

ACTIVITY

A group of film students want to organise a residential trip to a film festival in Europe. Investigate destinations that hold film festivals and recommend which would be suitable for them to visit.

Assessing the outcome

You are working as an assistant for a tourism marketing organisation and have been asked to help in creating an exhibit for the World Travel Market.

- Describe three European destinations which meet the leisure experience needs of specific customer types (**P3**).

Factors affecting the development of the European travel market

Over time the appeal of a destination may deteriorate and make it less popular. Fashions and the tastes of tourists change and so will the features they find appealing in a destination. When Spanish destinations first became popular, one of their appealing features was the quality of accommodation. In the early 1970s, accommodation in the UK was mainly provided by small hotels and guesthouses with bathrooms shared at the end of a corridor. Travelling to Spain where hotels had lifts, pools and ensuite bathrooms was an appealing feature. As tourists became more experienced, they were no longer satisfied with the quality of accommodation that was available in the Costa Brava and Costa Dorada coastal areas of Spain. Four-star accommodation and self-catering apartments became more appealing and so destinations that did not develop their accommodation found they were declining in popularity.

At the same time as some destinations failed to maintain and develop their appeal, others emerged with new features to give them appeal. Purpose-built resorts such as Disneyland Paris and La Manga provide quality accommodation with activities on site.

As new destinations emerge in their appeal they attract tourists from destinations that have lost their appeal and their popularity declines. Most destinations go through a life cycle, such as Butler's tourist area life cycle (Figure 7.06).

Figure 7.06 shows different stages that destinations will go through. Destinations that are still emerging as popular destinations will be in either the exploration, involvement or development stage. The consolidation and stagnation stages are where destinations are well developed and there is little growth in tourist numbers or development and improvement taking place. It is at this point that destinations could then go into decline and lose their popularity unless action is taken to revamp or rejuvenate them.

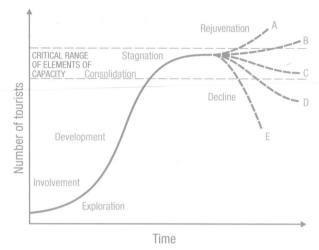

Fig 7.06 Butler's tourist area life cycle

Destinations in decline

There are a number of factors that can lead a destination to lose its appeal and decline in popularity. One of these factors is the increasing competition that has emerged as a result of European Union expansion and the introduction of low-cost airlines. Both of these have created new destinations that were previously less accessible. Destinations in Eastern Europe were relatively inaccessible when they were part of the 'Eastern Bloc' of communist countries. Passport and visa regulations restricted entry into such countries. The number of airlines operating to these countries was limited to 'national flag carriers' such as Lot in Poland and Aeroflot in Russia and these were able to control prices and keep them high. When the European Union expanded in 2001 to many of these countries, passport and visa restrictions were lifted.

ACTIVITY

Identify countries that joined the European Union at the time of its expansion in 2001.

Governments of these Eastern European countries, keen to develop their economies, have worked with low-cost airlines to ensure they are served by their routes. This competition has had an adverse effect on the more traditional short break and city destinations, such as Brussels. Where airports are at capacity with traditional scheduled services, they have been unable to support the growth of low-cost airlines into their

Table 7.05 Number of visits to selected European countries by UK residents

Country	2003	2004	2005
Belgium	1,964	1,799	1,733
France	11,957	11,602	11,094
Greece	2,857	2,709	2,435

(Source: adapted from Table 20 of MQ6, Quarter 3, 2006)

country and their advanced economies make the cost of visiting more expensive.

The International Passenger Survey (IPS) shows how countries that have traditionally been popular tourist destinations have had declining visitor numbers (Table 7.05).

Towns and cities are not the only type of destination that is in decline. Spain is also suffering a decline in tourism numbers:

> Two of Britain's biggest travel firms have axed more than a quarter of a million Spanish holidays from their 2005 brochures. Homing in on the Costa Brava, First Choice announced cuts here, Thomas Cook has halted its charter flights to the rugged coast's resorts from London Gatwick, and Club 18–30 has dropped Lloret de Mar from its brochure.

(Source: Colours of Spain)

ACTIVITY

Investigate tour operator brochures and identify those still selling destinations in the Costa Brava.

Case study

Malta at 2007 crossroads for hotels and holidays

The holiday and hotel market in Malta has seen a persistent decline in visitor numbers in recent years. With tourism consistently in decline, the Mediterranean island of Malta is hoping that 2007 will see new life breathed into her hotel and holiday industries. The Malta hotels and holiday industries are major players in the island's economy, and with unemployment already high, a further drop in the number of visitors next year could have a negative impact not just in tourism but for Malta as a whole. Throughout the year the monthly statistics for the number of tourists visiting Malta have made depressing reading for the hotels in Malta, and the next twelve months will be pivotal as to whether the island can stay in the mainstream of holiday destinations, or be relegated to niche travel status. The island was rife with rumours earlier in the year that a UK tour operator was going to withdraw the island from its 2007 brochures, and a survey in the island's biggest market showed that Malta would be more expensive for British tourists than the Canary and Balearic Islands for equivalent holidays next year.

(Source: ClickPress, 24 November 2006)

Case study

Canary Islands

It is not just the Spanish Costas that are experiencing a decline in tourism. Power FM is a local radio station for the Canary Islands. It asked listeners for their views on tourism decline on the islands.

> Having lived in Puerto Rico, Gran Canaria (GC) for about six years…I can only speak for GC but it was quite noticeable that tourist numbers were declining. Having been back to the UK, I can see that this island has not moved with the times. The main shopping centre area is extremely out-dated and quite dirty. The bars and restaurants can be poorly laid out and the constant pressure from 'PR' people working for them is quite off-putting. It seems many people in the UK are looking for resorts with natural beaches, good accommodation (not squashed together apartment blocks) and good services and entertainment. Although people in the UK are increasingly putting themselves in more debt, their decisions are not always based on what is cheapest.

> We have owned an apartment on Tenerife for around 4 years but have been visiting for about 15. We let our apartment to friends and family and we have found there are a number of reasons why some are going elsewhere. Air fares are a real issue, if you are forced to travel during school holidays, it's cheaper to fly to New York! And low-cost airlines such as easyJet doing return flights to mainland Spain for £50 doesn't help. Another point that has been raised is crime, particularly drug-related. It's important to respect and retain the culture of Tenerife – if it's perceived just as a sunny version of Southend, then all it will attract is the lager louts.

ACTIVITY

Consider the comments in the case study above and discuss why tourist numbers to the Canary Islands are in decline. Suggest ways that the islands can be developed to increase tourist numbers.

Developing destinations

The section on declining destinations indicates two key factors that are leading to the development of new destinations: low-cost airlines and EU membership. Many developing destinations can be found in countries that joined the EU in 2001 or 2006 as can be seen in the statistics in Table 7.06.

Table 7.06 Number of visits to selected European countries by UK residents

Country	2003	2004	2005
Bulgaria	158	297	367
Czech Republic	562	691	786
Hungary	150	218	302
Poland	175	304	637

(Source: adapted from Table 20 of MQ6, Quarter 3, 2006)

Table 7.07 Number of visits by UK residents to EU countries

	2003	2004	2005
EU of which EU25	47,859	48,221	48,928
EU of which EU15	45,090	45,137	44,991

(Source: adapted from Table 20 of MQ6, Quarter 3, 2006)

The IPS also gives statistics comparing visitor numbers to EU countries that were the 15 members prior to 2001 and the post-2001 expanded 25 members of the EU (Table 7.07).

These statistics show that the number of UK residents visiting the pre-2001 15 EU member states is in decline but when taking into account those joining in 2001, the numbers are increasing.

One reason for this growth is the introduction of low-cost airlines to the new EU member countries.

ACTIVITY

Investigate the routes offered by low-cost airlines. Categorise by those to destinations to countries joining the EU in 2001 and those that were already members in 2001.

"It's the ownership of second homes abroad, though, that is the real growth area. Almost 180,000 foreign homes are now English-owned – 20,000 more than in 2004. Spain (62,000) and France (42,000) remain the perennial favourites, but 41,000 homes are now located outside Europe, including 9,000 in the US. Croatia is said to be so popular with UK buyers that 'For Sale' signs in some towns are now written only in English."

(Source: Leo Hickman's guide to a good life, Guardian, 21 February 2006)

ACTIVITY

Investigate the appeal of Montenegro as a destination for a second home.

Case study

Why 68 per cent of Brits want to buy a property abroad

Fed up with the UK climate and lifestyle 68 per cent of Brits would like to buy property abroad, according to new independent research from HIFX, the currency experts. The study found that Britons rate overseas weather and lifestyles as more important than effective investment or making a profit when they pour their cash into properties abroad. HIFX's research found that almost two-thirds of Brits (62 per cent) see the main benefit of buying a property abroad as the chance to escape the cold and rainy UK weather. Half (50 per cent) think it would be good to escape their stressful UK lifestyle of long working hours and high taxes and, over a quarter (27 per cent), would like to eventually emigrate and live abroad. According to 2005 Office of National Statistics figures, the number of Britons owning second homes abroad now stands at 257,000. However, HIFX's research shows that a further 29 million Brits would like to buy a property abroad and 11 million could actually own one within the next five years (source: www.pattinson.co.uk). According to www.property-abroad.co.uk, the seven foreign hotspots for purchasing property in 2007 are: South Africa, Montenegro, Dubai, the Caribbean, Morocco, Turkey and Bulgaria.

Case study

Montenegro

One of the top ten holiday destinations is Montenegro. After the Second World War, Montenegro improved its legal and state status and became one of the six equal republics of the Yugoslav federation. After the turbulent years of the end of the twentieth century, and after the disintegration of the former Yugoslavia, Montenegro remained in the union with Serbia, thus these two republics formed the State Union of Serbia and Montenegro. Most citizens at the referendum held on 21 May 2006 voted for independence for Montenegro. Thus today Montenegro is an internationally recognised independent state. The UN received Montenegro as the 192nd country member on 27 July 2006.

Assessing the outcome

You work for a travel agency that is increasingly receiving enquiries from customers looking to buy second homes overseas. You have been asked to investigate destinations that are developing and those that are in decline so that more useful information on trends can be given to customers.

- Describe one declining and one developing destination in the European travel market and identify factors that have contributed to this (**P4**).

Improve your grade

The important skill that needs to be developed for this unit in order to access higher grades is 'reasoning'. For the merit criteria you have to give explanations. An explanation means you have to say why something has occurred or how one thing relates to another. It is not enough to simply describe relationships but the cause for the relationships needs to be given.

M1 requires an explanation of how different factors of leisure destinations appeal to different types of customers visiting the European Travel Market. The relationship between factors, destinations and types of customer must be explained – reasons given for why they exist. Factors and destinations are all given in the content for the second outcome and customer types are given in the third outcome; this content should be used to ensure you give sufficient coverage. Your work for **P2** and **P3** will give you the basic information you need to be able to complete this criterion.

M2 requires an explanation of how specific European destinations meet the leisure experience needs of different customer types. This time the reason needs to extend the descriptions given in **P3**. For each leisure experience and customer type covered for that criterion, you must say how the destination meets the needs of the customer type. You might not have mentioned customer needs in your work for **P3** so the starting point for **M2** might be to consider the needs of each customer type you have included. Then, give a reason why each need is met by the leisure activity.

The third merit criterion also needs reasoning to be demonstrated, but this time through an analysis rather than an explanation. An analysis is more complex than an explanation: it requires you to break down the parts of the question and consider the relationships and cause and effect as well as how each part affects the whole. This sounds complicated and it is, which is why it is a merit requirement. **M3** requires you to analyse the factors that shape the development and decline of destinations in the European travel market. Two destinations need to be considered in the analysis: one developing and one in decline. You will have considered two of each type of destination at pass level. An analysis will require consideration of the causes of the decline and/or development and the effect they have had. With analysis, the relationship between the changing fortunes of the two destinations will also be considered and any similarities and differences between causes and effects explored.

D2 also requires reasoning to be demonstrated but this time by evaluating the effects of current factors on the European travel market in the future. An evaluation requires that judgements are made and these should all be reasoned. For a judgement to be made, you will need to comment on whether you think a factor has been important in causing the decline or development of the European travel market. Where a factor has been significant you must give a reason. If you consider a factor has not been significant, you should also give a reason. Statistics to support your reasons are helpful as this suggests your evaluation is objective and based on available data rather than being subjective, where it is just your opinion.

The final higher-grade criterion for this unit is **D1** where you should give detailed and realistic recommendations how a European destination could increase its appeal for different types of customer. The destination chosen must be one used for **P2** or **P3**. The destination you use as the focus for this task should be selected carefully to ensure there is potential for improvement. Consider each customer type separately. For each customer type, give a detailed description of how its appeal could be increased. Consider each of the factors that affect appeal shown in the second outcome.

Top tips

- Focus on each type of customer.
- Consider the specific needs of each type of customer.

Long-haul travel destinations

Locating major long-haul destinations

The travel and tourism industry classes long-haul as destinations that require a flight of over seven hours to another continent. As the UK is in Europe, this means long-haul destinations are within the continent of Asia, North America, South America, parts of Africa and Australasia.

ACTIVITY

Using an atlas locate the continents on a blank world map.

A major receiving area is one that attracts or receives a significant number of tourists. It is possible to determine where 'major' receiving areas are by researching statistics that show visitor numbers. Another approach to determine which are major receiving areas could be the scrutiny of a range of brochures to see those destinations frequently used by major tour operators.

There are several travel statistics available relating to the numbers of people that visit a destination.

These figures can be used to see how popular a destination is. National Statistics Online is one place where research figures can be found. Table 8.01, overleaf, gives statistics showing the number of visits abroad by UK residents in 2005 from the National Statistics Travel Trends 2005 report.

This information gives details about the number of visits to each country. Further research is needed, however, to establish the specific area of the country that is receiving the visitors, e.g. where in the USA people are going. The information divides figures into two groups: holiday and business.

ACTIVITY

Using Table 8.01, overleaf, name the three long-haul countries that attracted the highest number of visits in 2005.

Research to find out why the highest-rating countries received the highest number of visitors.

The Travel Association (ABTA) publishes information that can help determine whether a destination is a major tourist receiver. According to ABTA, the following were the hot destinations in 2006:

- Ibiza
- Mallorca
- Austria
- Germany
- Croatia
- Slovenia
- Poland
- Egypt
- Tunisia
- Morocco
- Kenya
- Tanzania
- Brazil
- Sri Lanka
- Thailand
- Maldives
- India
- China.

ABTA also stated:

> Brazil is *the* hot destination for 2006 as a number of major tour operators have put on direct charter flights to northern Brazil. The country has so much going for it, including a rich and vibrant cultural heritage, amazing beaches, and the biggest rain forest and rivers in the world. Your money will also go far and, who knows, you may even get to see the world's best footballers play.

ACTIVITY

Look through ten brochures featuring destinations in Brazil. Identify three major receiving areas in Brazil.

ACTIVITY

Using an atlas, locate ABTA's top hot destinations in 2006 on a blank world map.

Table 8.01a Number of visits, nights and spending by purpose and by country of visit, 2005

	Holiday						Business		
	Total			of which inclusive tour					
	visits (thousands)	nights (thousands)	spending (£million)	visits (thousands)	nights (thousands)	spending (£million)	visits (thousands)	nights (thousands)	spending (£million)
Canada	320	5,215	323	125	1,700	156	60	706	65
USA	2,639	36,258	2,434	903	11,024	887	794	6,348	817
North America	2,959	41,473	2,757	1,028	12,724	1,043	855	7,054	882
Egypt	491	4,979	240	431	4,202	204	35	394	22
Tunisia	331	3,112	114	292	2,568	91	7	28	2
Other North Africa	164	1,699	86	76	631	34	45	463	25
South Africa	249	4,506	327	48	779	70	56	650	65
Other Africa	345	5,935	357	161	2,169	172	84	1,428	82
Israel	38	546	25	11	88	7	20	84	11
United Arab Emirates	255	2,356	218	108	889	91	77	634	79
Other Middle East	60	960	42	20	187	15	57	802	56
Hong Kong (China)	53	738	37	7	50	6	31	428	58
Other China	86	1,694	103	44	648	50	94	1,179	107
India	313	7,058	235	103	1,479	79	91	1,595	137
Japan	24	485	23	2	23	1	62	561	100
Pakistan	55	2,148	39	0	9	0	13	213	12
Sri Lanka	64	1,293	47	32	440	23	6	51	12
Thailand	266	6,602	324	82	1,237	74	24	256	35
Other Asia	279	5,852	263	118	1,704	120	78	1,840	77
Australia	272	11,073	493	32	756	57	51	993	92
New Zealand	106	4,820	241	9	237	26	10	380	19
Barbados	130	1,664	108	81	1,016	63	4	133	5
Jamaica	88	1,560	75	50	702	41	7	81	6
Other Caribbean	657	9,562	459	482	6,501	292	19	310	19
Mexico	236	3,256	173	189	2,586	138	12	88	11
Other Central & S. America	157	4,002	194	52	793	75	37	500	43
Rest of the world	316	3,783	426	311	3,532	413	0	4	0
Other countries	5,036	89,682	4,647	2,743	33,226	2,114	919	13,094	1,073

(Source: National Statistics Travel Trends, 2005)

Continued

Table 8.01b Number of visits, nights and spending by purpose and by country of visit, 2005

	Visiting friends or relatives			Miscellaneous			Total		
	visits (thousands)	nights (thousands)	spending (£million)	visits (thousands)	nights (thousands)	spending (£million)	visits (thousands)	nights (thousands)	spending (£million)
Canada	232	4,350	105	16	771	23	628	11,042	516
USA	704	12,446	364	104	1,933	82	4,241	56,984	3,697
North America	936	16,796	469	120	2,703	105	4,869	68,027	4,213
Egypt	36	976	15	2	85	0	564	6,434	277
Tunisia	13	158	4	3	29	1	353	3,327	121
Other North Africa	67	1,918	28	2	21	3	278	4,100	142
South Africa	131	2,845	73	13	490	16	449	8,491	481
Other Africa	225	6,136	157	37	1,303	37	692	14,802	634
Israel	44	559	19	4	135	2	106	1,324	57
United Arab Emirates	70	1,505	39	8	98	6	410	4,593	341
Other Middle East	103	3,179	35	58	1,261	51	278	6,202	184
Hong Kong (China)	90	2,659	46	3	173	5	178	3,998	146
Other China	101	3,236	29	9	901	8	290	7,010	247
India	353	10,121	196	39	1,264	39	796	20,038	607
Japan	40	1,026	17	6	325	8	132	2,398	148
Pakistan	316	14,277	213	18	964	20	402	17,603	284
Sri Lanka	42	1,479	22	9	124	5	120	2,947	86
Thailand	58	1,634	49	7	571	11	356	9,063	419
Other Asia	240	8,788	178	13	560	17	610	17,040	535
Australia	302	9,783	291	23	3,068	44	648	24,917	920
New Zealand	82	2,791	89	6	329	18	204	8,320	367
Barbados	14	333	14	2	31	3	151	2,160	129
Jamaica	42	1,371	24	3	71	3	139	3,084	108
Other Caribbean	49	1,324	25	12	228	19	736	11,425	522
Mexico	7	161	2	5	447	6	261	3,951	192
Other Central & S. America	54	1,554	34	10	553	16	258	6,608	287
Rest of the world	3	159	6	1	26	0	321	3,972	432
Other countries	2,483	77,974	1,606	296	13,056	337	8,734	193,806	7,663

Assessing the outcome

You have applied for a sales adviser position in the reservation department of a long-haul independent tour operator. As part of the interview process you have been asked to complete a short test of your knowledge of continents, major long-haul tourist receiving areas, countries and destinations of the world. You are told that for part of the assessment you may use appropriate reference sources that they will provide. You are advised that you will need to locate on a blank map, the continents, ten major tourist receiving areas and ten major tourist countries without using any resources. You are advised that resources will be provided to locate four examples of city, coastal, purpose built, natural, historical and cultural destinations. The destinations will be given on the assessment day.

- Identify and locate continents, major long-haul tourist receiving areas, countries and destinations of the world using appropriate reference sources (**P1**).

The nature of long-haul travel and the factors that affect customer choice

The previous section looked at what a long-haul destination was and the location of major worldwide long-haul destinations. There are a number of types of long-haul destinations and a wide range of different types of holiday available. These destinations can be broken up into destination types, as illustrated in Figure 8.01, overleaf.

City destinations

Sydney is a city within Australia and is the capital of New South Wales (NSW). NSW is Australia's most populated state, with a population of around four and a quarter million people. Sydney is Australia's financial capital and is home to the Australian Stock

Far East

Thailand
  Thailand tours & multi-centres
  Eastern & Oriental Express
  Bangkok
  Northern Thailand
  Cha Am & Hua Hin
  Pattaya
  Koh Samui
  Phuket
  Krabi
  Thai hideaways: Khao Lak/Koh Chang/Koh Lanta/Koh Yao/Phi
    Phi Trang
Cambodia
Vietnam
  Saigon & Hanoi
  Vietnamese coast
  Indochina multi-centres
Malaysia
  Kuala Lumpur & beyond
  Penang
  Langkawi
  Borneo
  Malay hideaways: Pangkor/Kuantan/Tioman/Redang
Singapore
  Star Cruises
  Singapore multi-centres
Bali
  Bali multi-centres
  Balinese hideaways: Lombok/Ubud
China
  Beijing
  Xi'an
  Hangzhou & Guilin
  Shanghai
  Yangtze Cruising
  China extensions
  China multi-centres
Hong Kong
  Hong Kong multi-centres
Far East & beyond
Thomas Cook Tours

Australia
Thomas Cook Tours

Indian Ocean
Mauritius
Seychelles
Sri Lanka
Maldives

India
Tours of India
Goa
Thomas Cook Tours

Dubai and the Middle East
Dubai
Fujairah
Adu Dhabi
Oman
Jordan

Egypt
Nile Cruising
Excursions and multi-centres
Cairo
Aswan
Luxor
Soma Bay
Hurghada
Sharm el Sheikh
Africa

East Africa
Kenyan beach
Anzibar
Thomas Cook Tours
Sourthern Africa
Worldwide multi-centres

Central & South America
Mexico
Costa Rica
Brazil
Thomas Cook Tours

Caribbean
Caribbean multi-centres
Barbados
St Lucia
Antigua
Turks & Caicos
Bahamas

Fig 8.01 Long-haul destination types in the Thomas Cook brochure

Exchange. It usually takes over 20 hours to travel to Sydney from the UK. The city has a range of types of accommodation, from hostels to five-star hotels. There are a number of flights arriving at its international airport daily.

ACTIVITY

In an atlas, find the location of Sydney, Australia.

Fig 8.02 Sydney, Australia

Coastal or seaside destinations

" Warm white sand beaches, crystal indigo seas, romantic Caribbean nights, world-class hotels, restaurants and nightlife; does all of this sound too good to be true? This is Cancun! World-renowned fishing, diving and snorkelling, archaeological sites dating back thousands of years, a balmy tropical climate and water sports galore…this is Cancun! A very complete resort where you could keep busy 24 hours a day just participating in the many activities and tours available, and yet Cancun remains a tranquil retreat where you can relax to your heart's content along the peaceful shore of the Caribbean … this is the real purpose of Cancun!

The beaches are probably one of the main reasons for your visit. Cancun's beaches are legendary and with good cause. The powdery, incredibly white sand of the Caribbean blesses all of the beaches in Cancun. These beaches seem to go on forever and each one is a beach lover's fantasy come true. The Caribbean Sea is unusually warm with incredibly blue water and at most times is very calm. Look down any beach, at almost any time, and you will see people enjoying the calming effects that seem to instantly relieve the tensions of everyday life. *"*

(Source: www.allaboutcancun.com, accessed May 2007)

Cancun in Mexico can be classed as a seaside destination. The extract above describes the beaches and sea, which are some of the features that make up a seaside destination. Figure 8.03 illustrates these features.

Fig 8.03 Cancun, Mexico

Purpose-built destinations

Las Vegas in America is an example of a purpose-built destination: it has been built specifically to attract visitors.

Fig 8.04 Las Vegas, USA

ACTIVITY

Research Las Vegas. Give a short presentation describing the purpose-built features of this destination.

ACTIVITY

Investigate one other long-haul coastal or seaside destination. On a flipchart identify the destination's main coastal and/or seaside features.

Natural destinations

Fiordland on South Island, New Zealand, is an example of a natural destination. It is made up of natural attractions (i.e. not made by man) including waterfalls, mountains, lakes, fiords and much more.

> **The eighth wonder of the world**
>
> **The power of Fiordland's scenery never fails to enthral travellers. Waterfalls tumble hundreds of metres into massive fiords; ancient rainforest clings impossibly to the mountains; shimmering lakes and granite peaks look the same today as they did a thousand years ago.**

(Source: www.newzealand.com, accessed May 2007)

ACTIVITY

Visit the New Zealand tourist board website. Research more about these natural attractions, such as the size of the waterfalls, the types of tree in the rainforest. Produce a newspaper article that describes the natural features of Fiordland.

Historical and cultural destinations

Thailand has a number of cultural and historic attractions that draw tourists there. It has many examples of history that link to the country's past. This includes two UNESCO-listed historical World Heritage Sites.

ACTIVITY

- Find out what the two UNESCO World Heritage Sites in Thailand are.
- Research either Bangkok, Chang Mai or Ayutthaya in Thailand. Find out why your chosen destination is classed as historic and cultural.
- Produce a traveller's mini-guide describing the historic and cultural features of the specific destination selected.

There are a wide range of long-haul holidays available. The ranges of types of long-haul holiday vary to suit different customer types. Each type of holiday will have factors that motivate people to visit these destinations.

ACTIVITY

Using Figure 8.01 on page 138 categorise the destinations featured into destination types.

The Caribbean

The Caribbean is made up of a number of islands, all of which have their own unique selling points. The Caribbean attracts thousands of UK visitors every year. The National Statistics Travel Trends report (Table 8.02) shows a growth in numbers from 2001 to 2005. The reason people are motivated to visit the Caribbean is partly because it has white beaches and a year-round tropical climate.

The Caribbean has been the setting for countless books and films, often related to piracy – for example, some of the James Bond films were set here. These films were shot in idyllic locations, painting a positive image of the destination, thus inspiring people watching the film to go there.

Case study

Puerto Rico

The island of Puerto Rico is one of the Caribbean Islands and is located in the Leeward Islands in the Caribbean Sea. The main town is San Juan, which has a main port and is used as a port of call by many of the main cruise operators.

Dating back to 1521, El Viejo San Juan – or Old San Juan – is not only the most attractive part of the Puerto Rican capital but also one of the most fascinating historic areas in the whole Caribbean. Best of all, you can walk there from San Juan's cruise port.

The narrow, cobblestone streets are lined with 16th- and 17th-century Spanish colonial houses, with plants trailing from wrought-iron balconies. These give some welcome shade from the ever-shining sun as you make your way to the 16th-century fortress, El Morro, still seemingly on guard against invaders from the sea.

A hugely atmospheric place with 20ft thick walls, you will be amazed at the medieval nooks and crannies, dungeons, lookouts, courtyards, ramps, hidden staircases and gun turrets it conceals. As one of the Caribbean's larger islands, Puerto Rico has enough room for an enchanting 27,000-acre rainforest: El Yunque.

(Source: www.pocruises.com, accessed May 2007)

ACTIVITY

Explain why tourists want to go on cruise shore excursions to San Juan, Puerto Rico.

Table 8.02 Number of visits by country of visit, 2001 to 2005

	Visits (thousands)					Change 2004–05	Growth 2004–05	Average Annual Growth 2001–05
	2001	2002	2003	2004	2005	(000s)	(%)	(%)
Canada	666	609	530	613	628	15	2.4	−1.5
USA	3,990	3,602	3,613	4,167	4,241	74	1.8	1.5
North America	4,656	4,211	4,142	4,780	4,869	89	1.9	1.1
Egypt	261	236	289	345	564	219	63.5	21.2
Tunisia	386	268	225	281	353	72	25.6	−2.2
Other North Africa	210	180	200	200	278	78	39.0	7.3
South Africa	309	397	475	439	449	10	2.3	9.8
Other Africa	369	431	496	591	692	101	17.1	17.0
Israel	106	65	76	112	106	−6	−5.4	0.0
United Arab Emirates	194	222	274	397	410	13	3.3	20.6
Other Middle East	189	228	165	200	278	78	39.0	10.1
Hong Kong (China)	150	171	114	177	178	1	0.6	4.4
Other China	145	180	168	240	290	50	20.8	18.9
India	479	465	494	657	796	139	21.2	13.5
Japan	107	131	114	112	132	20	17.9	5.4
Pakistan	236	255	305	358	402	44	12.3	14.2
Sri Lanka	81	85	149	171	120	−51	−29.8	10.3
Thailand	269	300	276	363	356	−7	−1.9	7.3
Other Asia	420	443	444	566	610	44	7.8	9.8
Australia	486	498	525	558	648	90	16.1	7.5
New Zealand	119	135	156	185	204	19	10.3	14.4
Barbados	123	131	140	147	151	4	2.7	5.3
Jamaica	135	182	162	159	139	−20	−12.6	0.7
Other Caribbean	463	466	515	669	736	67	10.0	12.3
Mexico	260	277	246	298	261	−37	−12.4	0.1
Other Central & S. America	200	185	198	227	258	31	13.7	6.6
Rest of the world	355	355	406	437	321	−116	−26.5	−2.5
Other countries	6,052	6,287	6,615	7,889	8,734	845	10.7	9.6

(Source: National Statistics Travel Trends, 2005)

ACTIVITY

Look on the internet or in a brochure at a Caribbean cruise itinerary. Find out which ports of call are included in the itinerary. Explain how the destinations used in the itinerary would motivate people to book a cruise holiday.

ACTIVITY

Research brochures featuring the Caribbean island of Barbados. Other than for international cricket explain why UK tourists would visit Barbados.

Barbados is another Caribbean Island. It has attracted UK tourists for a number of years. In 2005, according to the National Statistics shown in Table 8.02, Barbados received 151,000 visitors from the UK. Barbados has many natural attractions which contribute to its popularity and appeal. International cricket has been a sport played in Barbados for many

years and still draws cricket supporters during the test season.

All-inclusive holidays are popular in beach resorts such as the Caribbean. This type of holiday will be more than a package with travel and accommodation, and will usually include in the price all meals, drinks, entertainment and often sporting facilities such as water sports.

Peru

Peru is a country of diversity it has the Andes mountains, jungle rainforest, desert and coastline. One type of holiday Peru offers is trekking. Practically the entire centre of the country, including the valleys, plains and massifs, offers trekking opportunities for hikers. The most famous trek is the Inca Trail.

> **For many visitors to South America, a visit to the lost 'Inca' city of Machu Picchu is the whole purpose of their trip. With its awe-inspiring location, it is the best-known and most spectacular archaeological site on the continent. Despite being swamped by tourists from June to September, it manages to retain an air of grandeur and mystery.**

(Source: www.lonelyplanet.com, accessed May 2007)

Multi-centre holidays

Multi-centre holidays are those that involve several destinations within a holiday. A typical tour in China might follow the format shown in the box, opposite.

This tour involves four destinations: Beijing, Chengde, Xi'an and Shanghai. Multi-centre holidays can involve a range of methods of transport to get to and from each destination. Some involve flights, whereas others use sea or surface transportation, i.e. travel over land. Multi-centre holidays may include destinations in different countries, e.g. Maldives, Sri Lanka and Dubai.

Health tourism

Health tourism is a growth area. It is attracting a significant number of tourists to many destinations around the world. Kerala in India (see the case study, opposite) is a destination that attracts a significant number of visitors purely for this purpose.

Travel factors

There are a number of factors that potential travellers will consider when booking holidays – for example, extreme climate conditions. Hurricanes are an example of this factor affecting the choice of travellers to visit the Caribbean at certain times of the year. In recent years, a number of hurricanes have hit Caribbean islands popular with UK tourists.

China Experience Tour

Beijing: 3 nights
Chengde: 2 nights
Xi'an: 2 nights
Shanghai: 2 nights

Day 1 Fri Fly from Heathrow to Beijing. Meet your tour manager at Heathrow, who will accompany you throughout China.

Day 2 Sat Arrive in China's capital city where you will be met by your tour guide and transfer to the Lotus Flower hotel for a three-night stay.

Day 3 Sun Beijing is a wonderful city and today is spent visiting the major attractions, Tian'anmen Square, the Temple of Heaven and Forbidden City, before journeying further out to the Summer Palace. Optional evening out to the Peking Opera.

Day 4 Mon A not-to-be-missed experience in China is a visit to the Great Wall at Mutianyu. There will be plenty of time to walk along its ramparts and absorb the amazing views. After lunch return to Beijing and enjoy some free time before a Peking Duck dinner.

Day 5 Tue Depart by train in soft class through mountain scenery to Chengde, the former summer retreat of the Manchu Emperors (approx. four hours). Upon arrival book into the Emperor hotel for two nights. After lunch visit the majestic Summer Resort, the largest royal landscape in China today, enveloped within a smaller version of the Great Wall.

Day 6 Wed An inspirational full day of sightseeing includes the Temple of the Wooden Buddha, the Putuozongcheng Temple, a dramatic replica of the Potala Palace in Tibet and time to browse the local markets.

Day 7 Thu Travel by coach (approx. four hours) to connect with the flight to the ancient capital of Xi'an. Upon arrival transfer to the Garden hotel for two nights. Pass the afternoon at your leisure and enjoy a traditional meal in the evening.

Day 8 Fri A full-day tour including the sensational Terracotta Warriors, ancient city wall and the Wild Goose Pagoda. Optional evening experience to the Tang Dynasty show.

Day 9 Sat A visit to the historic Han Yang Tombs before flying to Shanghai. Transfer to the River hotel for two nights. Explore Shanghai.

Day 10 Sun Shanghai has a long and colourful history. On your escorted city tour, stroll along the Bund, cruise on the Hangpu river, discover the Old Town and visit the historical and artistic Shanghai Museum. In the evening enjoy a farewell banquet and an acrobat show!

Day 11 Mon Fly back to Heathrow arriving later the same day.

(Source: adapted from Kuoni brochure: *A Taste of China*)

Case study

Kerala: the pioneer state

Kerala has pioneered health and medical tourism in India. It has made a concerted effort to promote health tourism in a big way, which has resulted in a substantial increase in visitor arrivals to the state.

The bias towards health tourism in Kerala is so strong that Kerala Ayurveda Centres have been established at multiple locations in Kerala. The health tourism focus has seen Kerala participate in various trade shows and expos wherein the advantages of this traditional form of medicine are showcased.

Kerala has one of the best-qualified professionals in each and every field: Allopathi, Dental, Ayurveda, etc. This fact has now been recognised internationally. Regarding medical facilities, Kerala has the most competent doctors and world-class medical facilities. Tourists can get medical treatment in Kerala for a fraction of the cost compared to Europe or America. With competitive charges for treatment, Kerala is a very lucrative destination for people wanting to undergo treatment of certain medical problems who do not need immediate emergency treatment.

(Source: adapted from: www.hotelskerala.com, accessed May 2007)

Jet lag

Australia and New Zealand are destinations that involve flights of over 20 hours from the UK. Travelling to either of these countries means travelling through a number of time zones. New Zealand is 12 hours ahead of Greenwich Mean Time. Most people who travel long distances complain of jet lag – the sleeping problems and exhaustion that disrupt the first few days in a new time zone. Jet lag makes business travellers less productive and stops holidaymakers from enjoying their holiday. The symptoms of jet lag can sometimes last for a number of days.

Documentation requirements

For certain destinations it is necessary to have a visa for entry, e.g. Australia. Some visas are expensive, which could deter a person visiting as it adds additional costs to the holiday. Students on a gap year may not have sufficient funds to visit a number of countries that require money for visas. Some countries issue visas with restricted entry, e.g. a maximum of 30 days that visitors can stay. Another factor restricting the choice of destination to visit may be vaccination certificates. For example, Tanzania is an area where yellow fever is classed as endemic. This means that people visiting are at high risk of infection. Many of the endemic zones require a yellow fever certificate. Many countries will not permit entry to a destination if arriving from an infected area without a certificate.

The Foreign and Commonwealth Office (FCO) gives up-to-date advice on how to prepare for a trip abroad and advice on countries including those that pose potential risks to customers. It provides potential travellers with information about worldwide destinations.

Customer types

People visit long-haul destinations for a number of reasons: for leisure, for example, a holiday visiting friends and relatives or for the purpose of business. The National Statistics Travel Trends report on the 2005 international survey in Table 8.01 shows the significance of customer types for long-haul destinations. The statistics show that the purpose of leisure was more significant in the majority of countries than business.

Travelling for leisure can include a range of different customer types. There are students who take gap years from university. These customers often like to travel to a variety of different destinations. Many gap year students head to Australia, often via countries such as Thailand and Cambodia. Many will travel around the world and spend up to 12 months away from the UK.

ACTIVITY

Put together an itinerary for a gap year student. Think about places you might like to visit if you had a gap year. Research passport visa requirements, health restrictions including inoculations, Foreign and Commonwealth advice, and weather conditions for each destination you suggest.

Assessing the outcome

You work in the product development department of a leading long-haul tour operator. The managing director has requested that you investigate some of the long-haul destinations featured in its brochure. You have been specifically requested to research the different types of customer visiting different destinations featured in the brochure and the motivating factors affecting their choice. Prepare an email describing your findings.

- Select and describe different types of holidays offered by long-haul destinations for different types of customers, identifying both travel and motivating factors (**P2**).

The features making long-haul destinations appealing to different customer types

Accessibility can be important when choosing to travel abroad. Accessibility means the degree of ease with which travellers can get to and around a country. Some long-haul destinations are more accessible than others.

There are flights available to New York from a number of UK airports. Many of the flights are direct, meaning a traveller will not need to change planes to get to that destination. London Heathrow airport has five airlines operating direct flights to New York JFK airport and two airlines flying to New York Newark airport. (Figure 8.09) These airlines operate daily flights. The frequency of flights means more flexibility and choice for the potential traveller.

In contrast to New York with its choice of direct flights, destinations such as the Galapagos Islands, Ecuador, have no direct flights (see the case study, overleaf). Potential travellers would have to consider that they would need to make a number of flight changes to get to these islands. Due to the fact that there may be so many flights involved it is probable that travellers would need accommodation en route as flights may not connect. Having a number of flight changes also increases the travelling time, which for some people can deter them from choosing to visit.

BAA Heathrow

Scheduled Time	Flight Number	Departing To	Status	Terminal
		Thu 15 March 2007		
08:20	AA115	NEW YORK	SCHEDULED	Terminal Three
08:20	BA117	NEW YORK	SCHEDULED	Terminal Four
08:20	GF5115	NEW YORK	SCHEDULED	Terminal Three
09:30	CO8223	NEW YORK	SCHEDULED	Terminal Three
09:30	VS003	NEW YORK	SCHEDULED	Terminal Three
09:55	AA101	NEW YORK	SCHEDULED	Terminal Three
09:55	GF5101	NEW YORK	SCHEDULED	Terminal Three

(Source: www.heathrowairport.com, accessed Wednesday 14 March 2007)

Fig 8.05 BAA Heathrow, flights to New York

ACTIVITY

Look on a map to find out the location of the Galapagos Islands. Explain why these islands may not appeal to a family with young children.

Case study

Galapagos Islands

I had always wanted to visit the Galapagos Islands. From a young age I had heard about these remote islands. They are incredibly inaccessible but here live the most amazing species man could ever imagine: mammals, birds and plants vastly different to those of the UK. It is because man has not had easy access to these islands that they remain so unique.

When my special day arrived I was content for the journey to be a long one because I want the islands to remain a relatively undiscovered destination. I have seen too many places around the world ruined by tourism and I would hate to see this happen to the Galapagos Islands. I cannot bear to think of mass tourism spoiling such a beautiful place. Only those who will truly treasure and respect the islands should visit, so that they remain special for years to come.

My journey took me from Newcastle to London and then on to Madrid. I had to stay overnight in Madrid. The next morning I was at the airport for approximately 09.15 hrs. The flight left Madrid on time but it wasn't direct and we changed at Quito and Guayaquil. The final flight arrived at Guayaquil at 19.40 hrs. There were no connecting flights that night to the Galapagos Islands so another overnight stop was necessary. There was no opportunity to unpack and relax and although it was a long and tiring journey, this made me happy because I knew lots of tourists would not choose this destination because they would not want to travel for such a long time and have the inconvenience of several flights and overnight stopovers. On day three I finally landed at Isla Baltra, Galapagos Islands, Ecuador.

To see these enchanted islands there was more travelling: a coach to the port and a boat to the cruise ship. These islands can only be visited with a guided group from a ship.

These islands were my dream. That dream came true. They are filled with magic and wonder. On them live species that are not afraid of man and surrounding them undiscovered seas. To stay like this the Galapagos Islands must remain difficult to access so they attract only those who really desire to see them.

ACTIVITY

Research the accessibility of Fiji. Assess how easy it is to travel to Treasure Island in Fiji. Find out the frequency of flights, whether there are direct flights from the UK, flying time, other transport methods needed, etc.

Destination facilities can contribute to the appeal of a destination. Facilities can include natural attractions, e.g. whether there are mountains to climb or see or beaches to lie on. The Maldives (Figure 8.06) has many natural attractions that contribute to its appeal.

The appeal of a destination can also include built attractions such as theme parks and museums. Orlando has a range of built attractions that make it appealing to families.

Fig. 8.06 The Maldives

ACTIVITY

Look at the image of the Maldives. In pairs discuss the appeal of the natural attractions featured in the image.

Case study

Fig 8.07 Universal Studios

Universal Studios

Jump right into the action of your favourite movies at Universal Studios®. At this real working motion-picture studio you'll go behind the scenes and beyond the screen as you experience an incredible array of rides, shows, movie sets and attractions. Plunge into total darkness on a psychological thrill ride 3000 years in the making – Revenge of the Mummy[SM] The Ride. See, hear and feel the action through the miracle of OgreVision in Shrek 4-D™. Rocket through the worlds of your favourite Nicktoons® on Jimmy Neutron's Nicktoon Blast™. Zap aliens on MEN IN BLACK™ Alien Attack™, an amazing interactive ride based on the hit movies. It's never the same ride twice! Save the future of humanity in the action-packed TERMINATOR 2®: 3-D. Hold on tight as you're blown away by TWISTER… Ride It Out®. And have a ball in Woody Woodpecker's KidZone®, where you'll find the delightful stage show Animal Actors on location![sm]. It's all at Universal Studios®, the number 1 movie and TV-based theme park in the world!

Universal elements and all related indicia TM & © 2007 Universal Studios. All rights reserved.

(Source: www.virginholidays.co.uk, accessed May 2007)

Fig 8.08 Magic Kingdom Park

Magic Kingdom Park

Enchanting tales and magical adventures await the whole family at the Magic Kingdom Park through Disney tickets. The Magic Kingdom Park consists of seven fantasy lands, entrancing the young and young at heart in a world of fun and excitement.

With your Disney ticket, step back in time to an age of innocence on Main Street, USA. In Fantasyland, relive childhood dreams with all your favourite Disney classics, then feel the American spirit in Liberty Square. Experience a taste of the Wild West in Frontierland, where you will plunge down Splash Mountain with Brer Rabbit, and encounter an ancient Indian legend in a runaway goldmine car at the amazing Big Thunder Mountain Railroad. Make your way along mysterious rivers in the exciting Jungle Cruise and fly over ancient lands on The Magic Carpets of Aladdin in Adventureland. In Tomorrowland, you can pilot your own intergalactic cruise in Buzz Lightyear's Space Ranger Spin, or hurtle through space on Space Mountain!

You could not consider visiting the Magic Kingdom park without paying a visit to Mickey's house and all your favourite Disney characters at Mickey's Toontown Fair, then at loveable Goofy's Wiseacres Farm, brave 'The Barnstormer'!

The child in everyone comes alive through the magical, timeless Disney stories when you use your Disney tickets to visit Magic Kingdom Park – the only

Continued

ACTIVITY

Research other built attractions in Orlando. Explain how these built attractions contribute to the appeal of tourists.

Fig 8.09 Mickey Mouse

place where it is 'once upon a time' each and every day!

(Source: www.orlando-ticket-deals.co.uk, accessed May 2007)

SeaWorld

There's no place on earth like SeaWorld® Orlando. From Orlando's tallest, fastest, longest and only 'floorless' coaster, Kraken® to encountering creatures of the deep up close and personal, SeaWorld is a truly unique experience. Try two of the steepest, fastest, wettest drops in the world on the Journey to Atlantis® water coaster, then as you're wet go and get soaked again watching the world famous killer whale Shamu®.

Use your SeaWorld® Orlando Ticket to:

- Plunge into the frozen north on a virtual jetcopter ride to the Wild Arctic®
- View and touch Atlantic Bottlenose Dolphins at Dolphin Cove®, the most innovative dolphin habitat in the world
- Challenge Kraken®, the only floorless coaster in Orlando
- Experience the dazzling all-new dolphin spectacular, Blue Horizons
- Journey To Atlantis®, a super-charged water coaster of mythic proportions
- Attempt to stay dry when the world famous Shamu comes a splashing!

© 2005 Busch Entertainment Corporation. All Rights Reserved.

(Source: www.americanattractions.co.uk, accessed May 2007)

Fig 8.10 Raffles hotel, Singapore

ACTIVITY

Explain the type of customer you think the Raffles hotel would appeal to? Explain how Raffles adds appeal to Singapore. Find out how many awards the hotel has won.

ACTIVITY

Explain why hostels would appeal to gap year students.

Accommodation is another type of facility that can give a destination appeal. There are a number of destinations or 'resorts' that have exclusive accommodation, which is appealing to customers. One of the most famous hotels is Raffles in Singapore (Figure 8.10).

Hostels are budget accommodation typically in dormitory style. Younger people, such as gap year travellers, usually use this type of accommodation. This is why they are sometimes called youth hostels (Figure 8.11). These hostels encourage outdoor activities such as walking and offer the chance to

Fig 8.11 A youth hostel

share cultural experiences. Many hostels will have communal areas in which to cook and eat.

Food and drink can attract visitors to a destination. This can be because the destination offers different cuisine to that available at home or because it is a destination famous for its cuisine. Thailand has a number of features that make the country appealing. The food in Thailand is one of the contributing features. Thai cuisine is so popular that cookery courses are now offered while on holiday.

Case study

Capture the true flavour

Part of the pleasure of travel is to explore new cuisines and discover local ingredients. Thai food has inspired many travellers and with some skilled tuition it is eminently possible to recreate those flavours at home. Our two properties in Thailand offer dedicated professionally run schools.

(Source: www.mandarinoriental.com, accessed May 2007)

ACTIVITY

Research the cuisine available in China. Produce a menu featuring traditional food.

Culture is a feature that can make a destination appealing. Culture covers festivals, events, art, dance, music, religion, beliefs, customers, behaviour, etc.

Events around the world can draw people to the destination. These can include carnivals such as the Rio de Janeiro Carnival in Brazil, which is currently one of the biggest festivals in the world. It attracts hundreds of thousands of visitors every year.

Sporting events such as the Olympics Games add appeal to a destination. This is why destinations bid to host the Olympics. Beijing is to host the 2008 Summer Olympics and Vancouver the 2010 Winter Olympics.

ACTIVITY

Research how often the Olympic Games take place and which long-haul destinations have hosted the Summer and Winter Olympics. Assess the appeal of the 2008 Olympics in Beijing.

ACTIVITY

Research when the Rio de Janeiro Carnival takes place. Find out why this is such a popular event.

Assessing the outcome

You are a travel journalist. You have been asked to write a feature on a long-haul destination of your choice. The subject of the article is to describe the features that contribute to the appeal of the long-haul destination you choose.

- Describe the features that contribute to the appeal of a selected long-haul destination for different customer types (**P3**).

How to plan a long-haul tour

When planning a long-haul tour it will normally include a range of transport options. The first part of the tour will involve transportation to the destination. This could be a cruise, however it is more likely to be a flight as not all long-haul destinations are accessible by sea. Many flights used to access long-haul destinations are scheduled flights. These types of flights offer different classes of travel, e.g. first class, business and economy class. The prices of these vary significantly. It will depend upon the type of tour and the itinerary as to whether further air transportation or surface transportation is needed. This will also depend on the distances intended to travel. For example, a tour may start in Cairns, Australia, then go to Sydney. The distance is approximately 1600 miles. To drive this distance would take days. Visitors may not have the time or wish to spend the time travelling such distances by road or rail. For some long-haul destinations there is not always the option to choose methods of transport within a country.

Accommodation in long-haul destinations differs significantly. Some destinations have a range of accommodation to choose from. The range could include types of accommodation such as self-catering, hotels, hostels, etc., and also the standard of accommodation available.

ACTIVITY

Compare the types and standard of accommodation available in Hong Kong and Bamburi Beach in Kenya.

The quality of accommodation can also vary. For example, the hotels in Dubai are far superior in terms of service and standard to those in countries such as Bolivia. Dubai is home to the seven-star hotel, the Burj Al Arab Hotel. Here is a description of the hotel:

> **Soaring skyward like the sail of a huge dhow, the futuristic tower of this spectacular hotel is a landmark as exclusive as it is unique. Adjectives such as sumptuous, lavish and luxurious barely come close to describing the amazing interior of this innovative resort. With today's technology and ancient traditions, it is the very essence of Dubai.**

When organisations such as tour operators plan accommodation to be used in their brochures it will depend on the type of accommodation that is available within the destination. Tour operators arranging holidays need to make sure that the accommodation is appropriate to meet the needs of the customer. For example, in Australia and Canada many customers like to have the flexibility of having a motor home so they can travel where they wish and when they wish. Families may want accommodation that has entertainment on site and/or a swimming pool.

Fig 8.12 The Burj Al Arab Hotel, Dubai: a seven-star hotel

Inevitably most people visiting long-haul destinations for the purpose of leisure will want to see some attractions. They could be natural attractions such as mountains or beaches or built attractions like Disneyland in Los Angeles or Disney World in Florida. Look at the natural attractions featured in the Kuoni Primate Safari Tour in Rwanda (see box, opposite). The tour includes visiting forest reserves, rivers, lakes and volcano peaks as well as the opportunity to see an abundance of wildlife.

ACTIVITY

Plan a three-week itinerary for a couple in their fifties wishing to visit South Africa. Include at least five top attractions.

When planning a long-haul tour it is easy to become too preoccupied with the content of the tour and forget about associated costs. It is important to work within the customer's budget. For some destinations this may mean reconsidering the type of accommodation or the standard of accommodation. For example, hotels on certain exclusive islands such as Mauritius can be expensive.

Primate Safari

Day 1 Fri Fly overnight from Heathrow to Nairobi.

Day 2 Sat On arrival transfer by private car to the Nairobi hotel for one night.

Day 3 Sun Fly to Kigali and after a briefing depart to Butare, the intellectual and cultural heart of Rwanda. Visit the King's Palace at Nyanza. After lunch drive to the Nyungwe Forest Reserve via Gikongoro with optional visit to the genocide memorial site. Dinner and overnight at the Gisakura guesthouse.

Day 4 Mon After an early breakfast enter the Nyungwe Forest Reserve in search of the resident primates. The reserve extends across the majestic hills of south-east Rwanda and is the largest mountain forest remaining in East Africa. Of the larger mammals, primates are the most visible in Rwanda, with 13 recorded species representing 25 per cent of the African primate checklist, including chimpanzees, colobus monkeys, grey-checked mangabeys and red-tailed monkeys. Nyungwe is also home to more than 275 bird species. After lunch you will be driven to Cyangungu on the shores of Lake Kivu where you can bathe from a small beachfront.

Day 5 Tue Today drive to Gisenyi and then on to a lodge in Kigali at the base of the volcanoes.

Day 6 Wed After breakfast report to the Volcano Park for formalities and then on to the edge of the Volcanoes National Park where there is a briefing by the park's guide before tracking the gorillas. If time permits, a visit to Lakes Bulera and Ruhondo will take place before heading back to Kigali.

Day 7 Thu Depart for Kigali and the flight to Nairobi for one night at the Serena hotel.

Day 8 Fri Return to Heathrow, arriving the next day.

(Source: adapted from Kuoni brochure: *Luxury Lodges/Rwanda*)

ACTIVITY

A customer wishes to book three nights in Muscat, Oman, departing the first week in June. They want a double room in a hotel for less than £90 per night. Using the internet find out the choices the customer has within their budget. Now compare this to where they could stay on the same budget in Phuket, Thailand.

When planning a long-haul tour a customer will want all vital information for travel as well as costs and what is included in the tour. Travel agents and tour operators will present the tour as a basic itinerary. In the travel brochures this will just highlight the places to visit. Once booked, this will be presented as a more detailed itinerary. For example, the itinerary could include travel details such as transport arrangements, as shown in the example below.

1. *Check-in details* – customers will need to know how many hours before their flight they are required to check in at an airport. For long-haul flights this tends to be three hours before departure. If customers' itineraries include additional flights while abroad, they will need to know the relevant check-in times. Some may be domestic flights with less time needed for check-in.

2. *Flight numbers and the airline's name* should be presented on the itinerary. All flight numbers should be given.

3. *Departure and arrival times* should be given, preferably using the 24-hour clock to avoid any confusion e.g. 02.00 hrs rather than 2 o'clock, as the latter could be morning or afternoon.

4. *Class of travel* should be apparent on the itinerary to avoid any confusion at the airport or when boarding the plane. If customers have booked first class, details of access to the first-class lounge should be given.

5. *Luggage information* – information as to when the customer should reclaim their luggage. Customers need to be aware of whether they need to collect luggage at each airport or whether the airline will check in luggage to the final destination

6. *Accommodation details* should be presented, e.g. the hotel name as well as contact details. When a tour operator is used then the booking agent's details should be given. Meal basis such as bed and breakfast or all-inclusive should be highlighted and the type of room allocated, e.g. twin- or double-bedded room.

7. The itinerary needs to include details of *any other planned transport*, e.g. train details from one resort to another, planned activities, e.g. a visit to an attraction such as Victoria Falls. Any costs to be paid by the customer should be stated, e.g. costs

payable locally. It should give advice on passport, visa and health requirements for all the destinations featured in the itinerary. Customers should be advised of currency restrictions, bank holidays or any activities that may affect their holiday, e.g. festivals.

There are a number of resources available to help you find out information in relation to planning a long-haul tour for customers. Tour operators' brochures are a starting point for reference to find out the types of holidays available and the key destinations.

Guidebooks have a wealth of information. *Lonely Planet*, *Rough Guides* and *Fodor's Guides* offer guidebooks specific to a wide range of destinations. There are books about a country or on a specific area or city – for example, *The Rough Guide to the USA* or *The Rough Guide to New York City*. These guidebooks cover everything a customer needs to know about a destination.

ACTIVITY

Visit the library and review two different travel guides on the same destination. Compare the information available for customers by looking to see whether the information is the same or different.

ACTIVITY

You work for a tour operator and receive the following enquiry.

To: enquiries@longhaul-specialists.co.uk
From: juanreed@email.com
Date: 05/05/2007
Re: Holiday request

I would like to find out what there is to see and do in Australia. I want to fly to Sydney early October for a three-week duration. I would like to see the key attractions.
Number of passengers: 2 adults
Duration: as above
I look forward to your quote and suggestions.
Thanks
Juan

Respond to Juan's email, making suggestions and requesting any missing information.

Assessing the outcome

You work in a travel agency. A customer telephones asking for information about a three-week holiday to Canada in August for her family. The customer states that she is restricted to the school holidays. She mentions that she is looking for a holiday to include the highlights of Canada and that all her family enjoy the outdoors. She tells you that she has heard that Canada has some wonderful hikes. She specifically has shown an interest in Banff, Calgary, Vancouver and Toronto. There will be four people in the party – two adults (in their forties) and two teenagers aged 14 and 17 years. The customer has suggested that they book domestic flights between major destinations. They have asked you to suggest a 21-day itinerary to include the four destinations and any other key areas they should visit. The family want to see as much as possible but their budget will only allow them to use standard accommodation and flights. You are required to plan this multi-centre long-haul tour for the customer.

Your manager is currently reviewing the resources available in the travel agency. You have been asked to send an email to your manager showing all the references used to put the long-haul tour together.

- Plan a multi-centre long-haul tour to meet a given visitor profile, showing references used (**P4**).

Improve your grade

Explain means to make a point clear and to give reasons or justification. In the context of this topic to achieve a higher grade it is necessary to explain in detail why different long-haul destinations attract visitors with different motivations, and how travel factors can influence choice of destination (**M1**). So it is necessary to look at different destinations and give reasons and justification as to why these destinations attract visitors with different motivators and reasons, or justification as to how the factors can influence the destination they choose.

For example, if you choose a destination such as Las Vegas, then you could consider the type of destination it is. Is it a business or leisure destination or both? What choices of holiday do potential customers have when choosing a place to visit here? Is there anywhere similar? Is it easy to get to? Will the customer be at risk of deep-vein thrombosis because of the flight? Is there any advice from the Foreign and Commonwealth office that may be off-putting to the potential customer?

Case study

Travel considerations

Denise and Lee are getting married on 11 August. They want to go on honeymoon straight after the wedding. Lee collected some brochures from his local travel agent, which they looked through one evening. To begin with, they thought the Caribbean looked appealing, however Denise remembered that her friend had been on holiday on Peter Island in the Caribbean in August 2004 when Hurricane Francis had swept close to where she was staying. Her friend had told her about being delayed and having to stay in her hotel room because there was a severe hurricane warning. The chance of hurricanes made them reconsider their choice. Denise had always wanted to go to Australia. When she looked into the flight times she realised that the flight was possibly over 24 hours, so it was too far to travel because her fiancé had suffered from deep vein thrombosis in the past and therefore could be at risk during a journey of such length. The doctor had advised he was able to travel but he needed to wear flight socks and was advised to avoid unnecessary long flights. After some deliberation the couple both agreed on the Seychelles.

ACTIVITY

Research the Seychelles to establish whether or not the choice is appropriate to the couple's needs.
Explain in detail the factors that may influence their choice. The explanation should be extended to include a more detailed account of why it is a more appropriate choice.

Assess means making a judgement based on evidence gathered. In the context of this topic to achieve a higher grade it is necessary to assess the significance of the key features that influence the appeal of a selected long-haul destination for different customer types (**M2**). To make a judgement, it is essential to explore the key features of a destination. For example, in making an assessment of Oahu, Hawaii, it is necessary to explore and gather facts about the features of the destination. Once this has been completed a judgement can then be made as to whether these features make the destination appealing. You could use a website, e.g. www.visit-oahu.com, which gives facts about the beaches on the island of Oahu (see the case study, overleaf). This information could be used to make a judgement as to the appropriateness of this destination for people wishing to book a beach holiday with water sports. It states that there are 112 miles of beaches surrounding Oahu. An assessment could be made as to how the beaches would rate against the beaches of other long-haul destinations and whether the features of the beaches would attract people to Oahu. Beaches are just one feature. In the assessment, other features covered in this unit must also be explored.

To access the distinction criteria (**D1**), it is essential to assess the success of long-haul destinations in meeting the needs of different types of visitor, and make feasible recommendations as to how a destination could minimise the effects of the factors that negatively affect its popularity. This judgement should consider a number of types of visitors, e.g. those for leisure and/or business, and what the needs of the customer may be, e.g. what a family would need in a destination. Facts will need to be explored so a judgement can be made as to how well the destination meets each of the different types of customer need.

A recommendation is advice on a course of action. So in this instance it is a recommendation as to how a destination could minimise or reduce the effects of the factors that negatively affect popularity. So, for example, if a destination had restrictions on entry such as visas, then the country could review its entry restrictions. If the visa was expensive to purchase, it could reduce the cost or consider giving visas without charge. This has been the case in India and Japan (see the case study, overleaf).

Case study

Beaches in Oahu

With crystal-clear waters, glistening white sand, and the warm rays of the sun, the beaches of Oahu offer a friendly, inviting experience in paradise. Oahu beaches also provide a range of exciting activities such as snorkelling, surfing, windsurfing, boogie boarding and kayaking. With the average water temperature ranging from 75 to 80 degrees F year round, it's easy to understand why visitors and locals alike are drawn to the gorgeous waterscape off the island of Oahu.

From the powerful, pounding waves of the North Shore, to the gentle break in Waikiki – whether you enjoy the crowds or prefer isolation – there is a beach on Oahu waiting for you. Snorkel next to schools of tropical fish at Hanauma Bay Nature Preserve, voted Best Beach in America for 2004. Learn to ride the same waves as ancient Hawaiian chiefs did along Waikiki Beach at one of Oahu's fine surf schools. Watch in awe as the world's best professional surfers carve up the North Shore's massive waves every winter. Bringing the whole family to Oahu? Numerous beaches around the island have picnic areas that are near the beach and facilities to accommodate the keiki.

With 112 miles of beaches surrounding the island of Oahu, the hardest thing to decide on is which beach to go to. Regardless of your choice, kick back, relax and soak in Oahu, paradise found.

(Source: www.visit-oahu.com, accessed May 2007)

Case study

Japan and India to relax visa restrictions

Razib Ahmed, 24 September 2006
It is always nice to find that more and more countries are now relaxing visa regimes. Of course, for business people, getting a visa quickly is always a top priority. I am happy that Japan and India have learnt their lessons and are going to make it easier for the business people of the two countries to visit each other's country. According to a report by Forbes.com: 'Japan and India will extend the period of validity of business visas issued to individuals working in each other's countries to five years, while easing regulations on tourist visas, the Nihon Keizai Shimbun reported.

The moves, aimed at promoting a greater flow of people between the nations, are expected to be agreed upon at a Japan–India summit slated to be held in December and implemented in 2007, the paper said.'

From the same report, I came to know that the two countries are going to relax the regulations for tourist visas too. Last year, 102,000 Japanese tourists came to India while 58,572 Indian tourists came to Japan. Hopefully, after the visa regime is relaxed, more people will visit the two countries.

(Source: www.indianraj.com, accessed May 2007)

ACTIVITY

Suggest other visa agreements that could be considered by governments to increase the number of tourists coming to a destination.

The *Collins Dictionary* definition of evaluation is 'to ascertain or set the amount or value. To judge or assess the worth of.' Evaluate means to put a value on after assessment. In the higher grading criteria it is possible after having assessed the key features to evaluate how a long-haul destination could capitalise on its facilities in order to influence its future development (**D2**). Having rated a feature as appealing, e.g. the beaches in Oahu, Hawaii, then it is possible to evaluate how Oahu could take advantage (capitalise) on these beaches to influence its future development. For example, it could capitalise on its beaches by using pictures of them in promotional activities such as featuring the beaches in brochures, on posters, in TV adverts, etc. The Tourist Board could work with film companies to try to encourage them to feature the beaches in a film. The evaluation is then a judgement of the worth of the destination and capitalising on these facilities.

ACTIVITY

Research a long-haul destination that attracts visitors because of its appealing climate. Discuss how the destination can capitalise on its feature climate. Evaluate how this suggestion could capitalise on its climate to influence its future development.

Top tips

- Focus on what the unit assessment is looking for.
- Make judgements.
- Use research to substantiate your conclusions.

Learning outcomes

By the end of this unit you should:

- understand the retail and business travel environments
- understand how advances in technology have affected retail and business travel operations
- understand how retail travel organisations seek to gain competitive advantage
- know how to produce complex itineraries for retail and business travel customers.

Retail and business travel environments

Travel agents are organisations that sell products and services to customers on behalf of suppliers. The products and services are those provided by the tour operators or producers, e.g. airlines. Travel agents receive a percentage of money from the suppliers for any products and services sold, e.g. the tour operators pay travel agents a small percentage of money for selling their package holidays. The percentage of money paid to the travel agents is called commission. Travel agents also provide a service to customers as they give travel advice, e.g. whether a destination is suitable for a customer. There are retail and business travel agents that are private-sector organisations; this means that in order to make a profit, they need to sell products and services to customers.

Business travel agents mainly deal direct with the producers, e.g. accommodation providers, transport providers. Retail travel agents will also deal with producers but most of their business links to the products and services of tour operators (sometimes referred to as wholesalers in the chain of distribution). Further information about the chain of distribution can be found in Unit 12, on tour operations.

Retail travel agents specialise in arranging travel for leisure customers. This is not to say that they will not arrange business travel but the bulk of the travel agent's income comes from people booking travel for the purpose of leisure. The majority of the products and services that they sell are tour operators' package holidays. Let us look at some examples of the range of package holidays commonly sold by retail travel agents.

Summer sun holidays are one of the most popular package holidays sold. The summer sun holiday product is usually available between late April and October. Tour operators such as Thomson, Cosmos, First Choice and Airtours put these holidays together.

ACTIVITY

Pick up a summer sun package holiday brochure from your local travel agent. Alternatively you can download it from the internet. Scrutinise the brochure to see if you can find out why this type of package holiday is a popular holiday sold through travel agents.

Winter sun holidays are another popular product sold through retail travel agents. These holidays are to destinations during the winter months of November to April. The destinations are those that have a warmer climate than that of the UK hence the term 'winter sun'.

Having a product to sell covering the winter and summer months means that retail travel agents have the potential to make commission all year round.

ACTIVITY

Look at the types of destinations featured in a First Choice winter sun brochure.

Retail travel agents have been selling significantly more long-haul destinations in recent years. There are a number of tour operators' brochures that retail travel agents will promote. Long-haul holidays are those to destinations in other continents than Europe around the world. Popular destinations booked by travel agents are to the Caribbean Islands, Florida, Goa, Kenya and Thailand.

ACTIVITY

Interview ten people to find out which top five long-haul destinations they would book a package holiday to through a retail travel agent.

ACTIVITY

Visit a travel agency. Look at the brochures displayed to find out which other package holidays it sells.

Retail travel agents also sell a range of other products and services such as scheduled airline seats, insurance, car hire, car parking and foreign exchange. These products and services are sold separately but retail travel agents will also sell them as additional products and services to the main purchase, e.g. the summer sun package holiday. When sold in addition to the main purchase, they are often referred to as ancillary products and services. Let us look at an example of when ancillary products and services are added to a holiday booking.

Case study

Helen and Colin Heinsson booked a holiday with their local travel agent. They booked a package holiday flying from Manchester to Gran Canaria. The holiday included seven nights' half-board in a four-star hotel. The travel agent booking the holiday found out the following information from the couple.

- They both enjoy exploring places that they visit but Colin suffers from travel sickness on coaches.
- Colin has a driving licence.
- They live 50 miles from Manchester airport.

What ancillary services could the travel agent offer Mr and Mrs Heinsson in this instance? First, it could suggest car hire while away. This would mean that the

couple can explore the island of Gran Canaria without Mr Heinsson getting travel sick. The travel agent could offer the couple car parking at Manchester airport as they live quite a distance from the airport. The travel agent could suggest a night's accommodation close to the airport before and/or after the flight. Many airport hotels offer a number of free nights' car parking at the hotel. The couple are travelling to Gran Canaria, which is in Spain. The currency used is Euros so the travel agent could offer to exchange some money.

ACTIVITY

In pairs, role play the selling of one of the additional ancillary products featured in the case study. One person should take the role of the customer and the other the role of the travel agent. Reverse roles once complete, this time using another ancillary product.

The travel agent can book ancillary products and services such as insurance, car hire and car parking through the tour operator. Alternatively they can book the ancillary products and services direct through the supplier, e.g. directly through a car hire company. Travel agents often prefer to book the ancillary services direct as they get paid more commission from direct ancillary suppliers than tour operators.

ACTIVITY

Research why a travel agent sells foreign currency and traveller's cheques.

Explain why you think travel agents try to sell additional products and services such as currency to customers.

There are different types of retail and business travel agents. The most common names are those of multiple retail travel agents. These types of retail travel agent are organisations that have a number of branches (shops). They are usually found throughout the UK in major towns and cities. Thomson is an example of a multiple travel agent. It currently has over 700 shops, which can be found all over the UK,

Fig 9.01 A foreign exchange is inside this travel agency

e.g. London, Manchester and Edinburgh. The reason multiple travel agencies such as Thomson have grown is because they have merged with a number of independent or 'miniple' travel agents. For example, Thomson bought Callers Pegasus Travel Service, which was a miniple travel agent in the north-east.

Independent travel agents are private organisations. They usually consist of one or a few branches. The owner will often work in the travel agency, in many cases in the role of manager as well as director. An example of an independent travel agency is Travel Centre (Norwich) Ltd.

Miniple travel agents have fewer branches than multiple travel agencies. They can, however, have a number of branches. They are located in one region or area, e.g. the south-east of England. An example of a miniple travel agency is Hays Travel in the north-east of England.

A recent addition that is growing fast is the e-agent. These are travel agents that sell through the internet. Lastminute.com is an example of a retail e-agent. It can arrange a number of holidays for customers ranging from package holidays through to accommodation only.

Recently travel agents have been facing difficult times and for some travel agents this has meant

Case study

Travel Centre

Travel Centre is one of the longest-established truly independent travel agency groups in East Anglia, serving customers across Norfolk, Suffolk and beyond. We aim to provide a personal service, no matter how you contact us – whether by phone, email or visiting one of our branches. By looking after every aspect of your holiday we can save you time and money, as well as making the whole process more enjoyable!

How will you benefit from booking with Travel Centre?

Save time and money – we can arrange everything from package holidays, flights, tailor-made trips, cruises, insurance, finding you the best deal and doing all the work for you.

Peace of mind – with 45 years in the travel business, you are dealing with a reputable and strong company – your holiday is in safe and reliable hands.

We know...we go – we regularly send staff on educational trips overseas so they have first-hand experience of numerous destinations and, of course, they love travelling for their own holidays too.

(Source: www.travel-centre.co.uk, accessed May 2007)

ACTIVITY

Research other travel agents in the UK. You should look through the *Yellow Pages*, search on the internet and read trade magazines such as *Travel Weekly* and *Travel Trade Gazette*. Categorise the examples found into a list of business and retail travel agents. Now subcategorise your findings into multiple, miniple and independent travel agents. Did any of the travel agents found have both retail and business departments?

ACTIVITY

Look on the internet at Lastminute.com and see which products and services it sells.
Compare these products with those of a high-street travel agent.

Case study

Hays: 'I'd never sell my staff out'

Hays Travel managing director John Hays has said he would never sell out to a giant such as Thomas Cook because all his staff would soon be made redundant.

Addressing industry peers at an ITT Odyssey supper in the House of Commons, just days after the announcement that Cook is to merge with MyTravel, the north-east-based independent agent said: 'I have no plans to sell. We employ a lot of people [700] and I would feel very guilty if we were to sell to a Thomas Cook, as those jobs would go.

'We know those jobs would go from Sunderland if I was to sell to Cook,' he said. 'I would want to sell to someone who would keep those jobs going.'

Hays' comments come as thousands of MyTravel and Cook staff face an uncertain future from 22 May, when the deal is expected to be completed.

The Hays Travel chief claimed to have received guarantees from Cook and MyTravel that the combined business would continue to work with independent agents once the merger was completed.

'Both Airtours [MyTravel] and Thomas Cook have a good reputation in terms of working with the trade and with independent agents, and I have had assurances from Ian Derbyshire at Cook and Steve Barrass at MyTravel that will continue,' he said.

'Consolidation was needed in the industry and I genuinely see a future for independent agents.'

Hays claimed his 32 shops made their highest-ever profit last year, with foreign-exchange sales particularly strong.

'Retail makes good profits,' he said. 'We are opening two more shops.'

The company's Independence Group consortium of 130 independent agents was profitable for the group and members, according to Hays.

But he admitted: 'Call centres are a problem. We lost one of ours last year. The Teletext market is very difficult. It is a declining market on analogue and the cost of acquiring new clients is very expensive.'

(Source: Lucy Huxley, *Travel Trade Gazette*, 1 March 2007)

---

closing branches. Look at the article from The *Independent* newspaper, which describes what is happening to Thomson travel agents (see the case study, opposite).

> **Since 2001, the greatest decline in high street presence has come from MyTravel's Going Places outlets (139 closures) and Worldchoice (277 closures). Thomas Cook and Thomson closures have been less severe, and the latter remains Britain's largest high street agent with 776 stores.**

(Source: *Mintel's Travel Agent Report, October 2006*)

ACTIVITY

Research past articles from *Travel Trade Gazette* or *Travel Weekly* to find out if there have been any recent mergers or closures of retail or business travel agents.

Business travel agents book travel arrangements for organisations wishing to organise travel for their employees. The products mainly sold by business travel agents are rail, scheduled flights and accommodation. They operate in the same way as retail travel agents, however their customers are specifically businesses. The business customers may travel around the world but the purpose of this is business rather than leisure. The needs of the business customer are different from those of people travelling for leisure.

ACTIVITY

Ask a member of staff how their needs differ when travelling for business rather than for leisure.

How do the customer needs differ between retail and business travel? A customer travelling for work will probably need flexibility and convenience. For example, a business meeting time may change so flights or train tickets might need to be amended or cancelled. In order to have a flight or rail ticket that provides flexibility and no cancellation charges, flexible tickets need to be booked. The type of ticket used to allow such flexibility will cost significantly more than the average cost. Ticket prices change regularly but at the time of writing the cost of a

Thomson Holidays axes 2600 UK jobs

The owner of Thomson Holidays today said it would cut 2600 jobs in the UK as part of a Europe-wide restructuring programme.

TUI is cutting a total of 3600 posts in its tourism division, but said the UK will be more strongly affected by the job cuts since market changes have been far more dramatic in the UK compared with central Europe.

The German travel group did not immediately provide details of the cuts in the UK, where it owns former Lunn Poly travel agent shops.

Thomson has about 730 travel shops in the UK, which have had to compete, of late, with the rise of internet bookings.

TUI employs about 8000 staff in the UK.

Thomson has been the UK's biggest holiday company for many years but its takeover by the German company TUI has coincided with a complete change in the way people book holidays.

The huge increase in internet bookings coupled with the rise of the low-cost carriers has brought about a sea-change in the holiday business.

There are far more people now prepared to tailor-make their own trips, with the package holiday now playing second fiddle to adventure trips and short, city breaks.

TUI said the job losses were part of a cost-cutting programme aimed at saving 250 million Euros (£168m) in the tourism division by 2008.

It also announced a new German flight business under the brand TUIfly.com, as well as the establishment of a new Europe-wide internet portal for flights, the expansion of its hotel business and entry into the high-volume cruise market through a joint venture with the world's biggest operator, Carnival.

TUI said the changes to its tourism division were necessary in order to reflect lower margins, as internet operators and low-cost airlines have heightened competition, particularly in the UK.

Chief executive Michael Frenzel said: 'We therefore have to get fit for the future now, from a position of strength. Improvements in our cost structure in combination with profitable growth in new and existing business segments are the only way to ensure our future strength.'

Gerry Doherty, general secretary of the Transport Salaried Staffs Association, said: 'We are very disturbed that the UK seems to be bearing the brunt of these job cuts, when budget airlines have hit package holidays across Europe.

'We hope it is not the fact that the UK's weaker labour laws make it easier to get rid of workers than it is on the continent.'

Mr Doherty said he was seeking urgent talks with Thomson about the job losses, adding: 'If the company doesn't enter into serious talks, we will propose a TUC boycott of Thomson Holidays.'

(Source: Graeme Evans and Peter Woodman, Press Association. The *Independent*, 15 December 2006)

standard open return ticket from Leeds to London with the railway company GNER was advertised as £175, however on the same service GNER was advertising restricted tickets from £19 return, see Figure 9.02.

Why do flights differ in cost? There is a range of fare types available to customers. Business and first-class seats are significantly more expensive than economy. Leisure customers will be more reluctant to pay extra for a flexible flight. Business people however want, or even need, the flexibility. The person travelling for work is often not the person paying for the travel. Instead the organisation meets the cost and

Fig 9.02 London to Leeds £19 return with GNER, over a restricted period

therefore the individual travelling for business is less concerned about the price. The leisure person, although wanting flexibility, is less likely to cancel travel arrangements. They tend to book cheaper restricted fares because they are paying and in some cases cannot afford to pay the high fares paid by business people.

fee. According to ABTA it 'now represents over 6000 travel agencies and 850 tour operations, throughout the British Isles'. The main aims of ABTA are 'to maintain the high standards of service amongst Members which its famous symbol has come to signify, and to create as favourable a business climate as possible for its Members'.

ACTIVITY

Investigate the cost of a return flight from London to Los Angeles.
- Find the cheapest flight available.
- Find the cost of a flexible economy ticket.
- Find the cost of a flexible business ticket.
- Find the cost of a first-class flexible ticket.

Explain why the fares differ in price.

ACTIVITY

Interview a senior member of staff at your school or college to find out about the products they buy for both business and leisure travel. Find out whether price and flexibility play an important part in the purpose of travel. Ask the staff member whether they would pay the business prices if they had to pay them themselves. Discuss your findings with the rest of your class.

In terms of accommodation, the product also differs between retail and business travel agents. Leisure customers will have leisure time to stay in accommodation because they are on holiday and do not have work to do during the day. Business people, however, are travelling for a purpose (work) so they have limited time for leisure. The product sold then differs. People travelling on business want business facilities in a hotel, such as internet connections and room service. Many leisure customers' priority will be entertainment and leisure facilities such as tennis courts and a swimming pool. The properties booked by business people tend to be in major cities such as Paris rather than holiday resorts like Magaluf.

The products sold by business travel agents are mainly scheduled airline seats for a wide range of airlines, e.g. British Airways, Emirates, Singapore Airlines. The accommodation that they sell tends to be four- or five-star hotels. Business travel agents will sell well-known chains such as Marriott and Hilton.

Both retail and business travel agents can be members of The Travel Association (ABTA). The Association is one which requires the travel agent to join. Each member is required to pay a membership

ABTA operates a bonding scheme whereby customers booking with ABTA members have their holidays protected should the travel agent or tour operator cease trading. Travel agents often display the ABTA logo in their shop windows to tell customers that they are ABTA members, see Figure 9.03.

Fig 9.03 ABTA logo

ACTIVITY

Look at the ABTA website: www.abta.co.uk. Find out the benefits to a travel agent of becoming an ABTA member.

IATA stands for International Air Transport Association. Many travel agents have an IATA licence but business travel agents will nearly all have one. Having an IATA licence means that the travel agent is able to sell and issue scheduled airline tickets. For business agents, it is important they have this licence as the majority of their business is scheduled air tickets. In order to obtain an IATA licence, strict criteria applies – for example, staff are required to have sufficient experience and training.

ACTIVITY
Find out about other licences that retail and business travel agents have.

Travel agents are paid commission. Airlines until recent years used to pay agents approximately 9 per cent for international flights and 7 per cent for domestic flights. With the growing pressure within the travel industry and with the development of technology, airlines have cut commission levels dramatically. Recently many other suppliers have been reducing commission so some travel agents have been forced to charge a booking fee on certain bookings. Look at the newspaper article featured in the *Observer*, which examines how the cuts affect travel agents (see box, below).

ACTIVITY
In small groups, discuss the impact of commission level changes on the customer and the retail travel agent.

Retail travel agents have preferred tour operators that they promote and sell. For many multiple retail travel agents these are tour operators that they are vertically integrated with. Vertical integration is where linking occurs along the production process, e.g. when a tour operator owns a travel agent – for example, MyTravel owns Going Places. One other reason a travel agent promotes a preferred operator is because it has preferred commission rates, i.e. the tour operator or producer pays the travel agent higher commission compared to other tour operators and/or producers. So how do preferred operators work? First, the agent will promote the preferred operators in preference to other suppliers by positioning their brochures and other promotional materials in a prominent position, i.e. at eye level and in a position the customer will see as soon as they walk into the travel agency. Second, the travel agent may suggest booking the preferred operator first. This is provided that the supplier's product matches the customers' needs and wants. Travel agents will promote their preferred operators, e.g. window displays will show, more often than not, preferred operators.

ACTIVITY
Visit a multiple retail travel agent. Try to determine which brochures the organisation is giving preferred positioning, i.e. which brochures are in prominent positions. After visiting the agency investigate if the tour operators found in the prominent positions are linked with the agency.

How much...commission do travel agents get?

Travel agents become misty-eyed when they think back to a decade ago. Then, airlines paid handsomely for their services, with a standard commission of 9 per cent for international flights and 7 per cent for domestic. Booking a business-class return to Bangkok, for example, could net several hundred pounds' commission for just 15 minutes work. But the budget carriers started selling direct through call centres, then the internet, and the big boys followed suit. As airlines became less reliant on agents, they slashed commissions.

Today, there is a huge variation, so your choice of airline can have a big impact on how much the agent makes. For selling an American Airlines ticket to New York, for example, the agent will receive no commission. Persuade you to go for Eos, and they will get 10 per cent. Other big payers include the Middle East airlines Eithad and Emirates. If you want a nose into what your agent is making from you, go to www.abtamembers.org/commissions/index.htm.

(Source: The *Observer*, 25 February 2007, copyright Guardian News & Media Ltd 2006)

Fig 9.04 A travel agent's window display

Assessing the outcome

You are a travel and tourism student on placement working for the World Travel Market. You have been asked to produce promotional materials that describe the relationship between retail and business travel agents and other sectors of the travel and tourism industry, giving examples, where appropriate. These materials are going to be used on a stand at the World Travel Market.

- Describe the retail and business travel environment including the relationship between retail and business travel agents and other sectors of the travel and tourism industry, using examples where appropriate (**P1**).

How advances in technology have affected retail and business travel operations

Technology advances have brought new challenges to travel agents. The development of technology has

meant that travel agents have many more sophisticated booking systems available to help them make customer travel arrangements as well as systems to store customers' data. The internet is one example of a technological advance that has impacted on both business and retail travel agents.

The internet provides an easy and quick way for customers to research as well as book their own travel arrangements. They can do this from the comfort of their own home, at the office or even in internet cafés. The internet is available 24 hours a day, 365 days of the year, so this makes the buying process convenient for customers to access. Consequently, more and more customers are booking travel arrangements themselves rather than using the travel agent. There has been a lot of research carried out to see whether this is affecting the retail and business travel sector. Nielsen/NetRatings, Adviva and Harvest Digital carried out some research in 2006 to find out the online travel habits of UK consumers. Their research revealed that only 7 per cent of internet users now book on the high street (Figure 9.05).

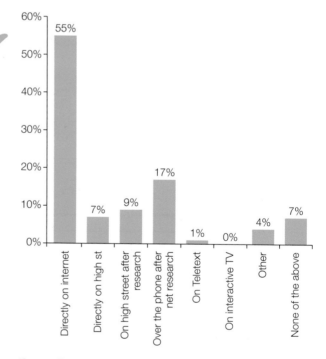

(Source: Research by Nielsen Net Ratings for Harvest Digital and Adviva, 2006)

Fig 9.05 How do you usually buy your holidays?

This would suggest that there has been a significant increase in internet bookings; however, Mintel research found that, in 2006, 42 per cent of overseas holidays were sold through travel agents. This represented 19.7 million trips. The research also revealed the following:

> Almost one in ten (9.1%) consumers use agents to book holidays of 21 nights or more, suggesting considerable potential in the 'holidays of a lifetime' and 'round-the-world' sectors.

(Source: www.mintel.com, accessed May 2007)

This evidence suggests that a significant amount of business is still booked through travel agents rather than directly with suppliers.

ACTIVITY

Look at a recent ABTA statistics and trends 2005 report (available at www.abta.co.uk). Compare the findings relating to internet usage to book holidays with the statistics highlighted in Figure 9.05.

Technology has meant changes to air transportation. So how does this affect the travel agent? Now a weekend break booked by travel agents is not just a break to Blackpool or Paris, instead Dubai or New York are becoming much more common. Aircraft can now travel at faster speeds and can run more efficiently meaning that destinations such as Dubai and New York are a lot cheaper. Travel agents can persuade customers to buy a flight or package to these destinations much more easily as the prices are not significantly more than the price of short-haul city destinations. The time to get to destinations such as New York or Dubai is also more feasible now for a short break.

Technology has meant that the booking process is much quicker. Travel agents are able to access tour operators' and producers' booking systems and know instantly whether there is availability for the products and services they require to book for their customers. Technology has advanced to enable airlines to have booking systems that process and generate e-tickets. This provides much easier booking systems as well as aiding travel agents to sell more globally. For business travel agents this has meant they can easily book flight tickets for customers to travel the same day. They do not need couriers to deliver airline tickets, instead the business travel agent can email the booking confirmation reference to the customer. They are only required to present this reference instead of a flight ticket.

Since 2000, there has been a significant growth in budget airlines. One reason for this is the internet, which is enabling airlines to cut costs by selling direct to the customer. Budget airlines such as Ryanair and easyJet only sell direct to the customer meaning they do not pay travel agents any commission for sales.

So how do budget airlines affect travel agents? Well in the initial stages of growth travel agents were losing business to the budget airlines. Flights were offered at prices customers could not refuse: sometimes as little as 1p per flight. This specifically affected the short break holidays sold through travel agents. At first the travel agents did not book these flights, as they did not gain any commission.

What did travel agents do to retrieve some of the business? A number of them started selling the budget airline seats and adding a booking fee for the privilege of the travel agent booking the flight seat on the customer's behalf. They also offered customers ancillary services such as accommodation, airport car parking, etc. So why would people book these if they can book them themselves without a fee? It might seem ridiculous to pay more for a flight but booking through the travel agent gives the customer the added advantage of security. For those customers worried about the risk of credit card fraud, they can pay the travel agent by other forms of payment. Another reason travel agents are able to book these flights is because the customer may not wish to spend time looking on the booking system. Instead they can simply tell the travel agent what they are looking for and the travel agent does all the searching. Another reason customers may not wish to book online is they want the opportunity to have that face-to-face contact and ask the travel agent questions. This is not always possible when making purchases online.

The case study overleaf shows some examples of how technology has improved the travel agent's process. In this case study Matt has been able to find the holiday using ViewData. ViewData is an online booking system that shows up-to-date availability of tour operators' products. Having a system like this means that Matt can see immediately the availability of the products. This system is much quicker and more cost effective than telephoning every tour operator individually. If Matt had to rely on the telephone system then he would either need another telephone to ring Mrs Tjernstrom or he would have to ring Mrs Tjernstrom and then ring the tour operator back. The probability is if there is only one room left, then it may be sold to another travel agent.

Case study

Technology

Matt is a home-worker travel agent. He receives a phone call from Mrs Tjernstrom enquiring about a ski holiday in France. She wishes to travel on the 18 February to Val Thorens for a week with her husband. Matt takes Mrs Tjernstrom's details and checks on ViewData. He finds a special offer for £179 per person based in a four-star hotel on half-board. The holiday matches all Mrs Tjernstrom's requirements. He phones her immediately as he knows it is a great deal and there is only one room left. He speaks to Mrs Tjernstrom, who decides to book the holiday. She pays for the holiday by credit card.

ACTIVITY

Investigate how technology has improved payment methods. Discuss how this affects the Technology case study.

Assessing the outcome

You work for a business travel agency. It is considering purchasing a retail travel agency. Before it makes this purchase it is keen to research more about the affects of technology. You have been seconded for two weeks to research technological advances affecting both the retail and business operations.

- Describe how technological advances have affected retail and business operations (**P2**).

How retail travel organisations seek to gain competitive advantage

Travel agents are all selling products of producers or wholesalers. They sell them in return for commission. By selling the products, they make money so it is important that they sell as many holidays as possible because without sales there is no income for the organisation. Travel agents are also competing with other travel agents, producers and wholesalers.

So how do travel agents gain competitive advantage? Promotional activities are one option available. However, by discounting or offering low deposits then a travel agent loses some of its profits. For example, if a customer books a holiday then the tour operator requires a deposit if the booking is outside of 56 days before departure. This is often in the region of about £130 to £150 per person. As an incentive to get customers to book the holiday early, travel agents may offer the customer the option to pay a low deposit of £10 per person. The low deposit is on the understanding that the customer pays the remainder of the deposit by the date set by the travel agent. The idea is that customers will be able to commit to the booking even if they have not got the immediate funds at that point in time. Having a low deposit gives the travel agent competitive advantage over other travel agents who may be asking for the full deposit. Customers would be more likely to book with the travel agent offering the lowest deposit fee. Travel agents offering low deposits need to get customers to sign a disclaimer, which is a legally binding document. This disclaimer assures the travel agent that the customer intends to pay the remaining deposit by the agreed date set. The disclaimer must be signed as once the booking is confirmed then the travel agent will be committed to pay the tour operator the full deposit. If the customer cancelled the holiday, then they are still liable for the remaining deposit.

Having low deposit schemes means that travel agents have to pay out money without receiving the full monies in. This can affect their cash flow. For some smaller travel agents, this could mean they need to arrange overdraft loans from banks. There are, however, some tour operators that are preferred operators as they may extend the payment date of the deposit until the customer pays. Either way the travel agent is committed to pay the tour operator the full deposit.

Market share for a travel agent is the percentage of business the travel agent has with its suppliers, e.g. the percentage of bookings made with a supplier in the town or city in which they operate in relation to other travel agents. The higher market share of bookings per supplier means that the travel agent will have received more sales, which should equate to more profit unless they have given the profit away in discounts. Either way, travel agents aim to gain as much market share as possible. The advantage to the organisation of having more market share includes more automatic delivery of holiday brochures. For example, if a travel agency sells lots of holidays from Kuoni worldwide brochures it will automatically be allocated significantly more brochures than a travel agency selling only one or two holidays per month. This means that it is going to have more brochures available. Travel agents use the brochure as a key selling tool as part of the booking process. Customers like to see images of the product they are purchasing. If a customer has collected a brochure from a travel agent, then there is a strong possibility they will return to that travel agent to enquire and book the holiday.

ACTIVITY

Research the promotional activities of an independent and a multiple travel agent.

Dynamic packaging is another way travel agents can gain the competitive advantage. Dynamic packaging is the travel industry's term for a more flexible way of booking packages. In terms of the travel agent, it allows them to package components from different suppliers and find deals to cut prices for the consumer, thus having a competitive price compared to its opposition.

Travel agents, however, are warned not to discard the traditional package holidays, as the *Travel Weekly* article in the box below points out.

ACTIVITY

Describe an example of a dynamic package a miniple travel agent might offer.

Assessing the outcome

You work for a trade magazine. You have been asked to write an article that explains how retail travel agents seek to gain competitive advantage.

- Explain how retail travel organisations seek to gain a competitive advantage (**P2**).

How to produce complex itineraries for retail and business travel customers

It should now be established that retail travel agents arrange holidays for customers. While a number of

Travel agents warned not to replace traditional packages with dynamic packaging

Hays Travel is piloting a new dynamic packaging system for its agents, which it hopes to roll out in the next two to three weeks.

The miniple's managing director John Hays said his agents had no choice but to use dynamic packaging as a booking method despite his preference to remain loyal to suppliers. Dynamic packaging makes up a third of the chain's business.

'I would be mad not to develop this, but our preferred option is still to work with suppliers who want to work with us because our expertise is as a travel agency,' he said.

However, he admitted agents also needed dynamic packaging as long as they could 'earn sensible margins'.

Hays said he has been reassured by Thomas Cook and MyTravel following the recent merger announcement that his agents will be part of the distribution mix.

He said: 'They are telling me they want a certain amount of third-party distribution, but they will probably want fewer relationships with more productive partners.'

Hays Travel's new technology will allow agents to search several bed banks, the group's own contracted hotels, as well as charter, no-frills and scheduled flights at the same time.

(Source: Kelly Ranson, *Travel Weekly*, 1 March 2007)

these holidays are straightforward, e.g. the travel agent books the customer a specific holiday featured in a tour operator's brochure, there are also a number of customers booking tailor-made holidays. These types of holiday are ones that are put together specifically for the customer, hence the term tailor-made. They are more complex to organise. Earlier in this unit it was discussed how a number of travel agents are using dynamic packaging. This type of holiday is also a complex type of booking as the travel agent is required to work out costs for different elements of the booking and ensure that they all work out to meet the customer's requirements. Other complexities include flexibility of duration, i.e. booking other than the normal 7/14 nights. This can prove sometimes prove difficult for the travel agent as some accommodation runs from Saturday to Saturday.

When a customer buys any holiday from the travel agent, they want all the holiday details clearly presented. This will include all costs and a final total amount that the customer is paying for the products and services they have agreed to buy. The itinerary is the documentation, presented to the customer, showing the details of all the products and services purchased. The itinerary will include travel details such as transport arrangements, e.g. flight numbers, departure times; hotel details, e.g. the hotel name; as well as describing other planned activities, e.g. a visit to a theatre.

A complex itinerary is one that is not straight from a brochure; instead it may include a number of suppliers' products and services. The itinerary could also include a number of different customer requirements, e.g. the booking might include flights from different airports to a range of destinations.

E-agents such as Lastminute.com or expedia.co.uk send their customers very detailed itineraries. These itineraries clearly show the customer the necessary travel information. They give the customers the flight information such as flight numbers, departure and arrival times, and details of check-in times at the airport. The accommodation details are not just the name of the hotel booked but instead the address, telephone number, check-in and check-out date, as well as details of where the hotel is located.

Business travel itineraries tend to be multi-sector, meaning that more than one travel and tourism sector is involved. They generally use a number of components, e.g. scheduled flights, accommodation, rail, and there is often more than one destination involved. For example, a customer may wish to book a flight from Birmingham

ACTIVITY

Working in pairs, one to take the role of a travel agent and the other the customer, send an email requesting a complex holiday. Discuss what makes the enquiry complex.

to Paris, Paris to Madrid, Madrid to London, then a train from London to Birmingham.

A business itinerary is very similar to a retail itinerary. The difference is not the itinerary itself but the products and services purchased.

Itineraries reflect the organisation, therefore they need to be of a standard that shows the organisation in a good light. They need to look professional and communicate to the customer accurately. They need to be clear in what they communicate and presented in a logical order. To comply with legislation they must also be accurate in the information given. Failure to supply the correct information could result in customers missing flights, etc.

There are a number of resources available to travel agents to find out information in relation to the itinerary they prepare for customers. All sales staff working in travel agencies must be able to refer to a wide variety of information sources when dealing with travel arrangements. Retail travel agents will use tour operators' brochures as a starting point for reference when handling enquiries, but will need access to other printed and computer-based information in order to provide a complete service to customers. Computer-based information sources are growing in popularity and now there is a good range of travel manuals and timetables readily available.

Let us look at some of the information travel agents need in order to deal effectively with their customers.

Passports and visa requirements for entry to a country

To comply with the EU Package Travel Regulations travel agents have a responsibility to advise customers about passport and visa requirements for travel. They can find this information from a number of sources. For example: a customer wishing to travel to India for a three-week holiday. The customer holds a UK passport.

A brochure from a tour operator such as Kuoni will give advice on passport and visas (Figure 9.06).

ACTIVITY

The internet gives passport and visa information – for example, the Foreign and Commonwealth Office website (www.fco.gov.uk) or the World Travel Guide on www.worldtravelguide.net. Look at these two websites and check the passport information for UK passport holders wishing to travel to India. Is the information the same as that in the Kuoni brochure extract (Figure 8.06)?

The National Tourist Offices (NTOs) of overseas destinations are happy to provide travel agents with country information in the form of brochures, maps, posters and DVDs. The travel industry press, including *Travel Trade Gazette*, *Travel Weekly* and *Travel Agency*, also has valuable information sources for agents.

ACTIVITY

In pairs look at a *Travel Trade Gazette* and a *Travel Weekly*. Produce a resource guide of what relevant information the two trade magazines give.

OAG Flight Guide

Another resource that travel agents often buy is access to the online OAG guides. For business travel agents resources such as the OAG Flight Guide prove useful when arranging scheduled flights in itineraries. It gives published flight times, details of airlines and much more.

> With more than 400,000 direct and connecting flights worldwide, the OAG Flight Guide Worldwide is regarded throughout the world as the ultimate printed resource for most comprehensive, accurate and unbiased flight schedules.
>
> In addition to its flight listings, the OAG Flight Guide Worldwide includes other vital air travel information such as:
>
> - flight routings
> - minimum connecting times
> - airline, aircraft and airport decoding tables
> - international time calculator
> - airline addresses and phone numbers.

PASSPORTS AND VISAS
We can only advise of the requirements for British and Irish passport holders. For British and Irish passports endorsed in any way and all other passport holders, requirements should be checked with the relevant embassy. You should ensure that you have a valid ten year passport and, as many countries require expiry dates on passports to be a considerable length of time after the return from holiday, we would recommend that your passport is valid for 6 months after return to the UK. Many countries including USA now require children to hold their own passports and additional countries are adopting this policy on an ongoing basis. We therefore recommend that all children travel on full passports.

USA REQUIREMENTS
The US Government has reinforced their entry regulations making some important changes which are now in effect:
- All passports must be machine readable ie: red passports. If you still have an old blue passport you will need to obtain a visa before travelling, or apply for a new passport.
  Passports issued on or after October 26 2006, must also include an integrated circuit chip capable of storing the biographic information from the data page, a digitized photograph and other biometric information.
  NB: Some passports issued by British Consular posts abroad may not be machine readable – please check with the UK Passport Service on 0870 521 0410 or www.passport.gov.uk for further information. Also applicable to passengers in transit in the US.
- The US Govt now requires all passengers entering the US to provide details of their country of residence, as well as full postal address of the first US hotel.
  This information is currently being collected by the airline upon check-in. The airline will also collect details of your passport number and country of issue, citizenship, full names as they appear on your passport, gender and date of birth, all of which is obtained by swiping your passport at the check-in desk.

Fig 9.06 Advice from Kuoni on passports and visas

Assessing the outcome

You work for a retail travel agent. You are required to find a holiday and produce an itinerary for each of the following customer requests.

Client brief one

Ruth Ryan and her friend Caroline Cozens wish to book a holiday. They want to travel to Thailand for a three-week holiday starting the beginning of June. They wish to go to Bangkok for three nights; Chiang Mai for four nights, then in the remaining two weeks visit two beach resorts. Ruth does not like ferries. They wish to purchase insurance and domestic flights to and from Leeds Bradford. The girls would like to stay in four-star accommodation with a swimming pool. Central accommodation is desirable. The girls both have UK passports.

Client brief two

Anita and Ricardo Inglis and their two children, Hannah aged 15 years and Lucas aged 13 years, wish to book a family holiday to America. Ricardo and Lucas are fans of Elvis. Hannah is a great horse lover. Anita has a friend that moved to Birmingham, Alabama, who she would like to visit. The family want to go for three weeks starting at the end of July. They wish to fly from London and stay in budget accommodation. They all have UK passports.

- Use appropriate resources to produce two complex travel itineraries for retail customers to given client briefs (**P4**).

You work for a business travel agent. You are required to find suitable travel arrangements and produce an itinerary for each of the following customer requests.

Client brief one

Calum Rayner's secretary rings up requesting that the following travel arrangements are booked for her boss:

15 September – Newcastle to London first available flight

1 night's accommodation in a four-star hotel in Mayfair (internet access required)

16 September – early a.m. flight London to Paris Charles de Gaulle

16 September – late afternoon flight Paris to Madrid One night accommodation five-star hotel near the historic town (internet access required)

17 September – Madrid to Amsterdam a.m. flight (he has a business meeting at the airport between 14.00 and 15.30hrs)

17 September – Amsterdam to Newcastle Economy flexible tickets are required throughout. Calum holds a New Zealand passport.

Client brief two

Sufghan Patel has a business meeting in Chicago and Portland, Oregon. He needs you to book him the following:

15 March – Bristol to Chicago Accommodation in a four–five-star hotel in central Chicago.

Car rental – a medium-sized car with pick-up and drop-off at the airport

21 March – Chicago – Portland, Oregon Accommodation in a four–five-star hotel in central Portland

Car rental – a medium-sized car with pick-up and drop-off at the airport

25 March – Portland to Belfast Business-class seats are required on all flights. Sufghan Patel holds a UK passport.

- Use appropriate resources to produce two complex travel itineraries for business customers to given client briefs (**P4**).

Improve your grade

How to evaluate and make recommendations

To evaluate the effectiveness of retail and business travel organisations (**D1**), it is necessary to research a range of travel and tourism organisations and determine how effective they are. So what is meant by evaluate? It is a matter of judging the worth or quality so this means that it is necessary to make a judgement as to whether retail and business travel agents are effective in terms of providing travel services to customers.

What to consider?

In terms of effectiveness, the booking systems used by travel agents could be evaluated. Consideration needs to be given as to whether the systems are effective when compared to systems such as the internet. Think about whether the travel agent provides a better service that is competitive with that of online travel services providers. Another consideration could be how effective travel agents are at responding to the changing needs and wants of customers. Consider whether the dynamic packaging option provides products and services that meet these changing needs and wants. How does this type of package enable the travel agent to be competitive with its competition, e.g. other travel agents, the internet, direct-sell tour operators. Travel agency commission levels are having significant impacts on the travel agents. Consider whether the reduction in some of the commission levels given to travel agents reduces the option of a travel agent been able to have the competitive advantage on price.

Tour operators draw up formal agency agreements with the retail travel agents to sell their services. These agreements specify the terms and conditions of trading, including such issues as the normal rates of commission paid, extended credit to the travel agent and how settlement of accounts should be paid. Under the terms of these agreements, the travel agent agrees to support and promote the sale of their products and services. In return, the tour operator agrees to provide the support and cooperation necessary for the successful merchandising of the company's products – that is, provision of adequate supplies of brochures, sales promotion material and sometimes finance for cooperative regional advertising or promotion campaigns.

ACTIVITY

Tour operators try to make sure that travel agents are knowledgeable about the products they sell, e.g. educational visits, training materials. Explain how training on a tour operator's product can give a travel agent the competitive edge over other travel agents.

Top tip

- You should keep up to date with the latest developments in the tourist industry.

Selecting a destination

This is an internally assessed unit. You will need to complete a portfolio that demonstrates your understanding of the impacts of tourism development in one short-haul destination and one long-haul destination. You will need to show which agents are involved in tourism development in your selected destinations, how their objectives for achieving sustainable tourism development are implemented and the role that travel and tourism industry plays in supporting this.

When selecting your choice of one short-haul and one long-haul destination, you should consider the following information.

Short-haul – this can be any destination under six hours' flying time from the UK. It is recommended that you select a Western European destination that has had an established tourism industry for over 20 years since this will provide you with a good basis for comparison with the less-developed long-haul destination. You do not have to limit your selection to these but examples could include the Spanish Costas, the Mediterranean Islands, city break destinations in the UK and Europe (e.g. Edinburgh, Dublin, Paris, Madrid) and certain areas in Greece, Turkey and Bulgaria.

Long-haul – these must be more than six hours' direct flying time from the UK and you should consider a less economically developed country (LEDC) or developing country with an increasing level of tourism development, as this will provide you with a good comparison to the more developed European destinations. As above, you do not have to select from this list but these are typical examples of destinations you could choose, e.g. Mexico, Cuba, the Gambia, Nepal, Thailand, East Timor and many other countries in the Southern Hemisphere.

Definition of sustainable tourism development

In basic terms, sustainable tourism development is about maximising the potential long-term economic benefits from tourism without undermining the resources on which it is based (i.e. the people and the environment) for short-term profits. The World Tourism Organisation's definition of sustainable tourism development is:

> **Sustainable tourism development guidelines and management practices are applicable to all forms of tourism in all types of destinations, including mass tourism and the various niche tourism segments. Sustainability principles refer to the environmental, economic and socio-cultural aspects of tourism development, and a suitable balance must be established between these three dimensions to guarantee its long-term sustainability.**

Thus, sustainable tourism should do the following:

- make optimal use of environmental resources that constitute a key element in tourism development, maintaining essential ecological processes and helping to conserve natural heritage and biodiversity

- respect the socio-cultural authenticity of host communities, conserve their built and living cultural heritage and traditional values, and contribute to inter-cultural understanding and tolerance

- ensure viable, long-term economic operations, providing socio-economic benefits to all stakeholders that are fairly distributed, including stable employment and income-earning opportunities and social services to host communities, and contributing to poverty alleviation.

Sustainable tourism development requires the informed participation of all relevant stakeholders, as well as strong political leadership to ensure wide participation and consensus building. Achieving sustainable tourism is a continuous process and it requires constant monitoring of impacts, introducing the necessary preventive and/or corrective measures whenever necessary.

According to the World Tourism Organization, 'Sustainable tourism should also maintain a high level of tourist satisfaction and ensure a meaningful experience to the tourists, raising their awareness about sustainability issues and promoting sustainable tourism practices amongst them.'

This basically sums up the principles of sustainable tourism development, i.e. maximising the economic, environmental and socio-cultural benefits of tourism while at the same time minimising the negative economic, environmental and socio-cultural costs of tourism. This unit will enable you to understand how this can be achieved.

ACTIVITY

- What do the terms economic, environmental and socio-cultural mean?
- What is the World Tourism Organization (WTO) and what does it do?
- In groups, rewrite the WTO's definition of sustainable tourism development (see previous page) in your own words.

The impacts of tourism development on selected destinations

Tourism is unique as an export industry in that the consumption of the product takes places at the point of production. This means that consumers or, in this case, tourists must travel to the host destination in order to enjoy their purchase. As such, this has more impact on host communities than most other industries. Some of these impacts are positive and some negative. In this section you will examine the economic, environmental, social and cultural impacts.

Positive economic impacts

Increased employment

The most obvious benefit that tourism has for an area is the creation of jobs. The tourism industry is a labour-intensive industry, which means that there is a high demand for staff to work in tourist facilities and amenities such as hotels, restaurants, visitor attractions, airports, shops, etc. For some areas where traditional industries are in decline, such as coal mining in Wales or ship building in Glasgow, tourism can provide an effective way to generate employment and offset some of these job losses.

Increased income

In many developing countries jobs in tourism are preferable because they often provide better wages and working conditions than other more traditional industries such as farming or fishing. For the area as a whole, the investment by overseas companies in the development of resorts and the taxes the government receives, such as VAT on the purchase of goods and services by tourists, provide valuable foreign currency earnings.

Multiplier effect

Tourism development not only benefits those employed directly in the industry, but the community as a whole. For instance, due to an increase in the disposable income of those employed in tourism, many of the shops that provide products and services to the workers also benefit from the extra business; this is what is known as the multiplier effect. Likewise, tourists stopping to buy petrol for their car or going to the cinema contribute to the employment of petrol station attendants and cinema ushers even though these workers may not realise it. This is what is known as secondary spending, where tourists spend money on goods or services that may not obviously be regarded as tourism purchases.

Improved infrastructure

In order to meet the needs of tourists, destinations often need to develop and upgrade their infrastructure to cope with the increased seasonal demand. This can mean improvements to road and rail networks, airports, electricity, sewage, etc. This therefore creates all-year-round benefits for the locals who may not have had these improvements without tourism development.

Negative economic impacts
Increased living costs

In some destinations, restaurants, shops, hotels, taxi drivers and visitor attractions raise the prices of goods and services to what is sometimes known as 'tourist prices'. In addition, many governments have to raise local taxes in order to pay for the improvements to the infrastructure and other tourist services. Not only that, but many tourism jobs can often be seasonal, unskilled, part-time, low-paid jobs such as cleaners, gardeners, waitresses, drivers, etc. This makes the cost of living very expensive for the locals, who may not have the purchasing power of the tourists.

Decline of traditional employment

Where tourism provides a more attractive option to harder, lower-paid traditional jobs, young people are often keen to leave the traditional jobs for the sake of better-paid jobs as hotel porters, coach drivers, tour guides, etc. This can mean that the traditional industries suffer as young people no longer want to learn the skills of the old jobs, like weavers, thatchers, blacksmiths, etc., with the result that those traditional industries often disappear.

Over-dependency on tourism

When destinations become over-dependent on tourism at the expense of other industries this can be very risky for the economy. The dangers with tourism are that it can be a very seasonal industry, e.g. beach resorts that are only busy in summer and ski resorts that are only busy in winter, with very little employment in between. In addition tourism is very sensitive to external pressures such as terrorist attacks like the one in Bali, natural disasters such as the Boxing Day tsunami, poor currency exchange rates, etc. It can also result in loss of local services – for example, when shops that previously provided groceries for the locals convert to only providing tourist gifts and souvenirs for the visitors instead.

Positive environmental impact
Regeneration and restoration

To provide an attractive heritage tourism product many man-made or built attractions such as historic buildings, castles and stately homes that have become derelict and dilapidated are restored to their former glory. Likewise whole areas, particularly in inner cities and docklands, have benefited from urban regeneration programmes, such as the Albert Dock in Liverpool or along the South Bank of the River Thames in London.

Environmental education and awareness

The old adage 'Take only photographs, leave only footprints' has been the advice for years to those ramblers who enjoy countryside walks. The reliance of tourism on the natural environment, such as the fauna, flora, rivers, mountains, lakes, forests, valleys, beaches, coastlines and even the air we breathe, has led to conservation groups and governments making positive efforts to educate tourists and the industry about the importance of protecting the environment and providing wildlife protection areas to preserve the habitat of the animals that live there.

Use of renewable resources

Sustainable development emphasises the use of renewable resources such as oxygen, fresh water, solar energy and timber as sources of energy generation rather than non-renewable resources such as plastics, coal, oil, natural gas and other materials produced from fossil fuels, which deplete at a faster rate than the environment's capacity to replenish them. The tourism industry recognises this and there are some good examples of hotels, tour operators and airlines that have taken steps towards moving in this direction; one good example is the Loreto Bay Homes holiday resort in Baja, Mexico (Figure 11.01) (see also the case study on p. 186).

Fig 11.01 Loreto Bay Homes holiday resort

Negative environmental impacts

Overcrowding

During peak tourist periods, large numbers of tourists can be drawn to what are known as 'tourist honeypots' or sites of major tourist interest, causing severe traffic congestion, e.g. the Lake District. This can make these places overcrowded, which can be particularly damaging for sensitive natural areas where erosion can take place on pathways or hillsides.

Pollution

Tourism can cause pollution in many ways, from air pollution caused by airplanes or cars to water pollution caused by holiday resorts pumping sewage into the sea or hotels pouring laundry detergents into rivers. For example, each day, cruise ships generate as much as '30,000 gallons of sewage, 255,000 gallons of dirty water from showers, sinks, laundries and dishwashers and 7,000 gallons of oily bilge water' (source: www.sustainabletourism.net). It can mean litter dropped by walkers or climbers on mountain trails – for example, in the Himalayas on what is now known as the 'Coca-Cola Trail' – but it can also include noise pollution caused by night flights or bars and nightclubs in residential areas.

Loss of habitat

When tourist developments such as holiday resorts encroach on areas where wildlife is present or when too many tourists in a natural area disturb wild animals' feeding and mating patterns, then the animals are often forced to move in order to survive – one example of this is the plight of the cheetahs in the Masai Mara

game reserve in Kenya (see www.basecampexplorer.com).

Erosion of resources

Tourism can sometimes destroy the resources on which it is based – for example, the deforestation of mountainous areas to create ski slopes or the use of scenic landscapes for tourist accommodation and other facilities. One of the biggest problems in recent years has been caused by golf tourism. Golf courses require considerable amounts of water to keep the grass green. This can deplete fresh water resources and can even cause saline intrusion into the groundwater. This is a particular problem in developing countries where quite often fresh water is in scarce supply.

Fig 11.02 Golf courses require substantial watering

Case study

Golf tourism

A study in the Philippines found water used on the 19 golf courses it surveyed could have irrigated 1500 smallholdings or supplied 330,000 Manila residents (*Social Cost of Golf Courses*, Omi Royandoyan, Philippine Peasants Institute, 1997). Another Philippines study found that the average golf course uses 24 million gallons of water per month – enough to irrigate 65 hectares of farmland or to supply a 2000-room four-star hotel (Philippine Human Rights Information Center, 1999). Even in Spain, a golf course in Benidorm uses as much water as 10,000 people. A typical golf course in Thailand uses 1500kg of chemical fertilisers, pesticides and herbicides a year and as much water as 60,000 rural villagers.

(Source: www.peopleandplanet.net)

Inappropriate development

Unplanned mass tourism can often result in buildings that are eyesores, the most common example of this is the sight of the high-rise hotels along the coast of the Costa del Sol in Spain. Even small-scale developments can spoil the view. The growth of second home properties in scenic areas has led to what has been termed 'bungalow blight', where large numbers of holiday properties dot the landscape.

Fig 11.03 Benidorm beachfront

Positive social impacts
Improved provision of community facilities and services

In addition to the general improvement and tidying up of the infrastructure and public transport, an important addition to the quality of life for locals is the provision of community facilities and services that locals can benefit from as a result of tourism development. New restaurants, bars, nightclubs, cinemas, theatres, museums, art galleries, parks, nature trails, leisure centres, hotels, amusement parks, golf courses, tennis courts, etc. can be used by locals as well as tourists – this is what is called dual provision.

Improved standards of living

For the locals or hosts in the tourist destination area the improvements to the infrastructure, increased investment in local services, education and skills training schemes and the opportunities for higher-paid employment with better working conditions can often mean the locals can have an increased disposable income with more choice of goods and services to spend their money on. In this way tourism development can improve the social status for local people and whole communities within their society.

For example, the Chiapas Indians in Mexico have been able to capitalise on the increased interest in their culture and traditions as a result of the growth of cultural tourism. By doing so, they have also increased their political power in a country where for many years they were marginalised.

Negative social impacts
Crime

In some developing countries where there is a significant gap in wealth between the tourists and the locals, this can sometimes result in jealousy. Where locals do not have access to the better-paid jobs or when the tourists behave in an irresponsible, anti-social way by being noisy and drunk in the streets or dealing in drugs, this can turn to resentment and hostility towards the 'guests'. This can lead to conflict and often the result is that local criminals will see tourists as easy targets.

Sex tourism

In some regions, particularly in South-East Asia, parts of Africa and the Caribbean, tourist destinations actively promote themselves as part of the sex tourism trade (Figure 11.04). Red-light districts become established, where young women and even children are often exploited and forced to work as prostitutes to serve the requirements of mainly European and American male tourists. To a lesser extent, female tourists, sometimes called 'milk bottles', travel to destinations such as Gambia or Jamaica seeking holiday relationships with 'beach boys'.

Fig 11.04 Bangkok red-light district

Overcrowding and loss of privacy

Any tourist site, beach, town or village will have a perceived social carrying capacity (SCC) or what is the maximum number of visitors (MNV) it can accommodate without feeling overcrowded. When the locals feel there are too many tourists and that they are losing their privacy, they will often come into conflict with the tourists. In the historic city of Bath, residents living in the spectacular Georgian houses along Royal Crescent protested against their loss of privacy caused by open-top tour buses travelling along their street, and successfully managed to have this route blocked.

Displacement

In some situations locals have even been forcibly moved off their land to make way for tourists.

Fig 11.05 Maasai tribespeople

Tourism Concern highlights the case of the Maasai tribespeople in Tanzania (Figure 11.05):

> **At the beginning of 1988, pastoralists were evicted from the Mkomazi Game Reserve. Some of their homes were razed to the ground and some livestock was rounded up and sold by the government to pay for the evictions. People received no compensation and were literally left by the roadside with 40,000 cattle. They are now confined to a narrow strip of land surrounded by the farms and villages of the agricultural community along the Pangani River. Tourists are permitted to enter the park to view the wildlife, but if cattle wander into the reserve in search of grass and water they are impounded and the pastoralists have to pay a heavy fine.**

(Source: Tourism Concern)

Positive cultural impacts
Preservation of traditional customs and crafts

In most parts of the world, as modernisation occurs young people in particular become less and less interested in the traditional customs, arts and crafts of their heritage. In some cases, if it were not for tourists taking an interest in these traditions, then they would cease to exist altogether. An example of this is the traditional Hungarian folk arts of weaving, embroidery and woodcarving, which are experiencing renewed appeal thanks to foreign tourists whereas interest from the domestic market is in decline.

Reinforcement of cultural identity

Countries that enter the cultural tourist market need to present a clear definition to the overseas visitor of who they are as a people, which also serves to reinforce to the host community their own sense of identity. This can also apply to minority groups within a country – for example, the National Museum of the American Indian in the USA was 'Established by an act of Congress in 1989, the museum works in collaboration with the Native peoples of the Western Hemisphere to protect and foster their cultures by reaffirming traditions and beliefs, encouraging contemporary artistic expression, and empowering the Indian voice' (source: National Museum of the American Indian).

Negative cultural impacts
Demonstration effect and the dilution of cultural identity

In many developing destinations, local people may perceive the wealthy tourists as being more fashionable and may try to copy their clothes, speech, tastes, views and other forms of more hedonistic behaviour in what is sometimes called 'westernisation'. This is what is known as the demonstration effect. Where the cultures of the tourists and locals are very different – for example, where more strict religious and cultural norms exist – the copying by the local young people of tourist behaviour such as drinking alcohol, gambling and disrespect for elders can be even more problematic and may result in a dilution of their distinctive cultural identity as fewer young people follow the traditional way of life.

The role of agents involved in sustainable tourism development

In order to achieve sustainable tourism development, there are a number of key stakeholders that must act responsibly. In this section you will study who are the main agents involved in sustainable tourism development. We can divide these into three separate sectors:

- private
- public
- voluntary.

Private-sector agents

The private sector is primarily made up of those organisations whose main aim is to make a profit.

Landowners

In straightforward terms, these essentially are the people who own the land. Farmers in the UK will be keen to ensure that ramblers walking in the countryside act responsibly and keep to certain pathways. Some farmers rent out fields and manage campsites, even selling home-made farm produce to campers to supplement their income during the summer months (Figure 11.06). In other situations, they will sell their land to property developers if it is in a prime tourist location.

Fig 11.06 A UK tent campsite owned by a farmer

Property developers

These are the organisations responsible for financing the building of large-scale, often multi-million-pound, tourism projects such as resorts and purpose-built visitor attractions. Often they will retain the lease and the leisure and tourism organisations will pay them rent for the use of the property. A spectacular example of this can be seen in the Palm Islands resorts in Dubai, a project developed by Nakheel Properties (source: Nakheel).

Tour operators

Tour operators negotiate rates with the suppliers of accommodation, transport and other services and use these component parts to assemble package holidays to the destination area. They are then sold through travel agents or direct to the customer. The market that they target and the images they promote of the destination will play a significant part in the type of tourist that will be attracted to the destination, e.g. if they highlight the cultural attractions of the destination, they will be more likely to generate interest among customers with an ABC1 socio-economic profile.

Hotel chains

Destination areas seeking to develop their tourism market will need to supply a sufficient quantity and quality of accommodation provision. Developing countries often seek to attract the prestigious global hotel chains such as Holiday Inn (600 hotels), Hilton (500 hotels) and Sheraton (400 hotels and resorts), however these often contribute significantly to the leakage of tourist earnings from the local economy caused by repatriation of profits to the company's head office overseas.

Airlines

The increased ease and lower costs of international air travel have meant that airlines carry approximately 2 billion passengers every year, a figure that is rising by an estimated 5 per cent annually. The growth of low-fare, budget airlines such as Ryanair and easyJet, has radicalised the short-haul market out of the UK in recent years to many new European destinations.

Entertainment companies

A major feature of any tourist resort is the range of entertainment facilities on offer where the holidaymakers can have fun. This can include bars, nightclubs, restaurants, amusement parks, cinemas, swimming pools, golf courses, etc. Most British seaside resorts will include a range of indoor entertainment venues due to the unpredictability of the weather.

Travel publishers

In a competitive industry where often similar destinations are competing for similar target markets, good public relations can give one destination a competitive edge over another. For this reason, tourist boards regularly invite journalists to their destination to stay and enjoy the experience on a complimentary basis in the hope that they will write positive reviews about them in travel guide books and travel trade press such as *Travel Weekly* or *Travel Trade Gazette*.

Entrepreneurs

In many developing countries where tourism is still in its early stages, much of the industry consists of small-scale, family-owned businesses, such as B&Bs. It can also be the case in more developed destinations, where locals do not have the skills or qualifications required to work in the formal-sector organisations such as hotels, that they have no option but to become self-employed, selling goods and souvenirs or providing services such as taxi drivers, masseuses, guides, etc.

Fig 11.07 Caribbean beach vendor

Public-sector agents

In most developed destinations the tourism industry is private sector led with public-sector support in terms of marketing and promoting and facilitating partnerships between the various stakeholders. In contrast, in developing countries there is a greater responsibility on the public sector to be more actively involved in the industry as the private sector may lack the capital investment to get started. In this section you will examine who the main public-sector stakeholders are and the roles they perform.

National governments

In the UK, tourism is the responsibility of the Department for Culture, Media and Sport (DCMS). This department takes overall responsibility for tourism policies, strategy and funding. In its 2004 report *Tomorrow's Tourism Today* it identified the four priority areas for the UK tourism industry as being 'marketing and e-tourism, quality, skills and data, plus a fifth priority for the DCMS – advocacy for tourism across Whitehall and the EU' (source: DCMS). In addition, the DCMS provides VisitBritain with approximately £35 million every year to promote Britain overseas (source: VisitBritain).

Local authorities

Local authorities are becoming increasingly aware of the economic, environmental and socio-cultural benefits of tourism to their area. They are responsible for the funding and management of many of our leisure and tourism facilities, tourist information centres and for planning local events and festivals. For example, Leicester City Council has a very active Festivals Unit, which manages a wide range of community events such as Bonfire Night and the Diwali celebrations (source: Leicester City Council).

Regional development agencies (RDAs)

The nine RDAs in England were first established in 1998 and their main role is to coordinate economic development, employment and regeneration in their respective regions (Figure 11.08). They are each allocated a portion of the £2 billion per year government funding and they are then free to decide how that money is spent. For some regions, tourism is seen as having greater potential to achieve returns on investment. For example, the South-West Regional Development Agency provided nearly £1 million of funding support to the Tourism Skills Network between 2003 and 2006 (source: South-West Regional Development Agency).

National tourist offices/regional tourist boards

The role of national tourist offices is primarily to promote the country worldwide to overseas tourists, whereas the regional tourist boards work closely with the Regional Development Agencies concentrating more on attracting domestic tourists and developing tourism at a local level. In addition to its marketing responsibilities, VisitBritain works closely with other

Key
A – One North East
B – Yorkshire Forward
C – East Midlands Development Agency
D – East of England Development Agency
E – London Development Agency
F – South East England Development Agency
G – South West England Development Agency
H – Advantage West Midlands
I – North West Development Agency

Fig 11.08 Regional Development Agency areas

stakeholders, such as advising the government on industry issues and providing support to the tourism industry in terms of information and advice.

Voluntary-sector agents

The voluntary sector consists of non-profit-making organisations whose members or employees may or may not work for money but generally share a common desire either to improve their local area or tackle a global issue such as protecting the environment.

Charity foundations

Charities are organisations that exist in order to provide help to disadvantaged people or other causes that are in the public benefit. They receive money from donations, gifts, grants and through organising fund raising events and activities, as well as the revenue they generate from consultation work and product sales. Organisations such as the Travel Foundation and Tourism Concern are actively involved in promoting sustainable tourism development and in particular the cause of Fair Trade in Tourism, which encourages fair wages and working conditions, sustainable use of natural resources and the opportunity for local people to benefit from tourism (sources: Travel Foundation; Tourism Concern).

Conservation organisations

Conservation organisations, such as the British Trust for Conservation Volunteers (BTCV), work unpaid on projects aimed at improving the environment, such as the £5.2 million Mineral Valley Project in County Durham. The BTCV also operates nature conservation-based holidays, aimed at carrying out environmental improvements to the natural and social history of an area. This has the dual benefits of bringing tourism revenue into the local economy as well as benefiting the habitats and access routes that they work on (source: BTCV).

Community groups

Community groups consist of the local people who live in the area where tourism takes place. They are sometimes formed in response to specific projects that affect their area or exist over a longer period of time to attract and promote a variety of development projects. Active involvement and participation in the planning process by the local community is one of the fundamental principles of sustainable tourism development. The Mumbles Development Trust is one such example of a community organisation concerned with the regeneration of the village of Mumbles in Swansea.

ACTIVITY

For *one* of your destinations (choose which one carefully because this has to be the same for all three sectors):
- find examples for each of the private-sector agents and describe the role they play in sustainable tourism development
- find examples for each of the public-sector agents and describe the role they play in sustainable tourism development
- find examples for each of the voluntary-sector agents and describe the role they play in sustainable tourism development.

How objectives for sustainable tourism development are implemented

Political objectives

Tourism can quite often be seen in political terms as it packages and re-presents images of peoples and their countries, which are by definition political.

Creating a national or regional identity

One objective of tourism development is to package a set of images and events and promote these as being the collective history and culture of a people in order to create either a national or regional identity. The St Fagan's National History Museum in Cardiff provides visitors with an 'insight into the rich heritage and culture of Wales' (Figure 11.09) (source: St Fagan's National History Museum).

Raising the profile of an area

Tourism can also be employed as a method of enhancing the image and promoting awareness of an area. The new town of Milton Keynes suffered from a

Fig 11.09 St Fagan's National History Museum

negative image as being boring. In response, the local council proactively supported leisure and tourism projects in order to counteract this and now the city boasts a new theatre, art gallery, indoor ski slope, multiplex cinema, amusement park as well as a vibrant nightlife with bars and clubs. The effect has been that the city is now able to attract a lot more visitors and more businesses are prepared to relocate there as a result.

Environmental objectives

Tourism can also be used to conserve our history and preserve our natural surroundings, as you will see in this section.

Habitat and heritage preservation

The economic benefits that a sustainable tourism industry can offer often stimulate the political and commercial will among the various stakeholders to cooperate towards the common goal of protecting the natural resources on which it is based, thereby preserving the wildlife and the habitat that they live in. For example, Responsible Travel operates brown bear watching tours in Finland. As these tours bring economic benefits to the area, it makes sense for the locals that bears that are alive have more value than bears that are dead (source: www.responsibletravel. com). Similarly, conservation projects aimed at presenting historic buildings as tourist attractions by organisations such as English Heritage, also serve the environmental objective of preserving our heritage for future generations.

Environmental education

As the market for alternative tourism increases, there is an opportunity for the travel industry to provide holidays that are not only fun but educational too. Travel companies such as Discovery Initiatives offer natural history and wildlife tours around the world where holidaymakers can take part in conservation projects and learn about the environment. In addition, the company works closely with a range of conservation partners such as the Eden Project (Figure 11.10), the Galapagos Conservation Trust and the Global Tiger Patrol to promote the principles of sustainable tourism (source: www.discoveryinitiatives.co.uk).

Fig 11.10 The Eden Project

Socio-cultural objectives

Tourism can be a means by which people learn more about each other, as you will see in this section.

Promoting cultural understanding

Tourism often brings people from very different cultures together and this gives visitors a valuable opportunity to learn more about the traditions and cultures of the host community. This is especially the case in community-based tourism, where locals have greater control over what is promoted and visitors can often stay in local people's homes to gain an even more authentic experience. Companies such as Muir's Tours offer these 'homestay' holidays throughout the Americas, Asia and the Far East (source: Muir's Tours).

Maintaining traditions or beliefs

Modernisation in any society often means that the younger generations no longer place the same importance on traditional values or beliefs as the older generations. However, as tourism trends indicate, visitors are increasingly keen to learn more about other cultures, therefore sustainable tourism development can play a major role in preserving traditions and cultures. The interest generated in traditions, festivals and arts can often reinforce a sense of identity and pride among younger locals in their own heritage and this can serve to maintain local culture despite the modernisation process.

Economic objectives

Arguably the most important objective in tourism development is the financial rewards that it can bring, which you will examine in this section.

Employment creation and revenue generation

Tourism is one of the most important and fastest-growing industries in the world. According to the World Travel and Tourism Council (WTTC), over 800 million people travel internationally every year, with tourism-related businesses representing over 10 per cent of the total global gross domestic product (GDP) in 2006, generating nearly 77 million jobs, or 2.8 per cent of world employment (source: www.sustainabletourism.net). The DCMS, in its *Tomorrow's Tourism Today* document, points out that, in the UK, tourism contributes £76 billion per annum to the economy (4.4 per cent of the GDP) and accounts for 7.4 per cent of the working population (source: DCMS).

Economic regeneration

The potential economic benefits of tourism can be a motivating factor for inner-city regeneration developments and often parklands, canal towpaths, riverbanks are cleaned up in order to make them more attractive to tourists. An example of this has taken place along the South Bank of the River Thames in London, where a major regeneration project has taken place in recent years, which has brought life back to the Southwark area, one of the most deprived boroughs in the country. The South Bank area now boasts a wealth of popular tourist attractions, both old and new, such as the Globe Theatre, Vinopolis, the London Dungeon, Southwark Cathedral, the Tate Modern, the *Golden Hinde*, the London Eye (Figure 5.11), the London Aquarium, the IMAX Centre as well as nearby Borough Market. The stimulation of the area through tourism has resulted in investment in the area by other businesses such as bars, hotels, restaurants, shops, etc., and other businesses who find the area more attractive to relocate to, thereby providing employment for the locals.

Conflicting objectives

As tourism is such a diverse industry involving many different stakeholders with different objectives, quite often they can come into conflict with each other. In

Fig 11.11 The London Eye

many cases, this involves the voluntary sector coming into conflict with the private sector, which they feel is destroying the environment or exploiting the local community in order to achieve short-term profits.

Often the public sector finds itself in the middle and in conflict with both, being accused of either giving too many concessions or not enough support to one side or the other. In addition, there can be conflict between the different user groups themselves

ACTIVITY

For one of your destinations (choose which one carefully because this has to be the same for all objectives):

- find a selection of tourist board and tour operator brochures of your chosen destination; what image do these give of the local people and their culture?
- find an example of an environmental conservation project this can be a natural or a built attraction
- identify examples of traditional dress, food, music, dance, festivals, sports, arts and crafts, architecture and folklore; how many of these are used to promote tourism in your destination?
- what are the government job creation targets in your chosen destination?
- describe how tourism has improved the infrastructure in your destination.
- find out what is the government budget for tourism development projects in your destination.

– for example, between cyclists, walkers, horse riders and motorists in countryside areas.

Usually these conflicts can be avoided through consultation and active participation in the planning process by all stakeholders, or resolved through discussion and compromise.

Assessing the outcome

You have been appointed tourism officer for a county council. The first task you have been assigned is to set up a tourism partnership of stakeholders to support tourism in the area. Write a report describing how different agents can be involved in tourism, and explaining how the objectives for sustainable tourism development can be put into practice, using a selected destination as an example.

- Describe the roles of agents involved in sustainable tourism development at a selected destination (**P2**).
- Explain how the objectives for sustainable tourism development are put into practice at a selected destination (**P3**).

How the travel industry supports sustainable tourism development

In this section you will examine how the industry can play an active part in supporting the ideals of sustainable tourism development.

Tour operators

Although tour operators are primarily concerned with profit-making, this does not necessarily mean that this is mutually exclusive to sustainable tourism practices. For example, in 2005, First Choice Holidays was included in the FTSE4 Good index of businesses that meet globally recognised sustainable development standards. Tour operators are increasingly aware that they have a responsibility to provide guidance to tourists with regards to how they should behave while on holiday in environmentally sensitive areas. Often they will issue holidaymakers with a code of conduct on the dos and don'ts as part of their travel documents.

Case study

Dive tourism

Specialist dive operators have recognised the importance of adopting sustainable practices and educating tourists on how to dive responsibly. In order to minimise the negative impacts from the growing worldwide threat to coral reefs posed by dive tourism, the United Nations Environment Program (UNEP) and the International Coral Reef Initiative (ICRI) has prepared a set of guidelines to help the global tourist industry inform visitors and dive operators on ways to help protect coral reefs. Among their key recommendations were:

For dive operators

- limit tourist numbers on each dive
- give a presentation of the reef's ecosystem before every dive
- anchor boats only on soft sand or use mooring buoys
- prevent divers from bringing back 'souvenirs' from the sea.

For divers

- do not touch the coral, stand on it or rest on it
- avoid kicking up sand with fins and do not dive into shallow water
- do not feed the fish
- do not attempt to touch marine creatures
- for souvenirs, take pictures and notes rather than pieces of coral.

(Source: Cyber Diver News Network, 2 March 2002)

Hotel companies

Accommodation is an essential component of most package holidays, and more and more hotels are providing good examples of how to adopt sustainable tourism policies profitably. A good example of an environmentally friendly development is the Loreto Bay Homes development in Mexico (see the case study overleaf).

Increasingly, sustainable tourism development is not just about the smaller, niche-market eco-tourism companies: the larger, mass-market operators are also developing tourism products that are environmentally friendly. For example, Thomson, the largest UK tour operator, has introduced Green Medal status for hotels that adopt environmentally friendly practices.

Case study

Loreto Bay Homes, Baja, Mexico

This development is a luxurious development that includes two 18-hole championship golf courses, a beach club and spa, a tennis centre, marina, and a sport fishing centre. Its aim is to generate energy mainly from renewable sources, such as air, wind and the sun. It does this through a combination of using earthen walls, which are thermally efficient, building design using domes, courtyards and fountains, thereby reducing the need for air conditioners, a wind farm to generate electricity and solar-powered hot water units.

(Source: Loreto Bay Company)

Case study

Thomson's Green Medal status

The hotels are 'measured against over 100 criteria for the environment and staff well-being such as whether the hotel has power saving key fobs that turn off all the lights when the holidaymaker leaves the room, use of alternative energy sources such as solar power, reuse of grey water for irrigation of the garden areas, using local products as a preference and questions relating to staff well-being, such as a policy to employ local staff, training for local staff to enable them to achieve management positions and providing staff benefits.'

(Source: Thomson)

Airlines

As people become more aware of the damaging effects of global warming, there has been a greater focus on the contribution that carbon emissions caused by the aviation industry is making. At present, this is about 15 per cent of Britain's carbon total but, according to the House of Commons Environmental Audit Committee, aviation will generate 43 million tons of carbon by 2050, or 66 per cent of the government's 65 million ton target. The Tyndall Centre for Climate Change Research disputes these figures and estimates that by then air travel will more likely account for the entire 'sustainable' carbon quota of the UK (source: *Independent*, 28 January 2006). In response to this increasing pressure, the airline industry has replied by taking a number of initiatives to support sustainable tourism, such as the introduction of new aerodynamic wing flaps and continuous descent approaches to reduce fuel consumption, noise and emissions.

Charitable foundations

There are many charity organisations actively involved in supporting sustainable tourism development through consultation and participation in the tourism planning process. An example of a charity dedicated to promoting sustainable tourism is Tourism Concern. It is very active in campaigning for the rights of host communities in destination areas. Currently it has campaigns aimed at boycotting travel to Burma, an end to the exploitation of tourism workers in luxury resorts, fair living conditions for locals in the Maldives, improved working conditions for Sherpas on trekking holidays, etc. In addition, it produces books, leaflets, videos/DVDs for schools and universities, as well as staging events, debates and public exhibitions to raise public awareness of issues such as corporate social responsibility in the tourism industry (source: Tourism Concern).

ACTIVITY

In your selected long-haul and short-haul destinations, find an example of what the following agents have done to show they support the principles of sustainable tourism development:
- tour operators
- airlines
- accommodation providers.

Case study

Richard Branson/Virgin

In 2006, Richard Branson pledged the profits from his transportation businesses, including Virgin Atlantic, to be invested in businesses that developed renewable energy – with plans to contribute $3 billion during the next decade for the initiative. Among his recommendations, Branson suggested the creation of new airport infrastructure to reduce fuel burn before take-off and after landing. He envisions 'starting grids', to which commercial airplanes would be taxied – engines off – before take-off, only to start their engines about 10 minutes before take-off. 'This would substantially reduce the amount of time aircraft need to taxi with their engines running and the time spent queuing before take-off.' Branson also touted the 'continuous descent approach', through which aircraft begin their descent at a higher altitude, moving groundward steadily, as opposed to a staggered approach that burns excessive fuel. 'This earlier descent means that aircraft descend at a more efficient speed, therefore reducing fuel burn. Virgin Atlantic believes that all air traffic control authorities should adopt this approach, saving considerable CO_2 emissions,' the carrier said in a statement. Other Branson-encouraged initiatives included reducing the weight of aircraft, which in turn would reduce the amount of fuel needed to fly. He also called on Europe to singularise its air traffic control organisations, painting the system as a 'mess of European air traffic control' that 'is punishing the environment, with 35 different air traffic control organisations, compared with just one in America'. Branson said that his plan would 'optimise air routings by aircraft and improve environmental performance further'.

(Source: Business Travel News Online, 9 October 2006)

Fig 11.12 A Sherpa

Assessing the outcome

You work for an environmentalist organisation and you are attending the World Travel Market to make a presentation to the travel industry describing how it could practise sustainable tourism more. Use the examples of the two destinations chosen for **P1** to support your point.

- Describe how the travel and tourism industry supports the development of sustainable tourism at one specific short-haul and one specific long-haul destination (**P4**).

Improve your grade

Referring to your assessment grid, you will note that the criteria are grouped together according to the topics described below. Higher grades are awarded for greater levels of depth, evaluation, analysis and reasoning.

P1/M1/D1 – Impacts of tourism development

At pass (**P1**) level, you only will need to describe the positive and negative impacts of tourism development in your two destinations, however for a merit (**M1**), you will need to explain how these positive impacts have been maximised and how these negative impacts have been minimised in one of your selected destinations.

For example, this could include giving details of how the accommodation providers purchase food produce from local suppliers to encourage linkages, thereby reducing leakages, or how tax revenue earned from tourism has been used to build schools for local children, or how companies train local staff and promote them to more higher-paid full-time managerial positions. Or, this could be examples of visitor and traffic management schemes such as park and ride or pedestrianisation projects to reduce overcrowding and traffic congestion, or planning controls to prevent inappropriate development. In all examples used, you will need to explain clearly how these measures will maximise which positive impacts and minimise which negative impacts.

At distinction level (**D1**), you will be expected to go further and give your opinions on how successful or unsuccessful you think these measures have been, and how they put the objectives of sustainable tourism into practice, giving reasons for your answer. For example, you may assess the actions of the tourist board and local authorities in tackling the problems of seasonality by staging festivals and events in the shoulder or low seasons.

P2/P3/M2 – Agents and objectives of development

In this topic you can choose to concentrate on *one* of your destinations; either the short-haul or the long-haul one. You only need to explain the agents that are actually involved in development in your destination, rather than a general description of agents. In other words, the named agent you are investigating must be a specific one and it must relate to tourism development in your destination. You will explain the role they play in tourism development and explain using real examples how they attempt to achieve the objectives of sustainable tourism development.

For example, you could explain how the local authorities allowed planning permission to developers to build a hotel on condition that 25 per cent of the hotel staff lived locally, thereby creating employment for the locals. To improve this to merit level (**M2**), you will need to explain how these agents could have conflicting objectives. There is some flexibility in this criterion if you cannot find real examples of conflict

between the agents. In these situations you can discuss the points in theoretical rather than specific terms, but they must be realistic and use examples of agents in your destination who could have conflicting objectives, even if you have no actual evidence that they are in conflict. For example, environmentalist groups objecting to the use of speedboats on a lake could realistically be in conflict with the company hiring out the speedboats to the holidaymakers.

P4/M3/D2 – Industry support

At pass level (**P4**), you need to describe specific examples of policies and guidelines to show how the travel and tourism industry supports the development of sustainable tourism in both your short-haul and long-haul destinations. However, at merit level (**M3**), you will need to give your critical analysis on these measures and argue whether you think they have or have not been effective in supporting sustainable tourism development, giving reasons for your answer. For example, you may argue that sustainable tourism practices in an all-inclusive resort in your destination is ineffective when most managerial positions are filled by overseas workers.

At distinction level (**D2**), you will need to take this further and make recommendations for further measures that the travel and tourism industry could take to support sustainable tourism development in one destination. Your recommendations will need to be described in detail and you will need to give a full explanation of how your proposal would support the development of sustainable tourism, using examples of good practice found elsewhere in the travel and tourism industry to support your points – for example, re-routing hill walkers away from areas prone to erosion in the Brecon Beacons or omitting mention of routes through eroded areas in guidebooks of the Dublin Mountains to allow time for re-seeding and repair of the footpaths.

Top tips

- You should be able to discuss the positive and negative impacts of tourism on a destination.
- You should know who are the main agents in the tourism business and how their roles connect.
- You should be able to state how sustainable tourism has changed the industry in the past five years.

The tour operations environment

Tour operators make purchases from producers such as airlines and accommodation providers. A tour operator is often referred to as a travel wholesaler that negotiates the purchase of different products such as airline seats, hotel rooms and entertainment and then combines them to make a 'package'. The tour operator will buy in bulk (e.g. 100 rooms per night for a season). Buying like this means that the tour operator gets a preferred rate thus making a saving, which can be passed on to the customer. The tour operator will produce a brochure that promotes its products and services. The tour operator has three main roles:

1. as a wholesaler, it is buying in bulk and packaging the holiday
2. as a negotiator and contractor, it is dealing with a number of other organisations (producers)
3. as the main marketer, it is promoting the products and services on offer.

Let us look in more detail at the links tour operators have with other sectors.

Producers include accommodation, transport and attractions providers. A tour operator needs to work closely with the producers. It needs to negotiate rates for the products and services for which it is contracting. There are a number of tour operators, many of whom want to buy the same products and services from the producers. It is therefore a very competitive business.

Table 12.01 shows some examples of producers or other service providers with which the tour operator negotiates contracts.

Table 12.01 Examples of producers and other service providers

Producers	Service providers
Accommodation providers e.g. hotels, apartments, villas, caravan sites	Iberostar Hotels, Melia Hotels, Sofitel Hotels
Transport e.g. airlines	First Choice Airlines, MyTravel Airways, British Airways, Virgin Atlantic
Ancillary producers e.g. car rental operators	Hertz, Avis
Insurance brokers	AXA insurance

As well as tour operators putting together the product, e.g. package holidays, they need distribution channels to sell the product. A travel distribution channel is the communications process that a tour operator uses to distribute its products/service to the target market. It can be done in two ways: first, direct to potential customers, i.e. from the tour operator to the consumer, e.g. Direct Holidays; it can also be distributed through intermediaries, i.e. through travel agents to the consumers, e.g. MyTravel. Look at Figure 12.01, which shows the distribution channels used by tour operators.

Traditionally brochures were distributed through travel agents or sent directly to potential buyers. Now, with the development of technology, the internet is one of the main distribution channels for tour operators; therefore, direct selling is becoming more common.

Over the years there has been a steady increase in integration between the sectors of the travel and tourism industry. Integration is the term used to describe the merger or linking arrangements between one organisation and another. There are two types of integration: vertical and horizontal.

Vertical integration (Figure 12.02) is where the linking occurs along the production process. For example, when a tour operator creates or buys another organisation at a different stage in the production process. For example, Thomson Holidays is a tour operator owning Thomsonfly, an airline. Another example is where a tour operator acquires, through merger or purchase, a retail travel agency.

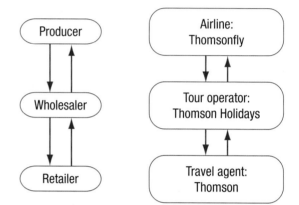

Fig 12.02 Example of vertical integration

Horizontal integration is the process of integration of two or more organisations at the same level. For example, a tour operator buying another tour

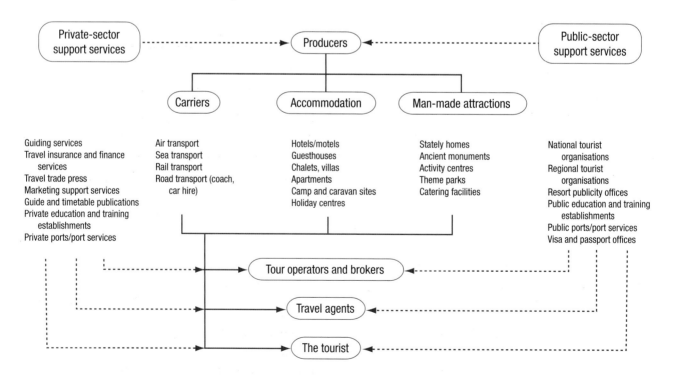

Fig. 12.01 Chain of distribution (Source: J.C. Holloway (2001) *The Business of Tourism*. FT Prentice Hall)

operator to improve its market share and reduce competition. There are a number of tour operators that are horizontally integrated (Figure 12.03).

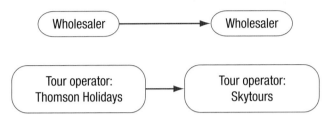

Fig 12.03 Example of horizontal integration

One of the first operators to start 'integration' was Thomson Travel Group, now known as TUI. It was formed out of an amalgamation of Universal Skytours and Riviera Holidays. Thomson also bought Britannia Airways, now renamed Thomsonfly, which became part of the same company, ensuring guaranteed control over a source of flight seats.

At the same time Thomson also bought Lunn Poly, now branded as Thomson Travel Shops. By doing this Thomson had a guaranteed source of sales outlet for their products.

In 1988, Thomson Travel Group bought Horizon Travel Group for £75 million. At the time it was the travel industry's biggest ever merger. Horizon was the third biggest tour operator in the UK and its companies included Orion Airways, Horizon Holidays and HCI.

TUI Group now has significant representation in all three levels of the travel distribution chain, namely a producer, a wholesaler division and a retail outlet. Thomson may have been the first to have all three levels of integration but other organisations have followed suit.

ACTIVITY

Research one other main tour operator of your choice to find out if it is vertically or horizontally integrated.

There are many kinds of tour operators within the UK. The largest ones have a wide portfolio of holidays to meet a range of customer needs while the smaller tour operators tend to specialise in a specific type of holiday.

There are thousands of UK tour operators organising package holidays. Some 149 organisations are members of the Association of Independent Tour Operators (AITO), at the time of print. This association is for independent tour operators, i.e. those that are not integrated. Only certain independent companies can join AITO. The Association has strict criteria for entry as the AITO logo has been established as a 'kitemark of excellence'. Look at the page from the AITO website shown in Figure 12.04 and see how AITO works.

There are a number of other trade and regulatory bodies that are linked to tour operators, for example:

- The Travel Association (ABTA)
- Federation of Tour Operators
- UKInbound
- the Civil Aviation Authority (CAA).

ACTIVITY

Research the links between tour operators and the following:
- ABTA
- UKInbound
- the Civil Aviation Authority.

Many UK tour operators are members of the Federation of Tour Operators (FTO). They have to be invited to be members and must pay a membership fee.

ACTIVITY

Visit the FTO website, www.fto.co.uk, and find out:
- how the FTO links to tour operators
- what the FTO does.

Tour operators, like any organisation, must work within a UK legal framework. Below are some examples of legal requirements with which operators need to comply.

The Consumer Protection Act 1987 makes it a criminal offence for an organisation or individual to give misleading price information about goods, services, accommodation or facilities being offered for sale. The act defines a 'misleading' price as one that is greater than the price given.

Products must not be described as being generally available when in reality they are available only in certain circumstances. This is why a tour operator

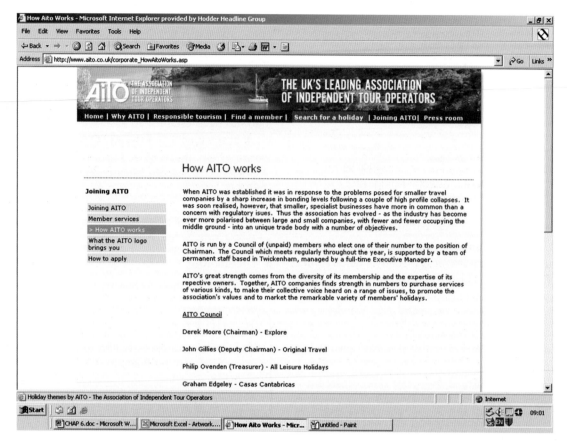

Fig 12.04 How AITO works

must fully state which facilities are included in the price and any additional supplements such as taxes or surcharges that may be payable. Many tour operators will have a statement in their brochure specifically stating what the price includes. Look at the example of what is and is not included in a Thomas Cook Signature worldwide holiday (Figure 12.05, p.194).

This Consumer Protection Act applies even to information mistakenly given, therefore it is crucial that tour operators ensure the accuracy of any information they give. This means all promotional material, such as their brochures and websites, must be checked so that they do not mislead customers.

The Trades Descriptions Act 1968 protects customers against false descriptions made knowingly or recklessly by those who are selling or providing services. This covers the tour operators' products and services.

Any description – for example, of a resort or accommodation property – must be truthful at the time it was written. If circumstances change, then the tour operator must inform the customer of these changes. This places a duty on tour operators to produce promotional materials such as web pages and brochures that do not deceive the customer, either knowingly or unknowingly.

EU Package Travel Regulations came into operation on 1 January 1993.

These regulations are specifically for the travel and tourism industry. The main aim of the regulations is to give people buying package holidays more protection and access to compensation when things go wrong. See the case studies from *Holiday Which?* reproduced opposite.

Case study

The wrong choice
Hotel horror on the Spanish Costa

While searching the internet for a two-week package holiday on the Costa del Sol, Andy Parsons thought he had found an ideal hotel – the four-star H10 Estepona Palace. First Choice described it as 'a unique hotel in a fantastic beach setting' and promised 'guests will enjoy a lively disco...and an extensive wellness centre'. It sounded perfect, so Andy paid £3654 for himself, his wife, their two children and his parents-in-law.

However, about a week before the family were due to set off, First Choice sent Andy a letter explaining that the work on the spa had fallen behind schedule and so would probably not be ready, the children's playground had been removed, and there would be building works, though it was promised the contractors would do their best to ensure the noise level would be kept to a minimum. As Andy was away on business when the post arrived at his home, he only opened the letter a couple of days before the holiday. He felt his only option was to go to Costa del Sol and hope for the best.

Unfortunately, the situation that awaited the Parsons was even more dire than expected. The building work was very disruptive – with drills, diggers and JCBs, and even a huge crane swinging right over the pool area.

Andy complained as soon as he returned home, but the best First Choice could come up with was a £330 voucher. Andy then contacted Which? Legal Service. We advised him to start court action. First Choice responded immediately with an offer to settle of £1250. Andy refused and eventually First Choice upped their offer to £1800, plus £120 in court fees, which was much more acceptable.

Point of law

If the tour operator makes a late change – and in practice it is too late to make suitable alternative arrangements – then under the Package Travel Regulations you can go on the holiday, making it clear to the tour operator you are going under protest, and claim for compensation upon your return.

(Source: *Holiday Which?*, March 2007)

Case study

Birthday blues
No celebrations on ski trip

For his 60th birthday, George Dodsworth was treated by his family to a Neilson skiing holiday in Les Arcs 2000, France. As it was a special occasion they booked the Chalet Altitude with Platinum Chalet Service – described in the brochure as having 'highly trained chalet hosts, as well as a number of service enhancements, to make your chalet holiday extra special'.

However, when George and his wife, Sylvia, arrived at their accommodation they soon realised it was going to be far from special. Having been on the road for nearly 17 hours, they were told the lift wasn't working, so they had to carry their suitcases up four flights of stairs. Every day they had to climb these stairs, often wearing ski boots as the chalet had nowhere for them to store equipment.

To make matters worse, despite having booked an en suite room, the couple were given a room with a separate bathroom – with a toilet that wasn't fitted properly, a sink hanging on pipe connections and a broken extractor fan. There were bare wires jutting out of a junction box and a nail sticking out of an electric socket. The couple were not even given clean towels until the last day of their stay.

In addition, the swimming pool was too cold to use and George described the sauna in the chalet as hanging off the wall and a potential fire hazard.

Back home, George and Sylvia complained to Neilson and were offered a mere £350. They refused and came to Which? Legal Service for advice. We helped them assess the value of their claim and suggested they ask for £1000 in full and final settlement of their claim. They did this and Neilson complied. The Dodsworths were delighted.

Point of law

Under the Package Travel Regulations holiday companies have to make sure all parts of the holiday are provided properly. if they fail to do this you are entitled to compensation. There are three basic components to holiday compensation: these are loss of value, out-of-pocket expenses and loss of enjoyment.

(Source: *Holiday Which?*, March 2007)

What the price includes

- **Accommodation** - Prices are shown within the price panel for each property. For hotels, the price applies to each of the two adults sharing a room. Apartment, villa and studio prices are based on the maximum number of adults sharing the accommodation and for fewer adults under-occupancy supplements usually apply
- **Meals** - If you book full board you will be provided with breakfast, lunch and dinner; half board usually means breakfast and dinner
- **Services of a Thomas Cook Representative** or 24-hour assistance from our UK Duty Office.
- **Return Flights** - Price panels show a basic holiday price with a nil flight supplement. Most other flights carry a supplement, and this must be added to the basic price.
- **Air passenger duty, UK airport taxes and security charges** - known at the time of going to press
- On scheduled airlines your baggage allowance will be shown on your ticket. Baggage allowances vary according to the airline, so always check before you travel. On charter flights the luggage allowance is a minimum of 15kg excluding infants. Additional luggage allowance may be available at a supplement payable at the time of booking.
- **In flight meals** - an in flight meal is included in the brochure price of your holiday.
- **Return Transport between your destination airport and accommodation in resort is included.** This will be in the form of a mini bus or coach transfer unless otherwise specified in the accommodation description or confirmed on your invoice.
- **Charges for extra security, aircraft insurance, aviation and other associated costs.**

And what's extra

- **Holiday Insurance** - you MUST be insured (see page 322 for brief details).
- **Flight supplements** - where applicable
- **Meal supplements** - where applicable are in the accommodation description.
- **Bottled mineral water** - in some All Inclusive hotels bottled mineral water does not form part of the 'unlimited soft drinks service'.
- **Under-occupancy supplements** - for studios, apartments and villas where applicable are shown in the price panel.
- **Optional excursions**.
- **Charges made by accommodation** - such as à la carte dishes, sunloungers, sporting facilities, indoor pool, telephone calls, safes, mini-bars, car parking and any other services not shown as being free. There may be a charge locally for infants for use of services and facilities in the accommodation.
- **Locally collected taxes.**
- **Accommodation Deposits** - in some cases on arrival at self catering accommodation you may be asked for a deposit. This is refundable, less the cost of any damage or loss.
When you register, many hotels will ask you for an imprint of your credit card to cover any personal extras. If you do not have a credit card, they may ask for a large cash deposit.
- **Excess baggage on coaches and aircraft** - excess baggage charges will apply if you exceed your allowance and/or you take sports equipment.
- **Late booking fee** - a charge will apply for all bookings made within 14 days of departure. We will make arrangements for you to collect your tickets from our airport representative on arrival, or in some cases may be able to post your documentation to you, at your request. The charge will be £15 per person but if special delivery is required the cost may be more.
- **Credit card charges** – there is a 2% charge on all credit card transactions (up to a maximum of £50 per transaction).
- **Possible surcharges** - see 'Surcharges - price increases after booking' section.
- **An additional variable charge depending on airline and destination, will apply.** This is for current and exceptional increases in fuel charges and will be added to all new bookings. (Please see price panels for current amounts).

Fig 12.05 Extract from Thomas Cook Signature brochure

There are a number of external influences that affect the operation of tour operators. These can be environmental, political, economic, social and technological.

Environmental influences

Case study

Hurricane Katrina: latest travel advice

Tourists scheduled to visit areas affected by Hurricane Katrina should speak to individual tour operators to rearrange travel plans, ABTA (Association of British Travel Agents) has said. The death toll from Monday's devastating storm has reached 110 and continues to rise. Authorities have said it could take up to four months before parts of the worst affected areas in Louisiana, Mississippi and Alabama are habitable again. 'Britons due to holiday in the affected areas should contact their tour operator directly,' said spokesperson Frances Tuke. 'Most operators are offering alternative destinations, refunds and deferrals where possible.'

As yet, ABTA has no official figures on how many British visitors were caught up in the hurricane although it's estimated the figure could be up to 2000.

(Source: www.thisistravel.co.uk, accessed May 2007)

How did Hurricane Katrina affect tour operators? First, customers needed to be brought home immediately so the tour operators would have faced costs to get people booked on flights back to the UK. Customers booked to travel to New Orleans immediately after the event would require their holidays to be cancelled and have the choice to either book a new holiday or have money refunded. Some tour operators only specialise in one destination so they may not have another product to offer their customers.

Hurricanes regularly hit the Caribbean. As a result of this, tour operators need to inform customers about risks of external influences like hurricanes. They often give advice in their brochure relating to any risk to customers. Here is a weather disclaimer quotation from a Virgin Holidays 2007 brochure:

" The area of the Caribbean is occasionally affected by hurricanes. Hurricanes, due to their unpredictability, are a force majeure event and we shall not be liable for any changes to your holiday arrangements, either before departure, or during the holiday, which in our judgment are necessary to protect your interests and/or safety. "

Political influences

Political influences include war, terrorism, the introduction of legislation, unstable governments, economic situations, e.g. price of oil, government taxes, currency rates.

Terrorism is a major influence over which tour operators have no control. Tour operators are able to

ACTIVITY

Research other environmental influences that could affect tour operators.

ACTIVITY

Look at the FCO extract about travel to Egypt, below. Explain how this advice would affect tour operators featuring Egypt in their brochures.

TRAVEL ADVICE BY COUNTRY

Still Current at: 25 April 2007
Updated: 20 February 2007

Egypt

This advice has been reviewed and reissued with amendments to the Summary, River & Sea Safety and Health sections. The overall level of the advice has not changed.

SUMMARY
- There is a high threat from terrorism in Egypt. Attacks can be indiscriminate and against civilian targets, including places frequented by foreigners.
- Since October 2004 there have been three separate bomb attacks in the Sinai Peninsula. These attacks have killed and injured a number of British nationals. The most recent incident was on 24 April 2006 when there were explosions at three separate locations in the resort town of Dahab, in which 23 people were killed and more than 60 injured. You should see the Terrorism Section of this travel advice for more information.
- Developments in the region may trigger public unrest. You should take care to avoid demonstrations, which can turn hostile, and be particularly vigilant in public places.
- Outbreaks of Avian Influenza (Bird Flu) in Egypt have resulted in a number of human fatalities. As a precaution, you should avoid live animal markets, poultry farms and other places where you may come into contact with domestic, caged or wild birds; and ensure poultry and egg dishes are thoroughly cooked. For further information see Avian Influenza section below and also read the FCO's Avian and Pandemic Influenza Factsheet.
- Approximately 1,033,000 British nationals visited Egypt in 2006. Most visits are trouble-free. The main types of incident for which British nationals require consular assistance in Egypt are for hospital cases, especially in relation to psychiatric illness; and death, mostly from natural causes and drowning. The majority of consular cases occur in Cairo, Luxor and Sharm el-Sheikh, where most tourists stay. The crime rate in Egypt is low but you should safeguard valuables including your passport and money.
- Egyptian society is conservative and women should dress modestly.
- You should carry some form of photographic ID at all times. A copy of your passport is sufficient.
- We strongly recommend that you obtain comprehensive travel and medical insurance before travelling. You should check any exclusions, and that your policy covers you for the activities you want to undertake. Please see Travel Insurance.

(Source: www.fco.gov.uk, accessed April 2007)

liaise with the Foreign and Commonwealth Office (FCO) to determine the level of threat, however, terrorism occurs without warning. Tour operators need to consider the risk involved and decide whether they should include a destination in their brochure. Sharm al Sheikh in Egypt is a destination that has had a high threat level.

Other political factors include the introduction of taxes or laws – for example, in February 2007 an increase in air taxes came into force.

ACTIVITY

Read the extract from the Guardian in the box on the following pages, relating to air tax. Discuss the implications of this tax for tour operators.

Tax on short-haul flights raised from £5 to £10

Air passengers face a 7% increase in the cost of the average short-haul ticket after air passenger duty was doubled in the pre-budget report.

The move means that tax on short-haul flights leaving the UK will rise by £5 to £10 per economy class passenger from February 1, a cost to be passed directly on to ticket prices by airlines. On long-haul flights, it will rise to £40 for economy class and will double to £80 in business class, which generates nearly all the profits on long-distance journeys.

(Source: The *Guardian*, 7 December 2006)

Economic influences

Economic influences include factors such as currency fluctuations. This is when the exchange is not stable in a country. How does this affect the operation of a tour operator? Firstly, many tour operators will contract accommodation overseas. They will often agree a contract price in the local currency. If the rate used to exchange the accommodation price is good for the tour operator, i.e. the currency has a low rate of exchange against the pound, then it will cost the tour operator less for the product. Secondly, if a destination is expensive because the rate of exchange is poor, then the cost of products and services will be more expensive for people. Customers buying holidays from tour operators will be more likely to purchase a holiday to a destination that has a similar cost of living to that of the UK rather than one that is more expensive. Let us look at an example.

If a tour operator contracts a room at $20 per night and the rate is 1.82 to the pound, then the tour operator will pay £10.98 per room per night:

$20 @ 1.82 (rate of exchange) = £10.98

If the exchange rate was to 'crash' and fall to 1.50 to the pound, then the cost will increase to £13.33 per room:

$20 @ 1.50 (rate of exchange) = £13.33

It may not seem much of a difference between £10.98 and £13.33 but when this is multiplied by 365 days a year, then each room will be costing tour operators an extra £857.75 extra per year. Now think about how many hotel rooms a tour operator is likely to contract out:

£13.33 – £10.98 = £2.35
£2.35 x 365 days = £857.75

ACTIVITY

Make a list of significant events that have occurred in the world in the past 12 months and have had significant consequences for tour operators. Identify which of these events you think a tour operator could realistically have expected to anticipate. Explain which of these events was likely to have had the greatest disruptive effect. You may want to use *Travel Trade Gazette* and *Travel Weekly* as sources of information.

Assessing the outcome

You work for a travel and tourism trade magazine. Produce a feature travel supplement on the tour operations environment.

- Describe the tour operations environment (**P1**).

The range of products and services offered by tour operators

There are different types of UK tour operator. There are *outbound* tour operators that deal with holidays from the UK to overseas. There are *inbound* tour operators that arrange holidays for customers visiting the UK. There are also tour operators that arrange holidays in the UK for people that live here. These are known as *domestic* tour operators.

There are currently four major tour operators who dominate the market: Thomson, Thomas Cook, Airtours and First Choice. These tour operators are integrated tour operators, as discussed earlier in this unit. The opposite of integrated operators are independent tour operators.

ACTIVITY

Visit the Association of Independent Tour Operators' website: www.aito.co.uk. Name ten tour operators that are part of this association.

There are also specialist tour operators. This category of tour operator will specialise in a specific product. This can be the type of activities that they specialise in – for example, safari holidays or dancing holidays. The product can also be specialist in terms of the destination – for example, there are specialist tour operators for Greece and Peru.

Many major tour operators sell a wide range of holidays such as summer sun, winter sun, ski, long-haul travel and short breaks. They will have separate brochures for each of type of holiday. They generally deal with the mass market, which is all market segment target groups, rather than one specific target group. The appeal of mass marketing is that by attracting a wider range of target markets, it has the potential for higher total profits. Tour operators with mass-market products often expect the larger profit to result from the expanded volume of holidays available and the increase in potential customers that it can target. Mass-market products have broad appeal.

Package holidays put together by tour operators are usually made up of a number of components.

ACTIVITY

Mr and Mrs Birt booked the following holiday at their local travel agency:

21 September
Flights from London Gatwick
14 nights
Hotel Taj Fort Aguada Beach
Tranfers included (75 minutes)
Cost £1419 per person.

Explain why this is classed as a 'package' holiday.

There are a number of optional extras that tour operators provide. These include:

- pre-bookable seats – which allows customers to reserve seats together in advance
- in-flight meals – allowing customers to book meals on the plane in advance of arriving at the airport
- room upgrade – such as deluxe rooms, sea view rooms, room with balconies
- insurance – often there are standard and superior insurance options available
- flight upgrade – in the past this was only available on scheduled seats where first and business class are available; now many long-haul charter flights are able to offer seat upgrades with extra legroom
- learn-to-ski packages – these usually include tuition, boot and ski hire as well as ski passes.

ACTIVITY

Look through three different brochures and identify the products and services available.

Tailor-made holidays are becoming increasingly popular. These holidays are produced specifically to match the needs and wants of a customer. The tour operator will take the customer's requirements and produce a holiday specifically to meet their requirements. There has been an increase in tour operators offering tailor-made packages.

With the exception of mass-market brochures that are targeting a range of different customers in one brochure, many brochures are produced and designed to target a specific market. Club 18–30 is a recognised brand that makes its target market very clear. The Club 18–30 product features destinations that are popular with young people. They feature lively resorts and the accommodation tends to be in central locations to meet the needs of young people who enjoy going out to bars and clubs.

ACTIVITY

Look at a family holiday brochure. In pairs, look at the brochure and discuss the following.
- What makes you think that the brochure is targeting families?
- What is the product for families?
- What sort of images are used?

Case study

Outbound holidays

Ward Holidays (a fictitious organisation) has just been established. It is an independent tour operator and a member of the Association of Independent Tour Operators (AITO). It is classed as an outbound tour operator. The holidays featured in its brochures are in the following destinations:

- Costa del Sol
- Costa Blanca
- Canary Islands
- Rhodes
- Corfu.

In the summer sun brochure it features flights from a range of local airports. The product includes a number of accommodation properties including apartments and hotels ranging from two to four stars.

Ward Holidays aims to appeal to the mass market. The packages featured in all brochures include accommodation for 7 or 14 nights, return flights and return coach transfer to the resort.

ACTIVITY

Ward Holidays is looking to expand and add additional products and services to its portfolio. You work in the product development department. Research additional products that the tour operator could add to its existing programme and promote in its brochures. Prepare a PowerPoint presentation featuring your suggestions.

Assessing the outcome

You work for a TV company. It has asked you to produce a holiday programme that describes the products and services offered by different categories of tour operators. Write a script for the programme.

- Describe the products and services provided by different categories of tour operators for different target markets (**P2**).

The functions of tour operators

Tour operators need careful planning and preparation for their programme. The task of coordinating the activities involved to produce a tour operator's programme often normally falls to the marketing department.

When planning a package holiday, the tour operator needs to consider a number of issues. Let us investigate these.

- It needs to make sure that it has the correct capacity, e.g. the right amount of holidays available. Over-capacity could result in holidays not been sold, resulting in a tour operator losing money.

- As there are a large number of tour operators, they need to make sure that the holidays offered are competitively priced.

- Tour operators need to make sure that they appeal to customers. In order to do this, they must be aware of the trends in market.

- Tour operators are private-sector organisations, therefore they need to produce profits.

There are a number of stages involved in the planning of a package holiday. Let us look at these now.

Research

The purpose of research is to gain and gather information on a given subject. Tour operators need to find out about trends and the wants and needs of people. For example, they need to find out about the types of holidays people are booking, the destinations people want to visit. The aim is to predict the total market size, type and extent of holiday demand.

Many tour operators design questionnaires (see Fig. 12.06 overleaf). Some research is gained from the questionnaires given to customers at the end of their holiday.

Tour operators can also use media reports, e.g. TV, radio or newspaper articles. They can also use their staff and previous sales performance statistics.

ACTIVITY

Look at the National Statistics website: www.statistics.gov.uk. How can this research help tour operators? Try to consider the categories of tour operators.

It is very important tour operators study the brochures and web pages of other tour operators. They will scrutinise the products of the competitors as soon as their brochures are published. They will make price comparisons with their own products. They will look at the special features promoted and see if there are any accommodation properties they share. Tour operators will also look at optional extras, such as car rental costs and insurance premiums.

Once research is complete and conclusions drawn, the next task is to produce a marketing plan. This should define the organisation's strategy and set SMART objectives for the programme (see Unit 2). The tour operator will need to determine how many holidays it plans to sell, the capacity of accommodation required and the seat capacity for the season. Larger tour operators often plan for a number of programmes together. Once overall capacity is agreed, then individual programmes are apportioned capacity, e.g. departure points need to be planned – for example, which regional airports will be used. Tour operators will do this by referring back to the research.

Contracting is an important element when a tour operator is planning a programme. This is generally carried out by several senior members of staff as it requires an in-depth knowledge of the company's background, financial standing and goals and objectives. The senior members need to have effective communication skills. They also need knowledge of contract law although they will use a lawyer.

ACTIVITY

Explain why a senior member of staff working for a tour operator in the contracting department requires effective communication skills and knowledge of contract law.

Contracting for existing products is often done very quickly using previous suppliers, provided that the tour operators are happy with the product and service previously provided. It is more difficult, however, to acquire new products – for example, new accommodation in a new resort. One of the reasons it is more difficult is the tour operator could be competing with other tour operators for the same accommodation. When it becomes competitive, the cost of the product can increase, i.e. the tour operator is forced to pay more for the hotel rooms.

The contracting of accommodation is often done in a resort. It can be done directly with the accommodation provider, e.g. the senior member of staff from contracting will speak directly with the hotelier. Alternatively, contracts can be organised indirectly using an appointed local agent, e.g. an agent is used to negotiate the contract on behalf of the tour operator.

ACTIVITY

Explain why large tour operators deal directly with suppliers and smaller tour operator usually have to use indirect methods. Explain the limitations of a tour operator using an indirect method.

There are three methods of contracting: commitment, allocation and ad hoc.

Commitment is when a tour operator contracts to pay for an agreed number of beds for the season regardless of whether it has the customers to fill them. This means even if the tour operator does not sell

SECTION A

1. Your Details

Title   First Name

Surname

Partner's Title   First Name

Partner's Surname

Address

Postcode

Country

Home tel. no*

Mobile tel. no*

Email*   @

Please provide your email as this is the easiest way for us to let you know of up to the minute great deals.

Today's date

* Please provide if you are happy to receive information from ourselves and other selected third parties.

2. Booking

A How did you book this holiday/flight?

In a Travel Agency ☐   Phoned a Call Centre ☐

On a Thomson website ☐   Other ☐

B Number of nights abroad:

1-2	3-6	7	8-13	14	15-20	21+
☐	☐	☐	☐	☐	☐	☐

C Accommodation and food arrangements:

Self Catering ☐   Room Only ☐

Half Board ☐   All Inclusive ☐ (All meals, drinks etc included)

Full Board ☐   Flexible Dining ☐ (combining B/B and H/B)

Bed & Breakfast ☐   Flight Only ☐

D I am travelling with (please tick the one that best applies):

Alone ☐   In a couple ☐

My partner & child(ren) ☐   Just my children ☐

With a friend ☐   My family & my children's grandparent(s) ☐

In a small group (up to 5) ☐   In a large group (6 or more) ☐

E Ages of children travelling with you (Under 18):

☐ yrs   ☐ yrs   ☐ yrs   ☐ yrs

3. Airport

Taking everything into account, how would you rate:

	Excellent	Good	Fair	Poor
A UK Airport check-in	☐	☐	☐	☐
B UK Thomson Service Desk before check-in (if applicable)	☐	☐	☐	☐

3. Airport (cont.)

Taking everything into account, how would you rate:

	Excellent	Good	Fair	Poor
C Overseas airport check-in	☐	☐	☐	☐
D Convenience of flight times	☐	☐	☐	☐

4. In-flight Experience

Taking everything into account, how would you rate:

	Excellent	Good	Fair	Poor
A Welcome & assistance on boarding the aircraft	☐	☐	☐	☐
B Helpfulness & attentiveness of the crew	☐	☐	☐	☐
C Cabin crew service overall	☐	☐	☐	☐
D Flight overall	☐	☐	☐	☐
E Toilet cleanliness	☐	☐	☐	☐
F Cabin cleanliness	☐	☐	☐	☐
G Seat comfort	☐	☐	☐	☐
H Overall cabin environment	☐	☐	☐	☐
I In-flight food	☐	☐	☐	☐
J Range of snacks/goods on sale	☐	☐	☐	☐

K Did you read the in-flight magazine?

All of it	Most of it	Hardly any of it	None of it
☐	☐	☐	☐

L How would you rate the in-flight magazine?

Excellent	Good	Fair	Poor
☐	☐	☐	☐

5. Car Hire

A Did you hire a car for your holiday?

Yes ☐   No ☐

B If YES, which car hire company did you use?

Europcar ☐   Alamo ☐

Holiday Autos ☐   Other ☐

C Was the car:

Pre-booked in UK via agent/website/holiday company ☐

Pre-booked in the UK direct with car hire company ☐

Booked overseas by Thomson ☐

Booked overseas direct with car hire company ☐

Please rate:

	Excellent	Good	Fair	Poor
D Car hire: value for money	☐	☐	☐	☐
E Car hire: service	☐	☐	☐	☐
F Car hire: overall	☐	☐	☐	☐

6. Holiday Experience

A Not counting this one, how many short breaks/holidays abroad have you taken in the last 12 months?

	None	1	2	3	4	5+
Short breaks (up to 6 nights)	☐	☐	☐	☐	☐	☐
Holidays (7 nights or more)	☐	☐	☐	☐	☐	☐

6. Holiday Experience (cont.)

B Not counting this one, how many business flights have you taken in the last 12 months?

None	1	2	3	4	5+
☐	☐	☐	☐	☐	☐

C Not counting this one, which of these types of holidays have you taken in the last three years?

Villa ☐   Ski ☐

Longhaul ☐   City Break ☐

Low-cost flights ☐   Cruise ☐

D Not counting this one, have you been on holiday to this resort in the last two years?

Yes ☐   No ☐

E Not counting this one, have you been on holiday to this accommodation in the last two years?

Yes ☐   No ☐

F Not counting this one, which of these companies have you taken holidays with in the last two years?

Thomson ☐   Portland ☐

Expedia ☐   Ebookers ☐

Last Minute ☐   Thomas Cook ☐

Airtours ☐   First Choice ☐

Other ☐

G How likely are you to recommend this current holiday company to a friend or relative? (e.g. Thomson, Portland, Thomsonfly)

Definitely	Probably	Possibly	Not likely
☐	☐	☐	☐

7. Journey Type

Are you on:

a) A package holiday, or a holiday where you bought your accommodation from Thomson / Thomson website? ☐
If so, please go to Question 8, Your Holiday Company

b) Just a flight with us or arranged your accommodation independently? ☐
If so, please go to Question 13, Independent Arrangements

Fig 12.06 Tour operator's market research questionnaire

sufficient holidays, it is still committed to pay for the accommodation contracted. This type of contracting is high risk because if there is an incident in a resort – for example, a terrorist attack – or if sales are generally low, the accommodation must still be paid for, even though the tour operator has not used the accommodation. Due to the commitment made by the tour operator, it will, however, get a good price. The greater number of rooms a tour operator commits to will result in a lower price agreement. This type of contracting is also known as guaranteed accommodation. There is less risk of overbooking. Mass-market operators often use this type of contracting. Any accommodation unsold is used for late bookings.

Allocation is another type of contracting. This is where a number of beds are allocated to the operator until a certain date. After this date (release date) they are given back to the accommodation provider. If the tour operator needs additional rooms after the release date, then the tour operator needs to contact the accommodation provider to check availability.

ACTIVITY

Explain why allocation contracting reduces the financial risk for tour operators.
Explain why accommodation providers may not offer tour operators an allocation contract.

Finally, *ad hoc* contracts are those that are requested as a customer needs them. This type of contract is often used for tailor-made holidays. These contract rates are much higher than with other methods.

ACTIVITY

Describe a problem that a tour operator could have when contracting on an ad hoc basis.

Transport is an essential component of the package holiday. It is predominantly air transport that is used by outbound UK tour operators but there are also tour operators offering coach and rail travel. Large tour operators often have their own transport companies but it is not always the case that the tour operator uses them.

It may be that the company airline can secure a higher contract rate from another tour operator. For tour operators who do not have their own airline, or it cannot supply all their needs, they need to contract air seats.

ACTIVITY

Look at a Thomson summer sun brochure. Identify the airlines used in the brochure. Explain why Thomson may contract airlines other than its own airline, Thomsonfly.

Charter flights are the most common flights contracted by tour operators. There are different types of contracts available to tour operators.

Time series charter is when a tour operator charters the full aircraft for a period of time, e.g. May to October. To make sure that the aircraft is maximised, the tour operators will plan flight patterns that take full advantage of the availability of the aircraft (see Figure 12.07).

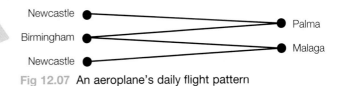

Fig 12.07 An aeroplane's daily flight pattern

Although this type of contracting is high risk, it can provide a cheaper cost per seat and it offers flexibility in terms of the choice of departure points and destinations available. If the aircraft is not fully used by the tour operator, it can be subcontracted to other tour operators.

Part charter is when an air broker sells flight seats on charter flights on behalf of an operator. This can be done on an ad hoc basis. Some tour operators will not want to contract the whole aircraft.

ACTIVITY

You work for the Civil Aviation Authority. Today a tour operator ceased trading. A radio station has invited you to discuss the benefits of medium-sized and smaller tour operators using part charters. Make some notes in preparation for the radio discussion.

Schedule flights tend to be used for long-haul products. They offer a choice of class of travel – e.g. business, first class – and more flexibility in the duration of flights.

Tour operators will also contract ancillary services, e.g. excursions and surface transport, i.e. transfer coaches. Tour operators will often use some form of ground handling agent to do this.

Once the tour operator has agreed contracts, then it is time to put the brochure together. The brochure needs to consider its overall appearance – for example, paper quality, the target market it is trying to attract, the photographs to be included. The tour operator needs to make sure that the photographs portray the correct image. Descriptions and images need to comply with legislation: correct description, accurate prices, etc.

While the brochure production department is getting the brochure 'off the ground', the pricing department needs to determine the pricing strategies to be used. Within the marketing department they will also need to set up an internet site and decide how the holiday will be promoted. Some examples of tour operators' promotional materials are shown in Figures 12.08–12.11.

Pre-departure is the service offered to customers before they go on holiday. Tour operators usually have an administration department that will deal with customer enquiries. They send confirmations to customers confirming the holiday booking and also post out tickets. This department will work closely with the overseas department by sending passenger manifests and rooming lists to the resort. This department also needs to deal with amendments to bookings, e.g. if a customer needs to change a name on a booking.

The UK office also has to deal with any brochure errata or changes to holiday booking made by the tour operator.

Post-departure is the service offered to customers after they have received the holiday (product/service). The post-departure team deals with holiday complaints. The role of this department is one of conciliation since it is expected to placate a disappointed or upset customer. This department will aim to come to some agreement, whether it is an apology or some kind of compensation without having to resort to outside intervention, e.g. *Watchdog*. Sometimes an ex gratia payment is offered to a customer. This payment is made on the understanding that the tour operator is not accepting any liability for whatever has gone wrong during the holiday. The payment is simply made as a goodwill gesture on its part. The litigation section within the post-departure department will be responsible for dealing with any serious complaints that will actually go to court.

The time involved in planning a tour operator's programme is lengthy. It can take up to three years from start to completion. Figure 12.12 is an adaptation of the timescale that the Federation of Tour Operators (FTO) gives (see p.204).

Fig 12.08 A brochure cover

ACTIVITY

Tour operators have different names for their post-departure department, e.g. client relations, customer services department. Find out what three different tour operators call their post-departure department.

Assessing the outcome

You work for a tour operator. Two new members of staff have joined the company and you have been asked by your manager to give a short presentation describing how tour operators plan, sell and administer package holiday programmes. Also, describe how they operate a tour operator's programme.

- Describe how tour operators plan, sell and administer a package holiday programme (**P3**).
- Describe how tour operators operate a package holiday programme (**P4**).

Fig 12.09 A newspaper advert

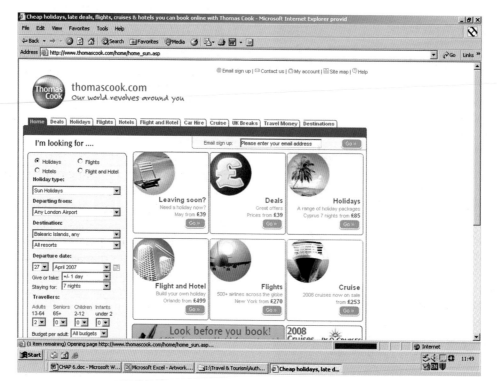

Fig 12.10 A web page (Thomas Cook)

Late 2007	Planning with countries and resorts to use, and broadly how many holidays to offer
Jan/Feb 2008	Contracting with hoteliers and airlines
May/Apr 2008	Preparing brochures – prices, photographs, descriptions etc.
May 2008	Brochure launch
Nov 2008	Airline scheduling meetings to avoid congested flight timings
Feb 2009	Bookings received and forecasts for programmes reveiwed. Early adjustments made if necessary
Mar/Apr 2010	Employ overseas staff, update training, finalise arrangements with hoteliers, coach operators etc.
May 2010	Issue tickets and final invoice
Jul 2010	Confirm names of customers to airlines, hotels, overseas staff
Aug 2010	Welcome holidaymakers

Fig 12.11 An operator's year
(Source: adapted from the Federation of Tour Operators)

How to plan and cost a package holiday

Costing of brochures

Tour operators must pay for transport, accommodation and other products and services featured in their brochures. When costing a holiday, they must take a number of factors into account.

There will be fixed costs that the tour operator will need to pay for. Many of these costs are for both the UK and overseas operations. They include staff salaries, rent of the premises, heating, lighting, cleaning and chartered transport.

There are variable costs that will change – for example, the accommodation cost can vary depending on the rate of exchange and the number of rooms used.

Tour operators also need to build in costs to the travel agency as they pay it commission for selling the holiday. Commissions do vary but are in the region of 7–15 per cent.

The larger tour operators are competing with other tour operators so they often use competitive pricing strategies. This could mean that holidays in the low season are offered at the break-even point where no actual profit is made, but holidays in the peak season are inflated to cover all the costs, including the travel agency's commission. The smaller tour operators tend to cost the basic core costs of the holiday and then add a mark-up of 20–35 per cent.

There are times when holidays do not sell and it is necessary for a tour operator to sell them without making a profit. This is not ideal but it is better at least to cover the costs, especially if the tour operator actually owns airlines and hotels. Reducing prices can have serious implications for a tour operator.

Tour operators are not able to predict exactly how many holidays they will sell. They will set a predicted realistic target that they think they will sell. This is known as a load factor (see the case study overleaf); this means the percentage of flight seats they estimate they will sell. If a tour operator charters a full flight, it needs to make sure that it has fully covered all of its costs. It needs to make allowances for all the seats that are not sold. For example, the first flight of the season will have passengers travelling out but no passengers on the inbound flight as there are no customers, as yet, overseas. At the beginning of the season it will be difficult to sell every seat. Tour operators generally assume that they will sell only 90 per cent of their seats. This will be their break-even point. They will work out their costing on this figure. Whatever they sell over and above 90 per cent is profit.

ACTIVITY

" The A380 will carry more passengers over longer distances, allowing for projected passenger growth worldwide and helping to ease an increasingly congested environment. It will achieve this without increasing the number of air traffic movements and without negatively impacting the environment, thanks to significantly reduced noise and emissions levels. "

(Source: www.airbus.com, accessed May 2007)

Discuss how the introduction of the Airbus A380 will affect tour operators' holiday costs.

ACTIVITY

Assume you work for a tour operator. The tour operator has over-estimated the number of holidays it will sell in a year. As a consequence, it has contracted to buy more flights and more accommodation than it needs. The price in the brochure is priced at the cheapest possible price; there is no margin to offer holidays at a discount. Sales are slow.

Suggest what the tour operator could do and explain how it could deal with the problem.

Tour operators' pricing usually varies throughout the brochure. For example, prices are cheaper in the early weeks of December, and the most expensive over Christmas and New Year, during school holidays, at the height of the summer and over bank holiday weekends. This is because the operator knows there will be enough people looking for holidays in peak times to increase the prices without fear of losing business. Figure 12.13 highlights this as the price shown rise significantly from 16 July to 23 August.

Case study

Costing the load factor

A tour operator contracts a flight series for a 150-seater aircraft every Tuesday at a cost of £18,000 per return flight. Its season covers 28 weeks. However, there is an empty leg at the beginning and at the end of the season. This gives a total of 29 return flights. This cost is 29 x £18,000 = £522,000.

The actual cost of each flight would be £522,000 ÷ 28 = £18,642.85.

The aircraft holds 150 passengers but a load factor of 90 per cent would means that only 90 per cent of the 150 passengers fly, which = 135 passengers. It would therefore be expected that 135 passengers would need to book in order to cover the cost of the flight. The cost per person for the flight is £18,642.85 ÷ 135 = £138.09.

If more than 135 people book, then the extra fares are profit for the tour operator. If fewer than 135 book the flight, then the tour operator will make a loss. In this case, a decision may be made to consolidate flights and ask clients to fly at another time or from another airport.

Assuming that the hotel is £65.00 per week and transfers £6.00 return then the cost would be £138.09 + £65 + £6 = £209.09 per person. The £209.09 is required to cover the actual costs. The tour operator must calculate a price at which the fixed costs and the travel agent's commission can also be covered. Fixed costs are generally marked up at about 25 per cent, plus the travel agent's commission. Most travel agents receive 10 per cent commission from the tour operators. If the travel agent is to receive 10 per cent of the final selling price this means that the tour operator must add another one-ninth (or 11.1 per cent) to the actual cost of the holiday. This final price is known as the break-even point. So in the example the break-even point would be:

Cost per person	£209.09
Fixed costs	£52.27
Subtotal	£261.36
One-ninth for travel agents' commission	£29.01
Selling price	£290.37

The tour operator could then round up the selling price to £291.00, which could be charged throughout the season. The pricing strategy might then be: (a) to sell the holiday at this price knowing that immediate costs would be covered; (b) add low season mark-up to make small amounts of profit; (c) raise the price of high season mark-up knowing that fixed costs and profits will be well covered.

Summer 2006		May					Jun		Jul					Aug					Sep		Oct			
Type of room	No. of Nights	1 May-13 May	14 May-17 May	18 May-20 May	21 May-23 May	24 May-31 May	1 Jun-27 Jun	28 Jun-30 Jun	1 Jul-12 Jul	13 Jul-15 Jul	16 Jul-19 Jul	20 Jul-22 Jul	23 Jul-2 Aug	3 Aug-9 Aug	10 Aug-19 Aug	20 Aug-23 Aug	24 Aug-26 Aug	27 Aug-1 Sep	2 Sep-15 Sep	16 Sep-30 Sep	1 Oct-11 Oct	12 Oct-18 Oct	19 Oct-25 Oct	26 Oct-31 Oct
Los Zocos Club Code: **6301** Board Basis: **Self Catering**																								
1 B'room/4 Adults	7	199	205	209	219	359	245	265	299	325	345	375	369	375	379	349	339	255	249	245	225	259	369	239
	14	265	269	309	319	359	309	399	465	469	479	529	515	535	509	419	415	349	335	319	309	365	359	299
2 B'room/6 Adults	7	199	205	219	229	339	229	229	269	289	309	329	339	349	365	349	329	309	269	259	235	279	369	239
	14	269	275	339	349	349	299	339	409	419	439	479	489	509	499	509	415	359	349	345	345	385	369	289
1st Child	7	129	129	149	159	305	155	155	169	189	225	285	309	309	309	299	299	269	165	135	135	195	289	155
	14	129	129	149	159	319	165	165	179	199	285	299	319	319	319	309	309	205	175	145	145	289	289	155
2nd Child	7	165	165	185	195	339	189	189	209	225	259	325	345	345	355	335	335	269	219	169	169	229	325	189
	14	165	165	189	199	355	195	199	219	235	319	335	345	345	355	335	335	235	219	169	169	259	259	189
Los Zocos Club Code: **6300** Board Basis: **All Inclusive**																								
1 B'room/2 Adults	7	399	405	419	429	549	459	469	519	549	569	589	595	599	605	575	569	479	469	459	445	459	549	419
	14	649	655	699	709	759	729	799	849	879	915	975	965	985	975	915	829	709	709	695	679	725	689	639
1st Child	7	205	205	209	215	369	245	225	249	269	289	349	359	359	389	365	315	225	209	225	229	289	389	219
	14	285	285	309	315	429	319	299	315	355	425	469	479	479	479	455	329	299	275	295	299	415	405	279
2nd Child	7	235	235	239	245	399	275	255	279	299	319	379	389	389	419	395	345	255	239	255	259	319	419	249
	14	315	315	339	345	459	349	329	345	385	455	499	509	509	509	485	359	329	305	325	329	445	435	309

*(See page 139) Seasons: **Low:** 1 May-25 May, 19 Sep-19 Oct, 28 Oct-31 Oct; **Mid:** 01 Apr-09 Apr, 24 Apr-30 Apr, 31 May-20 Jul, 20 Aug-18 Sep; **High:** 10 Apr-23 Apr, 26 May-30 May, 21 Jul-19 Aug, 20 Oct-27 Oct.

For full details of holiday insurance, flight supplements, booking conditions and essential reading information, all of which must be read before booking, please see pages 130-145. Prices may be subject to increase or decrease in accordance with First Choice pricing policy on page 139 and are in £'s per full paying passenger (adult) and include airport taxes and Air passenger duty.

Fig 12.12 First Choice prices, 2006

ACTIVITY

Look at a summer sun package holiday brochure. Find out when the prices change in the brochure. Explain why the prices fluctuate.

Having a high load factor will mean low prices but a risk of not selling sufficient to break even. Having a low load factor will be less risky, however, prices will be higher.

Profit margin

If tour operators are able to sell more holidays then they make more profit. Sometimes, however, only a small profit is made and sometimes it is insufficient to cover all costs. A profit margin is added to the total of the fixed costs. It covers variable indirect costs – for example, if the overheads such as heating costs increase. It also takes into account factors beyond the control of the organisation, e.g. fluctuations in exchange rates, new contracts, etc. There is also an allowance for net profit. The amount of net profit made per customer is usually very small: sometimes as low as £1 per person. However, large companies selling millions of holidays a year can make a sizeable profit with such a small margin.

Costing is complex and not only includes the costing of flights and accommodation but many other elements.

ACTIVITY

Discover the answers to the following questions.

- A tour operator charters an aircraft with 112 seats, of which 99 are sold. What is the load factor?
- The price of a holiday is based on a load factor of 85 per cent; 149 seats are chartered and 118 are sold. What percentage load factor was achieved?
- How many more seats must be sold to make break-even point?
- Price is based on a load factor of 80 per cent. 85 seats are chartered and 63 are sold. The load factor is increased and prices reduced. How many more seats must be sold to achieve a load factor of 90 per cent?
- If 72 seats of a 96-seat charter are sold, what load factor has been reached?
- If a flight is contracted for £4250 and has 120 seats available, what price would be allocated for the flight component of a package if a 90 per cent load factor were forecast?
- A company decides to put a 20 per cent mark-up on all air holidays and 27 per cent on coach holidays. Accommodation costs for seven nights are £143. Air transport costs are £116. Coach transport costs are £44. What would be the total cost of a holiday by air and a holiday by coach?
- A holiday's net cost is £150. Selling price is to be based on an 80 per cent load factor and a 20 per cent mark-up is added. Due to low sales the load factor is to be increased to 95 per cent. At what price would you sell a holiday to give the same total profit at break-even point with a capacity of 80 seats?

ACTIVITY

Look at a summer sun package holiday brochure. Produce a list of all the contracted products a tour operator will pay for.

Assessing the outcome

You work for a tour operator in the planning and pricing department. Plan and cost a package holiday for inclusion in the tour operator's brochure.

- Plan and cost a package holiday for inclusion in a tour operator's programme (**P5**).

Improve your grade

Explain means to make a point clear and to give reasons or justification. In the context of this topic to achieve (**M1**) merit criterion an explanation of the challenges facing the tour operating sector is required. So it is necessary to look at different challenges and give reasons and justification as to why these challenges face tour operators. This unit has already covered some challenges.

For distinction (**D1**) you need to evaluate the effectiveness of tour operators in responding to challenges facing the sector. *Collins Dictionary*'s definition of evaluation is 'to ascertain or set the amount or value. To judge or assess the worth of.'

Evaluate is to put a value on after assessment. In the higher grading criteria it is possible after having explained the challenges facing the tour operating sector that you can draw conclusions and make judgements as to how well the tour operators have responded to the challenges they face. Consider what they have done to deal with the challenges. It is good and, if so, why. If the changes are not effective, then again consider the reasons why. Your justification should not be just what you consider but should be based upon evidence from your research.

KarstadtQuelle to merge Thomas Cook with MyTravel

- KarstadtQuelle holds 52 percent in the new Thomas Cook Group plc
- KarstadtQuelle to hold key positions in the new company
- High value increase for KarstadtQuelle shareholders

The leading German retailer KarstadtQuelle AG is to merge its tourism subsidiary, Thomas Cook, with the leading British travel company MyTravel. The newly established company will be named Thomas Cook Group plc and will be traded on the London Stock Exchange. KarstadtQuelle will hold 52 percent in the new company and will consolidate it fully. The MyTravel shareholders will hold 48 percent. The merged company will achieve sales of approximately Euro 12 billion and will be a leader in Great Britain, Scandinavia and Canada with leading positions in continental Europe. It will be one of the largest travel groups in the world. The merger is subject to approval from the antitrust authorities and the shareholders of MyTravel plc as well as the final closing of the previously announced transaction with Lufthansa.

Thomas Cook AG is one of the world's leading tourism groups, with 2005/2006 sales of Euro 7.8 billion and a record operating profit (EBITA) of Euro 228 million. The company employs 19,775 people worldwide.

MyTravel Group plc is the third largest tour operator in the UK, after Thomson/TUI and Thomas Cook UK. In 2006, the company generated sales of £2.8 billion (Euro 4.2 billion) and employed 12,947 staff. Its geographical focus is in the UK, Northern Europe and the USA. The group was founded in 1972 under the umbrella of Airtours, and commenced operations of its own airline at the beginning of the 1980s. In the 1990s, there were purchases of several travel companies, including the Scandinavian Leisure Group with the operator Ving and the airline company Premiair. In 2002, Airtours was renamed MyTravel Group.

(Source: adapted from KardstadtQuelle press release, 12 February 2007)

This section should help you consider the challenges faced by tour operators in more detail and aid your explanation and evaluation to achieve the higher grades.

Challenges facing tour operators

There are a number of challenges that tour operators face. For independent tour operators mergers of organisations can be a great threat. Small independent tour operators find this very challenging.

So what is the advantage of integration? Well, financially it can be good as organisations are able to offer a wider portfolio of products. For example, they can increase the number of destinations that they can offer. They can support and service their own organisations – for example, a tour operator can use its own travel agents to promote the holidays it packages. It provides the opportunity to invest in new technology. The opening of a new branch or the takeover of an existing chain will add little to the overhead costs of central administration and accounting. Only a few extra staff may be required to

ACTIVITY

Read the Thomas Cook announcement in the box above relating to the merger of MyTravel and Thomas Cook.

Debate the topic: should mergers of this size be allowed?

ACTIVITY

Two tour operators have merged. Currently both tour operators have head offices: one in London and one in Manchester. The products that they offer are very different, however they do have some overlap in terms of resort offices. Explain the financial benefits of the merger between these two tour operators.

cope with the extra paperwork. The larger the organisation, the fewer costs involved.

When a takeover or merger takes place, the buyer acquires the existing expertise of the organisation that is taken over. This may be a strength if it is weak in a particular market segment. It may provide an opportunity to maximise market share in other areas.

Takeovers reduce competition, as there are fewer tour operators to compete with. This will result in an increase in market share and a rise in turnover and profits. Larger organisations have greater bargaining power with producers. Organisations such as Thomson tend to have more buying and negotiating power than the small organisations because they are contracting in large numbers.

ACTIVITY

Explain the benefits to a tour operator of being vertically or horizontally integrated. Think about distribution channels and brand awareness. Prepare a short presentation of your findings.

Another challenge tour operators face is the growth of dynamic packaging. This new concept is causing tour operators to look at and develop the products they have traditionally sold.

Dynamic packaging is the travel industry's term for a more flexible way of booking packages. In terms of tour operators, it allows them to package their own holidays and add their own profit margins. It helps them to be competitive. Many tour operators are offering the option of dynamic packaging – for example, Thomson and First Choice offer to help you build your own holiday. As reported by *Travel Weekly* in February 2007 dynamic packaging is rapidly increasing with online tour operator sales.

Budget airlines are a serious challenge to tour operators. Table 12.02 shows the growth of passengers using easyJet.

ACTIVITY

You work for the product development department of a medium-sized tour operator. The managing director, José Cozens, has asked you to send an email that explains the benefits of tour operators offering dynamic packaging. Draft an email that meets his request.

Table 12.02 easyJet passenger statistics

Full year	Annual total ('000)
1995	30
1996	420
1997	1,140
1998	1,880
1999	3,670
2000	5,996
2001	7,664
2002	11,400
2003	20,300
2004	24,300
2005	29,558
2006	32,953

ACTIVITY

Research low-cost airline prices and accommodation offered by these airlines. Compare the cost with that of holidays featured in a brochure. Discuss how you think these budget airline prices affect tour operators.

Top tip

- Use your research to help you calculate and make judgements.

13

Special interest tourism

Learning outcomes

By the end of this unit you should:

- understand the relationship between special interests and tourism
- know the factors that affect participation in special interest tourism
- know the nature of special interest activities in different locations
- understand the factors affecting and influencing the tourism provision for a special interest.

The relationship between special interests and tourism

What is special interest tourism?

The term 'special interest tourism' embraces a vast selection of holidays, ranging from activity holidays, through religious and cultural trips, to trekking and cruising. The types of trip described as 'special interest trips' tend to be aimed at small groups or individuals who share similar interests. Due to the typically small number of participants or the generally remote locations of these holidays, they tend to be more expensive. People choose such holidays not because of price but to pursue their interests. The appeal of such holidays will be discussed in more detail later on in the unit. The high price may also be justified by a rich programme of excursions and activities incorporated into this type of holiday. The price may also be high due to the inclusion of extras such as admissions, meals and tour guide services.

Unlike typical mass-market holidays of one or two weeks somewhere hot by the sea – such as a family's annual holiday in Majorca – special interest holidays, often called niche market holidays, tend not to be to everyone's liking and are chosen by a relatively small number of the travelling public.

While a typical mass-market holiday will be taken in destinations such as Spain or Greece, the destination of special interest holidays is important only if it lends itself well to the pursuit of the chosen activity. For example, Kenya is perfect for safaris while the Gambia, also in Africa and also offering hot weather throughout the year, is not, as there are no wild animals there.

Special interest operators, because of the nature of their product, tend to steer away from large hotels occupied by mass-market holidaymakers, choosing accommodation characteristic of the destination – for example, a riad in Morocco or a luxurious B&B in the Bahamas.

ACTIVITY

Using evidence from websites and brochures of special interest holiday operators, form your own definition of a special interest holiday.

ACTIVITY

Exodus (see the case study overleaf) does not encourage everyone to book its holidays. In fact, quite the opposite. It explains the main advantages as well as disadvantages of this type of holiday to its potential customers, who may not be used to trekking or adverse conditions. Identify those advantages and disadvantages.

Development of special interest tourism

The growth of special interest tourism is a natural stage in the development of the tourism industry. Unlike 50 years ago, large numbers of people in Britain now have experience of travelling to various destinations, often long haul. Travelling itself has become more common and accepted as a part of our

Case study

About Exodus

Have you ever dreamed of watching the sunrise over the plains of Southern Africa from the majestic summit of Kilimanjaro? Or travelling the fabled Silk Road to China along the Karakorum Highway? Or just having a relaxing week seeing the hidden corners of Tuscany? Or do you simply yearn for a holiday with a difference? Exodus offers you all these things.

Since our inaugural trip in 1974, to the Minaret of Jam in Afghanistan, we have fulfilled the dreams and aspirations of adventurous-minded people around the world.

Exodus is the leading adventure travel company in the UK. We offer an unrivalled selection of over 500 tours, planned and operated by experts who share a passion for travel. Our eight programmes cover some 90 countries worldwide.

Our tours are neither regimented 5-star packages nor unplanned forays into the unknown: they are authentic experiences of foreign places and cultures, where quality and interest come first. Quality should not be confused with luxury: we believe that the best way to discover the essence of a country is to use accommodation with character and transport appropriate to the terrain, whether that is a 4×4 jeep or a camel.

Like the many areas we cover, our holidays come in many different guises. Quite a few are in areas where good roads and hotels do exist: here we can combine excitement with comfort. Those to deserts, mountains and wilderness regions are necessarily more rugged and participatory, while others again, like our classic game safaris, treks and bike rides may have a particular special interest.

Whatever your preference, if you have a natural curiosity about the world and a desire to explore it, the chances are that you'll find an Exodus trip to suit you.

Whichever Exodus holiday you choose, there are several important features common to all our trips.

Group size

All our groups are small, with stated minimum and maximum group sizes. The maximum size varies from 8 to 22, though it is usually 16. We feel that small groups provide a better social experience for you, and in many cases are essential to preserve the integrity of the more remote places that we visit.

Your travelling companions

Many different kinds of people travel with us. They may be 18 or 65 years old, of either sex, alone or with a friend, experienced travellers or complete beginners, but you can be reasonably sure that they will share an interest in travel and exploration, and have a similar attitude of mind. In any group, many participants are likely to have done an Exodus holiday before!

Exodus staff

Our staff are one of our key assets, and are very carefully selected and trained to ensure that your trip is as trouble-free and enjoyable as possible. Many leaders have been with us for a very long time, and many of our office staff have been leaders first. Regardless of their position, all our staff share a passion for travel.

Where we stay

Our holidays outside Europe are not really about accommodation in the same way as beach holidays are: a hotel is a place to spend a night or two, not the main focus of your holiday. Most of our holidays are based on some form of hotel accommodation. Whether they are palaces, pensions or anything in between, they are selected for their charm and local character: multi-national tower blocks rarely feature. In places where there aren't any hotels you may find yourself roughing it for a short time, whether in a tent or a village house. It all adds to the experience, and it doesn't have to be arduous.

A few trips – African safaris and mountain treks are the obvious examples – are based on camping, because of the area and the activities. When we do camp, we supply all the necessary equipment, of a high standard, so that all you need to bring is your sleeping bag and maybe a karrimat.

Our European destinations all stay in small, comfortable hotels and lodges, carefully selected for their charm and location, to give you easy access to the best places from the comfort of your accommodation.

Is it for you?

Our trips are for active, flexible-minded people who enjoy the unusual and the adventurous. For trips that have an emphasis on walking or cycling, you need to remember that even the easiest walking or cycling involves some exertion, so you should be reasonably fit and sure that you will enjoy the activity; please see our walk grading or our cycling profile section. There will also be times when you will have to put up with temporary lack of civilised comforts, such as a hot shower, or ice in your drinks. If you simply cannot cope with anything unexpected or unusual, or if you have to be waited on hand and foot wherever you are, then we'd rather you looked elsewhere for your holiday.

(Source: www.exodus.co.uk, accessed May 2007)

lives, with increasing numbers of people taking more than one or two holidays a year. According to National Statistics:

> UK residents made a record 66.4 million visits abroad, an increase of four per cent on the previous year. UK residents also spent a record amount abroad: £32.2 billion – an increase of six per cent on 2004.

As the tourism industry developed, companies soon realised that holidaymakers would want more than a week or two of the 'sun, sea and sand' type of holiday and so they devised holidays offering greater variety. In the race to meet our needs and ensure competitiveness, travel and tourism companies rushed to develop services that more closely matched our needs. As early as the 1980s, some variation was introduced to our holidays: city breaks as well as all-inclusive holidays were added to the travel and tourism offer in an attempt to meet the individual needs of customers. The travelling public wanted more breaks, so the idea of visiting places during a weekend or a long weekend (taking a Friday or a Monday off) offered a perfect solution. In addition, as the break was short, it was often relatively cheap in comparison to other types of holiday. The popularity of city breaks was also down to cities' cultural appeal and the variety of activities on offer, ranging from visiting attractions, shopping, enjoying entertainment or nightlife, sampling different foods or simply soaking up different cultures. The cities that topped the city breaks lists were the ones that were also easily accessible by various means of transport so travelling there and back would not take up too much precious holiday time.

All-inclusive holidays, on the other hand, gained popularity because of the convenience they offered; having all the services such as accommodation, transport, food, entertainment and often activities paid in advance meant holidaymakers could simply enjoy the beautiful scenery, hot climate and unlimited food and drinks. Only later did holidaymakers start questioning the value for money of such holidays, their impact on local economies, and many other issues.

Tour operators also started introducing long-haul destinations in order to further increase the variety of holidays on offer. Packages to Florida, Goa or the Far East have become increasingly common. By the 1990s, holidaymakers had grown more discerning, leading to the emergence of special interest holidays. These were brought onto the market by niche operators.

Since the 1990s, the special interest holiday market has been enjoying steady growth. Despite the well-established operators getting stronger, a number of newly created operators came on the market. The big industry players such as Thomas Cook and First Choice have also noticed the growing demand for special interest holidays. For example, following the purchase of Laterooms.com by First Choice Holidays for £120m, First Choice now wants to focus on other, specialist operations, including its activity holidays division, clearly recognising the significance of the special interest holiday market.

ACTIVITY

Investigate a number of special interest holidays and find out how long they have been operating. What percentage of them have been operating for more than 20 years?

One possible explanation for the desire to travel – the need to seek and pursue individual interests – is Maslow's hierarchy of needs (Figure 13.01). The theory contends that as humans meet their 'basic needs', also referred to as deficiency needs – these being physiological, safety, love/belonging and esteem needs – they seek to satisfy successively their 'higher needs', which occupy a set hierarchy. These lead people to make the most of their unique abilities and to be the best they can be.

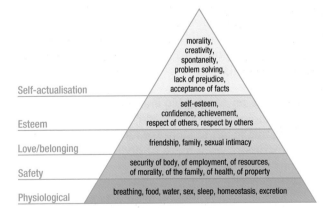

Fig 13.01 Maslow's hierarchy of needs

This means that people wish to spend their leisure time in search of activities that will satisfy their 'higher needs', as they no longer need to worry about meeting their 'basic needs'.

Part of the trend to pursue one's own interests is to want to travel when one finds it convenient, to stay in the accommodation of one's choice and effectively create one's own package according to one's own requirements. The increased availability of travel and tourism products through websites has led to holidaymakers booking services independently using different accommodation and transport providers. They often select only services such as transportation and transfers, as accommodation may be provided by friends, instead of booking the whole package. This is called an 'unpackaged' package.

In addition, more and more tour operators allow people to customise their own holiday by adding extra nights, choosing their hotel or simply allowing customers to choose from a range of excursions, instead of including them all in the price and having everyone participate in all of them. This flexible approach allows tour operators to better meet customer needs.

Travel agents are also involved in the process of 'unpackaging' packages as well as helping customers put together a holiday by selecting services not necessarily offered by one provider or operator. Forming packages in this way is referred to as 'dynamic packaging'. This is now a growing trend, according to ABTA:

> There was again a big increase in 'dynamic packaging' or 'tailor-made' holidays in 2005 and this is set to increase further in 2006. Customers want more flexibility and the trade has been there to deliver...
>
> The package holiday in itself was still a popular product in 2005 with approximately 18.5 million holidays sold in 2005. This is still considerably more than was sold ten years ago. However, as the total number of holidays has continued to grow (a possible 44 million holidays were taken abroad last year by British residents), the proportion of those taken as package holidays has dropped again for the third year running.

(Source: www.abta.com, accessed May 2007)

The low-cost airlines also played a huge role in the development of so-called independent travel, providing connections to many parts of Europe at low prices, allowing people to travel frequently to pursue their interests. For example, the majority of European cities are now served by at least one low-cost carrier. In your own time you may wish to investigate their routes.

Special interests

There is a wide variety of so-called special interest holidays on offer. Some of them require an active involvement in the activities they offer (such as diving or skiing) while others do not entail actual participation in events but simply involve travelling to events and being a spectator. For example, one may wish to travel to watch tennis at Wimbledon or the Olympics in Beijing without wanting to play tennis or participate in the Olympics.

Among 'passive' holidays are trips that provide access to cultural events. A small tour operator called Travel for the Arts offers trips to a variety of dance and opera festivals, mainly in Europe. You may wish to investigate its range of holidays by logging on to www.travelforthearts.co.uk.

Another type of special interest holiday consists of those taken for spiritual reasons; these could range from pilgrimages to retreats. Pilgrimages are trips made to a place of religious significance such as Lourdes, Jerusalem, Mecca or the River Ganges. Retreats provide opportunities for meditation and spiritual relaxation and are often sought after by people with busy lifestyles.

Educational holidays are also a part of the special interest market as they are aimed at a specific market and are not available as a mass-market product.

Fig 13.02 Opera holidays

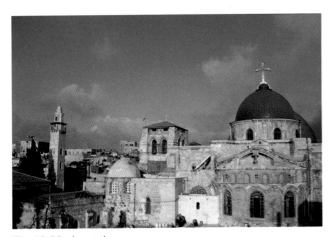

Fig 13.03 Jerusalem

Companies such PGL, EF Tours and NST Educational Tours offer a selection of tours to different destinations for schools and colleges, focusing on a particular area of study, such as business or travel and tourism, or simply organising a general trip for them. Such trips tend to be budget-driven, as they are student- or school-funded with accommodation in hostels or hotels suitable for groups.

The term educational also refers to holidays during which one acquires new skills. These could be cookery or painting courses during which participants explore a certain cuisine (e.g. French) or familiarise themselves with the watercolour technique in painting. Such courses do not offer additional qualifications but purely provide an opportunity for many people to try a new hobby.

On the other hand, a lot of special interest holidays are based on holidaymakers participating actively in a selection of activities. These could be yoga holidays or spa holidays. Investigate these types of holidays on the following websites: www.exclusiveescapes.co.uk; www.thermalia.co.uk. Some holidays are perhaps more challenging.

ACTIVITY

Investigate the range of active holidays listed below using the websites provided. What type of holidays do they provide?
- www.explore.co.uk
- www.neilson.co.uk
- www.longwoodholidays.co.uk
- www.inthesaddle.co.uk
- www.sunsail.com
- www.golfbreak.com

The companies mentioned so far specialise in a particular type of activity. However, there are also operators that offer a number of activities. The Last Resort includes the following activities in its holiday options:

- Learn to Paraglide
- Intro to Alpine Flying
- Fly Guiding Plus
- Activity Holidays
- Mountain Biking
- Cycling Holidays
- Canyoning & Rafting
- Via Ferrata & Rock Climbing
- Walking Holidays.

Companies such as Abercrombie and Kent, and Voyages Jules Verne also have more than one type of special interest holiday on offer. However, these holidays are not activity but more destination-based.

ACTIVITY

In preparation for your assignment, find the Abercrombie and Kent, and Voyages Jules Verne websites and investigate the types of holiday and variety of destinations they offer.

Special interest tour operators

The majority of special interest tour operators are either independent or horizontally integrated. You may wish to refresh your memory and remind yourself what horizontal integration means; it is described in Unit 1 in the book. For example, Voyages Jules Verne is owned by Kuoni, a niche market specialist, while Page & Moy, whose clients are expected to be 45 or over, is owned by Travelsphere, maintaining at the same time a clear brand distinction and aiming at slightly different target markets.

Most of these operators have solely web-based distribution or at least online booking facilities with a head office, possibly a call centre, also accepting telephone bookings. Because of the niche and unique nature of their product, they tend to sell directly to customers instead of using travel agents as intermediaries, fearing that agents may not have sufficient product knowledge to sell their product.

Fig 13.04 Travel company logos

Special interest operators tend to be small companies that started as sole traders and have grown to become a medium-sized enterprise through steady growth or possibly through a merger with another company of a similar profile. Small companies tend to employ up to 50 staff and medium-sized companies normally have up to 250 employees.

The large, vertically integrated operators have all responded to the growing popularity of special interest holidays. Thomson purchased a skiing operator called Crystal while MyTravel (formerly one of the 'big four') purchased Bridge Travel, a city break specialist. Thomas Cook, on the other hand, developed its Signature brand in order to compete in the niche market.

Assessing the outcome

You are working for a tour operator that is planning to introduce some new holiday products. Following a growing trend, you have suggested special interest tours. In order to 'sell' this idea to your superiors, you need to find out enough about special interest holidays so they feel confident trusting your judgement. Define and describe special interest tourism and its development.

● Describe the relationship between special interests and tourism (**P1**).

Factors that affect participation in special interest tourism

Industry factors

As demonstrated in the Exodus case study earlier, special interest operators use market segmentation quite effectively, choosing their target markets carefully. They aim at selected segments, carefully profiling their customers. The main basis for selecting certain segments could be lifestyle (some activities may require a certain level of fitness and general health or an interest in a subject). In some cases, the selection could be based on family circumstances as empty nesters (parents whose children have left home) may have more opportunities in terms of time and money to pursue their interests.

Quite often the targeted customers come from A, B and possibly C1 socio-economic groups: groups with enough disposable income to pursue their interests and whose basic needs have been provided for. Some tour operators tend to aim at slightly more mature customers who are believed to have higher incomes and whose travelling needs are more developed.

On the other hand, gender does not seem to play a large part in this selection, as the majority of holidays are available to both genders.

Many destinations attract tourists because of what they have on offer, whether it be wildlife, ancient monuments or simply a warm climate. The reasons tourists travel to such destinations are called their appeal. The more there is on offer, the greater the appeal of a destination as more tourists are likely to be attracted to it, possibly several times.

Many destinations have managed to improve their appeal by adding new facilities. For example, despite great weather, good wine and stunning coastlines, Portugal has now become one of the top golfing destinations because of the number of golf courses built there in the last few years, thus attracting not just the typical mass-market holidaymaker but also tapping into the special interest market.

Destinations such as Croatia have recovered quickly from civil war, re-creating their appeal to British holidaymakers. Croatia is now topping summer holiday lists for its scenery, quality of services and reasonable prices. The successful promotion of the destination has also had a significant impact.

There are various events that add to the appeal of destinations, which is why countries choose to host sports or cultural events such as the FIFA World Cup or the Eurovision Song Contest. These events often place them on the tourist map and revive their appeal. Such events provide a perfect opportunity to update a destination and make it more appealing to a wider public.

Participant factors

People now take more holidays – two or three a year is an accepted norm – with one of them often being to a more exotic destination. Some people now take advantage of breaks between jobs such as redundancy (when your employment is discontinued due to your position being no longer necessary to the company) or extended leave such a sabbatical (unpaid leave, lasting normally one year) to go on working holidays. Examples include helping to build a village in New Guinea and participating in various environmental or conservation projects such as planting trees in a tropical forest or working with scientists in various locations.

Increasing numbers of people choose to work from home or work so-called 'collapsible hours' (you choose how many hours you work a day as long as you have done a certain number of hours – e.g. 40 – per week). In this way, you may have longer weekends to spend in the countryside or holiday more often abroad pursuing your interests.

Special interest holidays used to be considered as solely the privilege of the rich. The majority of people took holidays in order to rest after working hard, and lying by the pool was their idea of relaxation. Special interest holidays were for those who did not need to rest as they often did not need to have regular jobs. Instead, they craved mental stimulation and self-realisation. Now, with the increased amount of leisure time and greater disposable income, more of us can participate in such activities.

In the past, long-haul holidays were also considered beyond the reach of many people, simply because of the travelling costs involved and the time one spent getting to such destinations. The time was a considerable obstacle as paid holiday, particularly for more than a week or two, was not the norm. With longer paid holidays, faster planes and lower flying costs, there are now very few people in the UK who have not ventured further afield.

People also tend to spend more time pursuing their interests in sports and are therefore more likely to travel as spectators to games or international tournaments. Apart from viewing, they also want to participate in various activities. Adventure trips such as whitewater rafting or glacier skiing are on the increase. As more of our basic needs are provided for, what people crave is additional stimulation, which they may obtain through participation in special interest holidays.

There seems to be a slightly different booking pattern to our holidays these days. While a lot of mass-market bookings are made on a last-minute basis, where customers are lured by discounts and special offers, special interest holidays tend to be booked in advance as customers clearly know what type of holiday they want and are prepared to research, book in advance and pay higher prices to be sure that their needs are met well.

According to Maslow's theory, esteem is one of the human needs. As explained earlier in this unit, special interest holidays may be associated with a certain status in society. Booking special interest holidays may also be meeting that need.

Apart from status, there are various other motivators (factors encouraging us to do something) contributing to the growing interest in special interest holidays. These may be interpersonal motivators, such as a wish to meet like-minded people and spend time in their company, or cultural motivators such as the desire to learn about other cultures. The growing interest in the world around us may be translated into the popularity of special interest tours.

ACTIVITY

As discussed earlier, a selection of destinations have been added to make the package offer more appealing. Have a look at the Regent Holidays website (www.regent-holidays.co.uk) to find some of its new destinations.

ACTIVITY

The political stability of a destination often contributes to its appeal. Some of the 'new' destinations have been added for that very reason. How do you think the accession of new European Union members such as Cyprus, the Czech Republic and Poland has added to their appeal?

ACTIVITY

Read the statements in the box below, made by various people. Identify the factors that affect their holiday choices.

'I had always wanted to know what the life behind the Iron Curtain was like so I decided to book this tour. We will even visit a KGB museum in Moscow.'

'With our position and social standing, it is about time we book ourselves on a cruise. The next-door neighbours have already been twice!'

'I did not realise I could visit a famous museum in Bilbao. It has been many years since I last came to Europe.'

'I love those expeditions; you always meet the right people, both travellers and guides. You could not ask for a better company!'

'I had always wanted to visit New Zealand but one needed a lot of time to do so. You can imagine how happy I was when I found out I could do it in between these two jobs.'

'I have heard of the Elephant Orphanage but, I guess, living and working in one may be a completely different experience. It must be such an eye-opener!'

'I travel with my fencing club almost every month because it is so inexpensive now.'

'I found us an amazing deal! You know how I have always wanted to listen to opera in Verona. We would have to be fools not to book it!'

'I have never been outside Europe so I would love to tour China to see how other people live.'

Assessing the outcome

Your superiors were interested in the findings you put together in the previous assignment. However, before they reach their decision, they would like to find out more about the factors affecting participation in passive, active and adventure special interest tourism. They would also like you to describe the future trends. To prepare, study the following article, published on www.travelmole.com.

" **Activity and adventure travel market – trends in 2007**

TravelMole guest comment by Annie Corcoran, head of Crystal Active

People today are better travelled than any previous generation and they are not just looking to visit a destination – they want an experience when they get there.

Just going to a destination is no longer enough. This desire for first-hand and unique experiences has led to a growth in both the activity and adventure travel sectors as holidaymakers now want more than a beach, sun and a sight-seeing tour.

Long-haul destinations are becoming increasingly popular because programmes like Michael Palin's series on the Himalayas make the remote seem more accessible and in our increasingly urban and sedentary world, people are looking for more challenges (this can also be seen in the dramatic increase in numbers of people competing in marathons and triathlons).

The desire for a healthy lifestyle and to be fit (and to look fit) is an important part of everyday life and even though this can sometimes be more perception than reality (we all join the gym but we don't always go!), we also like to think that we will continue this regime when we have more time, i.e. when we are on holiday.

Increasingly we are also seeing changes to the preferred length of holidays – people like short breaks which they take more frequently and longer holidays (15 days+) when they will go on more long-haul travels (the old 'trip of a lifetime' except that now we all expect to take far more than one!).

The increase in sports coverage and the cross-over of sport and leisure pursuits into everyday lifestyle and fashion has also increased the number of people wanting to try such sports as scuba diving, windsurfing, kite-surfing and mountain biking which in turn has led to an increase in activity-based travel.

Adventure holidays are not just for the young 'adrenaline junkies' but now families, young professionals and even the grey market are booking such activity holidays, whether it is paragliding over a glacier or walking the Haute Route. "

- Describe the factors that affect participation in passive, active and adventure special interest tourism (**P2**).

Special interest activities
Nature of activities and their location

The nature of special interest holidays depends on a number of factors. There is a wide selection of water-, land- and air-based activities on offer. These could be sailing, diving, skiing, horse riding or paragliding. Activities, such as trekking or golfing, can be done individually, pursuing one's own interest, while others require a team approach.

There is a variety of reasons why people travel on special interest tours. Art lovers may want to participate in a cultural tour that explores Renaissance painting. Such a tour would focus on destinations – it may go to Italy, for example, where many exhibitions of such paintings may be seen. It may also include a lecture on the subject.

Those pursuing a challenge may choose to go on an overland expedition, crossing a desert or a jungle. Others may want to travel to relax and therefore may choose a spa holiday – where they receive a selection of treatments – or a yoga break.

Some special interest tours involve elements of danger where the risk may be either real or perceived (i.e. not real). The majority of risks are actually perceived – whether you are on a safari or a TranSiberian train – you are mostly safe, otherwise tour operators would not offer such tours for fear of running into legal problems. Naturally, problems do occur, yet they are extremely rare. It is in the interest of both the tour operator and the local ground handling company (a company that provides services – such as transfers from airport to hotel and excursions – on behalf of the tour operator at the destination) to keep tours safe in order to maintain a good public image and therefore a certain level of business. It is also a legal requirement that British operators take responsibility for their suppliers (Travel Package Directive 1992). This places the onus on tour operators to check the health and safety standards and advise customers correctly regarding any foreseeable dangers. External risks such as crime or terrorism may lead to the destination no longer being offered by the tour operator. The risk of attack by wild animals on a safari is really minimal as the tour is guided by a fully trained ranger in possession of a weapon, who can deal with potential risks.

The nature of activities links closely with the location of special interest holidays. The locations of special interest holidays vary and depend on the nature of the activity they offer. They range from purpose-built centres, where people can do various activities, to a designated location. Holidays such as religious tours or heritage tours take travellers to places of religious significance such as Mecca or Jerusalem, or historic destinations such as Carcassone or Venice.

Some specific holidays require access to certain facilities. Consider a climbing holiday: you can travel to Snowdonia or the Peak District to pursue your interest or you can use climbing walls, which simulate natural conditions, in activity centres. Or if you are interested in sailing, you can use a centre such as Herts Young Mariners Base, described in the case study opposite.

The location of some special interest holidays may deliberately be remote and isolated. Retreats are a good example of this as people travel there for relaxation and to 'get away from it all'.

Fig 13.06 Heart Yoga retreats

The location of conservation holidays may be a remote jungle, which forms a significant part of the appeal of such a holiday.

Holidays such as safaris can only be organised to destinations where lions, elephants or giraffes can be observed in their natural environment, while bird-

Fig 13.05 Venice

Fig 13.07 Safari

Case study

Herts Young Mariners Base

Welcome to the 2006 brochure for the Herts Young Mariners Base.

We hope you will find something in these pages to interest and inspire you.

During 2005 we invested in a wide range of new equipment. For sailors this included RS Fevas, RS Visions and Topper Taz. Kayakers have the benefit of Avocet Sea Kayaks, Acrobat 275s, a Topolino Duo and a variety of play boats. The windsurfer fleet is scheduled to be upgraded for next season.

During 2005 we had some major building work: floodlighting the climbing wall; resurfacing the dinghy park and completion of the HCC Youth Service Camp Store relocation to HYMB.

With the wide range of personal skills and leader/coach training courses in kayaking, canoeing, sailing, windsurfing, climbing and caving along with day and weekend trips to other venues, we hope we can satisfy your needs.

If you have a disability, we will do our best to meet your individual requirements by providing a hoist to enable transfers to watercraft, and adapting other equipment to suit.

Widening opportunities include boat maintenance, Duke of Edinburgh's Award Open Award Centre and a film project for young people and leaders.

We continue to keep the costs low thanks to the support of Hertfordshire Adult and Family Learning, who also enable us to offer concessions to adults in receipt of benefit.

If you are involved in school or other youth groups, we are pleased to work with you to deliver courses to meet the aims and objectives of your group.

The Centre is fully licensed by AALA (Adventure Activities Licensing Authority) as well as being inspected by the RYA (Royal Yachting Association) and BCU (British Canoe Union). As part of Hertfordshire's Youth Service all staff are checked through the CRB (Criminal Records Bureau) system and the centre follows all the Health and Safety Policies of Hertfordshire County Council, thereby complying with all the requirements of the guidelines.

(Source: www.hymb.com, accessed May 2007)

---

watching holidays may only target destinations where certain types of bird are prevalent.

On the other hand, cultural and heritage tours normally take people to urban locations, such as towns and cities, as this is where the wealth of culture and heritage is available.

ACTIVITY

List ten special interest holidays. Explain what determines their destination.

Factors affecting tourism provision for special interests

Locations

Various factors affect the physical location of special interest holidays relating to season. For example, sailing tends to be associated with warm locations and the summer season and locations such as Greece or Croatia in summer or Antigua all year round. Skiing,

Assessing the outcome

As part of the decision-making process, you are expected to do some research and introduce your superiors to the wealth of special interest holidays that may inspire them when planning trips in future. The research is to include information about the nature of activities as well as locations of special interest tours. You must use some displays.

- Describe the nature of activities in special interest tourism (**P3**).
- Identify and show the locations for special interest tourism (**P4**).

on the other hand, is clearly associated with winter, although destinations such as Dubai try to do away with seasonality by offering artificial slopes. The skiing facilities in Dubai, however, seem to be more of an attraction on their own rather than a genuine attempt to compete with well-established skiing destinations such as the Alps, the Pyrenees or the Rockies.

Climate also determines the locations of some special interest tours. Hot, cold or mountainous climates lend themselves to different types of holiday. Water sports may be more popular in destinations with a hot climate while cold or rainy climates may focus on offering more indoor activities.

While some companies can offer a holiday that includes travel to the destination, others may offer ground-only arrangements (holidays that exclude travel to the destination or starting point of the tour). Ground-only arrangements normally include guides, expeditions and admissions to most attractions as well as accommodation.

Some companies may offer transfers from the airport to which you fly, to the place where your tour actually begins. For example, taxis often collect passengers arriving at Miami airport to take them to the harbour, where they board a ship to cruise around the Caribbean islands or the Mexican coast.

Some cities are perceived to be gateways, which means that the majority of people fly to the gateway to join their tour and return there to take a return flight home. Miami is a gateway for most of the passengers cruising round Florida, the Caribbean and Mexico. This means that customers from various parts of the world fly to Miami to join the same cruise.

customers who participate in this kind of activity on a regular basis and feel that it is worth investing in their own equipment.

A number of holidays cannot be participated in without the use of specialised training. Sailing is an example where training is required for health and safety reasons to avoid incidents such as collisions or drowning. Others require instruction so you can develop your skills, such as golfing or horse riding holidays. You select golf courses based on your handicap or you may join a group of riders of a similar skill level (e.g. beginner or intermediate) depending on how much riding you have done in the past and how confident you are.

Some people are excluded from participating in certain special interest holidays on medical grounds; for example, it is unlikely for someone to be able to paraglide if they are suffering from a heart condition. Age may be another factor that excludes one from participation in some activities; insurance companies often charge people aged over 65 a higher premium. Due to the higher risk of so-called 'dangerous sports', insurance companies also charge a higher premium. For examples, see: www.columbusdirect.com/index.cfm.

ACTIVITY

Read descriptions of tours offered by both Explore, www.explore.co.uk, and Kumuka, www.kumuka.com, and identify similarities and differences in their operations.

Some of the more mainstream special interest holidays (those with a low level of specialisation and therefore accessible to a wider range of customers) may not require any particular clothing or equipment. For example, cruising on the Nile or spending a honeymoon in the Maldives is similar to going on any holiday to a hot destination where the normal precautions apply such as adequate sunshine protection or vaccinations against diseases such as Hepatitis A and polio.

Other holidays, such as trekking, call for good-quality walking boots, and failure to have them may lead to injuries, given the amount of walking one would be doing. Snowboarding and diving require specialised equipment, which can either be hired at the destination or – in some cases – is brought by

Assessing the outcome

As a final task, you have also been asked to prepare information about the tourism provision for a specific special interest. This will complete the task set out by your superiors and will enable them to make decisions concerning your company's future.

- Describe the tourism provision for a specific special interest (**P5**).

Improve your grade

If you are reading this part of the unit, you are clearly interested in achieving higher grades. To do so, you need to be clear how to get there. This section of the unit endeavours to give you that understanding.

First, we encourage you to do all the tasks listed in this unit. They provide a firm basis for your understanding of special interest tourism and for your further research, which will lead you hopefully to a merit or a distinction. Without basic knowledge, you cannot achieve higher grades.

You can start by working on your pass criteria and gradually get to a merit or a distinction. For example, criteria **P1** and **M1** are linked.

While for **P1** you will be describing (*saying how things are*), for **M1** you are expected to explain (*give reasons, answer the why and how questions*). If you are not sure what you are expected to do, check with your tutor or refer to the Assessment Guidance on your awarding body website so you can get a better idea.

Having completed all the tasks in this unit, you will be able to describe the relationship between special interests and tourism. This will be sufficient for a pass grade, while for a merit you need to give reasons why special interest tourism developed. Some of your descriptions may include elements of explanations, which will be fine, but try to keep them descriptive and save explanations for your merit task.

To satisfy the requirements of the merit criterion, do not attempt to rewrite your pass work but select two relationships and concentrate on them in detail. Select your 'relationships' carefully so they link and your explanation will make sense, e.g. budget airlines have not influenced the development of long-haul travel as most of those airlines fly to short-haul European destinations, therefore this would not be an appropriate match. You do not need to write pages and pages, just keep your explanations clear and support them by research. You must describe the relationship between special interests and tourism before you can begin to explain.

When you are preparing evidence for **P2**, with some extra work you will also gain **M2**. For a pass you need to describe the factors that affect participation in passive, active and adventure special interest tourism (*say how things are*), while for a merit you should analyse (*say how things are and then draw conclusions*). Do not try to write your task again but choose two key factors (both industry and participant factors) and analyse how these have affected participation in three different types of special interest tourism, one from each category: passive, active and adventure (six in total). It is always easier to write about something that you can relate to. You must describe the factors that affect participation in passive, active and adventure special interest tourism before you start to analyse some of them.

This part of your assignment (**D1**) requires you to use all the evidence you have gathered so far in previous pass and merit tasks, and assess (*make value judgements, judge suitability*) the market for special interest tourism. Look at how it developed: is there more potential for development? Why? What type of companies offer such products? What interests are more popular than others? Why? You may find this task hard but don't give up and, remember, you are aiming for higher grades.

You must describe, explain and analyse (**P1, P2, P3, P4, M1, M2**) before you can assess the current market for special interest tourism and identify potential gaps in provision.

For **P5** you should describe (*say how things are*) the tourism provision for a specific special interest. Choose one that interests you, as you will find it easier to research it. For a merit you will have to analyse the nature of its provision (*say how it is and then draw conclusions*). For this you may analyse what location, if any, your special interest requires. Does it make it more or less popular? What companies cater for this type of interest? Are there many of them? What does it mean to customers? Are there any special requirements linked to your interest? Does the location contribute to its popularity? If you get stuck, ask your tutor or use the advice on the awarding body website. In order to achieve **D2**, you will have to evaluate (*make judgements often in relation to performance, examine*) the specific special interest, some of which you may have done in your **M3** task. However, the difference here is that you justify your recommendations for development. Whether your selected specific special interest is gradually gaining popularity or is already considerably popular, you need to say how you predict it will grow further. This needs to be based on facts as 'justify' means prove your point and demonstrate its correctness. For this you can use statistics, trends, perhaps evidence of growth in other countries. It is a task that you may not be able to sit down and find answers to easily: you need to do some research. You must describe the tourism provision for a specific special interest before you can analyse, evaluate it or make justified recommendations.

Top tips

- You must know what evidence you need to produce (in what form, i.e. report, presentation) and about which topic (location of special interest tourism).
- You must be clear as to what you are expected to do (e.g. describe, explain, assess) to achieve each criterion.
- You must research and use examples to support your statements.

Roles and responsibilities of holiday representatives

14

Learning outcomes

By the end of this unit you should:

- know the roles and responsibilities of different categories of holiday representatives
- understand the legal responsibilities of a holiday representative
- understand the importance of health and safety in relation to the role of the holiday representative
- know how to apply social, customer service and selling skills when dealing with transfers, welcome meetings and other situations.

What the price includes
- Accommodation
- Meals
- Services of our representative
- Return flights
- Air passenger duty, UK airport taxes and security charges
- Free luggage allowance of 20kg on Thomas Cook Airline flights
- Transport to and from your accommodation in resort
- Charges for extra security, insurance, aviation and other associated costs

Roles and responsibilities of different holiday representatives

Tour operators employ staff from the UK to work overseas in the role of holiday representatives. Examples of large tour operators include Thomson, First Choice, Airtours and Thomas Cook. These tour operators have a wide range of products on offer. They book hundreds of thousands of holidaymakers overseas each year.

Holiday representatives have important roles and responsibilities to the customer, organisation and to suppliers. These can differ slightly depending on the type of holiday representative. Usually within the price of the package is the service of the holiday representative. The tour operator contract with the customer therefore requires the holiday representative to provide a service to the customer. This is shown in the boxed extract adapted from the Thomas Cook summer sun brochure 2006.

Holiday representatives have a role in, and responsibilities to, the organisation because they are employed by the tour operator and have a contractual agreement to fulfil the terms and conditions set out in the contract. Holiday representatives also have responsibilities to the suppliers because tour operators have contracts with suppliers such as coach operators and hoteliers.

ACTIVITY

Investigate a tour operator of your choice. List the roles and responsibilities holiday representatives have to their suppliers.

There are a number of categories of holiday representative. The main categories are described below.

Resort representative

The category of resort representative includes a variety of different types of holiday representative. For example, 18–30, family, over-50s and property representatives can all be included in this category.

There are also more high-ranking roles, which are classed as senior resort representatives. A resort representative will be based in a resort, e.g. Faliraki, and be responsible for a number of customers, often in a number of properties within the resort.

Ski representative

A ski representative is similar to a resort representative. They are based in a winter ski resort and work during the winter months. Some tour operators require their ski representatives to accompany customers on the slopes, so they need to be able to ski.

Transfer representative

A transfer representative is employed to take customers to and from the airport and accommodation properties.

Children's representative

A children's representative is responsible for looking after groups of children, usually between the ages of 2 and 12. They are required to arrange fun activities for children while on holiday.

Campsite representative

Campsite representatives are employed to work in camping-style holidays abroad, e.g. camping and caravan sites. This type of representative is similar to a resort representative, however they are responsible for montage (putting up tents at the start of the season) and de-montage (taking down tents at the end of the season) as well as cleaning the guests' accommodation.

Below are examples of job descriptions of holiday representatives.

Resort representative

To be a success as a First Choice resort representative, you're no shrinking violet, love meeting new people and of course, enjoy exploring new cultures and environments. It's also important that you have excellent sales skills as well as an energetic approach – it's a hectic but very rewarding job. It's also important that you are calm and have the ability to deal with unexpected situations professionally, and you're as comfortable building a rapport with customers as you are with suppliers. If you think that all of this sounds like a breeze, overseas 'repping' might be something for you, and if you speak a second language in addition to English – that's a bonus too!

(Source: www.firstchoice4jobs.co.uk, accessed May 2007)

2wenty's and Heatwave

It's one big party for them but no easy ride for you. It's their holiday and you will be on hand to make sure it is the best one they ever have. Providing up to date information about the best bars and clubs to dance the night away and daytime activities to make the most of their fantastic resort. You will be focused on promoting not only ways to enhance our customers' holidays but also to join in with the Reunion party in November in the UK. Our recruitment takes place from November to February only.

(Source: www.firstchoice4jobs.co.uk, accessed May 2007)

ACTIVITY

Read the two descriptions of holiday representatives. Now rewrite the resort representative description as a ski representative, and the 2wenty's and Heatwave description as a family representative description.

Figures 14.01–14.04 give some job adverts and descriptions highlighting the roles and responsibilities of different types of holiday representatives.

Transfer Representative

Your duties will be numerous and varied and your hours of work could be long with much of the work happening during the night time. The main purpose of this role is to transfer our holidaymakers from the airport to their hotel on their arrival and from their hotel to the airport on their departure.

Transfer Representatives also guide our excursions, ensuring that our holidaymakers thoroughly enjoy their days and nights out with Olympic.

The position of a Transfer Representative is an ideal training ground for someone who is not quite old enough to be a Resort Representative, but still wants to work within Olympic's overseas programme. So, if you want a change of direction, with great job satisfaction and excellent career opportunities, take the next step and apply.

To apply for this position you must meet the following minimum requirements:
- preferably educated to GCSE level or equivalent
- customer service experience required.

(Source: www.careerintravel.co.uk, accessed June 2007)

Fig 14.01 Transfer Representative job description

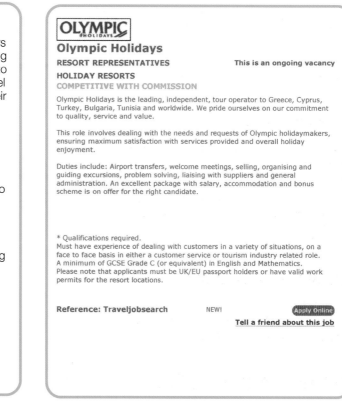

Fig 14.03 Resort Representative job advert

Children's Representative

Working overseas as a Children's Rep can be an exciting and challenging change from being a nanny in the UK. Your responsibilities will not only be to keep children from the ages of 2 to 12 happy, but their parents as well. A children's rep must have a cheerful and patient manner at all times and loads of imagination.

Main responsibilities of a Children's Rep are:
- organising daytime and evening activities
- supervising early suppers
- telling bedtime stories
- focusing on the health and safety of the children
- completing paperwork
- assisting in transferring customers to and from the airport and hotel
- assisting in the welcome meetings.

Main requirements needed to become a Children's Rep are:
- hold a NNEB or NVQ in Childcare or equivalent
- at least 6 months to 1 year's experience working with children
- First Aid Certificate
- highly imaginative
- able to work in a team.

(Source: www.careerintravel.co.uk, accessed June 2007)

Fig 14.02 Children's Representative job description

Campsite Courier

Approachable, well mannered, friendly and helpful: these are just a few of the qualities you will need as a Campsite Courier and remember, your main focus will be ensuring that our customers return home having had 'the best holiday they have ever had.'

So how are you going to achieve this? Your duties will mainly involve cleaning customer accommodation for their arrival, welcoming them onto the campsite and ensuring that all the customer's needs are attended to during their stay.

You will need to have initiative and be a quick thinker, able to resolve any problems that may occur on-site efficiently and effectively.

As a Courier you will also be involved in montage (putting up tents) and demontage (taking down tents) at the beginning and end of the season.

Every year we welcome mature couriers to our overseas team. They work as Campsite Couriers in a team, or on a number of our sites which we have designated 'Couple Sites' or 'Single Courier Sites'.

To apply for this position you must meet the following minimum requirements:

- have at least 6 months' customer service experience.

(Source: www.careerintravel.co.uk, accessed June 2007)

Fig 14.04 Camping Representative job description

ACTIVITY

In pairs, discuss the jobs advertised and identify one role and responsibility for each category of holiday representative given.

Now see if you can describe each of the roles and responsibilities you have identified.

One responsibility of a resort representative is to produce and maintain information booklets and notice boards in accommodation properties.

An information booklet is the main source of information for the holidaymakers when the holiday representative is not available. The holiday representative needs to make sure that customers are aware of what the booklet contains, and where it can be found.

The notice board contains important information. For example, a notice board in a resort such as Playa de las Americas in Tenerife would have information such as the representatives' visiting times, hotel information (such as pool opening times or reception facilities), excursions available, important telephone numbers (e.g. a local doctor, dentist and office emergency numbers) and inbound flight details.

Fig 14.05 A typical holiday representative's notice board

ACTIVITY

Look at Figure 14.05. In pairs assess the following:
- the appropriateness of the information provided to guests
- the presentation of the notice board.

The representative is responsible for keeping the notice boards and information booklets up to date, and for sure making they are clearly visible. Notice boards are usually positioned in the reception area of a property. They should reflect the tour operator's professional image and have good visual impact to stand out against those of other tour operators.

ACTIVITY

Select a tour operator, overseas destination and accommodation of your choice. Produce a notice board. You can use the headings listed below to help you.
- The holiday representative, including the service provided
- Suggested excursions
- Weather outlook
- Accommodation information
- Health and safety
- The flight home

ACTIVITY

Discuss the importance of an eye-catching and informative notice board.

Many tour operators also give customers small information brochures either at the welcome meeting or on the coach transfer into resort. These brochures contain a condensed version of what is in the information booklet.

The information booklet contains vital information for the destination. For example, an information booklet in a property in Tenerife may include details of swimming pool safety, the nearest doctor and pharmacy, as well as warnings about timeshare salespeople and illegal excursion operatives. It might describe the benefits of hiring a car, as opposed to the dangers of hiring a moped or motorbike. Another important point often mentioned in hot resorts is the danger of sunburn. Information books sometimes include some driving routes around the resort/island that guests could follow if they choose to hire a car. Towards the end they often have information about homewards bound flights and coach pick-up details.

ACTIVITY

Write a list of information that a holiday representative might need to regularly update in an information booklet in a ski resort such as Mayrhofen in Austria. Now try and give reasons why each needs to be updated.

Airport duties and transfer commentaries are other key roles and responsibilities of holiday representatives. Transfer and resort representatives carry out these duties. They have to check arrival and departure times of flights in advance in case of flight delays as it is better to have guests waiting at the hotel or apartment rather than at a busy and cramped airport.

Below is a checklist of some of the main airport duties of holiday reps.

Departing passengers

- Check airport departures.
- Find out which check-in desks are being used and let the customers know.
- Lead customers to the check-in area.
- Position yourself either at the check-in desk, along the queue or at passport control.
- Give general assistance to all customers.
- Check all customers have been checked in.
- Advise customers of facilities and the routine in the departure lounge.

- Report to the coordinating airport representative for updated information.
- Assist colleagues with any help they may require.

Arriving passengers

- Before passengers arrive, check coach positions.
- Decide, with colleagues, who will meet and direct the customers.
- Check uniforms are still smart and presentable.
- Greet/direct new customers (with a smile).
- Those customers who have booked a late deal will need the name of the accommodation in writing before being directed to the coach.
- Make sure information/hotel packs are given to the corresponding clients.
- Cross-check customers' names with colleagues.
- Assist any clients with problems with lost luggage/hand baggage.
- **Carry out a name check and headcount on the coach.**
- Report to the coordinator before leaving the airport.

For your assessment it is necessary to describe the duties in more detail.

Let us look at one of the roles and responsibilities in more detail as an example: 'Carry out a name check and headcount on the coach.' A transfer representative will have a checklist of customers that should be on the coach. The representative will check customers' names against the list, which is normally attached to a clipboard. They will often check the names of the customers before they board the coach. Some tour operators will also read out the names on the list once everyone is boarded to make sure they have all the right people on the coach and that no one is missing. Once the representative thinks all customers are on the transfer coach, as a double check they will walk up the centre of the coach and count the number of customers seated. They will then make sure that the number of customers on the coach matches that on their passenger list.

A holiday representative's job is very challenging and involves a number of roles no matter what type of category of representative they are. The case study overleaf describes the roles and responsibilities of a resort representative.

Case study

Resort rep in Lanzarote

Rakhee works in Lanzarote. She has been there for the past three seasons and finds it much easier than the busy resort of Magaluf where she previously worked. The company she works for has day flights and there are only two flights a week so that means only two welcome meetings and few transfers to and from the airport. Lanzarote airport closes at around 00.30 and opens at 06.00 so she does not have to go to the airport at 3 in the morning unless there is a major problem such as fog or floods. When occasionally this has happened, then she has to work more unsociable hours. This is a typical week for Rakhee:

Sunday is airport day so the morning is packed with taking holidaymakers to and from the airport. Often the afternoon is quiet, so Rakhee has a bit of time to herself. The evening tends to involve hotel visits.

Monday starts off with a welcome meeting and morning property duties followed by sorting out the weekly accounts. Between 17.00 and 19.00 she has property visits to see customers, book any excursions and check no one has any problems.

Tuesday morning, Rakhee leads a half-day excursion. It is an 8.30 pick-up so she has to be up early. Rakhee collects holidaymakers from several properties. During the afternoon she has free time but the evening is scheduled for the reps' cabaret.

Wednesday is arrival day of the second flight of the week. She does not need to transfer customers but is involved in the airport duties. In the evening she has property visits from 17.00 to 19.00.

Thursday starts off with a welcome meeting and morning property duties followed by sorting out the weekly accounts. Between 17.00 and 19.00 she has property visits to see customers, book any excursions and check no one has any problems.

Friday Rakhee is involved in guiding a full-day excursion. The pick-ups at customers' properties start at 09.00 and the final drop-off is not until 17.30. The evening is spent at the office sorting administration.

Saturday is a well-earned day off.

Rakhee is a good performer so she has rehearsals in her own time for the reps' cabaret. Guiding excursions requires lots of planning and throughout the day Rakhee needs to make sure she provides information to her group and responds to any questions they may have. When Rakhee carries out property visits, they often take a few hours longer than planned. If a customer has a problem, it is important that she tries to sort it out there and then.

ACTIVITY

Assume you work for a TV broadcaster. You are involved in the production of a short TV programme about transfer representatives' airport and coach transfer roles and responsibilities. You have been asked to produce a script for the programme. You have been given the following information about the programme.

The film will be about transfers to and from Benidorm and airport duties at Alicante airport. It will include both arrival and departures at the airport and transfers to and from the airport to the accommodation in Benidorm. There will be a variety of different customer types featured in the programme.

ACTIVITY

Identify Rakhee's key roles and responsibilities as a resort representative.

Assessing the outcome

You have recently applied to a tour operator for a job as a holiday representative. You have been shortlisted and asked to attend an assessment day. As part of the assessment day you have been asked to give a presentation describing three categories of holiday representative.

● Describe the roles and responsibilities of three different categories of holiday representative (**P1**).

The legal responsibilities of a holiday representative

Overseas representatives must be aware of the tour operator's contractual obligations to the customer. There are a number of laws and regulations in place to protect the customer, including:

- the EU Package Travel Regulations
- Supply of Goods and Services Act
- Health and Safety at Work Act
- Trades Descriptions Act
- Disability Discrimination Act.

EU Package Travel Regulations

When the EU Package Travel Regulations came into force in 1993, they caused quite a stir among UK tour operators. The main force of the regulations was to clarify that the tour operator was responsible for all parts of the package holiday. So what is meant by the term 'package'? In the case of the EU Directive, a 'package' means:

> the pre-arranged combination of at least two of the following components when sold or offered for sale at an inclusive price, and when the service covers a period of more than 24 hours or includes overnight accommodation:
>
> 1. transport
> 2. accommodation
> 3. other tourist services not ancillary to transport or accommodation and accounting for a significant proportion of the package,
>
>   and
>
>   (a) the submission of separate accounts for different components shall not cause the arrangements to be other than a package
>
>   (b) the fact that a combination is arranged at the request of the consumer and in accordance with his specific instructions (whether modified or not) shall not of itself cause it to be treated as other than pre-arranged

and 'retailer' means the person who sells or offers for sale the package put together by the organiser.

(Source: Package Travel, Package Holidays and Package Tours Regulations 1992 Statutory Instrument 1992 No. 3288)

For a tour operator, there are three main areas of liability outlined by the regulations: These are as follows:

1. Any descriptions given to customers must be accurate and clear. This means that tour operators must deliver all that they have promised their customers in their brochures, leaflets and materials such as their information booklets. It covers all descriptions not just those relating to accommodation properties described in the brochure. So, for example, if a notice board has information about a local market excursion but no market takes place, then the organisation is in breach of this regulation. The information must not be misleading. If a tour operator is in breach of this regulation it will have to compensate the customer if they have suffered as a result.

   In a resort, the holiday representative will need to check the information that is written in the brochure, leaflets, etc. to make sure that it is correct. For example, information about the area and resort must reflect what actually exists. Holiday representatives need to tell senior staff, such as team leaders at the resort office, of any discrepancies they find so that the UK office can be advised.

2. If a significant change happens to the customer's booking, the customer has the right to cancel with a full refund or accept the change. Examples of significant change could include a swimming pool not being available when the brochure said there was one available. Where a significant proportion of the booked holiday cannot be provided (e.g. if the customer arrives in the resort and finds the restaurant at a hotel is out of order), then the tour operator must make suitable arrangements at no extra cost to the customer, or compensate the customer. It is important that the UK office is made aware of these changes as soon as possible so that it can notify customers of the problem. The holiday representative must therefore liaise with the UK office as soon as there are any changes

affecting the accommodation properties the tour operator has contracts with.

3. In some cases, customers arrive on holiday only to find a problem, e.g. facilities are of a poor standard. It is the holiday representative's responsibility to try to sort out the problem. If the problem cannot be resolved, then possibly the holiday representative will need to compensate the customer for any expense, inconvenience, disappointment or loss (such as injury or illness) that they have suffered as a result of the problem. The customer is obliged to tell the tour operator and supplier (e.g. the hotelier) about any problems while they are in the resort. If the holiday representative cannot find a solution, then a written report needs to be completed. This is often referred to as a complaint or customer report.

A holiday representative therefore plays an important part in ensuring this regulation is adhered to.

ACTIVITY

In groups, discuss why a tour operator requires its holiday representatives to complete a written report when a customer experiences problems overseas and a solution cannot be found.

The following case studies describe customer problems encountered overseas and are taken from *Holiday Which?* (January–February 2006). These show examples of when the EU Package Travel Regulations were contravened.

Case study

Can Paz, won't stay
Cy and Enid fight on over a
Menorcan mis-description

Cy Binning and Enid Wallace paid £2634 for a 14-day package with self-catering specialist James Villa Holidays. They decided upon the Can Paz Villa in Menorca, as they were impressed by the description in the brochure and the inviting picture, which showed the villa and its swimming pool to be light, airy and spacious.

However, when they arrived Cy and Enid found the villa grubby, smelly and in a state of disrepair. Sunlight was limited inside the villa, which made it gloomy, while a lack of proper wardrobe facilities only added to the sense of it being second-rate.

Outside, the pool's cloudy water looked unsafe to swim in and the grounds were badly neglected. Very disappointed, Cy and Enid felt that 'only a complete refurbishment would have dragged it from its worn, tired and sorry state'.

The problems clearly could not be solved overnight, so when their James Villa rep was unable to offer them an alternative property, Cy and Enid felt they had no choice but to find one themselves. Exhausted after having left home at 4.30am, they moved out of Can Paz at 6pm, not knowing whether they would be able to find anywhere to stay. By chance, the couple met someone who was able to offer them a suitable alternative, and they agreed to pay €2800.

Upon their return, Cy and Enid wrote to James Villa Holidays, but the company failed to offer the couple any compensation. Very frustrated, they decided to approach Which? Legal Service. We helped them take court action against the operator for breach of contract and breach of the Package Travel, Package Holidays and Package Tours Regulations 1992.

Before the hearing, James Villa Holidays offered Cy and Enid the full £2020 claimed as full and final settlement, which they accepted.

Point of law

The Package Travel, Package Holidays and Package Tours Regulations 1992 say that a package holiday must correspond with its brochure description.

Case study

Expletives deleted
Kosmar coughs up after the Elkins endure an earful

When Peter and Kathy Elkins paid Kosmar £738 for a two-week stay at the self-catering Esperides Studios in Pefkohori, Halkidiki, they weren't expecting a Greek chorus of contempt to blight their break.

The problems started at once, with loud music thumping from the bar for up to 16 hours a day. When Peter and Kathy complained, owners Athenasea and Katerina not only refused to turn it down, but deliberately shut the bar one night and left the premises with music blaring defiantly! The couple spoke to the Kosmar rep, who was unable to improve the situation.

Worn down by the continuous cacophony, Peter and Kathy asked to be moved to a quieter room, which the Kosmar rep later managed to arrange. After a short-lived respite, matters came to a head on the penultimate day of their stay, when Peter and Kathy returned to their room in the afternoon to find deafening music playing in the adjoining room – and the balcony door being held open by a pile of blankets!

When Kathy went to reception to complain, she was told to ask her neighbours to turn it down – an obvious taunt, as she knew the room was unoccupied. She repeated her request, but Katerina shrugged her shoulders, so Kathy calmly said she'd pursue her complaint in the UK. At this, Katerina and Athenasea launched into a barrage of four-letter obscenities, ending the tirade by slamming the door in Kathy's face and catching her hand.

Peter phoned Kosmar demanding help. Katerina tried to turn the music off before the rep arrived, but took the wrong keys with her in her haste. When the rep discovered loud music coming from a locked, empty room – as Peter had described – the Elkins were transferred to a hotel in Hanioti for their remaining night.

Back home Peter complained to Kosmar, but the company would only 'apologise for any inconvenience caused'. The Elkins asked Which? Legal Service for help in bringing an action in the small claims court. After a hearing, where video evidence was crucial, the couple were awarded compensation of £250, plus £50 costs.

Point of law

Regulation 15(1) of the Package Travel, Package Holidays and Package Tours Regulations 1992 makes tour operators responsible for providing all components of a package properly even if they have subcontracted aspects of your holiday to hoteliers, airlines or other parties.

ACTIVITY

In groups, discuss key issues raised in the holiday 'upsets' articles in the case studies. Explain the legal responsibilities of the holiday representative in each situation.

Health and Safety at Work Act

This act affects employers and employees. As an employee, a tour operator must make sure that all work systems and practices are safe. It is required to regularly monitor the work environment in respect of health and safety requirements. It must also provide a written statement of safety policy and bring it to the notice of employees.

In order to comply with the act, tour operators must provide adequate information and training for all holiday representatives in matters relating to health and safety.

Holiday representatives have a duty under the Health and Safety at Work Act to take reasonable care to avoid injury to themselves or to others by their work activities. They also have to cooperate with their employers and other agencies to ensure that the requirements of the act are carried out. The next section looks at health and safety in more detail.

Documentation and the reporting and recording of incidents and problems are responsibilities that all representatives must carry out. Having an audit trail is necessary in case a further investigation of the problem is required. Figure 14.06 gives an example of an accident report. It contains key information relating to the accident.

Representativeís Report

Page 1 of $\boxed{2}$

Tour Operator	*THOMSON*
Resort (e.g. Palma Nova)	*BENIDORM*
Customer Name	*MR S. ELLIS*
Accommodation	*AMBASSADOR*
Representative Name (Print)	*C. LAMIN*
Holiday Insured with	*AXA INSURANCE*

Form No.	*095929*
Booking Ref. No.	*628291*
Area (e.g. Majorca)	*COSTA BLANCA*
UK Departure Date	*12·12·03*
Room No.	*642*
Date	*14·12·03*

Please tick relevent box   Illness [ ]   Injury [✓]   Accommodation Standards [ ]

Other (specify) _____

Summary of Case Issues (see guidelines for completion)

1. AT APPROX 11·30AM MR ELLIS CUT HIS FOOT ON A SMALL PIECE OF PLASTIC NEAR POOL.
2. MR ELLIS HAS A DEEP CUT, ABOUT 2CM LONG ON THE BASE OF HIS FOOT.
3. MR ELLIS WILL NOT BE ABLE TO SWIM OR GET HIS FOOT WET FOR THE REST OF HIS HOLIDAY
4. THE DOCTOR WAS CALLED BY RECEPTION AT 11·45AM. DR DEACON ARRIVED AT 12 NOON – HE ADVISED MR ELLIS TO GO TO THE CLINIC. HE WENT TO THE SAN MIGUEL CLINIC AND HAD AN EX-RAY. THE WOUND WAS CLEANED AND SIX STITCHES WERE GIVEN.
5. MR ELLIS MUST RETURN TO THE CLINIC IN TWO DAYS FOR A CHECK UP
6. NO INJURIES OF THIS KIND HAVE BEEN REPORTED AT THIS HOTEL BEFORE.
7. I DONT BELIEVE THE SUPPLIER IS LIABLE. ALL DRINKS ARE IN PLASTIC CUPS AND THE POOL AREA IS SWEPT AND CLEANED TWICE A DAY
8. MR & MRS ELLIS HAVE BEEN MOVED TO A GROUND FLOOR ROOM AND A WHEELCHAIR HAS BEEN RENTED FOR MR ELLIS TO GET AROUND

   MR & MRS ELLIS HAVE BEEN MOVED TO MAKE THINGS EASIER SO THAT THEY CAN HAVE ROOM SERVICE – WHICH THEY HAVE BEEN OFFERED FREE OF CHARGE.

With Customer Report Form No. _____   Copy received by _____

Holiday Amendment Form No. _____   On behalf of Hotelier/Supplier _____

Customer Service Form No. _____

IMPORTANT: PLEASE RETURN THIS FORM TO THE RESORT OFFICE WITH WEEKLY ACCOUNTS

DISTRIBUTION: WHITE – Customer YELLOW – Customer Service Support GLH GREY – Representative BLUE – Resort

Fig 14.06 An example of an accident report

Continuation Sheet   Page 2 of 2

Continued from:

Reps Rep Form No. _076531_   Cust Serv Form No. _N/A_

Cust Rep Form No. _No Report Completed_   Holiday Amend Form No. _N/A_

Customer Name _Mr S. Ellis_   Booking Ref No. _628291_   Reps Name _C. Lamin_

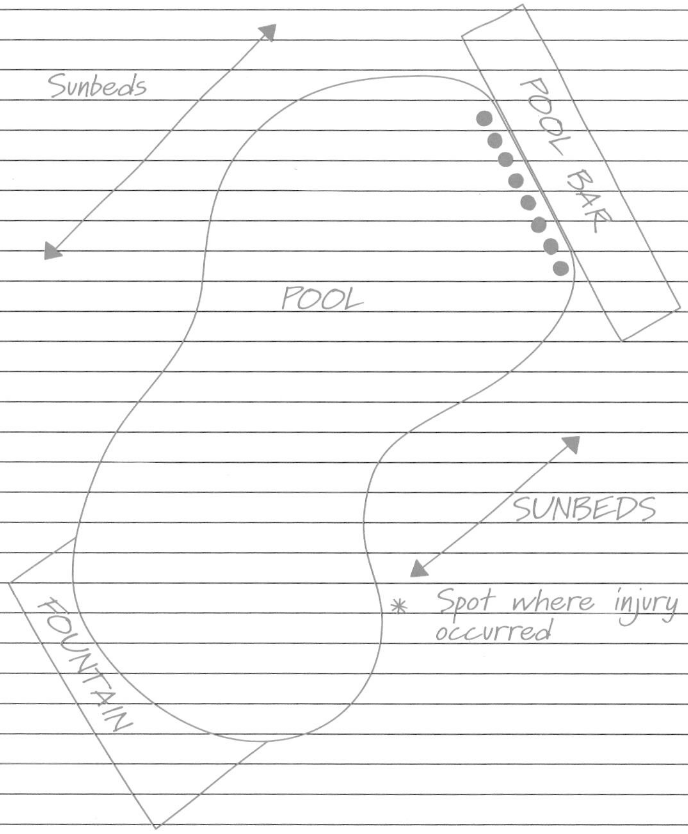

Sunbeds

POOL BAR

POOL

SUNBEDS

FOUNTAIN

✳ Spot where injury occurred

Mr Ellis has stated how happy he is with the treatment he has received from both Thomson & the Hotel

IMPORTANT: PLEASE RETURN THIS FORM TO THE RESORT OFFICE WITH WEEKLY ACCOUNTS

DISTRIBUTION: WHITE – Customer YELLOW – Customer Service Support GLH GREY – Representative GOLD – Resort

Fig 14.06 An example of an accident report, continued

ACTIVITY

In small groups, discuss the importance of holiday representatives completing this accident report.

ACTIVITY

Read the 'Problems in Majorca' case study below and imagine that you are the representative.
- Identify any laws or regulations that have been breached.
- Explain how you would deal with these problems.

Assessing the outcome

You work for a travel magazine and have been asked to write a feature article on the legal responsibilities of holiday representatives. The feature is to cover four different holiday situations.

- Identify and explain the legal responsibilities in four different holiday situations (**P2**).

Health and safety in relation to the role of the holiday representative

All representatives must ensure that the holiday environment is safe for their customers. For example, children's representatives must be aware of where equipment is placed and how it will affect children's play, i.e. are the swings located near to the entrance? Could one child collide with another?

Camping representatives need to ensure that fire extinguishers and hoses around the campsite are regularly serviced and are in good condition and easily accessible.

Resort representatives need to consider the safety of pools in properties.

Many tour operators will have a policy relating to safety. They also produce safety information leaflets for customers in resorts (Figure 14.07 opposite).

A holiday representative has health and safety responsibilities such as:

- making sure that customers are informed of all health and safety issues
- resolving any health and safety issues as they arise
- ensuring that customer information is accurate and up to date
- carrying out regular safety checklists
- ensuring that health and safety concerns are dealt with in a sympathetic way
- informing senior members of staff of any health and safety issues
- recording any incidents relating to health and safety.

Case study

Problems in Majorca

Mr and Mrs Glover and their son Seb are on holiday in Majorca. On the first day they go and see the holiday representative, who notices that the family are very upset and angry about their holiday. After listening and questioning the customers, the representative learns that the main areas of complaint are as follows.

The brochure stated that the transfer time to the resort was up to 60 minutes, however the journey took three hours because the coach passed through several resorts before arriving at their property and there were severe road works on the road to Alcudia.

On arrival at the hotel, the family discovered that they had been allocated a room on the top floor. The travel agent had made a special request for a lower floor as the family were worried about their 18-month-old son having access to a balcony.

The family were furious with the building work around the pool area. They had not been informed in the UK that the pool would be unavailable. They had come away for a quiet family holiday.

Resort Safety

Coach Travel

We do work closely with the suppliers of the coaches we use for your transfers and excursions. In all resorts however, we would ask you to:

- Wear the seat belt if one is provided
- As not all coaches will be equipped with seatbelts we advise you to avoid sitting on the front seats, the middle seat of the back row and those seats overlooking emergency exits. Children under 12 should not sit on these seats even if seatbelts are provided
- Always remain seated until the coach has stopped
- Never leave luggage in the aisle

Excursions and Activities

We work closely with our excursion and activity suppliers to ensure that they operate to appropriate safety standards. Please ensure that you are reasonably fit for the activity and that you comply with all safety instructions.

Should you independently choose to use an alternate supplier, you should satisfy yourself that your insurance and the insurance, legal cover and safety standards of the company you are choosing to use are adequate.

This leaflet relates to the Thomson Summer Sun, Winter Sun, Florida, Faraway Shores, Beach Breaks, Superfamily, Gold, Platinum, A La Carte, Young at Heart, Small & Friendly, Just , Skytours, and Portland Holidays Direct holiday products.

Beach Safety

Check if there is a lifeguard and if there is a flag warning system in place, make sure that you know what the flags mean, especially those that may tell you when and where it is dangerous to swim.

Be aware of local conditions; tides, winds and currents can make even the safest beach hazardous. Also, please ensure that you are aware of any 'zoned' areas that are marked out for watersports.

Road Safety

A high proportion of the accidents that are reported to us every year are road accidents. The rules of the road can be very different overseas, for example drivers are not always obliged to stop at pedestrian crossings and you may need to look the other way when crossing the road!

Driving overseas is a great way to explore and you can book car hire through your Holiday Rep at anytime. Please be aware of local regulations however, and never drink and drive.

With regard to mopeds, variable road conditions and drivers' attitudes towards them can make riding mopeds a dangerous option overseas. We do not recommend moped or motorbike hire in any resort, even for experienced riders. In addition to mopeds, we only recommend using quad bikes as part of a Thomson approved excursion.

Fig 14.07 Thomson resort safety information

The Federation of Tour Operators (FTO) has a preferred code of practice and guidelines for its members. This covers the following topics:

- fire safety
- food safety
- pool safety
- general safety
- beach safety
- Legionella management
- children's clubs
- incident management.

Tour operators train their overseas staff in relation to these guidelines so holiday representatives can give customers information and advice, relating to health and safety, at such times as on coach transfers, at the welcome meeting and in any literature produced.

ACTIVITY

Select a category of representative. Produce a poster highlighting how a holiday representative would create a safe environment. You should consider the key topics set by the FTO.

It is important that holiday representatives are aware of the areas that could cause a hazard. In order to avoid all potential hazards holiday representatives carry out safety checks.

A holiday representative needs to investigate the properties used by their customers. Finding out the location and advising customers about the type of roads around the resort can help avoid road accidents. For example, is there a busy road next to an accommodation property? Holidaymakers can be complacent about road safety when in a foreign country. A simple reminder as to whether cars drive on the left or right side of the road can avoid road accidents. Water is another potential hazard, so advice about the strength of the sea current or how the sand declines into the water can avoid people drowning. In some countries, there may be poisonous plants, berries or fungi, so customers need to be aware of what not to touch or eat.

Holiday representatives also need to do safety checks on surfaces. Some activities may be outside so concrete needs to be checked as it can have rough parts or loose chippings. Wood could have splinters. Pool areas are common places where people fall. Tour operators insist that holiday representatives carry out specific checks for accommodation properties with pools. Sand pits attract cats so if not covered properly can be unhygienic as cats use them as a toilet. Holiday representatives need to make sure that property managers look after equipment.

UK tour operators have to consider British standards as they are dealing with customers from the UK, however it may not be possible to change certain facilities abroad. If standards are not appropriate, then the UK office must be informed. Senior overseas staff will then evaluate the degree of safety to determine whether the property is safe to be used. In circumstances where certain property is not safe, the holiday representatives must think of alternatives. For example, if a playground is located near a busy road could the hotelier build/erect a fence or could the children's representative design activities that are away from the play area for children to participate in?

Holiday representatives must consider the safety of equipment – for example, in a playground:

- swings
- climbers
- spring and rocking items

- roundabouts
- seesaws
- slides.

The children's representative needs to check equipment before arranging activities in play areas. Are the swings, slides and climbers all properly secured in the ground? What type of surface surrounds the equipment? Are there any sharp items on any equipment that may cause harm?

If children's representatives are taking children to the beach or water park, they have to have trained staff to manage the children. The children's representative has to make sure that the ratio of staff to children on trips is correct. The location of the activities must also be risk assessed, i.e. is the beach a safe area to play around in? Does it have a gradual gradient? What is the sea like on the day of the activity (rough/clean)?

ACTIVITY

Produce an outline plan for a typical children's activity day, which highlights the legal responsibilities of children's representatives.

Safety applies to all categories of holiday representative. Let us consider what holiday representatives could do to improve safety.

Holiday representatives normally complete safety checklists monthly. The accommodation safety checklist often includes bedrooms and apartments, lift safety, corridors and stairways, internal public areas, kitchens and buffets, general health and safety, children's facilities, fire alarms and customer communication, as well as swimming pools. The swimming pool checklist outlines the checks that holiday representatives are required to make for pool safety.

ACTIVITY

Look at the swimming pool checklist opposite. In groups, scrutinise the checklist and discuss how carrying out a checklist assists in the promotion of a safe environment.

Swimming pool safety checklist

SWIMMING POOLS	Pool	Pool	Children's Pool	COMMENTS AND ACTION TAKEN
Is the bottom of the pool clearly visible, i.e. can you see the bottom of the pool at the deep end?	Yes / No / NA	Yes / No / NA	Yes / No / NA	
Are depth markings present?	Yes / No / NA	Yes / No / NA	Yes / No / NA	
Are depth markings visible, i.e. not faded?	Yes / No / NA	Yes / No / NA	Yes / No / NA	
Are there any notices or preventative measures to reduce the slope's danger? (i.e. painted or buoyed lines, additional depth marks etc.)	Yes / No / NA	Yes / No / NA	Yes / No / NA	
Are there prominently displayed pictorial 'No Diving' signs?	Yes / No / NA	Yes / No / NA	Yes / No / NA	
Are there any cracked or broken tiles or dangerous edges?	Yes / No / NA	Yes / No / NA	Yes / No / NA	
Is the pool cleaned regularly?	Yes / No / NA	Yes / No / NA	Yes / No / NA	
Is there prominently displayed, accessible rescue equipment around the pool?	Yes / No / NA	Yes / No / NA	Yes / No / NA	
Is there a multiboard/safety notices indicating: a) pool opening hours b) no night swimming c) children must be supervised d) emergency action information?	Yes / No / NA Yes / No / NA Yes / No / NA Yes / No / NA	Yes / No / NA Yes / No / NA Yes / No / NA Yes / No / NA	Yes / No / NA Yes / No / NA Yes / No / NA Yes / No / NA	
Does the pool have a trained dedicated lifeguard on duty when it is open?	Yes / No / NA	Yes / No / NA	Yes / No / NA	
If no, does the pool have a 'no lifeguard on duty' sign?	Yes / No / NA	Yes / No / NA	Yes / No / NA	
Are all pool fixtures and fittings in place and secure, e.g. lights, grilles, handrails, steps, filter covers?	Yes / No / NA	Yes / No / NA	Yes / No / NA	
Does the pool have a diving board or platform?	Yes / No / NA	Yes / No / NA	Yes / No / NA	
Are slides/flumes supervised when open?	Yes / No / NA	Yes / No / NA	Yes / No / NA	
Is the plant room securely locked at all times?	Yes / No / NA	Yes / No / NA	Yes / No / NA	
Only plastic glasses should be used at the pool bar. Is this the case?	Yes / No / NA	Yes / No / NA	Yes / No / NA	
Are all sun-loungers around the pool area in a safe condition?	Yes / No / NA	Yes / No / NA	Yes / No / NA	
If there is a heated jacuzzi does it have the following notices displayed close by: a) water temperature b) minimum ages for use c) emergency action information d) advice against use by those with high blood pressure, heart conditions, pregnancy etc.?	Yes / No / NA Yes / No / NA Yes / No / NA Yes / No / NA	Yes / No / NA Yes / No / NA Yes / No / NA Yes / No / NA	Yes / No / NA Yes / No / NA Yes / No / NA Yes / No / NA	

ACTIVITY

What would you do to improve safety in the following situations?
- A swimming pool has a loose tile.
- A hotel manager keeps blocking the emergency exit with deliveries.
- Fire extinguishers have expired use-by dates at the campsite you work at.
- There has been an accident in a hotel property you are responsible for. An adult has fallen from a balcony. He was drunk.
- A number of customers have food poisoning in a property you are responsible for.
- The beach has a number of jellyfish washed ashore.
- A number of customers have reported bag thefts in a certain area of the resort.

Assessing the outcome

You work for a tour operator. You have been asked to produce an information booklet for new holiday representatives so that they know how to create a safe and healthy holiday environment for holidaymakers.

- Describe the role played by holiday representatives in creating a safe healthy holiday environment (**P3**).

Applying social, customer service and selling skills

The holiday representative deals with a wide range of different customers. In Unit 4, on customer service in travel and tourism you will have learnt about the needs of different customers and how staff need to deal with a range of types of customer. Social skills are crucial for holiday representatives, as they regularly have to deal with different types of customer.

Customers form an opinion of the holiday representative very quickly. Usually within five seconds a customer will form a visual first impression of the holiday representative. Within 30 seconds, they usually stereotype them, e.g. 'Look at his uniform. It is typical – he looks just like that lazy rep Johnny we had last year.' As a general rule, within 90 seconds of their meeting, the customer will have formed the impression they are going to have of the representative. The first point of contact for the customer is the airport at the arrivals point, so it is important that that first contact is favourable as holiday representatives only have one chance to give an excellent first impression.

ACTIVITY

Billy works as a resort representative in the Costa del Sol. He regularly visits the airport to drop off and meet new holidaymakers. Today he arrived at the airport at 08.00 hrs. It is now 14.35 and his customers have just landed having had a three-hour flight delay. He is expecting 121 passengers, 49 of which he will be accompanying back on the transfer coach to the resorts of Fuengirola and Puerto Banus.

Describe how Billy can create a good first impression with his customers.

A good holiday representative is one that creates a good rapport with customers. This can be done in a number of ways – for example, on property visits the holiday representative can talk to customers around the pool or bar.

Case study

Building rapport

Rachel is a campsite representative. She is a little shy and has to push herself to talk to customers. Her manager has spoken to her on several occasions about ways in which she could improve her performance. Today her manager came to watch her in action and this is what he observed.

Name: Rachel Crusher
Position: Campsite Representative
Location: St Tropez
Situation: Selling an excursion to a family

Comments: Rachel, you did begin to explore the customer's needs and you asked about what they enjoy doing in France. However, you did not take this further to establish their real needs and wants or to find out if they are enjoying the holiday. Your voice was quiet and you did not talk to the customer about anything other than the excursion. You did have some eye contact, however your body language was quite cold – you folded your arms and sat back from the customer.

ACTIVITY

Using the previous case study on Rachel suggest how she could have built a better rapport with her customers.

Transfers

So what does the holiday representative tell you on a coach transfer? On the way from the airport to the resort they will welcome the customers to the resort and introduce themselves and the tour operator the customers have booked through. For example: 'Good morning. On behalf of [tour operators' name] I would like to welcome you all to the sunny island of Majorca. My name is Jo and I am your transfer representative today...'

Let us have a look at the other information given on an airport arrival transfer.

- *Safety and comfort on the coach*: this includes information such as air conditioning, toilets on board, the use of seat belts, emergency exits.

- *Country information*: customers will be looking forward to their experience abroad. For many customers it may be their first visit to the country and for some a first holiday abroad. Transfer representatives therefore give the customers some general information about the country they are visiting such as what the time is, i.e. are the clocks ahead or behind the time in the UK? Customers will also want to know what the weather is going to be like so reps will tell them the forecast for the next few days. Customers also need to be informed about safety issues such as extreme heat. The transfer representative might say, 'The weather has been extremely hot for this time of year so please take care not to go in the direct sunshine during the peak of the day. The sun is extremely hot and can cause severe sunburn and heat stroke if you are exposed too much.'

- *Transfer details*: customers will want to know how long they are going to be on the transfer coach. Some tour operators will have people staying in different resorts on the one coach. The speech should therefore give an indication of the duration, and the route to be taken.

- *Resort information*: some brief details about the resort will be given in the transfer speech. Detailed information is followed up at the welcome meeting. Customers will want a brief overview of what their resort is like. They will be told information that sells the resort well and will reassure them that they have made a good choice. The content will highlight the strengths of the resort such as it has a long sandy beach and excellent nightlife.

- *Promoting excursions and company services*: any contact with customers should be utilised and the transfer speech is in example of 'planting the seed' to sell excursions.

- *Accommodation check-in procedures*: the transfer representative will give information to customers about check-in procedures at the hotel. They give a general overview about what happens at check-in and advise customers to have their passports ready to be presented to the receptionist as part of the registration check-in process.

ACTIVITY

You work as a Club 18–30 transfer representative in Ibiza. Prepare a transfer speech for a journey from Ibiza airport to the resort of San Antonio.

It is important that holiday representatives present themselves in a positive way. Tour operators will give their employees uniforms to wear. It is important that the member of staff looks and feels good in their uniform. In order to present a professional image holiday representatives must make sure that their uniforms are maintained and that they pay attention to their personal presentation. Holiday representatives normally have more than one uniform: they usually wear a formal uniform at the airport and for welcome meetings, and a less formal uniform when guiding excursions.

ACTIVITY

Investigate the uniform worn in formal and informal situations for a tour operator of your choice.

Welcome meetings

This is where the representative has the opportunity to get to know customers, share vital knowledge about the resort and area, help those customers with any problems, and, probably most importantly for the commercially minded, make money – for both themselves and the tour operator.

Once a holiday representative has developed an effective format for a welcome meeting, it probably won't change throughout the season. It will only be the choice of excursions promoted that will change, depending on the audience.

Even the most confident holiday representative will find the experience of standing up in front of up to 150 people and presenting a welcome meeting very daunting. It is important that they are prepared and give an informative presentation. Not all welcome meetings are as big as this. They can range from two people up to 150.

Depending on the number of people attending the meeting, it may well take a different presentation style. If there are only a few people, there is no point doing a formal, stand-up presentation. In a case like that, it is much better to sit customers around a table, and have an informal approach. If, however, there are a large number of people, then the holiday representative will need to make a presentation and possibly use a microphone.

When holiday representatives plan the welcome meeting, it is important to arrange a location that is quiet, such as a temporarily closed bar or TV room. It is also important to have a location where the guests will not be too distracted, i.e. by the sun or by other guests. The holiday representative should try to ensure that everyone is seated and if possible provided with a drink. In many cases this will be arranged with the hotel reception in advance.

Welcome meetings are usually arranged within 24 hours of a customer's arrival. A welcome meeting will last about 30 minutes and at the end of the meeting the holiday representative chats to customers and takes excursion and car hire bookings. The speech itself will cover a number of topics, such as:

- an introduction to the holiday representative
- holiday hints
- the tour operator's service
- health and safety

- accommodation information
- resort information
- responsible tourism
- what there is to see and do – including the promotion of excursions on offer
- car rental
- how to book car hire and excursions.

The holiday representative presenting the welcome meeting needs to make sure that the presentation keeps people's attention.

Let us look at some of the topics included in a little more detail.

The introduction

This is where the holiday representative introduces him/herself, and also introduces the tour operator. They give details of the format of the welcome meeting and ask that any questions be kept until the end. They need to make sure that they inform customers of the benefits of staying and listening to the welcome meeting. The fact that the holiday representative knows a lot of information about the area, which can be shared with customers, is one benefit.

Health and safety

When customers go on holiday, they sometimes tend to leave their sense of danger back in the UK. It is so easy for accidents to happen when on holiday, especially when people are in high spirits. It is therefore very important for holiday representatives to inform customers of any safety issues. Remember, holiday representatives want customers to have a great holiday, not spend their time in hospital.

If an accommodation property has a swimming pool, then it can be great fun, but it can also be dangerous. The presentation should warn people not to dive in shallow water, and to watch their children around the pool. Most pools use strong chemicals, including chlorine, which are often put in the pool at night. Holiday representatives should alert customers to this. When presenting this part of the welcome meeting, it could be easy to sound patronising towards the guests. Therefore it is important that the holiday representative brings some humour into what they are saying – get people to laugh about it and they will take note!

There have been a number of incidents relating to customers climbing over balconies. Customers should be alerted to the dangers of this.

The reception of the accommodation property has staff who are available to help customers so it is important that holiday representatives make sure that the customers are aware of this. Some people are afraid to approach reception because they don't think the receptionists will understand them. It is vital to persuade customers to use the facility; reception will be able to solve many customer problems before the holiday representative even knows about them. Customers need to be aware that many receptionists speak excellent English.

The welcome presentation should also include information about the facilities that are available at reception, such as safety deposit boxes (a must to mention) telephones, money exchange, taxi calling service, postcards and stamps.

Accommodation information

The accommodation, which is often a hotel or apartment, is home to the customer for the duration of their holiday. This part of the welcome meeting is intended to provide the guest with all the information needed in order to make the most of their stay. Customers will need to know about the facilities the property provides such as swimming pool, entertainment, children's facilities, etc.

Information about the services provided in the accommodation should be given, such as how often the rooms are cleaned and how often the linen is changed.

ACTIVITY

Consider the resort information included in a welcome meeting.
- Research the resort of Faliraki. You could look at guidebooks, brochures, websites and newspaper articles.
- What key information would you include in a welcome meeting about the resort of Faliraki? Your accommodation manifest highlights that your guests will be couples and groups aged between 18 and 30 years old.

Selling skills

The selling part of the holiday representative's role is important to the tour operator both as a means of generating income and as an excellent service to customers. Welcome meetings, transfers, hotel visits and guiding all provide opportunities for the holiday representative to promote optional extras to their customers.

It is important that the holiday representatives understand why they sell products in the resort. During their training they will be helped by being told of the benefits of such selling. Some of these are as follows.

- It brings in additional revenue for the organisation. It is a competitive industry so the more revenue, then the more opportunities for growth within the company.
- The holiday representative makes commission. Holiday representatives' wages are supplemented by the commission they make from the sale of items such as excursions, car hire and reunion tickets.
- The customer gets 'out and about' and therefore maximises the holiday experience.
- The tour operator can compete with the competition as it is providing a service to the customer. If customers had to book an excursion or car hire themselves, they may have to pay more as they are not buying in bulk. Customers may also have to waste time finding out where they can buy the product.
- Customers meet other people and this can play a part in their enjoyment of the holiday.
- Customers may come back again if they have a fantastic time.

In order to sell the excursions effectively, it is important that the holiday representative knows the product that she/he going to be selling/promoting. They can do this by visiting or going on the excursion at the start of the season. In addition, they can collect publicity information as well as speaking to customers who have been on the excursions.

In the resort, the holiday representative will sell a range of products – for example:

- excursions – such as boat trips, day trips to theme parks, historical sights or local markets

- car hire – this is arranged in resort usually using a recognised car rental company, e.g. Hertz or Avis

- merchandise – such as T-shirts

- reunion tickets – such as the Club 18–30 reunion weekends in the UK.

There are a number of key points to consider with regard to successful selling. Holiday representatives need to do the following.

- Identify the target market – at welcome meetings the representative will look at the accommodation manifest to determine the target markets arriving in resort.

- Explore the needs and wants of the customer(s) – for example, the customer might want a luxury car but needs a baby seat.

- Demonstrate a positive opening.

- Appeal to the senses, such as smell, touch, feelings and sight, – for example, painting a picture using descriptive language.

- Present the features and benefits of the excursions.

- Sell.

- Overcome any objections.

- Relate to the customer(s).

- Close the sale.

Having ascertained a customer's request, then found and presented the product, what happens if the customer then raises an objection? First, the selling does not really become a challenge until the customer says 'No!' A holiday representative must always deal with an objection immediately. They should try to find out why the customer is objecting. It could be too expensive or the day of the excursion might not be right.

A vital point in the effort to be successful at selling is getting customers to book immediately. The holiday representative should create a sense of urgency to book. They should look for 'final buying signals' in order to close the deal. If a holiday representative knows that there is limited availability on an excursion then they can finish off a sale by telling the customer that places are strictly limited and that they may go quickly. This can help customers to make a decision.

It is important to remember that a good seller is one who:

- uses active listening

- uses positive body language

- maintains and builds the relationship

- asks the right questions at the right times

- has excellent product knowledge

- has confidence in their own ability

- has confidence in the tour operator's products they are selling

- recognises and reacts to buying signals.

ACTIVITY

Research possible excursions that are available in a resort of your choice.

In pairs, carry out a role play. One person is to take the role of the holiday representative and the other the customer. You are to sell an excursion(s) to the customer matching their individual needs.

This activity should be repeated using different customer types. You should swap roles each time so each of you has the opportunity to take the role of the rep.

There are a number of other situations that holiday representatives have to deal with including handling complaints, accidents, illness, evacuations, flight delays, a flight delayed indefinitely, lost luggage, lost passports and tickets, crime, resort not suitable, building work, etc.

ACTIVITY

Research types of problems a holiday representative deals with overseas.

Holiday representatives have to know how to complete documentation. An example of a customer service report is shown in Figure 14.08, overleaf.

Customer Report Form

Page 1 of ☐

Form No. ☐

Tour Operator	*THOMSON*
Resort (e.g. Palma Nova)	*ARENAL*
Customer Name	*MR P. JONES*
Accommodation	*CASTELL PLAYA*
Customer UK Address	*4 WOOD LANE*
	IPSWICH

Booking Ref. No.	*4731697*
Area (e.g. Majorca)	*MENORCA*
UK Departure Date	*14·11·03*
Room No.	*622*
Postcode	*IP1 3SQ*

Customer Telephone _____ Rep. Name *JAMES POTTER* Date *20·11·03*

Please give details below of issues raised (to be completed by the Customer or representative):

1 *GUESTS INFORMED ME THAT THE FOOD IN THE DINING ROOM IS COLD + SERVICE IS POOR*
2 *MR JONES FEELS THE HOTEL IS NOT UP TO THE NORMAL GOLD HOTEL STANDARD*
3
4
5

Actions taken to the issues raised above:

1 *ISSUE REPORTED TO MAITRE D' AND CHEF*
2 *I WILL EAT IN RESTAURANT TODAY TO CHECK ABOVE*
3 *EXPLAINED HOW GOLD 'T' RATINGS WORK – THIS HOTEL*
4 *IS 3 STAR / 4T*
5

Customer Signature _____ Rep's Signature *James Potter* Date *20·11·03*

Copy Received by _____ (on behalf of Hotelier/Supplier) _____

Dear Customer

Thank you for taking the time to complete this report.

Copies of the report will now be forwarded to the management team in resort who will use the information you have provided to develop and improve our service. Thank you.

If you wish to make any further comments please contact us by letter, phone or e-mail, the details are shown below. A member of the customer service team will be pleased to hear your feedback.

Many thanks,

General Manager Customer Service

Customer Service Department, Thomson Holidays, Greater London House, Hampstead Road, London NW1 7SD Phone: 0870 607 1642

Fig 14.08 An example of a completed customer service report

ACTIVITY

Assume you are a holiday representative in the resort of Bodrum, Turkey. A customer, Mr S. Schlosser, complains to you about severe building work in the Apartment Aegean where he and his family are staying. They were not advised of any building work before travel. The resort is full and the customers are not willing to change resorts. They are booked for a seven-night holiday.

Write out the statement that you would put on the customer service report.

Assessing the outcome

You work as an overseas representative in the resort of Playa de las Americas in Tenerife. Your team leader has informed you that your performance will be observed and assessed. Your team leader will attend your transfer speech, welcome meeting and observe you dealing with a range of different customers during your hotel visits.

- Use social, customer service and selling skills to deliver an arrival speech and plan and deliver a welcome meeting completing appropriate documentation (**P4**).
- Use social and customer service skills to deal with customers in different situations, completing appropriate documentation (**P5**).

Improve your grade

What does analyse mean? The *Collins Dictionary* definition of analyse is 'to examine in detail in order to discover meaning, essential features etc. To break down into components or essential features.'

In order to analyse the roles and responsibilities (**D1**) it is necessary to break the task into small parts. Analysis in this context is about looking at the big question and breaking it into smaller parts. You should consider looking at what causes tour operators to give holiday representatives their roles and responsibilities. You should also consider the effect upon the holiday representative of having a set of roles and responsibilities. In order to determine how they contribute to the overall holiday experience, it may be necessary to consider how these lead to an overall positive or negative holiday experience.

You could start this task by thinking about what the holiday representative actually does. You could approach this by producing a list of the roles and responsibilities carried out by holiday representatives. Consider which roles and responsibilities are key to making the holiday experience positive.

Let us look at two examples and think about the questions you need to consider as part of your analysis.

First, let us look at welcome meetings. You could start by thinking about what the welcome meeting hopes to achieve. This will help you to determine why holiday representatives are required to have welcome meetings. What would the holiday representative include in the content of the presentation? We have looked at this earlier in the unit. Why do you think the welcome meeting covers the topics discussed? For example, one of the topics is health and safety. Why is it important that a holiday representative tells the customer information about safety in the resort? Think about specific examples of what they are telling the customers and why that may be so. What is needed in the welcome meeting to improve the customers' holiday further?

Let us now think about dealing with customer complaints. What are the tour operator's complaints procedures? What is an effective procedure? How should a holiday representative go about dealing with a customer complaint? What would happen if a complaint was not handled correctly? What would happen if the holiday representative ignored a holiday complaint?

These are some of the questions that you need to consider when analysing the roles and responsibilities in relation to their contributing to the holiday experience. It is important that you examine the outcome. A starting point could involve listing bullet points. However, you must develop this further and show where those points lead, giving a detailed analysis.

Top tips

- Before starting **D1**, consider the roles and responsibilities of holiday representatives.
- Consider how important the holiday representative is to the customer's overall holiday experience.

The appeal and importance of UK visitor attractions

Learning outcomes

By the end of this unit you should:

- know the products and services provided by different types of visitor attraction
- know the range and purpose of techniques used for visitor interpretation
- understand the appeal of visitor attractions to different types of visitor
- understand the importance of visitor attractions to the popularity and appeal of UK destinations.

Products and services provided by different visitor attractions

According to J. Christopher Holloway (2006) in *The Business of Tourism* (Pearson), visitor attractions are what 'prompts the tourist to travel in the first place'. Holloway also suggests that a visitor attraction is one that 'appeals to people sufficiently to encourage them to travel there in order to visit'. Attractions can be natural e.g. waterfalls, or built, such as the London Eye. Built attractions are sometimes referred to as man-made. There are some UK visitor attractions that are a combination of both natural and built attractions. For example, a stately home is a built attraction, however it may be located next to a lake, which is a natural attraction. There are hundreds of visitor attractions in the UK. This unit will look at both natural and built visitor attractions.

" The Association of Leading Visitor Attractions (ALVA) comprises members from the majority of Britain's biggest and best-known attractions. The members receive some 100 million domestic and overseas visitors each year. Current members include many of

the UK's most famous museums, galleries and heritage sites, whose international recognition makes them a magnet for overseas visitors, as well as mass-market commercial leisure attractions, which are renowned throughout the world. These attractions seek to provide people with the highest quality in terms of visitor experience. "

(Source: adapted from www.alva.org.uk, accessed May 2007)

ACTIVITY

Research ALVA. Make a list of its members.

Built visitor attractions

Built visitor attractions include a number of different types of attraction. These include heritage sites, such as castles and cathedrals, theme parks, gardens and educational attractions.

Heritage visitor attractions link the present to history and the past. Attitudes towards heritage are changing. Not long ago people replaced old buildings with new, but now they are more aware of their historic and heritage significance as well as their tourism potential. Until recently, many old mills, such as the Baltic in Newcastle, were demolished because they were no longer useful but now they have been restored and turned into visitor attractions such as art galleries.

English Heritage is one organisation preserving built attractions. It protects and promotes England's historic environment and has over 400 UK historic attractions. English Heritage is officially known as the Historic Buildings and Monuments Commission for England. It is an Executive Non-Departmental Public Body, which is sponsored by the Department for Culture, Media and Sport (DCMS).

ACTIVITY

Research the aims of English Heritage. Select one historic built English Heritage visitor attraction and explain how English Heritage meets its aims at this attraction.

Case study

Edinburgh Castle

Edinburgh Castle is the best known of Historic Scotland's buildings and is part of Edinburgh's World Heritage Site. It is a landmark that dominates the city and is visited by over one million people each year. It is located on an extinct volcano and has amazing views over the city. From the north, on a clear day, the mountains of the Kingdom of Fife can be seen in the distance and immediately below the castle there is a superb view of the world-famous Princes Street Gardens. The castle's architecture reflects Scottish history. One of the oldest buildings found within the castle is the small Norman chapel of St Margaret, which dates back to the 1100s. The castle's main courtyard, Crown Square, was developed in the fifteenth century and James IV built the Great Hall with its hammerbeam roof in 1511. This hall is now used to display examples of historic weapons and armour. The Half Moon Battery was created in the late sixteenth century and the Scottish National War Memorial was added after the First World War. There is a display of the Crown Jewels in Edinburgh Castle and the Stone of Destiny, which was returned to Scotland after 700 years in England, is also available to view. The castle is the home of the One O'clock Gun. This is fired every day except Sunday at precisely 1.00 p.m.

(Source: adapted from www.edinburghcastle.biz, accessed May 2007)

Fig 18.01 Edinburgh Castle

Case study

The Eden Project

The Eden Project is another example of a built attraction. It is located near St Austell, Cornwall, England. It is a large-scale environmental complex conceived by Tim Smit and designed by the architect Nicholas Grimshaw. It has rapidly become one of the most popular visitor attractions in the United Kingdom. The complex includes two giant, transparent greenhouse domes made of plastic-like cushions, which house plant species from all around the world. The first is a tropical environment, the Humid Tropics Biome, which is 200m long, 47m high and 100m wide. The second dome is the Warm Temperate Biome, which contains plants from the Mediterranean, South Africa and California. Outside there are 10 hectares (25 acres) of landscaped gardens and rockeries. The project took 2½ years to construct and opened to the public in March 2001.

ACTIVITY

Produce a summary describing Edinburgh Castle.

ACTIVITY

Visit the Eden Project website: www.edenproject.com. Research this visitor attraction to find out why the Eden Project is classed as a built attraction. Produce a newspaper article that describes the visitor attraction.

Natural visitor attractions

These are visitor attractions that have not been created or made by anyone, but have been formed naturally. Examples of natural visitor attractions include waterfalls, gorges and rivers. Many of these are located within National Parks.

Case study

The Brecon Beacons National Park

The Brecon Beacons National Park is one of Wales' most beautiful countryside areas. It is situated in mid-Wales among mountains and hills, and runs from the Welsh/English border to Lladeilo. Included within the National Park are the Brecon Beacons, the Black Mountains, Fforest Fawr as well as valleys, waterfalls, lakes, moorland, caves, gorges and forests. In October 2005, the Brecon Beacons National Park Authority was awarded membership of the highly prestigious European Geopark Network and given UNESCO Global Geopark recognition for the Fforest Fawr Geopark. Fforest Fawr is Welsh for the Great Forest, and is the range of mountains between the Black Mountain and the central Brecon Beacons. The Geopark includes the whole of the western half of the Brecon Beacons National Park.

Fig 18.02 The Brecon Beacons

ACTIVITY

Research the definition of a Geopark.

Fig 18.03 Cheddar Gorge

Case study

Cheddar Gorge

This area has been a destination for travellers and holidaymakers for centuries, each one curious to view the magnificent limestone gorge carved into the southern slopes of the Mendip hills above the village of Cheddar.

Reaching 500 feet in places, the sides of the ravine boast the highest inland cliffs in the country and can be viewed both from the public road running through the base of the gorge or from footpaths along the cliff tops.

At the lower end of the gorge, closest to the village, are riverside walks, tea rooms and gift shops and the famous Showcaves, a series of labyrinthine underground chambers accessible to the public.

Cheddar cheese is known throughout the world, its manufacture originating in farms in the region. You can watch traditional Cheddar cheese making at the Cheddar Gorge Cheese Company in the lower Gorge.

The Mendip hills are a great centre for walking, riding, adventure activities and outdoor pursuits, particularly caving and climbing. An Area of Outstanding Natural Beauty, the limestone plateau is noted for its landscape beauty and wildlife.

(Source: www.enjoyengland.com, accessed May 2007)

ACTIVITY

Explain why Cheddar Gorge is classed as a natural visitor attraction.

Products and services

Visitor attractions' products and services vary depending upon the type of attraction, i.e. whether it is a built or a natural attraction. There are two types of products and services at visitor attractions: primary and secondary.

Primary products and services

Primary products are services that initially draw visitors to the attraction. Primary means it is the main reason why people would visit the attraction – for example, exhibits or landscape.

ACTIVITY

Read the case study, below, then, in pairs, discuss why the exhibits at Tate Modern are the primary products and services attracting visitors.

Another primary product and service is landscape – for example, Lake Windermere. Many visitors are drawn here because of its magnificent scenery, i.e. the lake, which is surrounded by a number of other natural attractions such as the hills and mountains.

Wastwater is situated in the Wastdale Valley in the Lake District. It is 3 miles long, half a mile wide and 260 feet deep, and is the deepest of all the lakes. Wastwater is perhaps the most breathtaking of all the lakes as it is surrounded by the mountains of Kirk Fell, Great Gable, Red Pike and Scafell Pike, which is England's highest mountain.

ACTIVITY

Research each of the following visitor attractions to determine the primary product or service of each.
- Oxford University
- Buckingham Palace
- Blackpool Pleasure Beach
- Durham Cathedral
- Giant's Causeway
- Scottish Whisky Heritage Centre and Royal Mile
- Hadrian's Wall
- Museum of Welsh Life
- Chessington World of Adventures
- Science Museum

Case study

Tate Modern

Tate Modern is the national gallery of international modern art. It is located in London and is one of the family of four Tate galleries that display selections from the Tate Collection. The Collection comprises the national collection of British art from the year 1500 to the present day, and of international modern art. The other three galleries are Tate Britain, also in London, Tate Liverpool, in the north-west, and Tate St Ives, in Cornwall, in the south-west.

Created in the year 2000 from a disused power station in the heart of London, Tate Modern displays the national collection of international modern art. This is defined as art since 1900. International painting pre-1900 is found at the National Gallery, and sculpture at the Victoria & Albert Museum. Tate Modern includes modern British art where it contributes to the story of modern art, so major modern British artists may be found at both Tate Modern and Tate Britain.

The Tate collection of modern and contemporary art represents all the major movements from Fauvism on. It includes important masterpieces by both Picasso and Matisse and one of the world's finest museum collections of Surrealism, including works by Dalí, Ernst, Magritte and Miró. Its substantial holdings of American Abstract Expressionism include major works by Pollock as well as the nine Seagram Murals by Rothko, which constitute the famous Tate Rothko Room. There is an in-depth collection of the Russian pioneer of abstract art, Naum Gabo, and an important group of sculpture and paintings by Giacometti. Tate Modern has significant collections of Pop Art, including major works by Lichtenstein and Warhol, Minimal Art and Conceptual Art. Tate also has particularly rich holdings of contemporary art since the 1980s.

A continuous programme of temporary exhibitions also complements Tate Modern's permanent collection.

(Source: www.tate.org.uk, accessed May 2007)

Case study

UNESCO World Heritage Sites

The United Nations Educational, Scientific and Cultural Organization (UNESCO) is an organisation set up to look for and encourage the 'identification, protection and preservation of cultural and natural heritage around the world considered to be of outstanding value to humanity'.

Sites as unique and diverse as the Medina of Marrakech in Morocco, the historic Sanctuary of Machu Picchu in Peru, the Great Barrier Reef in Australia, the Taj Mahal in India and Hadrian's Wall in England are all UNESCO World Heritage Sites.

Here are some of the UK properties on the World Heritage List:

Cultural

Blenheim Palace (1987)
Canterbury Cathedral, St Augustine's Abbey and St Martin's Church (1988)
Castles and Town Walls of King Edward in Gwynedd (1986)
City of Bath (1987)
Durham Castle and Cathedral (1986)
Frontiers of the Roman Empire (1987)
Heart of Neolithic Orkney (1999)
Ironbridge Gorge (1986)
Maritime Greenwich (1997)
Old and New Towns of Edinburgh (1995)
Stonehenge, Avebury and associated sites (1986)
Studley Royal Park including the ruins of Fountains Abbey (1986)
Tower of London (1988)
Westminster Palace, Westminster Abbey and Saint Margaret's Church (1987)

Natural

Giant's Causeway and Causeway Coast (1986)
Gough and Inaccessible Islands (1995)
Henderson Island (1988)

Mixed

St Kilda (1986)

ACTIVITY

Select one UK UNESCO World Heritage Site. Find out its primary products and services. Produce a newspaper advert promoting its primary products and services.

Secondary products and services

Secondary products and services are those that are additional to the main purpose of visit. These contribute to the visitor attraction's customer experience. They are not, however, what initially makes a potential customer visit an attraction. Secondary products and services vary in amount and type depending upon the size and scale of the visitor attraction.

Shops are one example of a secondary product and service. Many such shops sell memorabilia in the form of merchandise materials, e.g. pens, rubbers, T-shirts. Some attractions will also sell their secondary products and services over the internet. Shops provide additional income opportunities. For some visitor attractions this can be significant. One example is the Beatles Story in Liverpool, which is a Beatles-themed visitor attraction. It has a shop selling memorabilia relating to the pop band The Beatles (Figure 18.04). It sells items such as badges, music, T-shirts and stickers. The visitor attraction also has a facility for people to shop online to buy products and services.

Shops selling merchandise materials also help to promote the visitor attraction. People will leave with

ACTIVITY

Find out the UK UNESCO properties on the World Heritage List from the year 2000.

Fig 18.04 The Beatles Experience shop

items in plastic bags with the visitor attraction's name on it. T-shirts can also promote the visitor attraction.

Catering is another secondary product and service available at many UK visitor attractions. Some use external or franchise companies – for example, Alton Towers has a McDonald's within the theme park. Either way, if a visitor attraction offers catering facilities, then these will provide additional income as well as providing the opportunity for customers to stay longer and have a more enjoyable experience.

Case study

Flamingo Land

Flamingo Land is a theme park, zoo and holiday village. Helen and Stavros decide to take their three children to visit Flamingo Land in August. The children have been driving Helen crazy as they have been off school for a few weeks. Helen thinks a day out to see the animals and go on the rides will amuse and thrill them. The day they arrived at the theme park, the weather was glorious with clear blue skies and sunshine. Luckily for the family the shop sold sun cream. At lunch time the family visited the restaurant and bought sandwiches and soft drinks.

ACTIVITY

Read the above case study, then explain how the shop and restaurant could contribute to the overall enjoyment of a trip to Flamingo Land.

There are a number of other additional services that add to the overall enjoyment of a visitor attraction – for example, guided tours that give information and show visitors around the attraction. Knowing what the attraction is about can make the experience more memorable. Some additional services are at an additional cost, however some are included in the entrance fee – for example, Wordsworth's Cottage in Cumbria includes a tour round the cottage, giving interesting facts about the poet Wordsworth so that the visitor understands more about the house that he lived in.

Guides are an example of an additional product and service. Guides are used to give visitors a commentary about the attraction. They will provide

the visitors with information, such as the history of the building. There are also audio guides that have recorded information the visitor can listen to while looking around the attraction. Audio guides are often provided in a number of languages. At some visitor attractions there are guides who give commentaries in a number of languages. However, this is not always practical for small visitor attractions employing perhaps one or two guides.

Visitor attractions have recently increased their educational links with schools, colleges and universities. Larger visitor attractions employ staff to deal directly with educational establishments. The job description of the education officer at Bede's World, which is the museum of early medieval history at Northumbria, Jarrow, shows the service they provide to educational establishments (Figure 18.05 opposite).

Another additional product and service available in some visitor attractions is corporate hire. In some attractions this means there is the facility to hire the whole attraction, rooms or an area of space in the attraction for business or conferences. Some attractions even offer the use of the attraction for weddings. For example, at Vinopolis in London, an attraction dedicated to the pleasures of wine, corporate and private events such as the following are offered: Christmas parties, summer parties, private parties, corporate wine tastings, weddings, civil partnerships, product launches and charity events.

Visitor services are also provided by visitor attractions. These additional services include cloakrooms, parking, first aid and pre-bookable ticket services.

ACTIVITY

Select a visitor attraction. Identify and describe the visitor services available.

Assessing the outcome

You work for a travel and tourism trade magazine. Produce a feature supplement on the products and services provided by one UK built and one UK natural visitor attraction.

- Describe the products and services provided by one built and one natural visitor attraction (**P1**).

Bede's World
The Museum of Early Medieval Northumbria at Jarrow
Education Officer, Job Description

Responsible to: Senior Education Officer

General responsibilities: To assist the Senior Education Officer in delivering the educational programme of Bede's World and in operating, developing and promoting a range of services which further the education objectives of Bede's World and achieve required standards and targets. He/she will also assist as necessary in the general running of Bede's World.

Main duties:

- To provide teaching services for schools and other groups using Bede's World.
- To assist in arranging courses, programmes and meetings to further the educational objectives of Bede's World.
- To assist in the administration of educational visits to Bede's World and to ensure that accurate records are maintained.
- To deputise for the Senior Education Officer when necessary.
- To remain conversant with new developments in education, museums and heritage.
- To ensure that the staff of the Education Service function well as a team and work effectively with all other members of staff.
- To ensure that the Education Service maintains standards of quality and performance, achieves targets and implements the Education policy.
- To plan (with other staff), develop and provide educational services in the form of teaching, talks, seminars, courses, meetings demonstrations, family activities, outreach and other activities.
- To develop, prepare and manage educational resources.
- To assist in providing educational advice in the development and preparation of museum displays, exhibitions, publications, and interactive learning developments.
- To participate in programmes for the training and development of staff.
- To attend the Education Advisory Panel and to work as required with the Panel.
- To ensure the maintenance and security of educational equipment and material.
- To be responsible, along with all other staff members, for compliance with health and safety regulations for staff and visitors.
- Other duties of a similar nature and level will be required from time to time.

Fig 18.05 Education officer, Bede's World, job description

The range and purpose of techniques used for visitor interpretation

Visitor attractions use a range of interpretation techniques. Interpretation is giving people an understanding of information that is not obvious. Different techniques are used to enable the visitor to understand more about the attraction they are visiting. Visitor attractions need to consider the needs and types of visitors so that they can provide appropriate interpretation. For example, if a visitor attraction targets children, then the interpretation needs to be right for that age group, i.e. clear and not using complex words. If the attraction draws a number of overseas visitors, then it needs to think about how it will communicate to non-English-speaking visitors. Interpretation makes an essential contribution to the experience of the visitor attraction. For competing visitor attractions it is vital that they have a competitive edge and that visitors have a good experience, otherwise they may not re-visit and could pass on negative remarks about the attraction to other people. Sometimes, to achieve a positive experience, more than one interpretation technique has to be used. For many visitor attractions, it is necessary to use a number of techniques.

Displays are one type of technique used. They are commonly used in museums and art galleries. Displays will present the exhibits that the visitors have come to see. For example, a museum may have displays of pottery, clothing, animal bones, antique coins, and so on.

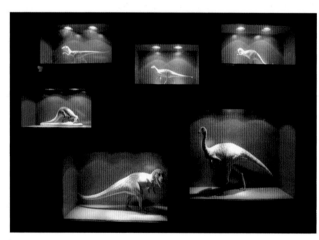

Fig 18.06 A Natural History Museum display

The Natural History Museum in London uses displays to showcase its exhibits. Many schools visit this attraction to learn and understand about the items exhibited in the displays. For example, if students are studying minerals, they can visit the display of minerals and read information relating to this at the museum.

Role play using actors is another interpretation technique used by visitor attractions. This technique enhances the visitor experience. Actors are frequently used to entertain visitors by interacting with them and providing humour. At historical attractions, actors commonly represent people from the past. They are dressed in historical costumes relevant to the attraction, e.g. they may be in Elizabethan costume in a castle. Some English Heritage visitor attractions use actors dressed up as buccaneers, highwaymen, Normans and jousters. Actors are often used for themed days that are held in historic sites around the

UK – for example, Old Sarum Castle near Stonehenge.

In some visitor attractions actors surprise people, like at the London Dungeon where actors in costume jump out in front of visitors to give them a fright and make the attraction more scary.

ACTIVITY

Select a visitor attraction currently not using actors. In pairs, suggest how actors could be used at your chosen visitor attraction.

Another technique used is interactive technology. This is the two-way communication between the user and the communication system – for example, a touch-screen computer. The advantage of using interactive technology is that it enables the visitor to become more involved with the attraction. For example, instead of just reading information about the attraction, the visitor can use technological equipment to find out about the visitor attraction. Many visitor attractions have introduced the use of interactive technology as it is thought to make the attraction more exciting. This technique has quickly spread due to advances in technology. W5 is an example of a visitor attraction located in Northern Ireland. It uses interactive technology and has 160 interactive exhibits.

Eureka is another example of a visitor attraction that uses interactive technology for interpretation. The attraction is designed for children to learn about many aspects of life in a fun and interactive way.

A number of awards have been won by visitor attractions in recognition of the interactive technology they use. The ARCHI-TECH AV Awards honour outstanding examples of the creative and effective integration of technology into otherwise traditional construction projects. Think Tank in Birmingham won this award in 2003.

Guides and tours are another interpretation technique used to explain more about an attraction; for example, a guided tour can explain the history of the attraction to the visitor. A guide at Chatsworth Hall (see case study, opposite) would tell visitors what the rooms were used for, the family history and the history of the masterpieces displayed. Guides are also helpful if visitors want to ask any questions they may have relating to the attraction.

Fig 18.07 Interactive technology at Eureka

For some attractions, such as Buckingham Palace, due to the high security required, it is necessary to have a tour guide or member of staff in all areas that are accessed by the public.

As mentioned earlier in this unit, many visitor attractions now use audio guides. These are often available in different languages, making it easier for the overseas visitor to understand and engage more with the visitor attraction.

ACTIVITY

Assume you work as a tour guide for Buckingham Palace. You have heard that the attraction is considering replacing tour guides with audio guides. You are concerned about the security of the attraction. Produce a report that explains and justifies the need for tour guides at Buckingham Palace.

Another interpretation technique is leaflets that are available to visitors. They tell the visitor about the attraction. Some include maps while others will supply separate maps. The LEGOLAND Windsor park guides and brochures have information relating to the attraction on one page and a map of the attraction on another. This helps visitors to see where the products and services are located, as well as giving useful information about the attraction.

ACTIVITY

Use the case study below to discuss how Chatsworth Hall not catering for the couple's needs affects their overall enjoyment.

ACTIVITY

Using the LEGOLAND park guide extract (Figure 18.08), assess how good it is at helping people know more about the location and the products and services available at LEGOLAND Windsor.

Tate Britain produced a leaflet for an exhibition called 'A Picture of Britain'. In the leaflet it divided the exhibition into six areas, Highlands and Glens, The Home Front, The Romantic North, The Heart of

Case study

Chatsworth Hall

Juan and Estelle visit Chatsworth, one of Britain's most beautiful historic houses and estates. It is located in the magnificent landscape of the Derbyshire Peak District National Park. The couple are from Madrid and speak only very limited English. When they arrive at the attraction, they book a tour of the house.

This private guided tour brings Chatsworth and the family's history alive, and takes in masterpieces from the Devonshire Collection, which are on view throughout the richly decorated rooms. We strongly recommend that your tour is arranged to begin no later than 10.30 a.m., before the house opens to general visitors. The tour lasts approximately 1½ hours and is available in English, French, Italian and German.

(Source: www.chatsworth.org.uk, accessed May 2007)

Fig 18.08 Extract from the LEGOLAND, Windsor park guide and brochure
(Source: LEGO, the LEGO logo, the brick and knob configurations and LEGOLAND are trademarks of the LEGO Group.© 2007 The Lego Group)

England, The Flatlands and The Mystical West. These were each represented in a colour. The colours of the map were matched to the exhibition rooms so visitors could easily locate the different areas of the UK (see Figure 18.09). The leaflet also gave visitors information about each room and area in the exhibition and each of the room's exhibits. It informed the visitor about the region covered, artists and historic facts relating to the artists and the region. This is an extract from 'The Romantic North':

> **The north, outside its towns, was long regarded as forbidding – 'mostly rocks' according to one early traveller. But changing attitudes to nature and wilderness made it more fashionable during the eighteenth and early nineteenth centuries. The Lake District became an English Arcadia, reminding 'Picturesque' tourists of paintings by Claude Lorrain. Wilder scenery, like Yorkshire's Gordale Scar or the bleak Northumberland coast, appealed to a taste for the awe-inspiring and 'Sublime'.**

(Source: Tate Online, www.tate.org.uk)

Case study

The National Trust

The National Trust is a charity and is completely independent of government. It relies on income from membership fees, donations and legacies, and revenue raised from its commercial operations. It has 3.4 million members and 43,000 volunteers. More than 12 million people visit its pay-for-entry properties each year, while an estimated 50 million visit its open-air properties. It protects and opens to the public over 300 historic houses and gardens and 49 industrial monuments and mills. It also looks after forests, woods, fens, beaches, farmland, downs, moorland, islands, archaeological remains, castles, nature reserves and villages.

(Source: adapted from www.nationaltrust.org.uk, accessed May 2007)

Museum and art curators manage the collections exhibited in a museum or art gallery. All types of museums require at least one curator. A museum

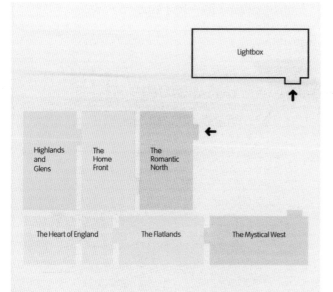

Fig 18.09 Floor plan and UK map in the leaflet for the exhibition 'A Picture of Britain', Tate Britain (Source: Tate, London 2007)

ACTIVITY

The National Trust uses leaflets partly for the purpose of promoting conservation and partly for information about its visitor attractions. Discuss in small groups how and why leaflets could help support the promotion of conservation. Feed back your discussion points to the rest of your class.

curator usually has a background or interest in history, archaeology and anthropology. Curators are key in the organisation of the visitor attraction and are another example of an interpretation technique.

ACTIVITY

Research the job role of a museum curator. Produce a job description for a curator for a museum visitor attraction of your choice.

Signage is vital in any attraction. It enables the visitor flow to work as well as contributing to the visitor experience. If signage is not correct or is missing, then it could result in the need for more staff as visitors will need to ask more questions. It could also lead to visitors missing areas of the visitor attraction because they may not see or may not be able to find key parts of it. If the visitor flow is not good, then it can result in overcrowding in certain areas. The staff at the ticket desk in the entrance of the attraction can monitor the visitors entering. If there is appropriate signage from the entrance, then visitors will follow the presentation in a logical order and leave by the required exit. This means that people are moving around the attraction in the same direction. If the signage is poor, then congestion and disruption occur as visitors are going in different directions, against the flow of the incoming visitors. In some visitor attractions, the corridors or access to areas may not be wide enough for this – for example, a bathroom or small room in a stately home.

Signage is also used to avoid damage to items, such as people touching priceless pieces of art (Figure 18.10). In some attractions photography can damage exhibits so signs asking people not to use flash photography are displayed. Signage is important; however, if it is not used correctly, it can ruin the sense of the product or service. For example, if the attraction was a spooky tour, then to have large signs giving visitors directions would spoil the sense of the attraction being scary. Signage should be used to enhance the experience rather than detract from it.

Fig 18.10 Do not touch the exhibit

Signage is vital in protected areas such as natural attractions. Without signage, visitors may enter areas that are protected. Signage is used to help conserve an area.

ACTIVITY

Research a UK natural attraction. Draw the signs you would suggest it uses. Produce a plan showing where you suggest the signage should be displayed.

ACTIVITY

Research two UK visitor attractions. Compare the interpretation techniques used. Determine which attraction has the competitive edge.

Some visitor attractions aim to work with the local community or local schools. The Centre for Life in Newcastle has a teaching laboratory that is used with schools to support a wide range of educational courses.

ACTIVITY

Research the Centre for Life visitor attraction. Assess whether its interpretations help meet its mission statement (see the case study below).

Case study

The Centre for Life

At the Centre for Life, our mission is:

- to inspire curiosity in science through an imaginative programme of exhibitions and events, to raise standards in science education for young people and to engage everyone in contemporary science issues, such as climate change and stem cell technology
- to provide substantial annual funding and state-of-the-art facilities on-site to support world-class scientific research in medicine.

We aim to create a vibrant and exciting focus where science is explored and debated in the north-east of England.

The Centre provides:

- an exhibition based on the theme of 'life', offering live science shows, an interactive dome theatre, hands-on displays and family-based laboratory workshops
- a schools programme based on a suite of laboratories and debating rooms
- an annual lecture and debating series featuring popular and respected science communicators
- management for the Newcastle Science Festival
- outreach activities to disadvantaged or under-achieving groups in the north-east
- 100,000 sq ft of laboratory space providing a campus for world-class, university-based research in stem cell, genetics and regenerative medicine
- major conference facilities.

(Source: www.life.org.uk, accessed May 2007)

The appeal of visitor attractions to different visitor types

The appeal of visitor attractions is to do with how interesting and attractive they are to visitors. There are a number of factors that contribute to the appeal of a destination.

Accessibility

The location and the degree of ease of accessibility of an attraction are contributory factors to its appeal. Good transport networks near an attraction will mean better accessibility. A motorway, major rail station, airport or even a seaport located near to the attraction can help attract visitors. The more transport options available, the more potential visitors an attraction can target. Having an international airport or seaport means that the attraction is accessible to overseas visitors. Having a good location in relation to the UK is also important.

Another factor linked to appeal is the opening times of an attraction. Opening at erratic times such as individual months or only on certain weekdays can limit the number of visitors able to visit the attraction. For example, attractions open only at the weekend are not likely to attract school groups. Many visitor attractions need to be profitable, so they need to maximise visitor numbers. They can do this by providing opening times they know will attract the most visitors from their target market.

Having a range of products and services available to visitors can contribute to the appeal of the attraction. For example, a museum exhibition with a very specialist tapestry would not appeal to everyone and therefore this limits the number of people who would want to visit. In comparison, a theme park such as Thorpe Park with lots of rides for different ages would appeal to a wider number of people.

ACTIVITY

Read the case study, below, then discuss the appeal of Dundrum Castle, Northern Ireland, in terms of products, services and accessibility.

Case study

Dundrum castle

Dundrum Castle in County Down is one of the finest Norman castles in Northern Ireland, with views to the sea and Mourne Mountains. It was built by John de Courcy in about 1177 and later occupied by the Magennises.

For safety reasons children under 16 must be accompanied by an adult.

Prices: Admission free

Opening times:

Winter (1 October–31 March)

Open only on Saturday & Sunday. Saturday 10am to 4pm, Sunday 2pm to 4pm

Site may be opened on request

Summer (1 April–30 September)

Closed on Mondays

Open Tuesday–Saturday 9am to 6pm, Sunday 1.00pm to 6pm

(Source: adapted from www.discovernorthernireland.com, accessed May 2007)

Fig 18.11 Dundrum Castle

vary dramatically. This is due to the type of visitor attraction, i.e. is it a profit-making or non-profit-making one? Attractions like Alton Towers or Buckingham Palace can be costly for a family to visit. Some visitor attractions are free and, therefore, this means people will be more likely to visit, and on more than one occasion.

National Statistics revealed that:

> In 1999 the British Museum, Tate Gallery and National Gallery all had approximately twice as many visitors as they did in 1981. In contrast, the Natural History Museum and Science Museum, both of which introduced admission charges in the late 1980s, have seen the number of admissions fall by more than half since 1981. However, they both currently make no admission charge for children (since 1999) or those aged 60 and over (since 2000).

(Source: www.statistics.gov.uk, accessed May 2007)

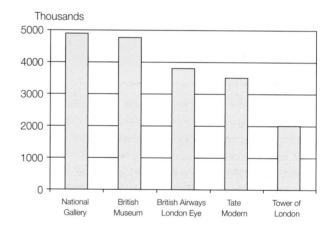

Fig 18.12 Top five tourist attractions in London: number of visits, 2001 (Source: VisitBritain)

ACTIVITY

Research the cost of visiting for the top five London attractions illustrated in Figure 18.12. Discuss how the cost of visiting can affect a visitor attraction.

The cost of visiting covers the cost involved in travel to the attraction as well as whether there is an entrance fee to get into the attraction. Entrance fees

At certain times of the year, some visitor attractions have special offers to attract people. At the start and end of the season, theme parks have offers to draw visitors when business is quiet. Some attractions have special deals where they offer discounts if visitors pay to visit two attractions together, such as Ripley Castle and Gardens in North Yorkshire (see case study, below).

Case study

Ripley Gardens Tariffs 2007

Castle and Gardens

Adults – £7.00
OAPs and Groups (25+) – £6.00
Children (5–16) – £4.50
Children (Groups) – £4.00
Children under 5yrs – Free

Gardens Only

Adults – £4.50
OAPs and Groups (25+) – £4.00
Children (5–16) – £3.00
Children (Groups) – £2.50
Children under 5yrs – Free

Case study

The Discovery Museum

Discovery is north-east England's most popular free museum. Discover all about life in Newcastle and Tyneside, from the area's renowned maritime history and world-changing science and technology right through to fashion through the eras and military history. The museum is bursting with interactive displays, which makes it the perfect place to learn and have fun.

Our displays are regularly updated and complemented by an array of free, fun learning activities.

One of our favourite exhibits – *Turbinia* – dominates the entrance to the museum. Invented on Tyneside, it is the first ship to be powered by a steam turbine. The 35m-long vessel was once the fastest ship in the world and her history is brought to life in the *Turbinia* Story display. She sets the standard for a day out that is guaranteed to be filled with breathtaking discoveries.

Discovery Museum is managed by Tyne & Wear Museums on behalf of Newcastle City Council.

(Source: Tyne & Wear Museums)

ACTIVITY

The Discovery Museum (see case study, right) has free entry to the attraction. In order to encourage repeat business, the museum needs to consider the appeal of its products and services. Describe how the Discovery Museum can encourage new and repeat business.

> **The July 7 bombers planned to attack Big Ben, the London Eye and other tourist attractions, it emerged yesterday, as three men were charged with helping the terrorists plan their attacks.**

In the same way, the *Guardian* reported that dozens of people were hurt at Alton Towers (see the extract reproduced overleaf). This could make people question the safety of the attraction and therefore choose not to visit.

Novelty factor also contributes to the appeal of an attraction. This could be a new attraction and

The image of an attraction can make people choose to visit or not. If an attraction has had some good media coverage, then potentially more people may visit. In the same way, if an attraction has a bad image, then people may be put off visiting. Websites such as tripadvisor (www.tripadvisor.co.uk) give reviews about attractions worldwide. If a potential visitor checks out an attraction and finds negative reviews, they will think twice about visiting. Media such as television or newspapers can also contribute to the appeal and image of an attraction. For example, the following quote from the *Daily Telegraph* from April 2007 could deter people from visiting the attractions mentioned:

ACTIVITY

Select a UK visitor attraction you have visited. Write a review of your experience. Set criteria and give it a score for each criterion set.

Alton Towers rollercoaster crash

Four people were hospitalised and 25 others were left with cuts and bruises following a rollercoaster accident at Alton Towers yesterday.

The incident happened when the front two carriages of the Runaway Mine Train – described on the Alton Towers website as an 'adrenalin buster' – separated from the rest of the ride and rolled back, colliding with the remaining nine carriages.

The ride, which was full at the time with 46 people, was stopped and passengers were evacuated.

Two women suffered whiplash, spinal or abdominal injuries. They were airlifted to the trauma unit of North Staffordshire hospital, while two other people were driven there.

An on-site team at Alton Towers treated other customers for minor injuries at the park's medical centre. A spokesman for Staffordshire Ambulance Services said: 'It could have been a lot worse.'

A statement released on behalf of Alton Towers said: 'As a precaution four guests were taken to hospital by ambulance and we understand that two others have since visited accident and emergency. Of these, four have already been discharged, and two, we understand, are progressing well and hopefully will be discharged shortly.'

Runaway Mine Train is one of the theme park's older rollercoasters, dating back to 1992. It is located in the Katanga Canyon area of Alton Towers and has a maximum speed of 22.4mph.

Passengers are held in with a safety bar across the lap. The attraction cost £3m and a ride lasts less than three minutes.

A spokesman for Alton Towers said the ride would remain closed until after a health and safety investigation had been carried out. The Health and Safety Executive said an inspector had been sent to the theme park.

(Source: Riazat Butt, The *Guardian*, 21 July 2006, copyright Guardian News & Media Ltd 2006)

---

therefore appealing because there is no other attraction like it. Attractions such as Eureka in Halifax and Go Ape, which is an award-winning high-wire forest adventure course made up of rope bridges, Tarzan swings and zip slides in 12 forests around the UK, are examples of attractions that are unique.

For all attractions, appeal will depend on their target market. Some attractions can appeal to a number of types of customer, however for others the visitor type may be limited.

ACTIVITY

Research the following visitor attractions to determine the main types of visitor they are trying to attract.
- Bannockburn in Scotland
- The National Museum Wales
- Belfast Castle in Northern Ireland
- The Deep in England

Assessing the outcome

You work as a researcher for a holiday programme. You have been asked to research the appeal of one selected natural and one built visitor attraction. The producer wishes you to give an explanation of the appeal of both of these attractions to different types of visitor.

- Explain the appeal of one selected natural and one built visitor attraction to three different types of visitor (**P3**).

The importance of visitor attractions to the popularity and appeal of UK visitor destinations

So why are attractions important to the UK and more specifically to a region?

Any destination will aim to maximise spending. In tourism terms, this means a destination wants as many people as possible to visit the area. More visitors coming to an area from overseas means that they will stay in a destination and spend money, which will contribute the destination's economy. A destination will also try to keep as much money as possible within the area and to attract as many domestic tourists as possible, (for example, Blackpool will want to attract as many UK and overseas visitors as possible to visit). Tourism spending in the UK is crucial and in order to attract people to visit a destination requires them to be stimulated to come and visit the UK or encouraged to want to stay in their own country. Visitor attractions are just one of the contributing elements that can encourage people to visit a destination.

VisitBritain provides a range of statistics, research, intelligence and insights on the domestic and inbound tourism industry. The following information provided by VisitBritain gives an overview of the volume and value of the UK's tourism industry. Table 18.01 shows that tourism generates a significant volume of spending by both inbound visitors, spending £17 billion, and by domestic visitors, spending approximately £67 million. According to National

Statistics, tourism is 'one of the largest industries in the UK, accounting for 3.5% of the UK economy and worth approximately £85 billion in 2005'.

Visitor attractions aid domestic tourism not only from a visitor spend point of view for the destination but with regard to employment.

ACTIVITY

In 2005, Table 18.02 shows that there were 3,438,000 US visitors to the UK. Heritage is one reason people visit the UK. Discuss which UK visitor attractions would attract people visiting from the USA.

ACTIVITY

Research the job opportunities available at visitor attractions. Produce a fact file of these opportunities.

Table 18.01 VisitBritain spending by overseas and domestic residents

Spending by overseas residents	£ billion
Visits to the UK	14.2
Fares to UK carriers	2.8
Spending by domestic residents	£ billion
Trips of 1+ nights	22.7
Day trips	44.3
Rent for second ownership	0.9

(Source: Estimated figures from www.visitbritain.com, accessed May 2007)

Table 18.02 Inbound tourism to the UK

Country	Visits (000)	Country	Spend (£ m)
USA	3438	USA	2384
France	3324	Germany	998
Germany	3294	Irish Republic	895
Irish Republic	2806	France	796
Spain	1786	Spain	697

(Source: www.visitbritain.com, accessed May 2007)

Table 18.03 Top ten participating tourist attractions visited in Northern Ireland in 2005

Rank	Attraction	Visitor numbers	% change on 2004
1	Giant's Causeway Visitor Centre	464,243	+4
2	Oxford Island National Nature Reserve[F]	234,925	+9
3	Ulster Museum[F]	212,344	−6
4	Belfast Zoological Gardens	210,930	+4
5	W5	205,243	−17
6	Ulster Folk & Transport Museum	197,673	+9
7	Derry Walls[F]	190,100	+10
8	Carrick-a-rede Rope Bridge	165,000	+20
9	Portstewart Srand	140,000	−3
10	Ulster American Folk Park	134,003	+7

[F] Denotes no admission or parking charge

(Source: Northern Ireland Tourist Board)

ACTIVITY

Use Table 18.03, relating to the top ten visitor attractions in Northern Ireland in 2005, to analyse the importance of the attractions to the country's economy.

Regeneration is important in the sustainability of run-down areas. Visitor attractions have been key in the regeneration of many UK destinations. The Department for Culture, Media and Sport produced a report entitled *Culture at the Heart of Regeneration* (June 2004). This included the significance and importance of UK visitor attractions in the development of UK destinations.

ACTIVITY

Select an area of the UK that has recently been regenerated. Find out about the attractions in that area.
Assess the importance of the attractions to increase visitors to the area. Consider both domestic and overseas visitors. Justify your assessment judgements by obtaining statistics showing visitor numbers since the regeneration programme.

Case study

NewcastleGateshead Initiative

Culture® is a curated programme of exceptional cultural events and festivals across the north-east region which supports the development of the NewcastleGateshead and subregional brands each year until 2010. It is intended to build upon and consolidate the successes achieved through the European Capital of Culture bidding process and to give the region an international launchpad for the rest of the decade, ensuring the momentum that made NewcastleGateshead the nation's favourite for Capital of Culture continues.

The partners are Newcastle City Council, Gateshead Metropolitan Borough Council, One North East, Tyne Wear Partnership, Northern Rock Foundation and Arts Council England, North East. These partners contribute to the planning process through active engagement in a Programme Executive Group. In addition, regular meetings of the chief executives and finance directors of each partner organisation ensure there is consistency and a transparency of approach.

(Source: www.newcastlegateshead.com, accessed May 2007)

ACTIVITY

Read the Newcastle Gateshead case study and suggest how Culture® can link attractions to the regeneration of Newcastle.

Case study

Promoting international cultural exchange and dialogue

Given increasing globalisation, Scotland's relations with the other countries in the United Kingdom, Europe and the rest of the world will have an increasing influence on our culture. Improved communications have accelerated the process of cultural interchange. Developing an awareness of the culture of other countries enables us not only to learn from others, but also to identify those aspects of our own culture that are particularly worth celebrating or that can be improved.

Trade and tourism are fundamental to these exchanges and will have significant impacts on Scotland's future cultural development. The tourism industry is worth £2.5 billion to the Scottish economy and supports over 170,000 jobs. Scotland's heritage is at present central to our branding, but we need to consider further how we promote our contemporary culture. As economic and other international relations develop, there will be many opportunities to promote Scotland's culture abroad and, associated with this, to present Scotland as a tourist destination. These should be grasped.

The Scottish Executive's New Strategy for Scottish Tourism, which was published in February 2000, recognises the value of Scotland's culture. It identifies a number of actions to promote cultural tourism.

To realise fully the potential and very significant contribution of arts, culture and heritage to tourism, a Ministerial Group has been established. It will make recommendations about ways in which this important market can be developed. It will also consider how to ensure that Scotland can exploit its advantages to attract international events in all aspects of culture, including sport.

(Source: www.scotland.gov.uk, accessed May 2007)

Destinations try hard to promote a cultural exchange. There are projects in certain areas that are specifically designed to look at ways of attracting people from different cultural backgrounds to destinations, as well as educating people in an area of cultural differences. To promote cultural exchange, a visitor attraction needs to ensure that it appeals to different cultures.

In Scotland, the Scottish Executive is keen to ensure the promotion of cultural exchange. It has a strategy in place to meet this objective.

ACTIVITY

Assume you are a member of a debate panel discussing the topic cultural exchange. Prepare notes on your views of the importance of visitor attractions in the UK promoting cultural exchange. You are required to research examples to use in the debate.

Conservation is crucial to the popularity and appeal of visitor attractions. If attractions are not protected, then potentially they could be ruined and not sustained for the benefit of tourists in the future. National Parks have many conservation policies in place to ensure the conservation of the area. This is also the case for heritage sites.

ACTIVITY

Research conservation at a National Trust attraction. Produce a leaflet explaining the importance of conservation to the popularity and appeal of the UK destination where the attraction is located.

Assessing the outcome

Assume you work for VisitBritain. You have been asked to give a presentation explaining why visitor attractions are important to UK tourism.

- Explain why visitor attractions are important to UK tourism (**P4**).

Improve your grade

To achieve **M1**, you are required to analyse how effectively the products, services and interpretation techniques of a built and a natural attraction are used to meet the needs of three different types of visitor. First, you need to consider what analyse means in relation to this criterion.

In Unit 14, analysis was defined as the examination by breaking down facts into smaller components and looking at the cause and effect of the facts. In order to make a judgement on effectiveness, then, it is important to consider at the outset what the needs of different visitors would be. You could look at the unit on customer service to find out more about visitor needs. In order to analyse the products, services and interpretation techniques of a built and a natural attraction, first it is necessary to examine the products, services and techniques used in each one. For example, find out if the attraction has used interactive technology and consider the appropriateness of that interpretation technique for a visitor type such as children. Will they be able to use the equipment? Is the technology using language that children will understand? Is it appropriate for the children's age? Is the technique designed for educational purposes? It is necessary to break the information down into small parts. You should consider looking at the relationship of the different products and services in relation to the different visitor types. The same should be considered for interpretation techniques.

For **M2**, you are required to explain how one built and one natural attraction could adapt to appeal to a wider range of visitor types. When choosing your attractions, you must make sure that you do not choose a visitor attraction that has already adapted its products and services to a wide range of customers. Instead use those attractions to give you ideas for visitor attractions that are not yet as developed.

For **M3**, you are required to explain the impact visitor attractions have had on the popularity and appeal of a destination or area. When selecting a destination, research the statistics and evidence of the impact available to you. You will possibly need to use statistics to determine the impact they have had on the destination, i.e. has there been an increase in employment, visitor numbers, visitor spending, repeat business? Alternatively, you could carry out a survey.

D1 requires you to make realistic and justified recommendations for improvements to the products, services and interpretation techniques used by a selected built or natural attraction to meet the needs of different types of visitor.

Realistic improvements are those that are likely to be implemented. They should be feasible. You may wish to start this criterion by coming up with a range of wonderful ideas, however if an idea is too expensive for the attraction selected, it will not be realistic. For example, if you were to suggest that the British Museum should have interactive technology for all its exhibits, would that cost be realistic? Also consider what is the likelihood and how would the British Museum make all its mummies or clocks interactive? The improvements must be justified, which means you should draw upon research to back up your ideas. You also need to consider the different types of visitors, i.e. adults, children, overseas visitors, groups, and their particular needs.

D2 requires you to evaluate. *Collins English Dictionary*'s definition of evaluation is 'to ascertain or set the amount or value. To judge or assess the worth of.'

Evaluate is to put a value on after assessment. In this higher grading criterion it is possible, after having explained the impact visitor attractions have had on the popularity and appeal of a destination or area, to evaluate the success of visitor attractions in terms of the popularity and appeal of a destination or area. Here the research and statistics can draw conclusions as to whether the visitor attractions have increased customer spending, visitor numbers, etc. Alternatively, you can use a survey to substantiate your conclusions. Finally, you need to make recommendations for improvement. These recommendations should include details and justification based on the conclusions drawn from your evaluation.

Top tips

- You should break down your information into small parts that fit together to prove your case.
- You should justify your research by providing statistics and data that can be checked.

Learning outcomes

By the end of this unit you should:

- know the options available to customers when travelling to and from airports
- understand the process of embarkation for all passengers and the roles of airport and airline staff
- know the facilities and services available to passengers during the flight
- know the airport and airline services and facilities during the disembarkation process.

Options available to customers travelling to and from airports

Transport options

When considering how to handle air passengers, it is important to take into account not only their needs when on aircraft, but their needs in respect of the whole air journey including when at the airport and when travelling to and from airports. Those involved with handling air passengers need to be aware of the variety of options passengers will have when planning their journeys. Knowing about transport options means that those working in the travel and tourism industry can assist with the decision-making process, if asked, and can anticipate potential problems an air passenger may encounter in getting to the airport and on arriving at a destination airport.

A customer in Tewkesbury may have a choice of flights from Birmingham or Bristol at similar fares and a travel consultant who is aware of ways of getting to these airports may help that customer to decide which booking to make. A passenger planning to fly from Newquay has limited public transport options to get to the airport so is likely to travel there

by car. A member of staff checking in passengers for a flight to London will anticipate this. If they hear about an accident on a key road to the airport, they would be prepared. They would expect more last-minute check-ins and possibly make arrangements for keeping the check-in desk open for longer than usual or delaying opening the check-in for another flight and using other staff to assist. The more assistance and information an organisation can give its customers, the better its reputation, and this should increase business opportunities.

Planning how to arrive at the airport to catch a flight is important for all passengers, no matter whether they are travelling for business or leisure. When making these plans, there are a number of issues to consider.

ACTIVITY

Joel lives in Crawley. He has a flight booked from London Heathrow to New York on a Friday morning at 10.30 a.m. He has to check in two hours before departure. He owns his own car and lives close to the M23 and also Crawley train station.

Ian and Debbie live in Middlesbrough. They have flights booked from Manchester airport to Malaga, also departing at 10.30 a.m. with a requirement to check in two hours before departure. When in Malaga, they have arranged for car hire as they have to drive five hours to their destination. They live close to Middlesbrough station and the A66 and have their own car.

Discuss the issues each of the passengers above would need to consider when deciding how to get to the airport.

Most airports are located near to major road networks, which allow passengers to easily access them by car. Many airports also have rail stations at or near to the airport terminal buildings, which gives passengers an alternative method of arriving for their flights. For airports that don't have rail stations close by, there are often public transport options from the nearest rail station.

Case study

Doncaster Robin Hood airport by train

Doncaster rail station is the closest station to Robin Hood airport, situated just 7 miles away. A dedicated shuttle service combined with local services links the airport to Doncaster rail station every 30 minutes. Read on for more details.

Journey Planner

Visit www.sypte.co.uk to plan your journey. Type in 'Robin Hood airport' and your chosen departure/arrival point, and the online Journey Planner will offer you the best method of public transport for your chosen journey.

If we can help you further, please email hello@robinhoodairport.com or call our team on 08708 33 22 10.

Easy Link to Rail Services

As Doncaster is a major rail station on the East Coast Main Line, there is a frequent rail service linking us to various other major networks.

The Airport Arrow®

The Airport Arrow® shuttle service links Doncaster Station with Robin Hood Airport. The Airport Arrow® (which is painted in eye-catching green so you won't miss it!) is a daily service and operates hourly. The journey takes under 25 minutes.

You can purchase a 'through ticket' to Robin Hood Airport from any GNER service. Simply state your final destination as Robin Hood airport when you purchase your ticket, either in person or online at www.gner.co.uk.

The Airport Arrow® was designed with passengers in mind and as well as being air conditioned for extra comfort it is also monitored by CCTV for added peace of mind. Extra space for luggage is also available and the vehicle is fully compliant with the Disability Discrimination Act (DDA).

(Source: www.robinhoodairport.com, accessed May 2007)

ACTIVITY

Investigate the accessibility of your nearest airport. Consider the options available for potential passengers living up to 20 miles away.

Knowledge of the location of the airports in the UK can assist in giving passengers information regarding their journey options.

ACTIVITY

Danny Pedrosa lives in Morpeth, Northumberland, and has found a flight from his local airport, Newcastle, to Madrid for £249, departing at 11.00. There is also a flight available from Leeds/Bradford departing at 10.30 for £189, saving £60. Discuss how knowledge of the location of these airports could be used to assist him in making his choice of flight.

ACTIVITY

Using an atlas, and rail network information, plot the major roads and rail networks connected to UK airports.

Knowing options available to travel to an airport can also assist air passengers. A passenger may find a flight is available with a low fare from an airport not close by and so considering transport options can help see if it is economically viable.

It is important to remember that transport options do not only apply to getting to a destination airport – they are also about transport options available from the arrival airport.

Car parking

Many passengers choose to travel to the airport by car. Most airports offer a variety of car parking options to their customers. There are usually long-stay car parks at the airport (on-site), which are recommended for passengers leaving their cars for over 24 hours and short-stay car parks for up to 24 hours. It is not forbidden to park in short-stay car parks for more

ACTIVITY

Marc Godween and his two children, Amy (aged 5) and Alex (aged 15 months), would like to travel to Florida for a three-week summer break. They live near Stirling in Scotland and they would like to find out what options they have for flying to Florida. They have a car and would take it to an airport depending on the cost of parking. They would also consider an overnight stay but this would depend on the cost and the times of the flights.

Research which UK airports the Godween family could fly from to Florida. With this information, identify the transport options they have for travelling to and from those airports. Assess the relative costs for each airport researched.

ACTIVITY

Consider the Godween family situation. The family are actually planning to spend a week in Orlando, followed by a week in southern Florida, spending time in the Florida Keys and Everglades. Investigate the destination airports that they could fly into and out of, and the transport options available to them on arrival.

than 24 hours but the cost is likely to be much greater than that for a long-stay car park. The same applies when staying in long-stay car parks for a short period. Pre-booking is possible but not essential.

ACTIVITY

London Heathrow is the busiest airport in the UK. Calculate the cost of on-site parking for non-pre-booked short-stay and long-stay car parks for
● Friday to Sunday
● staying two weeks.

In most major airports, where there are thousands of air passengers arriving and departing each week, the amount of space needed to accommodate all cars means that the car parks are not always close to the terminal building. Figure 24.01 shows the layout of Stansted Airport parking facilities.

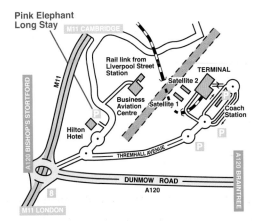

Fig 24.01 Stansted Airport parking facilities

Because of the distances involved, once passengers park their cars, they will either walk to the terminal or take a coach transfer. The coaches operate a regular service between the car parks and the airport terminal. This all adds to the journey time.

As an alternative to on-site airport parking, often provided by the airport, there are off-airport car parking facilities at most airports. These are usually provided by competing private organisations who generally try to offer a better and cheaper service, to gain competitive advantage.

ACTIVITY

Select a UK airport and investigate the parking service provided including costs, location of car parks and means of access to the terminal building.

Recently, meet-and-greet parking services have been introduced at a number of airports. These allow the passenger to drive to the terminal building and then their car is taken to the car park. The quote below shows how this service is advertised on www.purpleparking.com:

> We meet and greet you at the terminal. While you catch your flight, we park your car. Meet & Greet is so convenient. When you get back, we return your car. Meet & Greet is so cost-effective. You could easily save 45 minutes per journey. So try Meet & Greet! Save time with Meet & Greet.

ACTIVITY

Chan Chi Ming and family can fly from Exeter or Bristol to Hong Kong. They are taking four suitcases, four holdalls, a pushchair, a car seat and laptop computer with them for the journey. There is also a box of presents they are taking to friends and family. They plan to drive from their home in Taunton. Investigate the parking options for both airports including the cost for three weeks and the route they would take to the airports. Assess which airport would provide them with the most appropriate service in terms of cost and convenience.

ACTIVITY

Mr and Mrs Golden could fly from London Gatwick with Virgin Airlines or London Heathrow with British Airways for their holiday in Cuba. They will first fly to London from Belfast. Investigate the connections available at each of the London airports including which terminal their flight will arrive into and depart from, suitable inter-terminal transfer methods, and prices of accommodation if overnight stays are required.

ACTIVITY

Mr Panesar is living in Newcastle and plans to attend a wedding in Perranporth, Cornwall. Newquay is the nearest airport to Perranporth but there are no direct flights from Newcastle. He hopes to arrive on a Friday evening. The nearest airport he can fly to direct is Bristol. On the Monday after the wedding, Mr Panesar has a meeting in Manchester. There is a flight from Newquay to Manchester.

Assess whether it would be better for Mr Panesar to get a train from Bristol to Perranporth and then to Newquay airport or to hire a car.

Inter-terminal transport

Many passengers arrive at airports and need to connect to other flights to continue their journey. Methods of transferring passengers from one terminal to another vary depending on the airport.

Case study

Gatwick Airport inter-terminal transfer facility

The terminal connecting trains run every 3–4 minutes – taking under two minutes from each terminal:

North Terminal If you transfer to the South Terminal the monorail is on The Avenue shopping floor which is between the Departure/Check-in level and the Arrivals level.

South Terminal The monorail station can be found on the main Departures/Arrivals floor close to the main Gatwick Airport train station. Follow the signs.

(Source: www.holidayextras.co.uk, accessed May 2007

Car hire

As some passengers arrive at airports and need to carry on their journey using alternative methods, it is important that there are options available to them. Car rental (hire) companies have rental points at most airports and are usually located landside opposite the check-in desks. Most major car hire companies allow their customers to pick up a car at one airport and drop it off at another.

Assessing the outcome

You are on a work experience placement for the British Airports Authority (BAA). It is currently redesigning its website and plans to have a page specifically for transport options available to air passengers.

- Describe the options available to customers when travelling to and from airports and between terminals (**P1**).

Embarkation and the roles of airport and airline staff

Landside departure facilities

Embarkation is the act of passengers and crew boarding an aircraft or ship. Passengers fly for a variety of reasons and require different facilities to meet their individual needs through embarkation. To be able to understand the facilities that meet passenger needs through embarkation, it is important to know the embarkation process (see Figure 24.02).

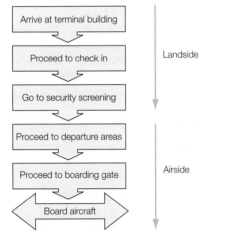

Fig 24.02 Embarkation process

On arrival at the airport to check in for a flight, the passenger will be landside. This is the area up to and including the entrance to the security point and the only area where customers who do not have documentation for a flight can wait. Airside is the area from the exit of the security point to the aircraft.

Another type of customer is an unaccompanied minor (UM); see the box below for British Airways' definition of an unaccompanied minor.

ACTIVITY

Discuss the facilities required by an unaccompanied minor at an airport. Investigate your local airport and assess if these facilities are provided.

ACTIVITY

Consider each of these customers and discuss their landside needs:
- business person, meeting finished at 4 p.m., flight at 5 p.m.
- family with two young children returning to Australia after four weeks of visiting friends and relatives; some relatives are with them at the airport
- two backpackers arriving into the UK for their first visit after four months in the Far East
- passenger arriving in a wheelchair.

Investigate landside facilities at two UK airports. Use the information you find to assess the suitability of the facilities to meet the needs of the customers you identified.

The aviation industry deals with passengers with specific needs, including those related to passengers from a diverse range of cultures and religions, and must offer a range of services to meet these needs. Facilities available can include chapels and praying areas, induction loop systems, translation services and assistance with communication.

ACTIVITY

Investigate the specific facilities available to the following customers with specific needs at two different types of airport within the UK:
- a passenger who is a Muslim arriving three hours before departure for a long-haul flight
- a customer with hearing difficulties
- a family with a small baby.

Recommend facilities your selected airports could introduce to meet their needs.

British Airways' guidance on unaccompanied minors

Children aged 5 years
Your child can travel from age five upwards on a single-sector, direct, non-stop flight only.

Children aged 6–12 years
Your child can travel from the age of six on any British Airways flight. Your child must be registered for the Skyflyer Solo service *unless* they are accompanied by a person of *16 years* of age or above. The person accompanying the child can be a family member or an appointed person.

Children aged over 12 years
The service is also available on request for children up to their 18th birthday.

Passengers with limited mobility can request assistance to board and disembark the aircraft. Most airlines will check in the passenger's personal wheelchair and transfer them to an airport wheelchair to take them to the gate. Some passengers who have restricted movement and do not require a wheelchair may be transferred to and from the gate using an airport buggy.

ACTIVITY

Discuss why airlines prefer passengers with wheelchairs to check in their wheelchair and use other means to access the airport facilities.

ACTIVITY

Mr Mullane is planning to travel from Glasgow Airport to London Heathrow to catch a flight to Singapore. He is a wheelchair user and is unable to walk. As he is travelling alone, he would like to know what departure facilities there are at Glasgow and London Heathrow airports and the specific facilities available to meet his needs.

SERVISAIR

Ground handling
Servisair offers airlines an integrated range of high-quality passenger, ramp and technical services across its network, which meets the specific expectations of its passengers at the best price–quality ratio possible.

Our range of services include:

Passenger services
Passenger checking
Ticketing
Lost and found
Irregularity handling (hotel accommodation, meal vouchers)
Security screening
Special services

Ramp/technical services
Baggage loading
Pushback, towing and repositioning
Aircraft cleaning, toilet/water
Aircraft de-icing
Load control, communications, flight operations, dispatch
Line maintenance
GSE maintenance
Supervision

Landside personnel and staff roles

When passengers arrive at the airport for their flight, they will come into contact with a variety of personnel. These may work for the airport, airline or other organisation providing a service at the airport. There will be other personnel involved with the embarkation process that they will not come into contact with, but who also play a very important role in the process.

At larger airports, many of the airlines will have their own passenger service staff while at smaller airports many airlines will be represented by ground handling companies who provide the passenger service staff on the airlines' behalf – for example, Servisair (see box). These have airside and landside roles in processing passengers for embarkation.

Whether an airline is self-handled or handled by another company, the roles and responsibilities of passenger services staff will be the same. The ultimate aim is for an on-time, safe departure of the aircraft.

One of the key passenger services staff is the customer service agent, also known as passenger service agent. This is the staff member who will check in the passenger for the flight or assist them with the self-service check-in desks. Passengers will be checked in using a computer system (automated) or manually. Manual check-in can be very time-consuming due to the fact that everything must be written out individually and more errors can occur due to incorrect details being logged on the manual check-in paperwork. With both check-in methods, the customer service agent will ensure that passengers have the correct documentation for the flight, ask the security questions, weigh the passengers' baggage and ensure that the cabin baggage meets the latest security requirements.

Whether a passenger checks in at the airport or online, baggage must be handed over to the airline. Baggage allowances vary between airlines and a passenger over the allowance would have to pay excess baggage charges.

ACTIVITY

Some airlines have introduced online check-in, reducing the responsibilities of the customer service agent. Investigate how the online check-in process differs from that described above. Describe the roles and responsibilities of a customer service agent at check-in when a passenger has checked in online.

ACTIVITY

Research the baggage allowances and excess baggage charges of a low-cost, a charter and a scheduled airline.

Once the passenger has been checked in, the customer service agent will give them a boarding card for the flight.

ACTIVITY

Julie is a customer service agent working at the check-in desk for a flight to Alicante. Mr and Mrs Reynolds have arrived at the desk wishing to check in for the flight. They have two suitcases and two pieces of cabin luggage. Their suitcases weigh in at a total of 47 kilos, however they are allowed only 20 kilos each. They are unhappy with the fact that they will have to pay excess baggage charges because when they previously flew with another airline, they were allowed this amount of baggage.

Role play this check-in situation. Check the relevant documentation from your passengers, explain the procedures for embarkation, the baggage allowance for your airline and the reasons why excess baggage charges are made.

Fig 24.03 A boarding card

ACTIVITY

After giving the passenger a boarding card, describe the information a customer service agent would provide related to the next stage in the embarkation process.

ACTIVITY

Discuss the skills and qualities required to fulfil the roles and responsibilities of a customer service agent.

Airside departure facilities and personnel roles

Depending upon the size of the airport, there will be airside (after the security points) departure facilities such as shops and cafés, foreign exchange facilities and cash points, information desks and baggage trolley facilities. Many airports also offer play areas for small children and computer games and activities for older children. Airlines and ground handling agents also provide airside private lounges. These lounges are usually available to business- and first-class passengers but can also be accessed by other passengers for a fee.

ACTIVITY

Investigate the facilities and services provided in two different private lounges available at London Heathrow.

ACTIVITY

Investigate the departure facilities at London Gatwick and Inverness Airports and use your findings to make a comparison.

Once passengers have proceeded to the departure areas, they can wait in the lounge, restaurant areas or at the departure gate. The customer service agent will liaise with the aircraft dispatcher to ensure that boarding starts at the correct time and to communicate any problems that could delay the aircraft's departure.

ACTIVITY

Investigate the airside role of the following staff members:
● customer service agent at the departure gate
● aircraft dispatcher.

Baggage handling agents work landside and airside, taking baggage from check-in desks to the airside apron area; this is outside the terminal building around the aircraft stand. Their role is to load the baggage onto the aircraft, ensuring that it is safely secured into the aircraft hold and positioned correctly to ensure the safety of the aircraft for weight and balance requirements.

Security staff have a very important role to play ensuring that only those passengers with the correct documentation, and staff members who need to move between landside and airside, can enter airside areas of the airport.

Fig 24.04 Airport security

ACTIVITY

Andrew is working at the main security point at Manchester Airport, monitoring all passengers and employees moving from landside to airside. He must ensure that everyone is in possession of the correct documentation and that all hand luggage complies with the latest security regulations.

Research the following information Andrew must be aware of to carry out his role effectively:
● documentation needed by passengers to pass through the security point and explanation of why it is important
● documentation needed by staff members to pass through the security point and why this is necessary
● the latest UK security restrictions for hand luggage.

Immigration officers and HM Revenue & Customs officers also work at airports but their roles are not related to the embarkation process.

Assessing the outcome

The British Airports Authority is planning to introduce a guide for passengers to be available at each of its airports. As part of your work experience, you have been asked to assist in producing the guide.

● Describe the process for embarkation for all passengers and the role that airline and airport staff have during embarkation of customers (**P2**).

Flight services and facilities available to passengers

Boarding

When passengers have checked in and gone through the security procedures, they then wait to be called to go to their designated departure gate. Each flight will have its own departure gate with a specific time for boarding the aircraft. Passengers will wait in the lounge area at the gate until they are called forward for boarding by the customer service agent.

ACTIVITY

Airports use different methods to notify passengers of where to board the flight, what time the flight is due to depart and what stage the boarding process is at. Investigate the different methods used by different types of airport.

Depending on the airline, passengers will either be allocated a specific seat on board the aircraft, or it will be a 'free seating' arrangement. Free seating is like boarding a bus: passengers choose where to sit once they have boarded.

ACTIVITY

Discuss the advantages and disadvantages of each approach for families, business people and the airlines.

When boarding the aircraft, the customer service agent will normally call passengers for boarding based on their seat numbers or passenger security numbers. The security number is the number each passenger is allocated at the time of check-in. For example, if they were first to check in, they would have security number 1, if they were 71st to check in, they would have security number 71. The passengers with the lowest security numbers would be boarded first.

When boarding commences, most airlines will 'pre-board' certain types of passengers such as those with specific needs or those travelling in business or first class. Pre-board means they are the first to be able to board the plane.

ACTIVITY

Discuss the types of passengers likely to be pre-boarded and the reasons why airlines pre-board such passengers.

The boarding process may vary according to the position of the aircraft. Aircraft may be parked on stand with no air bridge but with steps to access the plane (Figure 24.05). Aircraft may be parked on stand with the air bridge attached (Figure 24.06). The air bridge gives access to one entrance to the plane and is often used for larger aircraft. Steps could be at the front or front and rear. Customer service agents would need to ensure passengers don't walk under aircraft wings if accessing steps at the rear of the plane. Aircraft may be parked on a remote stand away from the terminal building, and accessed by coaches from the terminal building.

Fig 24.05 Aircraft with step access

ACTIVITY

Discuss how customer service agents would board passengers onto the aircraft for each aircraft position.

Fig 24.06 Aircraft with air bridge access

At the departure gate, it is very important that the correct passengers board the right aircraft. To ensure that this happens, the ground staff must check all boarding cards and photographic identification. If there are any discrepancies or missing documentation, the customer service agent would contact the aircraft dispatcher (who is responsible for the aircraft turnaround) to discuss the issue. It could be decided at this point that a passenger would not be allowed to fly and the customer service agent would have explain this to the passenger, including the reason why they are being denied boarding. The passenger would then have to be taken off the flight, his/her bags removed from the aircraft and then escorted back through to the arrivals area. This is known as decontrolling: the offloading of a passenger from the flight and the computer system and ensuring that no bags are left on the flight to travel unattended.

On-board facilities

The facilities on board an aircraft will vary depending on a number of factors: the class of travel; the type of airline; the type of aircraft; the route and the length of the flight. It is important to recognise this because some passengers may be disappointed with their flight if it is different from their previous experiences.

Scheduled airlines offer different classes of service on board the aircraft, e.g. first class, business class and economy; in general, all meals and drinks (except for Champagne in economy) are included in the price.

Some charter airlines offer an enhanced economy class and a regular economy class. These are usually known as premium seats, and additional services are provided for a supplement.

Charter airlines charge for meals and drinks; most offer a hot meal or a snack option. Passengers can pre-order hot meals or buy on board if there are meals available.

Low-cost airlines offer a one-class economy service and all snacks and drinks are paid for during the flight; easyJet's philosophy is that 'There's no such thing as a free lunch.'

Case study

Star Class Premier

Experience the luxury of Star Class Premier – with spacious leather seats that can be adjusted to your individual preference and a personal entertainment system so you can watch what you want, when you want – you can be sure of a relaxing start to your holiday.

Dine on nutritional dishes from our contemporary menus, order your favourite tipple from the complimentary in-flight bar while the kids are kept busy with our 'Skytime' entertainment.

- Amazing 36" legroom*
- Air-filled leather seats with winged head support
- 9" widescreen seat back TV
- Entertainment on demand – ability to stop, start and rewind programmes
- 30 channels with video and games on demand
- Priority check-in and boarding
- Delicious menu with a choice of 4 course meal, all served on china crockery, and a snack before landing
- Complimentary drinks
- Sparkling cocktail before take-off
- Complimentary pampering pack and noise reduction headphones
- Mood cabin lighting

(Source: www.firstchoice.co.uk, accessed May 2007)

ACTIVITY

Compare the following for two charter airlines:
- classes of travel
- food and drink services on board
- in-flight entertainment
- facilities at the airport for premium passengers
- facilities for check-in prior to arriving at the airport.

ACTIVITY

Discuss why passengers will choose to fly with one particular airline rather than another.

ACTIVITY

Miss Ramon is flying from Aberdeen to London Heathrow and then onwards to Miami. For her flight from Aberdeen to London, she doesn't mind where she sits; however, for her long-haul flight she would prefer to sit in a window seat near to the centre of the aircraft. She is a diabetic passenger who will need to carry her medication on the flight and she will also need to order a special meal for her flight.

Research the aircraft types Miss Ramon will fly on for the Aberdeen to London and the London to Miami routes. Compare the configuration plans (seat plans) for each aircraft type and explain the layout of the aircraft, including seating arrangements and toilet locations, and the number of seats on the aircraft. Explain what special meals can be pre-ordered to meet Miss Ramon's dietary requirements for each flight.

ACTIVITY

Mr and Mrs Clark are travelling from Manchester to Palma in August with their children Lois, aged 1, and Ben, aged 5. Before they book their flight, they want to find out which airline offers the best facilities for children.

Investigate which airlines fly from Manchester to Palma, and research the facilities for children on a low-cost, charter and scheduled airline.

Roles and responsibilities of personnel in-flight

The role of cabin crew may be viewed as a glorified waiter but their primary role is that of a safety officer. They are on board the aircraft to ensure that health, safety and security standards are met at all times. Most passengers will be aware of this role only if there is an emergency situation on board the aircraft. As airlines operate to high safety standards, the role that passengers are more aware of is from a customer service perspective and for making on-board sales.

Day in the life of cabin crew

Before the crew meet the passengers they have specific duties to carry out:

- start duty 1 hour 30 minutes before the flight is due to depart
- pre-flight briefing
- once on board the aircraft, carry out security checks of the cabin and report any issues to the senior crew member, who passes on the information to the captain.
- on completion of all relevant safety checks and when the cabin has been prepared for passengers, liaise with ground staff to start the boarding process.

ACTIVITY

Discuss the information to be included in a pre-flight briefing given to cabin crew and why cabin crew have to carry out specific duties before the passengers board the aircraft.

Once the pre-boarding duties are complete, the cabin crew:

- direct the passengers to their seats
- make passenger announcements regarding welcome on board, switching off mobile phones, stowage of baggage and being aware of the fasten seat belt signs
- assist passengers to stow bags.

ACTIVITY

Produce a script for a passenger announcement for a specific flight, giving relevant information to passengers as they board the aircraft.

Once boarding is complete and the aircraft doors are closed, cabin crew give a safety announcement supported by a demonstration. Increasingly, airlines are now using technology to show a video demonstration.

During the flight cabin crew serve food and drink and take payment for these depending on the airline

ACTIVITY

Consider why cabin crew demonstrate the safety features on board an aircraft in addition to a safety announcement. Devise a script for a safety announcement, including requirements for cabin crew demonstration.

type. They also carry out tax-free and duty-free sales and assist with completion of landing cards if necessary.

ACTIVITY

Jane works for a scheduled airline and operates long-haul routes. She has been flying for four years and loves her job. She is on her way to work and is flying to Capetown on a Boeing 777. The check-in time for her duty day is at 10.00 a.m. and her flight is due to depart at 11.30 a.m. She will be working in first class during the flight and so will be responsible for ensuring the welfare of the flight crew as well as the passengers.

Create a diary of events for Jane's duty day to Capetown. Explain what happens at the pre-flight briefing and what roles and responsibilities she has during the flight as she is working in first class.

Assessing the outcome

You are working with an airline, preparing for the next round of cabin crew training. You have been asked to put together a section of its training guide.

- Describe the boarding process (**P3**).
- Describe the role of staff and the facilities available to customers during a flight (**P4**).

Airport and airline services and facilities available during the disembarkation process

When passengers fly into an airport, they need assistance to get off the flight and reclaim their baggage. This is known as the disembarkation process. Passengers will follow different procedures for disembarkation depending on where the flight arrives from and the type of stand the aircraft is allocated for parking. The time it takes to disembark an aircraft can also vary, depending on the size of the airport.

ACTIVITY
Discuss why it can take longer to disembark an aircraft at London Heathrow than at Southampton Airport.

A customer service agent from the airline or the airline's ground handling company meets passengers when they disembark the aircraft. It is the responsibility of the customer service agent to ensure that all passengers follow the correct procedures for disembarkation from their flight.

ACTIVITY
Consider the following.
- Why must the customer service agent wear a high-visibility jacket?
- Why must passengers follow marked pathways when leaving the aircraft and passing through the airport?
- Why must the customer service agent stay with the passengers until they have cleared the baggage hall?

Passports and visas, and other restrictions on entry

There are general immigration procedures to follow regardless of whether the passengers are disembarked from the aircraft using steps, coaches or an air bridge. Any passenger arriving into the UK without the correct documentation, such as a valid passport and visa, will be repatriated (sent back) to the country the flight came from. Airlines are fined by the Home Office for wrongly bringing passengers to the UK without the correct documentation.

Some passengers arrive into the UK and claim asylum – shelter from harm or danger in their home country. They might have provided documentation to check in for their flight and then 'lost' it or they may

ACTIVITY
Discuss ways that airlines can ensure that passengers arrive at a destination with appropriate documentation. Discuss ways that UK immigration officials can repatriate passengers.

have stowed away in the aircraft. If a passenger claims to be an asylum seeker, they will be processed by an immigration officer and then moved to a reception centre.

ACTIVITY
Immigration officers will watch for potential asylum seekers when certain flights arrive. Investigate areas where asylum seekers come from.

ACTIVITY
Investigate the procedures immigration officers would follow in these situations:
- passengers arriving into Belfast on a domestic flight
- UK passenger arriving from Barcelona into London Gatwick
- passenger arriving with a US passport from Chicago to London Heathrow.

In addition to passports and visas, there are other issues that can affect a passenger's right to entry into the UK. These include contagious illness and restricted items on the person or in baggage.

ACTIVITY
Investigate restrictions on contagious diseases into the UK. Discuss how a passenger arriving into the UK with a contagious disease will be dealt with.

Baggage

Once a passenger has proceeded through immigration, they collect their baggage before going through the customs area. In case of any problems with passenger baggage, such as delayed (lost) or damaged bags, the customer service agent remains in the baggage reclaim area until all bags have been collected.

A Property Irregularity Report (PIR) is a form that is completed for checked baggage that has been damaged or delayed (Figure 24.07 opposite).

The customer service agent will fill this in using the relevant codes shown on the baggage identification card issued at check-in. It is then passed to the Baggage Facilities Department. The passenger must also fill in a Customs Declaration, which describes the missing bag and the goods being carried in it.

Most delayed bags are located within 48 hours; airlines trace these bags using the Worldtracer Baggage System.

In the event that the baggage is not traced or is damaged, passengers can claim compensation from the airline under the Montreal Convention.

As an alternative to claiming from the airline for compensation for lost or damaged baggage, a passenger can claim from his or her own travel or household insurance. The level of compensation that can be claimed through insurance can be greater than that provided under the Montreal Convention. A passenger can claim from only one source.

All airports input information relating to baggage found or arrived at their airport in error. Once a bag is logged into the system, a baggage officer searching for baggage can request further information or request to have the baggage sent to them. A bag that is sent unaccompanied is known as a 'Rush bag' and this has to have documentation to accompany it and needs to be security-scanned.

PROPERTY IRREGULARITY REPORT (PIR) FOR CHECKED BAGGAGE

(to be completed in BLOCK LETTERS)

OPERATOR TRANSMISSION NOT REQUIRED FOR BOXES LEFT EMPTY

Address(es)
→ A T L W M X S → → → ⬅

• Originator
L L → Date Time ⬅

Station where Bag was last seen

Originator please cross out those boxes that do not apply

Destination on Baggage Tag

AHL ⬅

Airport Carrier ⬅

NM → Passenger's Family Name and Name on Bag

Note: maximum of 3 Names
16 characters per name

IT → Initials ⬅ Initials on the Bag or Passenger's
Full Initials (maximum of 4) ⬅

TN → Carrier - Bag Tag Number   Carrier Bag - Tag Number

Carrier - Bag Tag Number   Carrier Bag - Tag Number   Carrier Bag - Tag Number ⬅

CT → Colour Type Description   Colour Type Description   Colour Type Description   Colour Type Description   Colour Type Description ⬅

RT → Routing and/or locations to be traced (maximum of 15 city codes) ⬅

FD → Carrier - Flight Number   DATE (DAY/MO)   Carrier - Flight Number   DATE (DAY/MO)   Carrier - Flight Number   DATE (DAY/MO) ⬅

BI → Brand Name of Bag Distinctive Outside Identification (1) Other markings/Hotel/stickers on Bag (maximum of 58 characters) ⬅

BI → Brand Name of Bag Distinctive Outside Identification (2) Other markings/Hotel/stickers on Bag (maximum of 58 characters) ⬅

BI → Brand Name of Bag Distinctive Outside Identification (3) Other markings/Hotel/stickers on Bag (maximum of 58 characters) ⬅

BI → Brand Name of Bag Distinctive Outside Identification (4) Other markings/Hotel/stickers on Bag (maximum of 58 characters) ⬅

BI → Brand Name of Bag Distinctive Outside Identification (5) Other markings/Hotel/stickers on Bag (maximum of 58 characters) ⬅

Damage Information Please indicate damage on these drawings.

Side 1   Side 2   End 1   End 2   Top   Bottom

Type of Damage		Condition	
Minor		Good	
Major		Fair	
Complete		Poor	

PA → Passenger's permanent address (maximum 2 lines of 58 characters per line) ⬅

— → ⬅

TA → Temporary address (maximum 2 lines of 58 characters per line) ⬅

— → ⬅

PN → Passenger's permanent phone number (maximum of 20 characters) ⬅ TP → Temporary phone number (maximum of 20 characters) ⬅

LD → Local delivery instructions (maximum 1 line of 58 characters) ⬅

FF → Free Form Text (maximum 99 lines of 58 characters per line) ⬅

Additional Elements

PT → Passenger's Title ⬅ NP → Number of Passengers ⬅ LA → Language ⬅ PP → Passport Number ⬅

TK → Ticket Number ⬅ PR → PNR Record Locator ⬅ FL → Frequent Flyer ID ⬅

BW → Weight of missing pc(s) ⬅ RL → Reason for loss ⬅ FS → Fault Station ⬅ AG → Agent ⬅

INSURANCE   YES ☐ NO ☐   If bag(s) locked ask for key(s) and attach to PIR Key(s) attached   YES ☐ NO ☐   Code of Combination Lock   Overnight Kit Male ☐ Female ☐   Cash Advance Paid ⬅

This report does not involve any acknowledgement of liability

AGENT SIGNATURE _____   PASSENGER SIGNATURE _____

Fig 24.07 Property Irregularity Report (PIR) form

Customs

Once luggage has been collected, a passenger can then pass through customs control.

> ### ACTIVITY
> Investigate the customs channels available for passengers arriving into the UK. Discuss why there are different channels and why domestic passengers are not required to go through customs control.

> ### ACTIVITY
> Mr and Mrs Mills have UK passports and have arrived on a flight from Lanzarote. Their aircraft has parked at a remote stand away from the terminal building. They have 600 cigarettes and 5 litres of gin in their suitcase and do not know which channel to go through at customs.
>
> Create a flow chart, which clearly describes the disembarkation process for Mr and Mrs Mills.

Arrival facilities

Depending on the size of the airport, there will be a variety of arrival facilities available to passengers and for customers waiting to meet passengers. Facilities include car hire, foreign exchange, short-stay parking and meeting points for friends and family.

> ### ACTIVITY
> Compare the arrival facilities at one small airport and one large airport, and explain any similarities and differences.

Transit passengers

The definition of a transit passenger by the Department for Transport is 'A passenger passing through an airport for the express purpose of connecting with another flight.'

At larger airports, such as London Heathrow, transit passengers can wait in a transit area, which has shops, restaurants, bars and facilities to keep children occupied. These passengers do not need to collect their luggage, as it will automatically be transferred to their onward connection.

> ### ACTIVITY
> Research the transit facilities at London Heathrow for the following passenger types:
> - family travelling with two children who are bored and becoming noisy and tearful
> - young couple who enjoy shopping and would like to have a meal before their onward flight
> - business passenger who needs to communicate with his office while waiting for his onward connection
> - first-class passenger who wants to unwind and relax before catching her onward connection to Los Angeles to be present at a film premiere.

Airlines set minimum connection times for passengers transferring from one flight to another. These minimum connection times can vary depending on the type of flight connection (e.g. domestic to domestic, domestic to international, international to international) and the size of the airport.

> ### ACTIVITY
> Research the following minimum connection times:
> - Newcastle – London Heathrow – Singapore
> - Edinburgh – London Gatwick – Rome
> - Glasgow – Amsterdam – Hong Kong
> - London Heathrow – Los Angeles – Las Vegas.

ACTIVITY

Mrs Fields has travelled from Sydney via Singapore to London Heathrow. For the final leg of her journey she needs to catch a connection from Heathrow to Durham Tees Valley airport. Her bags have been checked in at Sydney and she does not need to collect them until she arrives at Durham Tees Valley, however she is very concerned about how to catch her onward connection as she knows that she needs to change terminals.

Investigate the procedures for Mrs Fields to transit through Heathrow and catch her flight to Durham Tees Valley. Explain the procedures in place, including which terminals she will be using, what the minimum connection time is between these flights and why this is.

Assessing the outcome

You are working with the Air Transport Users Council and have been asked to produce a guide for air passengers.

- Describe the disembarkation and transit processes at UK airports (**P5**).

Improve your grade

To achieve a merit for this unit, you will need to achieve all pass and all merit criteria. Pass criteria all require description and demonstration of knowledge, but for merit level you have to show understanding by making comparisons and giving explanations. An explanation requires you to give a reason. A comparison needs you to give reasons for similarities and differences in the way two organisations operate. Without reasoning, the merit criteria cannot be achieved.

The comparison you are to present relates to the facilities at two different airports. Using similar types of airports, such as London Heathrow and London Gatwick, would mean you find many similarities, and using different types of airport, such as London Heathrow and Cardiff, may mean you find many differences but there will also be some similarities. This will give you scope to discuss each airport type

and expand your answers when you consider the comparisons. To achieve **P1** and **P2**, you have already described the facilities of the airports, thus you already have the raw data, the information, you need to be able to make a comparison. For the merit you need to consider each type of facility within the airport. One type of facility you might start with is car parking. Do both airports provide on-airport and off-airport parking? Does the airport manage them all or are other organisations involved? Is there just one other organisation or a range? Do both airports offer meet-and-greet and VIP parking? What about the distances from the car parks to the terminals: will this cause problems for different passenger types? What about the parking charges: is it better to use short-term or long-term car parks, on-site or off-site? For each answer, give a reason why there are similarities and differences. All these questions can be asked to provide the opportunity to compare parking at two airports, but parking is only one type of facility provided. The same consideration should be given to all facilities.

In addition to facilities, the comparison also needs to make reference to the embarkation (boarding) process. Always remember to explain why there are similarities within the UK. For example, security questions at check-in should be the same because this is a legal requirement, but which legislation requires this? Check-in procedures may be different because passengers may be flying with an airline using free seating or where seats are allocated. Seats may also have been pre-booked through a charter airline or a passenger may have checked in online. These will all require customer service agents to follow slightly different procedures at check-in.

To obtain one of the other merit criteria, explain why correctly disembarking passengers is important within the UK. Consider the fact that some aircraft will be parked on stand while others will be parked remotely. This will mean that there are different considerations to be made when moving passengers safely from the aircraft into the terminal building. Relate the disembarkation of passengers to health and safety for both the passengers and the passenger service agent meeting the flight. Give reasons why there are different processes for domestic, EU and non-EU arrivals that might relate to security and immigration, improved airport efficiency and customer relations. Give reasons why transit passengers must remain in the transit areas and not proceed to landside and why there are minimum connection times between flights that passengers must adhere to.

There is one other merit criterion and this also requires an explanation.

The distinction criteria require higher-level skills to be demonstrated. These are evaluation and analysis. To obtain **D1**, there needs to be an evaluation of processes for handling passengers during embarkation and disembarkation at a specific airport, making justified recommendations for improvement. An evaluation requires reasoned judgements to be made. It requires consideration of the effectiveness of current procedures. Are the procedures appropriate and working effectively or are there weaknesses? Each judgement made must be justified with good reasons given. Where weaknesses are identified and reasons for these given, recommendations for improvement should be supplied. Each recommendation should be supported by a detailed statement proving that the suggestion will lead to an improvement. One weakness might be waiting times for baggage reclaim. To simply recommend more staff does not give any detail and also may not be feasible because of the cost implications and thus would be difficult to justify. It may be feasible to introduce signage indicating to customers the potential waiting time for luggage to arrive, as although it won't reduce waiting time, it will be clearer to passengers how long they have to wait so that they can take advantage of washroom facilities, make telephone calls or find luggage trolleys, and are less likely to be frustrated about the long waiting times. Waiting times may be because the flight had more than 400 passengers. Two carousels could be used: one for passengers in seats at the front of the plane and the other for those in seats in the rear. Signs could clearly show which carousel relates to which seat. At check-in, baggage handling agents would need to ensure baggage is stored in relevant parts of the hold to enable those at the arrival destination to direct baggage to the correct carousel. This would require the same amount of staff but additional carousel space and would reduce waiting times by half. This gives two ways of possibly reducing waiting times, if this is an identified weakness, with some detail and justification.

Ensure that you have used the most recent and up-to-date security information when completing the assignment because the aviation industry is fast-moving and very reactive when there are security incidents or potential security breaches. This will allow recommendations to be made with justification as to why they are necessary.

The final distinction criterion asks for an analysis of the effectiveness of the disembarkation process at a UK airport. It would be beneficial to use one of the airports already studied. Consider the systems already in place at an airport: are they effective at all times of the year? Are there enough air bridges attached to the terminal building? If more airlines were to use the airport, would there be enough staff to ensure effective disembarkation? Would there be enough aircraft parking or would aircraft have to fly over the airport in a holding pattern?

Top tips

- You should make comparisons and give explanations.
- You should stay up to date on the latest security regulations at airports.

Glossary

Active/passive holiday – active holidays requires participation in activities on offer; passive holidays involve watching an event

Analyse – say how it is and then draw conclusions

Assess – make value judgements

Charter airlines – are mainly used for package holidays to transport holidaymakers to leisure destinations

Compare – look at a number of issues and how they are dealt with by each organisation involved in your comparison

Cultural holiday – a holiday during which one visits art galleries, and participates in cultural events such as concerts or theatre performances

Describe – say how it is

Dynamic packaging – creating your own holiday by selecting services offered by various operators

Eco-tourism – a niche market within tourism where the visitor travels to an area of natural interest in order to observe or participate in an environmental conservation project to learn more about the environment

Educational holiday – a holiday during which you learn a certain skill, or one organised for a college or school

Evaluate – make judgements, often in relation to performance, examine

Explain – give reasons, answer the why and how questions

Features of destination – these could be climate, landscape, accommodation, accessibility, local services, local culture attractions, events or facilities at a destination

Green tourism – good practice by tourism providers when acting in a responsible way with a consideration for the impacts of tourism on the environment in accordance with the principles of sustainable tourism

Guest – a term often used to describe the tourists

Horizontal/vertical integration – process of linking of organisations for economic gains either on the same level or different levels of the chain of distribution

Host – a term often used to describe the locals

Implant – a branch of a travel agency on the premises of another company for which it provides travel services

Independent holiday – a holiday in which one follows one's own itinerary instead of one set by tour operators or travel agents. This type of holiday is booked direct by the traveller

Intermediary – organisation acting as agent; link between suppliers and customers

Low-cost airlines – focus on reducing cost thus offering 'no-frills' to its customers, charging extra for all additional services

Man-made (built) attractions – museums, cathedrals, gardens, theme parks

Market Research – ways of gathering, analysing and evaluating information, could be primary or secondary

Marketing – The planning and implementation of a strategy for the sale, distribution, and servicing of a product or service (http://mvp.cfee.org/en/glossary.html)

Marketing mix – the 4Ps, Product, Price, Place, Promotion

Mass-market – offer holidays that appeal to the majority of holidaymakers

Natural attractions – beaches, national parks, range of mountains

Niche-market product – special interest holidays suitable for a small range of customers only

Niche operators – offer holidays which focus on a specific activity, destination or are designed for a specific group of customers

North – countries in the developed Northern Hemisphere (north of the Equator)

Overland adventure – a type of trip taken on foot, animal or vehicle, lasting some weeks and involving visiting an area as well as meeting local people

Place – location, accessibility or way of distributing products and services to customers

Popularity – demand for a certain destination. This may be affected by increased accessibility, social trends and attitudes, the availability of attractions, changing holiday patterns and many other factors

Price – amount of money customers are willing to pay for products or services

Primary research – ways of obtaining information directly from customers through surveys, questionnaires, observations or focus group

Product – goods or services offered by an organisation

Promotion mix – a combination of promotional techniques and materials used by an organisation

Promotional materials – items produced to support a promotional campaign i.e. leaflet, press release, merchandising, poster, etc.

Promotional techniques – ways of promoting the company such as advertising, sales promotions, public relations, direct marketing, etc.

Recommend – make suggestions

Religious holiday – a holiday to visit sites of religious significance, such as churches, synagogues or mosques

Scheduled airlines – operate according to a timetable transporting leisure and business customers to short-haul and long-haul destinations

Self-realisation – process during which one discovers one's true self, finds out what one is like

Serviced and non-serviced accommodation – the former is the type of accommodation which offers food and drinks, laundry services, concierge etc., while in the latter these are not provided

South – countries in the less developed Southern Hemisphere (south of the Equator)

Tailor-made holiday – holiday organised by a travel agent or tour operator to meet an individual's (or a group's) needs by mixing the products it offers, creating a tour for them that includes only the components that are required

Tourist destination area – the country or place the tourists are visiting

Tourist generating area – the country the tourists are from

Unpackaged packages – selecting services from the package that suit an individual customer's needs

Index

Page numbers in italics refer to illustrations or tables, e.g. *281*